AF478162

From Growth to Convergence

From Growth to Convergence

Asia's Next Two Decades

Edited by
Fan Zhai

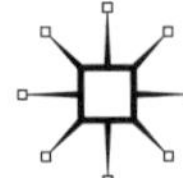

First published 2009 by
PALGRAVE MACMILLAN

Palgrave Macmillan in the UK is an imprint of Macmillan Publishers Limited, registered in England, company number 785998, of Houndmills, Basingstoke, Hampshire RG21 6XS.

Palgrave Macmillan in the US is a division of St Martin's Press LLC, 175 Fifth Avenue, New York, NY 10010.

Palgrave Macmillan is the global academic imprint of the above companies and has companies and representatives throughout the world.

Palgrave® and Macmillan® are registered trademarks in the United States, the United Kingdom, Europe and other countries

ISBN-13: 978–0–230–22176–5   hardback
ISBN-10: 0–230–22176–9   hardback

This book is printed on paper suitable for recycling and made from fully managed and sustained forest sources. Logging, pulping and manufacturing processes are expected to conform to the environmental regulations of the country of origin.

A catalogue record for this book is available from the British Library.

A catalog record for this book is available from the Library of Congress.

10   9   8   7   6   5   4   3   2   1
18   17   16   15   14   13   12   11   10   09

Printed and bound in Great Britain by
CPI Antony Rowe, Chippenham and Eastbourne

Contents

1 FROM GROWTH TO CONVERGENCE: AN INTRODUCTION 1

Fan Zhai, William James, and Frank Harrigan

2 WHY ARE BILATERAL TRADE AGREEMENTS SO POPULAR, AND DOES IT MATTER? 40

Jayant Menon

Commentary: Siow Yue Chia

Tables

Figures

Acronyms and Abbreviations

AFTA	ASEAN Free Trade Area
APEC	Asia-Pacific Economic Cooperation
ASEAN	Association of Southeast Asian Nations
BTA	bilateral trade agreement
CGE	computable general equilibrium
CU	customs union
EFTA	European Free Trade Area
EIT	Economies in Transition
EPPA	Emissions Prediction and Policy Analysis
EU	European Union
EV	equivalent variation
FTA	free trade agreement/area
GATS	General Agreement on Trade in Services
GATT	General Agreement on Tariffs and Trade
GDP	gross domestic product
GIDD	Global Income Distribution Dynamics
GTAP	Global Trade Analysis Project
ILO	International Labour Organization
JSEPA	Japan-Singapore Economic Partnership Agreement
Lao PDR	Lao People's Democratic Republic
MENA	Middle East and North Africa
MFN	most-favored-nation
NAFTA	North American Free Trade Agreement
NIEs	newly industrialized economies
OECD	Organisation for Economic Co-operation and Development
PPP	purchasing power parity
PRC	People's Republic of China
PTA	plurilateral/preferential trade agreement
SAFTA	South Asian Free Trade Area
SSA	Sub-Saharan Africa
TFP	total factor productivity
TIFA	trade and investment framework agreement
UN	United Nations
WEU	Western European Union
WTO	World Trade Organization

Preface

The economic landscape of developing Asia, as well as its relationship with the global economy, is undergoing significant transformation. Just a decade after the Asian financial crisis, developing Asia is again emerging as a new engine of growth in the world economy. Most countries in developing Asia have undertaken a wide range of reforms over the last decade, which have helped the region benefit more from globalization and cope better with the attendant risks. Regional economies are now increasingly linked through commodity, capital, and technology flows, which have been boosted by the formation of an integrated regional production network. The parallel rise of two giants—the People's Republic of China (PRC) and India—has conferred substantial growth leverage on their neighbors, directly via bilateral trade and indirectly across a web of supply chain linkages in intermediate products.

Developing Asia stands on the threshold of a new era of growth. With its high domestic savings rate, considerable potential for productivity catchup, large surplus in rural labor forces, and substantial demand created by rapid urbanization, the region is well positioned to continue its robust growth over the next couple of decades. However, various risks and challenges have emerged and may potentially derail the upward trend in Asian economic development. These include uneven economic performance of regional economies, growing dependence and potential vulnerability of each regional economy on the performance of its neighbors, increasing binding resource and environmental constraints, accelerated demographic transition toward an aging population (in many Asian counties), and worsening income distribution parallel to economic globalization and domestic structural reform (in most regional economies).

This book sets out a vision of the economy of developing Asia over the next 20 years, one in which challenges are met by regional governments and societies, and in which a new era of growth that is more sustained, more equitable, and beyond the expectations of prior generations, comes to fruition. This vision will not materialize automatically. The book makes clear that five conditions are key to sustained high growth and income convergence among the main subregions of Asia over the coming two decades and beyond. These are increased trade and regional integration through more open trade and investment policies; accelerated investment in hard and soft infrastructure; overcoming resource constraints; improved human resource development;

and inclusive growth policies that enhance opportunities and incentives for all citizens without exception.

The book is divided into five thematic areas. Chapter 1 provides an overview of the volume. Chapters 2 and 3 deal with Asian regionalism. Chapters 4 and 5 define the roles of infrastructure development and trade facilitation in Asian regional integration, growth, and economic convergence. Chapters 6 and 7 paint possible scenarios for Asia's agriculture and energy future and investigates the implications for the regional economy. Chapters 8 and 9 extend the scenario analysis to broader social development issues such as population aging and income distribution prospects.

Long-term forecasting is always risky: it often lacks adequate vision on technological innovation and almost by definition can hardly predict turning points. However, the scenarios presented in this book, and the analyses surrounding them, can serve as a useful starting point for the reader to think about the long-term opportunities and challenges of both the region and the wider world. I hope this book will provoke other reflective studies on Asia's future.

Ifzal Ali
Chief Economist
Asian Development Bank

Acknowledgments

The collection of papers in this volume was prepared as part of the technical assistance project "Long-Term Scenarios for Asian Growth and Trade" of the Asian Development Bank. The editor is grateful to all the contributors, for without their expertise and dedication this volume would not have seen the light of day. Thanks are also due to the anonymous referee who provided useful comments on the completed manuscript.

The project was initiated by Jean-Pierre Verbiest, then ADB's Assistant Chief Economist, who also worked out the formulation of the topics. Douglas Brooks contributed to the design and implementation of the project in its early stage. Ifzal Ali and Frank Harrigan provided overall guidance and support for the project. Somchai Jitsuchon and Chalongphob Sussangkarn (Thailand Development Research Institute), Xiaoji Zhang (Development Research Center of the State Council of the People's Republic of China), and Manoj Panda (Indira Gandhi Institute of Development Research, India) contributed background studies. The project also benefited from comments and suggestions received from participants of regional workshops held in Bangkok, Beijing, Mumbai, and New Delhi in 2005. Special thanks are due to Lea Sumulong, who assisted in the supervision, administration, and coordination of the project with great dedication and competence.

The views expressed in this volume are those of the authors and do not necessarily reflect the views and policies of the Asian Development Bank, its Board of Governors, or the governments they represent.

Contributors

Iain Bain, *College of Business and Economics, Australian National University*

Maurizio Bussolo, *Development Prospects Group, World Bank*

David Canning, *Harvard School of Public Health*

Siow Yue Chia, *Singapore Institute of International Affairs*

Jane Golley, *College of Business and Economics, Australian National University*

Alla A. Golub, *Center for Global Trade Analysis, Purdue University*

Frank Harrigan, *Asian Development Bank, Manila*

Thomas W. Hertel, *Center for Global Trade Analysis, Purdue University*

Rafael E. De Hoyos, *Development Prospects Group, World Bank*

William James, *Asian Development Bank, Manila (formerly Center for Strategic and International Studies, Jakarta)*

Carlos E. Ludena, *Center for Global Trade Analysis, Purdue University*

Patrick Low, *WTO Secretariat, Geneva*

Denis Medvedev, *Development Prospects Group, World Bank*

Jayant Menon, *Asian Development Bank, Manila (formerly Asian Development Bank Institute, Tokyo)*

Sergey Paltsev, *Joint Program on the Science and Policy of Global Change, Massachusetts Institute of Technology, Cambridge*

Michael G. Plummer, *The Johns Hopkins University, SAIS-Bologna, and East-West Center*

Richard Pomfret, *University of Adelaide, Australia*

Allan Rae, *Massey University, New Zealand*

John Reilly, *Joint Program on the Science and Policy of Global Change, Massachusetts Institute of Technology, Cambridge*

David Roland-Holst, *University of California, Berkeley*

Rod Tyers, *College of Business and Economics, Australian National University*

Dominique van der Mensbrugghe, *Development Prospects Group, World Bank*

Fan Zhai, *Asian Development Bank, Manila*

1

From Growth to Convergence: An Introduction

Fan Zhai, William James, and Frank Harrigan

1.1 DEVELOPING ASIA'S NEXT TWO DECADES: FIVE CONDITIONS FOR HIGH BUT CONVERGENT ECONOMIC GROWTH

The chapters of this volume provide insights into some of the critical issues confronting the world's most dynamic economic region—developing Asia. The future of the region is unfolding largely as an economic success: commercial and human development in conditions of rapid and sustained economic growth have become well established. Open capital markets and trade present ample opportunities for financial gains by investors who take a long view. The rich cultural traditions and varying natural environments of the region continue to captivate and entice travelers and businesspeople alike, driving growth forward in services, trade, and investment. The technological advances that have taken place in recent decades are becoming well grounded in the region and create grounds for optimism over the long term. Yet there are serious obstacles on the path forward, and these are analyzed in this volume.

The 1997–98 financial crisis that shook the region caused a setback to growth that some countries have still not fully recovered from. The unsettled conditions in global financial markets in 2007 that have resulted from the downturn in the United States (US) housing market are a reminder that the region's growth is still somewhat vulnerable to shocks from outside. A severe downturn in the US would hurt exports and expose the region's reliance on demand in large markets outside the region. While these are short- to medium-term concerns, this volume is explicitly intended to flesh out some of the key long-term issues that present difficult challenges to the region, including the issue of whether living standards of the poorer countries will converge with those of the richer ones during the next two decades or more. The reader should be amply rewarded in considering what the contributors to this volume have to say in this context.

The contributors have identified five key conditions to sustained high growth with convergence of per capita incomes among the main subregions of Asia over the coming two decades and beyond. These are in order of their appearance in the chapters that follow: (i) increased trade and regional integration through more open trade and investment policies; (ii) accelerated investment in infrastructure—both hard and soft; (iii) overcoming resource constraints that threaten to short-circuit growth and degrade the natural environment; (iv) population growth consistent with improved human resource development and broader labor participation rates; and (v) inclusive growth policies that enhance opportunities and incentives for all citizens without exception.

The authors evaluate the challenges of regional trade and investment integration, demographic transition, resource scarcity and substitution, and technological advance through various forward-looking scenarios of the global and Asian economy over the next 20–25 years. Building on observed recent historical trends in global and regional economic development, these scenarios are quantitatively constructed with dynamic computable general equilibrium (CGE) models. The use of CGE models ensures the internal consistency of the scenarios—the economic variables being investigated are consistent with each other in that they "add up." The methodology makes use of current knowledge about interactions in the economy and permits researchers to explore the economywide effects of different policy scenarios and shocks, helping reveal the key driving forces and major uncertainties for future development in the region.

In a sense this volume provides the reader with a future profile of what developing Asia could look like. The characteristics of the region are likely to evolve, so that it will be more integrated and will have a larger presence in global trade and investment, will be richer but less equal, will be older, and will have significant environmental impacts that must be considered in understanding global climate change.

Section 2 of this introductory chapter defines the main Asian subregions that have emerged as the most dynamic growth areas in the world economy in recent decades. The spread of industrialization from Japan to the newly industrialized economies (NIEs—Hong Kong, China; Republic of Korea; Singapore; and Taipei,China) of East Asia, then Southeast Asia, the People's Republic of China (PRC), and finally to India and the rest of South Asia is briefly reviewed in order to set the historical context of Asia's emergence in the latter half of the 20th century and its process of catching up with the developed regions of Western Europe and North America, as well as Australia and New Zealand in Oceania. Section 3 elaborates on the concept of high and convergent growth under the heading of Asia's growth dynamics. Section 4 discusses the five themes for Asia's high and convergent economic growth in more detail.

1.2 ASIAN DRAMA REDUX: THE EMERGENCE OF INDUSTRIALIZED ASIA IN THE 20TH CENTURY

Nobel laureate Gunnar Myrdal expressed the pessimistic view that the underdeveloped economies might never converge in terms of their living standards with the rich industrial countries.[1] In particular, Myrdal believed that the countries of South Asia and Southeast Asia were unlikely to emerge from poverty (Myrdal, 1968) in his famous three-volume magnum opus *Asian Drama: An Inquiry into the Poverty of Nations*. Events have since contradicted Myrdal's gloomy prognosis with the rapid industrial development of Japan and other Asian countries in the latter half of the 20th century.

The antecedents of Japan's emergence as an industrial power in the 20th century lie in the distant past. However, it was the encounter with the West in the mid-19th century that truly set in motion the wheels of modern Japanese technological and economic progress. Subsequent reforms coupled with strong preconditions, such as a fully literate population, provided fertile ground for Japan's post World War II takeoff in sustained high economic growth. Once Japan overcame immediate problems of high inflation and macroeconomic instability, as well as large fiscal and trade deficits, by adopting sound exchange-rate, fiscal, and monetary policies, it was able to tackle postwar reconstruction with vigorous enthusiasm. Light industrial exports flourished and allowed it to finance much needed imports of new machinery and raw materials to support industrial expansion. Nearly double-digit growth rates for more than two decades catapulted Japan into the ranks of the Organisation for Economic Co-operation and Development (OECD). Japan's success appeared to be threatened by the oil price and commodity shocks of the early 1970s. However, these shocks were quickly overcome and the economy continued to sustain growth in real per capita GDP that propelled it to higher living standards than those of many European countries.

This remarkable performance, underscored by high rates of domestic saving, as well as by high rates of investment and increasing openness to international trade, made Japan by the 1980s the world's second-largest economy, behind only the US. The lessons of Japan's "miracle" were not lost upon the next tier of East Asian economies, eager to jump start the process of catching up with the West.

The NIEs were all in one way or another in disadvantaged positions at the start of the growth process in the latter half of the last century. All faced security threats that caused governments to focus on building up strength through rapid industrialization. Political realities galvanized the governments of the NIEs to place emphasis on economic success, for which Japan provided an example of attainment.

The NIEs rejected the export pessimism that gripped much of the developing world, especially Latin America, by the early 1960s and, learning from the experiences of Japan and West Germany, adopted sound exchange-rate, fiscal, and monetary policies, all the while taking advantage of aid from the US and of the market access that the General Agreement on Tariffs and Trade (GATT) system provided. Exports of simple manufactures, particularly labor-intensive items such as clothing, footwear, toys, and furniture, took off and led to booming industrial development. Land reform and investment in education gave a fillip to rural development in Taipei,China and Korea and large numbers of young male and female labor-force entrants staffed the rapidly growing factories and service industries. By the early 1970s, manufacturing was moving into more capital-intensive and technologically advanced industries, fueled by investment and imports of advanced capital goods; exports soon followed. By the mid-1980s, the industrial and employment success of these four dynamos was being widely celebrated.

Events in the early 1970s–mid-1980s led to some dramatic changes in the economic architecture of Bretton Woods. The end of the gold standard and the relaxation of capital controls with the collapse of the fixed exchange rate system led to strains in economic relations with the US as it began to experience large trade deficits with Japan and the NIEs, particularly in the first half of the 1980s. The Plaza Accord of 1985 led to a sharp nominal and real appreciation of the yen, and other East Asian currencies followed. The currency realignment did not curb these economies' surpluses and instead led to a boom in foreign direct investment (FDI) not only into the US but also into the emerging Southeast Asian economies that had initiated reforms at just the right time.

The new wave of FDI from Japan and the NIEs fostered rapid industrial export development in Malaysia and Thailand, and soon thereafter in Indonesia and the Philippines—and somewhat later in Viet Nam, Cambodia, and the Lao People's Democratic Republic (Lao PDR). The resultant growth led the World Bank to include these countries in the new category of high-performing Asian economies. The "flying geese" model of Asian development through industrialization, trade, and investment that was initially popularized in Japan became standard fare in economics texts dealing with development and Asia—a far cry from Myrdal's version of a permanently impoverished region as expressed in his *Asian Drama* (1968).

The PRC began to emerge from three decades of autarky in the late 1970s. First, experimentation with price and market reforms in agriculture (decollectivization) in limited areas were followed up by more general reforms in rural towns and villages. Second, the development of special economic zones (SEZs) inviting private FDI first in Shenzhen and then in other coastal provinces led to a boom in investment, much of it originating from overseas Chinese keen to assist in development of their home country. Next, the PRC launched its decade-and-a-half-long march to rejoin the GATT—then World Trade Organization (WTO)—system with attendant reforms in financial and business laws, trade regulations, and labor and foreign exchange markets. The PRC's boom fueled rapid expansion of trade and investment flows in the region.

The populous nations of South Asia (Bangladesh, India, Pakistan, and Sri Lanka) remained largely outside the hyper-growth category until they began to experiment with economic reform in the 1980s. However, the reform efforts in South Asia were quite timid in the trade and investment fields until India suffered a severe balance-of-payments crisis in 1991. Then in timely fashion, it launched a series of liberalizing reforms that opened up the economy to FDI and trade. The opening coincided with the 1990s economic boom in the US and the move of the European Union (EU) to a single market beginning in 1992.

So, even though the collapse of Japan's bubble economy in the early 1990s led to slower growth there, global growth provided ample opportunities for India. Thus the PRC and India were well positioned to expand trade and attract inward FDI, and both moved into a phase of accelerating economic growth. Reforms in the rest of South Asia have been made, allowing Bangladesh, Pakistan, and Sri Lanka to begin to emerge as well.

1.3 ASIA'S GROWTH DYNAMICS

Developing Asia has sustained a remarkable growth performance over the past 20 years, with GDP growth rates averaging nearly 7% a year—or a near doubling of real GDP per decade. Still-rapid real GDP growth in Asia has helped reduce the income gap between these economies and the advanced economies of North America, Western Europe, Oceania, and Japan. During these two decades, Asia's real income per capita in constant 2000 US dollars increased 2.7 times. Its ratio to the OECD average measured in purchasing power parity (PPP) US dollars doubled from 8.6% in 1986 to 18.1% in 2006, in sharp contrast to the widening gap between non-Asian developing countries and the OECD (Figure 1.1).

Within the picture of rapid growth for the region as a whole, there are, however, significant variations across subregions (Figure 1.2). Growth was particularly strong in East Asia, largely driven by the robust performance of the PRC, which grew at an average annual rate of 9.7% during the period.

Figure 1.1 Per Capita Income of Developing Economies Relative to OECD, 1986–2006

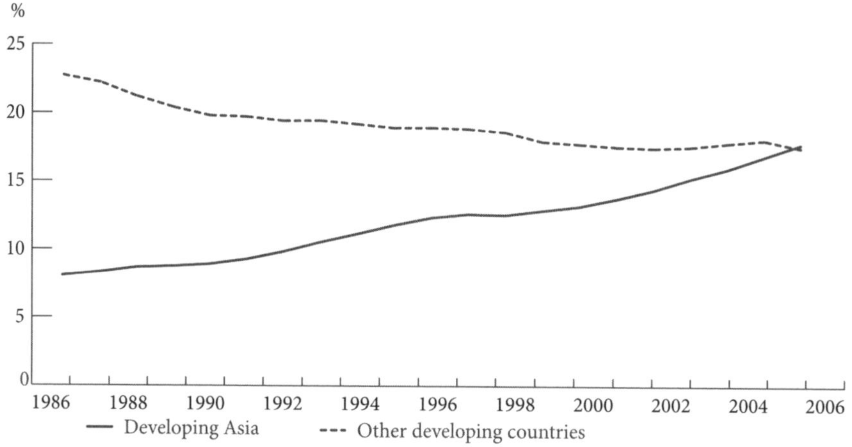

Source: World Bank, *World Development Indicators* database.

Figure 1.2 GDP Growth by Subregion, 1986–2006

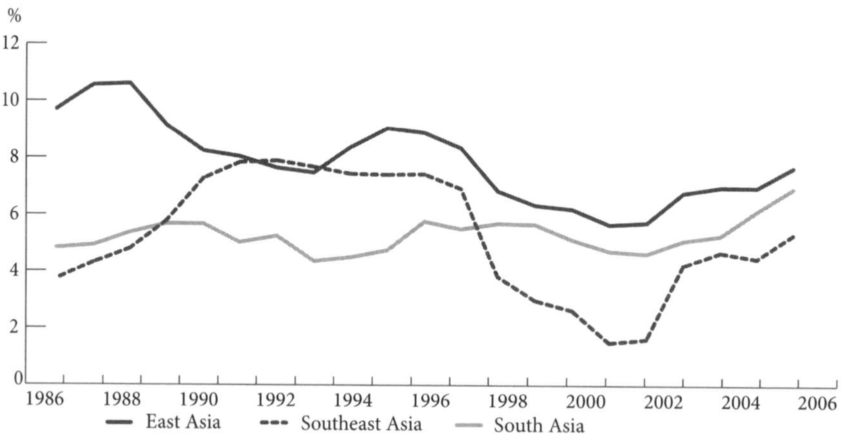

Sources: Asian Development Bank, *Asian Development Outlook* database and World Bank, *World Development Indicators* database.

Southeast Asia had more moderate growth due, in part, to the downturn during the crisis years. Growth rates in South Asia have begun catching up with the East Asian level in recent years. The growth rates were even more diversified among countries, ranging from an average of 4.0% a year in the Philippines to 9.7% a year in the PRC (Figure 1.3). Despite the fact that Asia includes some of the fastest-growing economies in the world, there are still a few in the region that suffer from prolonged sluggish growth (for example Nepal, Philippines, and Sri Lanka).

Figure 1.3 GDP Growth by Economy, 1986–2006 (%)

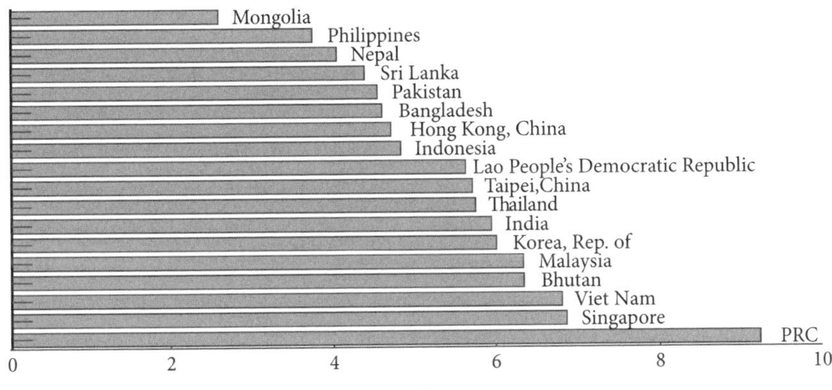

Source: Asian Development Bank, *Asian Development Outlook* database.

Asian growth and industrialization in the 20th century provides an example of a non-Western group of economies catching up with incomes of the advanced Western industrial economies. This catching-up process was never inevitable and must be understood as a consequence of historical conditions, policy choices made, and opportunities seized. Will a process of convergence in incomes and catching up in industrial development continue in the 21st century? These are the questions that this volume addresses by considering economic growth theory and empirical study of the still divergent growth processes in Asia's developing economies.

This divergent growth performance can partly be accounted for by the convergence force envisaged by the neoclassical growth model (Solow, 1956). The model predicts that, given the low ratios of capital to labor in the poorer countries (and the implicitly higher returns to capital), countries that begin with a lower level of per capita GDP will grow faster than those at initially higher income levels due to diminishing returns to capital. Thus, according to the model, lower-income economies of East, South, and Southeast Asia are expected to catch up with the NIEs and Japan in per capita income in the coming decades. Figure 1.4 shows the distribution of Asian economies in a plot of annual average growth of per capita GDP over 1986–2006 against the level of per capita GDP in 1986. As can be seen, the growth pattern of East and Southeast Asia is generally characterized by a convergence process, i.e., the catching-up through higher growth in per capita income by lower-income countries and the easing of growth momentum of richer, earlier developers.

This convergence characterizes PRC; Hong Kong, China, Korea; Malaysia; Singapore; Thailand; Taipei,China; and Viet Nam relative to Japan. However, some economies appear not to have performed as the convergence model predicts. Indonesia, Philippines, and Lao PDR—despite some growth in per capita GDP—have actually seen their relative standard of living fall further behind the lead economies. Thus, a priority in these countries is to accelerate their economic growth over the next two decades.

The South Asian countries have the lowest per capita income levels in Asia and have experienced some increase in overall GDP growth, but their per capita income growth rates have been lower than in most East and Southeast economies, mainly due to their higher rate of population growth. India is an exception as it has enjoyed a sustained period of rapid GDP growth, particularly following its economic reforms that began in the mid-1980s and that were deepened after 1991. India's population growth has also moderated in recent years from 2% a year in the 1990s to 1.5% in the period 2001–2006. Overall, convergence in Asian living standards has been accentuated by the emergence of the PRC and most of the Association of Southeast Asian Nations (ASEAN) member states and is extending into South Asia, largely as a result of India's recent success. Convergence of per capita incomes toward regional income countries has not yet become obvious, however, for much of South Asia, particularly for Bangladesh, Nepal, and Pakistan. Thus the growth pattern in Figure 1.4 may suggest the existence of a "club convergence" in Asia,

Figure 1.4 Economic Growth and Initial Income Level of Selected Asian Economies

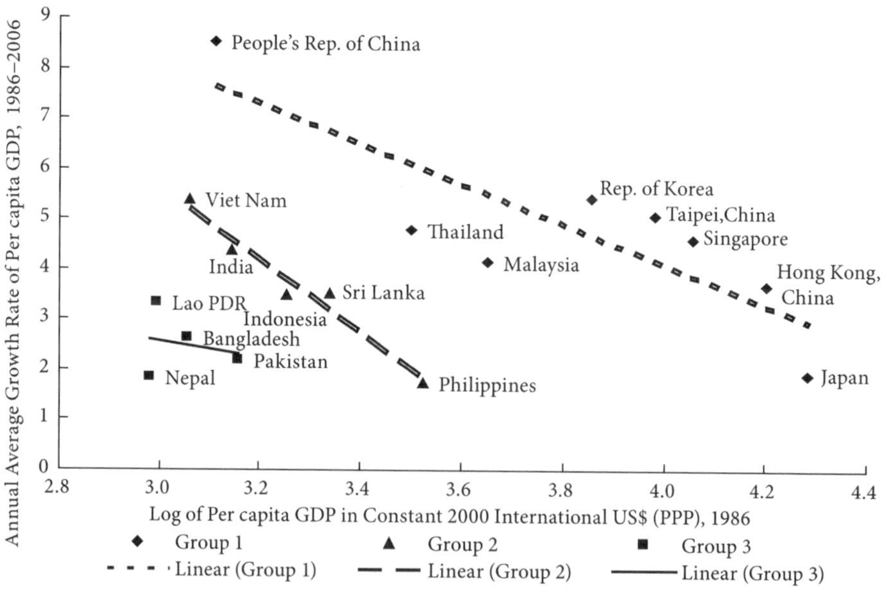

Sources: Asian Development Bank, *Asian Development Outlook* database and World Bank, *World Development Indicators* database.

under which the region is stratified into different clubs of growth according to long-term growth rates (Durlauf and Johnson, 1995; Quah, 1996, 1997). The members of the "rich club," including Japan and major East and Southeast Asian economies (Group 1 in Figure 1.4), tend to converge to a higher-growth rate in the long run, while other countries converge to lower long-run growth rates (Group 2 in Figure 1.4) or diverge (Group 3 in Figure 1.4).

The dominant trend in Asia over the past two decades can be characterized as convergence in East and Southeast Asia (with the exceptions of Philippines, Lao PDR, and Indonesia) and economic divergence between South Asia (with the exception of India) and other Asian economies. This trend has led to declining income inequality across countries within East and Southeast Asia, but increased inequality among all developing Asian countries.[2] Figure 1.5 plots the

Figure 1.5 Dispersion of Per Capita GDP in Developing Asia, 1986–2006

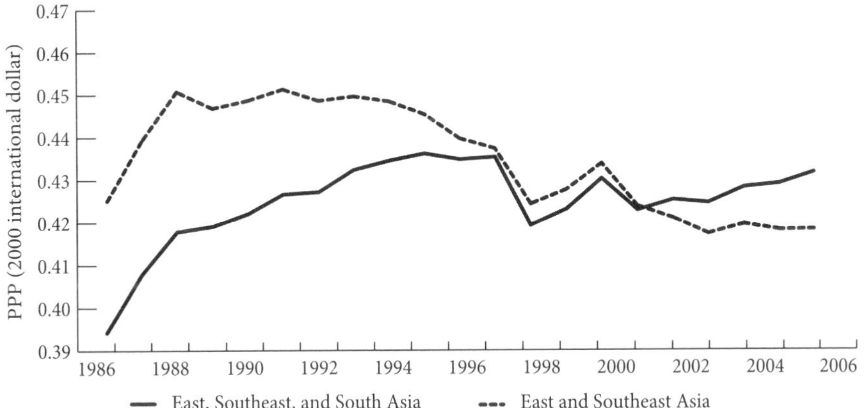

Source: World Bank, *World Development Indicators* database.

standard deviation of the logarithm of per capita GDP in the region over time. The standard deviation measure is known in the literature as σ- convergence (Barro and Sala-i-Martin, 1992). This measure for East, Southeast, and South Asia has tended to increase over the past two decades. At the same time, the standard deviation of income across East and Southeast Asian countries has stabilized since 1990 and trended downward in recent years. These changes in cross-country inequality can be better seen in Figure 1.6, which shows the ratio of per capita incomes in major developing Asian countries relative to Japan over the past two decades. It indicates that the NIEs and the PRC have been rapidly catching up with Japan in terms of per capita income while countries like the Philippines, Pakistan, and Nepal had hardly closed their income gaps with Japan over the last 20 years.

The patterns of growth of successful Asian economies in the cases of the

Figure 1.6 Per Capita Income Ratio Relative to Japan, 1986–2006

2000 International Dollar, Japan = 100

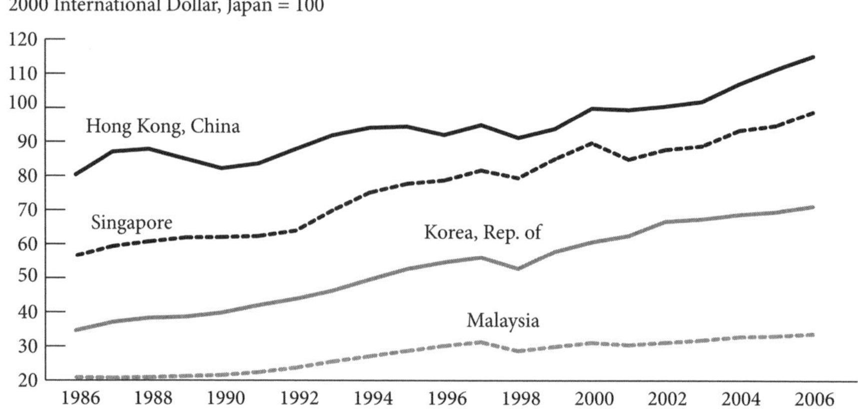

2000 International Dollar, Japan = 100

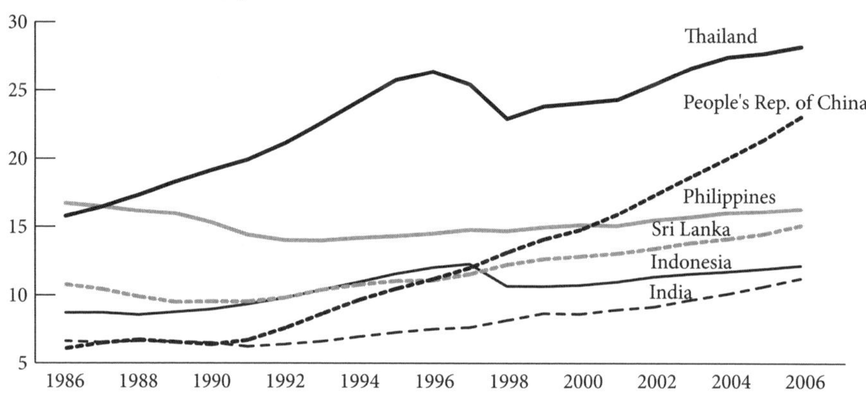

2000 International Dollar, Japan = 100

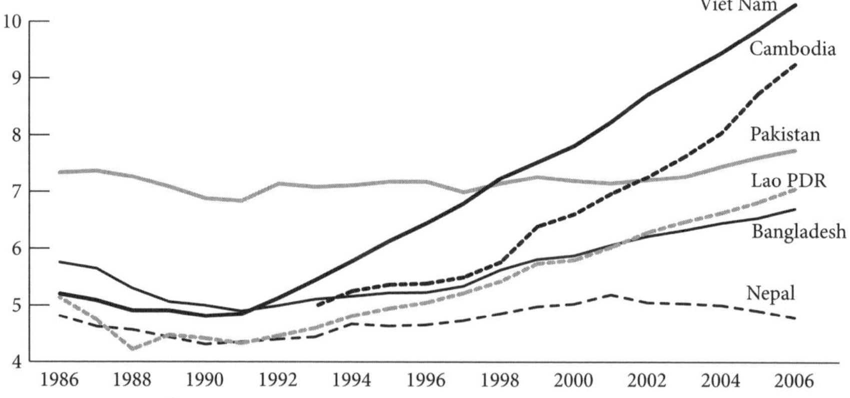

Source: World Bank, *World Development Indicators* database.

Figure 1.7 Long-term Growth Dynamics of Successful Asian Economies, 1955–2005

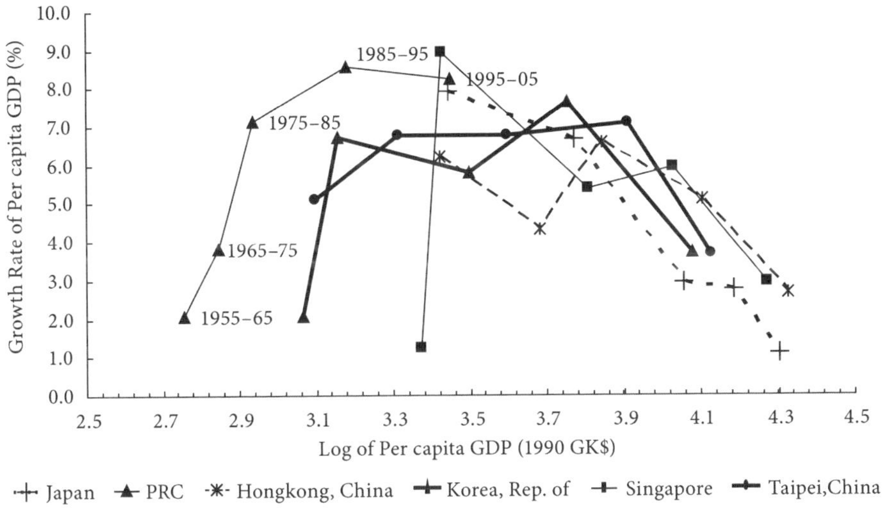

Source: The Conference Board and Groningen Growth and Development centre, Total Economy Database, November 2007, available: http://www.conference board.org/economics/

NIEs and Japan over a period of about five decades provides some useful insights into the process of growth and convergence to a high standard of living. The catching-up process is depicted (Figure 1.7) for the successful Asian economies (Japan and the NIEs). Interestingly, there is a clear pattern in per capita income growth in these cases. All have an inverted U-shaped time path, implying that the process of growth itself must first be generated in an initial set of circumstances. Starting from low levels of per capita income and slow economic growth, these economies underwent significant acceleration of their growth rates for a sustained period of time. Then growth decelerated as their per capita income converged to the level of industrial countries. For countries like the PRC, India, Viet Nam, and Cambodia, recent growth performance suggests that they are in the early phase of catching up, and appear to be moving along paths similar to those of their successful Asian predecessors. However, how long these pathways of high growth last remains to be seen.

Indonesia, Malaysia, and Thailand enjoyed rapid and sustained economic growth over the three decades of 1965–1995. However, the Asian financial crisis in 1997–98 set back their catching-up process with the advanced economies. Although there is no clear evidence that the crisis has derailed them from a growth path similar to that of Japan and the NIEs permanently, its impact on their growth has persisted for nearly a decade (ADB, 2007a). Some other Asian countries, including Philippines, Nepal, Pakistan, and Bangladesh, have not yet been able to succeed in achieving high rates of per capita income growth, partly because of inadequate savings rates and related excessively high population growth rates. Despite the recent strong pickup of economic growth in some of these economies, their long-term performance over the past decades suggests that they appear to be mired at a low level of income and stagnant economic growth, resulting in a widening income gap between them and other regional economies.

The poverty trap that some low-income countries have fallen into is often related to persistent political instability, ethnic, or ideological conflicts (for example, Philippines, Nepal, Bangladesh, and Sri Lanka). For example, the ethnic conflict in Sri Lanka between 1983 and 2006 is estimated to have cost households (averaging four people) the equivalent of over $26,000 at current exchange rates. If discounted, this translates into a 2% annual reduction in real per capita income growth (The Competitiveness Program, 2007). Structural problems also characterize the poverty trap and are exacerbated by instability and conflict. These include failure to invest enough in human capital (health, nutrition, and education), small market size coupled with inward-looking trade policies, low savings and investment rates, underdeveloped financial systems, geographic disadvantages, weak fiscal policies, and failures in institutions such as legal and political arrangements. High population growth and environmental destruction are additional features of these economies.

All these factors deter poor countries from exploiting their potential to catch up. Without sustained economic reforms, the countries locked in a poverty trap are unlikely to be able to break out of it. Reforms in governance are difficult to enact in countries with weak institutions and legal systems. However, carefully targeted assistance and development of reform constituencies can eventually lead to action on the reform front.

From the developing countries' viewpoint, successful catching-up requires a sustained period of higher than average growth. However, sustaining economic growth tends to be a harder challenge than igniting it for a period of time (Rodrik, 2005). Most of the growth accelerations in economic history have not been durable. Following the approach of Hausmann, Pritchett, and Rodrik (2005), ADB (2007b) examined growth episodes involving a rapid acceleration in economic growth that had been sustained for at least 8 years in developing Asia. It identified 24 growth accelerations since the mid-1960s, but only 10 of these were sustained over 8 years or more. Volatility in the external environment appears to have an important role in the growth collapses of many developing countries over the past 20 years. In these countries, growth and prosperity have often suddenly been hit by the shocks in the terms of trade, interest rates, and international capital flows.

The absence of fundamental reform, too, often causes setbacks in growth, as the growth dynamism triggered by the initial reform needs to be maintained through deepening of reform. Fundamental reform is also necessary for developing institutions that generate resilience to external shocks. In developing countries with weak institutions of conflict management, the distributive effects generated by the macroeconomic policy adjustments following external shocks often make these adjustments difficult to undertake. The different paces of post-Asian financial crisis recovery after 1998 in Korea and Indonesia highlight the importance of strong institutional capacity to cushion external shocks (Temple, 2003; Rodrik, 2005).

1.4 AN AGENDA FOR REGIONAL CONVERGENCE

Despite the impressive growth that has narrowed the income gap with developed countries in recent years, developing Asia as a whole is still far behind the rich countries in terms of per capita income, output per hour worked, and in comparisons of life expectancy, consumption of energy, nutrition, child mortality rates, and other comparisons of living standards. In 2005, the per capita GDP of developing Asia was on average equivalent to 17.4% of the OECD average in PPP terms and, still less, at 5.5%, in terms of income per head measured at market exchange rates. This suggests that Asia's convergence with the per capita income level of industrial economies will be a long process. In fact, even if both developing Asia and the OECD countries sustain their rates of per capita income growth at the same rates as over the past 5 years into the future, developing Asia will still require more than 50 years to catch up with the average OECD level of income in PPP terms.

The inclusion of the poorest regional economies into the process of growth is a prerequisite for a stable and prosperous Asia. The large and widening gaps between poor and rich in developing Asia highlight the need for a shift of the pattern of growth toward greater regional convergence. The achievement of higher standards of living for the people in the region will significantly reduce the global incidence of poverty. Past experiences have shown that existing institutional and market forces cannot spontaneously lead to similar living standards across countries. Heightened policy efforts, both domestic and international, are necessary to stimulate the catch-up process and spur the transition toward regional convergence. In-country inequalities must also be addressed through provision of more inclusive opportunities for education and health care and through enhancing labor market participation by females and migrant workers (among other initiatives for rural development).

Although intensified integration into the global economy and accelerated structural reform in most developing Asian economies in recent years have helped establish a favorable environment for future development, serious challenges may arise from the uncertain international environment, rapid demographic transitions, increasing resource pressures, and rising domestic inequalities. These realities can potentially derail Asia's promising future. An agenda for sustained growth and regional convergence needs to be built on the strengths of the regional economies and must also address the potential challenges. The key five components of this agenda are set out below.

1.4.1 Managing Asia's Trade Integration

Trade has been a key driver of economic growth over the last 50 years, for both industrial countries and some developing countries. Spence (2007) examines 11 individual cases of sustained high growth—defined as growth of over 7% a year and sustained for over 25 years—in post-World War II history. He found that in each of these cases—Botswana; PRC; Hong Kong, China; Indonesia; Japan; Korea; Malta; Oman; Singapore; Taipei,China; and Thailand—the export sector was a prime driver of growth with an increasing share of trade in GDP. The stellar growth performance of East Asia over the last 50-plus years has also clearly been associated with strong export-oriented growth (Petri, 2007). Imports have also played an important role, particularly imports of capital equipment embodying technological advances in industrial countries. Adapting these to East Asian conditions allowed rising productivity and enhanced capacity to produce higher-quality manufactured goods.[3] Every growth miracle involves leveraging the demand and resources of the global economy, and there are no exceptions to this principle.

In the last four decades, most East and Southeast Asian economies have gradually but consistently opened up their trade and investment regimes, and growth of these economies has responded positively to this increased openness (Petri, 2007). This process of trade reforms was led by Japan in the 1960s, and followed by the NIEs in 1970s, Sri Lanka and some of the members of ASEAN in the 1980s (Indonesia, Malaysia, and Thailand), and the PRC and new ASEAN member Viet Nam in the 1990s. South Asia (Bangladesh, India, and Pakistan), started their trade liberalization reforms in the 1990s and have significantly reduced import tariffs.[4] However, their tariff levels remain high relative to other regions and India and Pakistan continue to restrict the flow of trade between one another. This, together with the high cross-border trade costs of these two countries, has limited their participation in global trade.[5] Unlike East and Southeast Asia, South Asia's export and import to GDP ratios are lower than the world average.

Partly as a consequence of relative income and partly as a legacy of earlier trade regimes, most East and Southeast Asian exports have been targeted at the more affluent OECD markets in Japan, Europe, North America, and Oceania, inducing limited reliance on regional demand as a source of growth. However, this trade pattern has dramatically changed over the past decade. Intraregional trade in Asia has expanded more rapidly than extraregional trade and accounts for over half the region's total trade. This increased importance of intraregional trade reflects the faster economic growth in the region and, more importantly, the rise of regional production networks. This production fragmentation within Asia emerged in the 1990s, driven mainly by the desire of multinational corporations to improve their competitive position within the regional market through the positioning of plants where they were most efficiently located. This trend has been facilitated by a generally favorable policy setting (waiving of tariffs on imports or providing duty drawback for exporters, establishing export processing zones, encouraging export-oriented FDI, eliminating export restrictions, liberalizing foreign exchange regulations, and ensuring sound macroeconomic policies) and by an improvement in transportation and communications services, often through bringing in foreign providers. Not all policies favorable to exports were WTO-compatible, particularly the use of export subsidies, and these types of policies have consequently been replaced by those that are permissible under global trading rules.[6]

The policy reforms were timely and were accompanied by the increasing extent of relocation of industrial activities, substantial inflows of FDI into the region (particularly the PRC) and expansion of the back-and-forth trade of parts and components. Countries engaged in regional production networks are now specializing in tasks within the supply chain on the basis of their resource endowment and comparative advantage. And trade patterns within Asia are becoming much richer and more dynamic due to the sophisticated vertical division of production processes. The rise of intraindustry trade has involved vertical specialization in East Asia, particularly in machinery and transport equipment, with various activities along the supply chain being located according to cost minimization and other locational advantages, such as intellectual property protection, geographic advantages, or availability of inputs. Gradually, horizontal intraindustry trade in differentiated consumer products, particularly durable items such as passenger vehicles, is also rising, with incomes.

But trade within the Asian region is far from reaching its potential, especially between East Asia and South Asia, two of the most dynamic growth poles in the world in the 21st century. The rapid rise of the PRC and India will significantly reshape the global growth pattern, leading to a shift of global economic gravity toward Asia. This will promise tremendous trade opportunities for regional businesses and spread rapid growth across the Asian region (Roland-Holst et al., 2005). However, to fully realize the potential of regional trade and growth, some institutional changes are necessary. Unlike the cases of North America and the EU, economic integration in Asia has not been formalized by trade treaties. Asian integration has been largely market driven, with the private business sector as a primary force. Firms operating within the "factory Asia" production networks may increasingly be exposed to trade frictions within the region and beyond.[7] An institutionalized response may therefore increasingly be necessary, both to manage frictions that may arise and to ensure the smooth functioning of the regional production and trade system as a whole (Baldwin, 2006).

Within the region, countries have mounted some mutual efforts for more formal institutional arrangements to facilitate regional trade since early in the 1990s. This is partly motivated by the formation of regional trade blocs elsewhere—North American Free Trade Agreement (NAFTA) and the EU—but also reflects economic and geopolitical developments in the region. Since 2000 a new wave of Asian regionalism has been gathering momentum, leading to the proliferation of bilateral free trade agreements (FTAs).[8] Asian regionalism reflects growing integration that is taking place largely as a result of market forces and investment decisions taken by multinational enterprises, rather than as a result of formal regional preferential trade agreements (PTAs). The process of regionalism, however, is clearly extending itself to formal PTAs that are mainly bilateral but that also tend to correspond to membership of broader regional arrangements, such as ASEAN, Asia-Pacific Economic Cooperation, and related organizations such as the Pacific Economic Cooperation Council and the ASEAN Regional Forum. This indicates that institutional bases for regional integration are being strengthened.

While a broad regional framework of trade agreements appears to provide a promising approach to building the institutional underpinnings for regional integration, the current proliferation of bilateralism is flawed in several important respects. First, overlapping FTAs with multiple and complicated provisions and rules of origin saddle businesses with additional transactions costs in international trade, resulting in the "noodle bowl" (or "spaghetti bowl") phenomenon. Second, bilateral agreements limit the diversification of membership of FTAs. Third, many South Asian countries tend to maintain high most-favored nation external tariffs, resulting in high risks of trade diversion from FTAs. Finally, exclusion of sensitive sectors is common practice of many FTAs in Asia. For example, Japan and Korea tend to exclude key agricultural products in all their bilateral agreements. In addition, the ASEAN countries are allowed to exempt a number of sensitive products from the coverage of the ASEAN Free Trade Area. Services are largely excluded in most FTAs made by Asian developing countries.

In Chapter 2, *Why are Bilateral Trade Agreements so Popular, and Does it Matter?*, Jayant Menon provides a taxonomy of bilateral trade agreements (BTAs) in Asia with an assessment of the factors driving them and their impacts on both multilateralism and the global trading system. Menon argues that identifying the underlying motivations of the BTAs is important, not only to understand why bilateralism has been proliferating, but also to ascertain the potential impacts on the world trade system. The chapter attempts to classify the motivations for BTAs into general factors (such as the slow progress of multilateral negotiations under the WTO and domino effects resulting from countries' fears of exclusion from major markets) and specific factors (such as market access considerations in specific sectors and markets and of noneconomic strategic or political motivations). He observes that the sheer number of BTAs and their continued rapid growth are generally harmful to the world trading system, due to the spaghetti-bowl effect. The emphasis on BTAs also diverts scarce negotiating resources away from the multilateral front, lessening the chances of a successful conclusion to the WTO Doha Round.

Proliferation of BTAs will result in a more complex and costly trade environment for businesses as overlapping and idiosyncratic rules and standards impose high compliance and transactions costs. This will eventually force governments to seek remedies in order to restore a more rational system of trade. Menon compares three alternative remedies: (i) regionalism, i.e., consolidation of BTAs into regionwide PTAs or blocs; (ii) multilateralism, i.e., completion of the Doha Round with minimal compromises; and (iii) open regionalism, i.e., (for countries having engaged in multiple BTAs), equalizing preferences across these BTAs and offering concessions to non-BTA countries on a reciprocal basis—in essence making trade preferences available on a most-favored nation basis. The author argues that the third approach allows like-minded countries to roll their BTAs into what, in effect, would become a global open trade system, but without the difficulty of completing multilateral trade negotiations. Menon argues this would be more sensible than the first two options, given the possibility of regional trade blocs raising costs of world trade and the great uncertainties surrounding the outcome of global multilateral trade negotiations.

These three remedies are not necessarily incompatible. They could be pursued simultaneously. Chia Siow Yue comments on Chapter 2 and suggests three possible responses to the proliferation of regional trade agreements in Asia: ensuring the success of the Doha Round, improving the design of such agreements and convergence toward an Asian or East Asian agreement. The issues surrounding how to achieve these goals are taken up in Chapter 3, with a focus on the latter two objectives.

Chapter 3, *Regionalizing Bilateral Free Trade Agreements in Asia* by Frank Harrigan, William James, Michael Plummer, and Fan Zhai, notes that bilateralism has gained momentum in Asia largely as a defensive response to the emergence of trade blocs centered upon large "hub" economies such as Japan and the US. It is further motivated by the stalling of the Doha Round.

In view of the advantages of BTAs in terms of the possible depth of trade and investment facilitation and liberalization, a practical and appropriate policy response is to accept them, identify major pitfalls, and try to avoid these pitfalls or fix them. In addition, many of the new BTAs have "WTO-plus" features that include extending services and investment liberalization to all service providers operating within the member states on a nondiscriminatory basis (that is, regardless of whether or not the owners of the service providers are citizens of the states that are signatories to the BTA). Trade facilitation by definition is nondiscriminatory and benefits all who engage in trade transactions.

Building on these features would strengthen the beneficial aspects of the BTAs by extending benefits on a broader basis. After reviewing the requirements for bilateral or regional PTAs in the WTO, the chapter proposes 10 "rules of thumb" on good practices in BTAs, including: comprehensive product and services coverage, low and symmetrical rules of origin, transparent customs procedures, and objective and expeditious dispute-resolution arrangements. The chapter reveals that complex and overlapping rules of origin are a major concern in the proliferation of bilateral agreements involving developing Asian countries. Moreover, intra-Asian BTAs tend to offer less favorable treatment than extra-Asian PTAs, potentially threatening the development of efficient regional production networks.

To what extent can good practices in regional FTAs deliver benefits? Chapter 3 explores this issue by simulation of some hypothetical quantitative scenarios for regional trade agreements using a CGE model. Generally, the simulation results confirm the benefits of good practices and more open FTAs. The key finding in the scenario analysis is of the superiority of a single regionwide FTA as opposed to both bilateralism and to hub-and-spoke systems in general. One possible outcome that is likely to be third best is the emergence of hub-and-spoke systems around individual large hub economies like Japan and India. Because of the large product exclusions and the missing connections among the spokes in this case, each hub becomes the major benefactor of market access improvements while denying these full benefits to the smaller spoke economies.

The simulations also suggest that, sometimes, good practices may be insufficient to avoid net trade and investment diversion, as in cases where hub-and-spoke arrangements shift trade in intermediate products from low-cost suppliers outside the BTA to the hub and where there is strong potential for terms-of-trade deterioration in one or more of the spoke countries. Good practices in bilateral agreements can lessen the damage they are likely to do, but they cannot eliminate it altogether. In this sense, the authors suggest that pursuing good practices in BTAs and expanding the current overlapping regional BTA web into a unified regional FTA are equally important to Asian countries. An ASEAN-plus strategy may provide a promising way out of the current dilemma posed by bilateralism as a step on the way to an Asian FTA.

Patrick Low's commentary on Chapter 3 points out that what happens to trade costs tends to dominate the outcomes in these simulations. For this reason, comparison of various configurations of hub-and-spoke systems of preferential trade with complex and overlapping rules of origin and unconnected spokes are definitely inferior to a single, large FTA with all spokes and hubs connected under one set of rules. The analysis in Chapter 3 is critical of the architecture that many of the BTAs within the region are adopting and, as Low points out, the result may be incoherence and reduced opportunities for efficient development of production-sharing arrangements in Asia.

Asia's trade is rapidly expanding and its trade regimes are becoming increasingly complicated, with the blending of unilateral, regional, and multilateral disciplines. The analysis in Chapters 2 and 3, however, highlights the potential vulnerabilities in the international trading system and in the architecture of the region's bilateralism that might undermine trade dynamism in the future. The risks are manageable, but efforts to move toward a single harmonized trade agreement in the region will be crucial in the absence of a successful multilateral trade round. Achieving this single agreement will require bold leadership and a clear road-map that will allow all participating countries in the region to take the necessary steps within a delineated time frame.

1.4.2 Catalyzing Growth and Integration

Given the importance of trade in economic growth, connecting poor countries into international markets should be an important aspect of their growth strategies. Like the growth process, the development of regional integration has been uneven across Asia. The countries that have lagged in terms of economic growth have also been less engaged in the regional integration process. Locked in by adverse geographic conditions, poor infrastructure, weak institutional quality, or low levels of human capital, these poor countries have weak connections with the international economy and are also being bypassed by the process of regional integration. As both manufacturing and services production tends to agglomerate in a few leading countries (or a few leading regions within a country) to take advantage of economies of scale, knowledge spillovers, and large market size, trade liberalization alone may be insufficient to connect poor countries to international markets or to allow isolated countries access to regional markets.[9] Their potential for participation in regional integration to achieve rapid growth needs to be catalyzed by comprehensive efforts toward structural and institutional reforms as well as financial assistance, technology transfer, and substantial investment in infrastructure.

Chapter 4, *Infrastructure as a Catalyst for Regional Integration, Growth, and Economic Convergence: Scenario Analysis for Asia*, by David Roland-Holst, provides an overview of regional infrastructure investment as a means of accelerating growth and integration using a CGE model. Roland-Holst argues that because of geographic realities, unleashing the full trade and growth potential of the largest economies in developing Asia—the PRC and India—will depend critically on infrastructure development. With improved infrastructure, Southeast Asia could act as an attractive bridge to connect the two emerging giants, and capture many of the indirect growth spillovers from intensified Sino-Indian trade linkages. The author identifies three different economic roles played by infrastructure: as a demand stimulus, as a means of reducing trade costs, and as a spur to productivity growth. In the first case, significant economywide multiplier effects accelerate growth, particularly in less-developed regional economies whose initial conditions require larger amounts of investment to upgrade infrastructure.

To elucidate the role of reducing trade costs, the author uses investment scenarios to demonstrate how infrastructure investment can facilitate market access and regional integration, sharply increasing economic growth. Two types of countries are most likely to gain from this infrastructure effect: those with very high prior domestic margins, and those with high prior levels of external trade dependence. Finally, appealing to an extensive theoretical literature on endogenous growth effects, the author gives indicative results about how infrastructure-induced productivity growth can stimulate regional integration and convergence. Taken together, these results demonstrate that infrastructure development can be a potent catalyst for wider economic participation, both within and between Asian economies. It also promises large benefits to the poorest regional economies.

In his commentary, David Canning sets out three cases where marginal social benefits diverge from marginal social costs in the context of infrastructure investment: (i) the public goods argument (arising either from non-rival use or from non-excludability); (ii) externalities in consumption or production; and (iii) monopoly power. He notes that these three cases all arise in the context of infrastructure investment, though each may apply with more or less relevance depending upon the type of infrastructure and its technology. His commentary distinguishes how these cases apply to roads, telephones, and electricity. In the example of the provision of a road, he points out the road's effect of linking many specialized firms, permitting efficient development of production networks rich in intermediate and differentiated goods, thus increasing competition and reducing markups, and thereby expanding trade as trade costs fall. He adds that recent technological advances may have diminished the problems of non-exclusion and of monopoly, and that governments had to carefully consider these issues in designing their interventions in infrastructure provision and operation.

Trade facilitation reform can also play a significant role in promoting regional integration and achieving more rapid and sustained growth across Asia, because trade costs arising from logistical, institutional, and regulatory barriers are increasingly becoming the binding constraints on modern international business, especially in poor economies. With a focus on the trade performance of Asia's least-developed countries, Fan Zhai in Chapter 5, *Unlocking the Trade Potential in Least-Developed Countries: A CGE Investigation for Bangladesh*, asks why their trade growth has been slow and how they can be included in the rapid regional integration process.

Using Bangladesh as an example, he argues that in addition to restrictive trade policies, some domestic supply-side constraints severely limit the export competitiveness of the poorest economies. A weak institutional environment and poor infrastructure are often two major constraints. These constraints significantly increase trade costs, deterring a large proportion of firms from engaging in export and import activities. The chapter investigates alternative scenarios of unlocking the trade potential of Bangladesh through trade liberalization, domestic technology promotion, and comprehensive trade facilitation reform.

The simulation results demonstrate that, given its current high tariff rates, Bangladesh can achieve important gains in terms of exports and welfare from less costly imports through unilateral trade liberalization. However, to fully tap its trade potential, Bangladesh needs to address some important supply-side constraints through effective and comprehensive trade facilitation reform. Such reform—focusing on reducing broad trade costs—would significantly boost the economy's export competitiveness, diversify its export structure, and bring larger welfare gains to the country than tariff reductions alone. Zhai suggests that the policy focus should not be confined to traditional tariff and nontariff barriers. Infrastructure, ports and customs efficiency, simplification and coherence of rules, and the investment climate are at least equally important to trade development in most developing countries. In least-developed countries, policy makers have to make sequential reforms within a comprehensive and ambitious overall long-term plan if they are to greatly reduce barriers to trade both at the border and behind the border.

Richard Pomfret in his commentary demonstrates that, despite some reform of traditional trade barriers, industry in Bangladesh remains shielded from foreign competition through measures such as para-tariffs that raise nominal protection rates on average to 26.5%. He also points out that the costs of starting a business are high, that property registration and contract enforcement are plagued by inordinate delay, and that poor infrastructure and a plodding customs service all increase trade costs and deter investment. He asks whether the author's target of a 30% reduction in trade costs is plausible for Bangladesh. Despite this caveat, he feels that the analysis of the chapter successfully shows that lingering protection and high trade costs are preventing Bangladesh from truly liberalizing and becoming a "Bengal Tiger."

1.4.3 Addressing Resource Constraints

Natural resource vulnerabilities could be an important constraint for the future growth of developing Asia. The World Bank (2000) argues that a sustained growth path can only be achieved through balanced asset accumulation across physical, human, and natural capital. If past growth in the region was somewhat reliant upon the contributions from natural capital, i.e., the rapid depletion of natural resources and depreciation of environmental stocks, its long-term growth prospects will depend on whether or not resource and environmental conditions can be improved.

In fact, there have been increasing signs of pressures on resources in developing Asia. Scarcity of fresh water for human consumption, crop production, and industrial use is likely to become a binding constraint on economic growth in the PRC and India in the near feature (Winters and Yusuf, 2007). In the energy sector, developing Asia has less than 3% of the world's proven oil reserves. In addition, the limited supply of land, under threat from rapid urbanization and environmental hazards, could be a primary constraint hindering expansion of agricultural production unless agricultural productivity can be increased within the intensive margin, that is, by increasing yields at least in proportion to non-land inputs.

Technological progress will be a major means of overcoming resource constraints. Chapter 6, *Economic Growth, Technological Change, and the Patterns of Food and Agricultural Trade in Asia*, by Thomas Hertel, Carlos Ludena, and Alla Golub, examines patterns of trade and structural change of food and agricultural products and implications for long-term price trends. It finds that technological change is the critical determining factor in whether real food prices will return to their historical downward trend after the recent upswing. Moreover, the chapter finds that much of the past agricultural productivity growth in Asia has been fueled by catch-up with the existing technology frontier, rather than an outward shift in the frontier itself. Given the shrinking gap between current practice and the existing technology frontier, this finding suggests that future agricultural total factor productivity (TFP) growth in Asia is likely to slow, especially in East and Southeast Asia, if the region's economies do not make faster progress in agricultural technology innovation. Though there may be some scope for productivity to increase in the non-crop livestock and fisheries sectors through complementary investments and in food crops by rehabilitation or improvement of rural roads and irrigation works, the application of scientific research holds out the best hope for such productivity gains.

Alan Rae notes in his commentary that two forces that are not explicitly incorporated into the analysis of food demand in Chapter 6 may have some influence in altering the predicted consumption patterns: urbanization and the changing age structure of the population. He also notes that on the supply side, a more rapid loss of agricultural land could have different impacts on production of crops as opposed to raising of livestock, as the latter can be increased more easily through greater use of non-land inputs than the former. These issues could be explored further through a disaggregation of the sector and estimation of TFP separately for crops and livestock.

Rae also reminds the reader that technological advances may not follow past patterns of accelerating progress after an initial period of learning. Research and development (R&D) activity and expenditure are clearly important in determining the pace of technological advance. The paltry rise of TFP that is projected for East and Southeast Asia may need to be revised upward if R&D activity increases. That aside, there is little doubt that developing Asia will increase its imports of food and agricultural products significantly over the next 20 years and its economies' agricultural trade balances will continue moving into deficit. This will create new export opportunities for agricultural suppliers in other regions.

With expected rapid economic expansion and increasing resource pressures, developing Asia will have to raise its dependence on the rest of the world for the supply not only of agricultural products, but also of energy. In Chapter 7, *Energy Scenarios for East Asia, 2005–2025*, Sergey Paltsev and John Reilly sketch a number of alternative energy futures in Asia through a global CGE model. It starts from a baseline scenario, which essentially extends observed historical trends into the future. Several alternative scenarios are also examined with different assumptions about economic growth rates, energy efficiency, and energy prices, to provide a sensitivity analysis of the baseline results to some key uncertainties. In their baseline scenario, the authors predict rapid growth of global energy demand, relatively rigid energy supply and, as a consequence, a sharp rise of energy prices in the next 20 years. The oil price in baseline is predicted to double from an average US$40/barrel in 2000–2005 to around US$80/barrel in 2025 (measured in average constant 2002–2006 prices).[10]

The comparison of different scenarios in Chapter 7 finds that Asian demand will make substantial impacts on world commodity markets. It estimates that if the growth rates of developing Asian economies in the next two decades double from 3–5% per year to 6–10% per year, the international oil price in 2025 will increase from $80 per barrel to $100 per barrel. The chapter also finds the PRC to be a dominant source of future growth of Asia's energy demand. About two thirds of the difference in Asia's total energy use between the baseline and high-growth scenarios is attributable to economic growth in the PRC. Higher growth in the PRC alone could lead to a rally of international oil prices in 2025 of nearly $10 per barrel, with an overall oil price premium created by increased Asian demand of up to $25 per barrel.

Heavier reliance on commodity imports would leave developing Asian economies more exposed to terms-of-trade shocks, as world commodity markets are volatile in nature. Chapter 7 also evaluates the adverse regional growth effects that rising energy prices will create. Its baseline forecast projects a 20–30% rise in coal prices, a 100% rise in oil prices, and a 100–150% rise in natural gas prices over the period 2005–2025. The chapter estimates that these energy price increases could place a drag on growth of Asian countries of up to 0.6% a year.

As David Roland-Holst in his commentary points out, by historical standards these growth effects seem moderate. However, if the growth of the global economy was dragged down by steadily rising energy prices, spillover effects on growth become more dramatic and more complex. For example, a sustained recession in OECD countries accompanied the great energy shocks of the 1970s, and this downturn was transmitted to developing economies via falling OECD absorption. Given the increasing importance of Asian economies to the global economy and to world commodity markets, the region's governments and businesses need to improve substantially their abilities to manage the risks arising from volatile world commodity markets.

Improvements in regional infrastructure will help secure supplies of vital food and energy for developing Asia. Chapter 7 finds that if regional gas markets develop through better pipeline links between East Asia and the Russian Federation and the Middle East, gas use in Asia could grow substantially more than in the baseline scenario, an increase by about 75%. This would largely occur through switching of gas for coal. This finding underlines the importance of regional infrastructure to a more secure and clean energy future in Asia.

David Roland-Holst's commentary underscores the uncertainties in Asia's energy future and points out that conventional sources of energy (oil, coal, and natural gas) are likely to find it increasingly hard to meet demand from rapidly growing Asian economies, particularly the PRC, especially when the realization of promises of new renewable alternative sources of energy remain uncertain. Hence, global energy markets will continue to arbitrate access to these conventional sources. The effects of possible future energy price hikes will be determined by a combination of adaptability and purchasing power, and these effects may have important consequences for the global convergence process. Economic analysis of the consequences can help governments reach more effective decisions on the appropriate policies.

1.4.4 Preparing for Demographic Transition

Variables associated with demographic change are fundamental in determining an economy's potential growth rate, although a long time lens must be used in examining these demographic factors. During the next five decades, developing Asia is expected to undergo a dramatic demographic change. Lower fertility and longer life expectancy will lead to an aging of its population. The proportion aged 65 and above will grow rapidly across all Asian countries. This aging process is already visible in the NIEs and the PRC; is beginning to take hold in some Southeast Asian countries (for example, Thailand); and is expected to emerge in 20–25 years in South Asian countries. For the region as a whole, the proportion of the population aged 65 and above is expected to double over the next 20 years.

The graying of the population is not a new phenomenon, and has been experienced by almost all industrial countries. But the pace of aging in developing Asia will be much more rapid than that experienced by the rest of the world. According to United Nations (UN) medium population projections, developing Asia is likely to take only 23 years for the share of the population over age 65 to double from 7% (a level the UN defines as an "aging society") to 14% (a level it defines as an "aged society"). This transition took 40–100 years in most European countries (Table 1.1).

With the exception of Bangladesh, Pakistan, and Philippines, all major East Asian, Southeast Asian, and South Asian economies will become aging societies (UN definition) in the next two decades. For these economies facing aging demographics, the prospects for economic growth are generally optimistic. By the time their elderly dependence rates reach 14%, their per capita income in PPP terms would be in the range experienced by the EU and Japan at the time they were becoming aged societies. Hence, although the fast pace of aging will pose challenges, "growing old before growing rich" will not be a major concern for most of developing Asia.

The direct challenge arising from population aging is the shrinking of the labor supply, which is expected to begin happening in the NIEs, PRC, Sri Lanka, and Thailand in about 2015. Population aging is expected to result in declines in rates of saving and investment, because the elderly tend to save at a lower rate and because reduced labor supply growth lessens the returns to investment. These factors tend toward slowing the rate of GDP growth.

More serious challenges come from the inadequacy of social safety nets for rapidly aging populations. In developing Asia, the traditional family-based

Table 1.1 Speeding of Population Aging in Developing Asia and Industrial Countries

	Year of Share of Elderly Reaching [a]		Number of Years
	7%	14%	
Developing Asia	2014	2037	23
China, People's Rep. of	2001	2026	25
Korea, Rep. of	1999	2017	18
Indonesia	2018	2039	21
Malaysia	2020	2043	23
Philippines	2028	-	-
Singapore	2000	2016	16
Thailand	2002	2023	21
Viet Nam	2020	2038	18
Bangladesh	2031	-	-
India	2022	2049	27
Pakistan	2034	-	-
Sri Lanka	2008	2026	18
Industrial Countries			
Japan	1970	1994	24
Canada	1945	2020	65
United States	1942	2013	71
Finland	1958	1994	38
Germany	1932	1972	40
Greece	1951	1992	41
Poland	1966	2013	47
United Kingdom	1929	1976	47
Switzerland	1930	1982	52
Italy	1927	1988	61
Sweden	1887	1972	85
France	1864	1979	115

[a] The share of population over 65 in total population.

Sources: OECD (2001); United Nations (2006), World Population Prospects, medium projections, available: http://esa.un.org/unpp.

social security systems are gradually eroding, yet the public pension and health care systems are not well enough established to meet the demands from tomorrow's elderly generations. Only a few countries have pension schemes that will cover more than a fraction of the elderly population.

Faced with these demographic challenges, the region's governments must respond with policy actions. In the PRC, relaxation of the "one-child policy" may partly offset the contraction of the labor force and help slow the aging of the population. Chapter 8, *Projected Economic Growth in the People's Republic of China and India: The Role of Demographic Change* by Rod Tyers, Jane Golley, and Iain Bain, examines how changing fertility rates in the PRC and India may affect economic growth over the period to 2030. Simulation results indicate that a two-child policy in the PRC would achieve the twin goals of increasing GDP and reducing the proportion of the aged population dependency ratio (from 21% to 18%). They also imply, however, that by 2030 per capita income declines by almost as much as GDP goes up, a result that stems primarily from an associated large rise in the youth dependency ratio as well as from adverse changes in skilled emigration, capital income repatriation, and the terms of trade. Thus the authors argue that if higher fertility rates are considered desirable in order for the PRC to achieve its objectives, policy efforts will need to be directed toward mitigating the negative impact of higher population growth on per capita income.

With India currently forecast to become the world's most populous country by 2030, its population policy will continue to be directed toward promoting declines in fertility. A faster fertility decline in India necessarily leads to lower GDP growth, yet the benefits in terms of per capita income could be substantial. In both the PRC and India, the chapter concludes that while lower fertility reduces GDP and increases per capita income, India gains substantially more per capita income than the PRC per unit of change in fertility, a result that depends critically on India's higher youth dependency. India therefore has considerably more to gain, at least in per capita terms, from further reducing fertility.

In his commentary to this chapter, David Canning points out that the economic dividend of East Asia's demographic transition to lower fertility rates with a young and rapidly increasing labor force was an acceleration in per capita income growth. The higher proportion of the working-age population to young and old dependents, coupled with the rise in life expectancy and the increase in labor force participation by women, created more dynamic growth. In the cases of India and the PRC, these demographic factors help explain much of the acceleration in per capita GDP growth between 1960–1965 and 1995–2000, with increased trade and higher educational attainment also having significant impacts upon growth acceleration. In the future, the decline in the proportion of the working-age population to the total and the effect of higher per capita incomes will be to slow growth in income per head in these two giant economies, with the slowdown likely to be more pronounced in the PRC than in India due to the effects of the PRC's one-child policy on the labor force.

But Canning points out that the policy environment may be able to mitigate some of the effects of aging on growth. For example, greater female labor participation, productivity improvements related to higher levels of education and skill, and application of new technologies would help offset somewhat the effects on the labor force and unit labor costs.

1.4.5 Making Growth More Inclusive

In spite of overall rapid growth and significant poverty reduction, income inequality within countries has increased sharply in developing Asia over the

Table 1.2 Changes in Inequality in Selected Developing Asian Countries

	Period	Gini Coefficient	
	Start Year–End Year	Start	End
Gini for Income			
Bangladesh	1991–2005	0.283	0.341
Cambodia	1993–2004	0.318	0.407
China, People's Rep. of	1993–2004	0.407	0.455
India	1993–2004	0.329	0.362
Indonesia	1993–2002	0.344	0.343
Korea, Rep. of	1992–2005	0.284	0.348
Malaysia	1993–2004	0.412	0.403
Mongolia	1995–2002	0.332	0.328
Nepal	1995–2003	0.377	0.473
Pakistan	1992–2004	0.303	0.312
Philippines	1994–2003	0.429	0.440
Singapore	1990–2005	0.436	0.522
Sri Lanka	1995–2002	0.344	0.402
Thailand	1992–2002	0.462	0.420
Viet Nam	1993–2004	0.349	0.371

Sources: ADB (2007c), Krongkaew and Zin (2007).

past two decades. This trend has been most pronounced in the PRC, where the Gini coefficient, a measure of inequality, rose from 0.26 in 1985 to 0.46 in 2004 (Kanbur and Zhang, 2005). But it has also visibly increased in almost all other regional economies, ranging from low-income countries such as Bangladesh to high-income NIEs, and from rapidly growing economies such as India and Viet Nam to stagnating economies such as the Philippines (Table 1.2). Only the countries severely hit by the Asian financial crisis (Indonesia, Malaysia, and Thailand) and Mongolia have experienced a decline in Gini coefficients in the past decade.[11]

Overall income inequality has risen partly as a reflection of the increase in inequality between regions within a country. The growth in the PRC over the past two decades has been associated with a widening inland–coastal disparity, as the concentrated growth in coastal regions has left behind the inland regions. The richer southern states of India have grown 3 percentage points faster than the poorer more populous northern states in recent years. In Sri Lanka, GDP in the Western Province grew at 6.2% annually over 1997–2003 as compared with 2.3% for the rest of the country (World Bank, 2006). A large and persistent regional disparity can also be seen in Indonesia (Java vs elsewhere), Philippines (Luzon island vs the peripheral islands of Visayas and Mindanao), Thailand (Bangkok and surrounding area vs the Northeast region), Viet Nam (north vs south and interior highlands vs the coastal lowlands), and Pakistan (Punjab province vs Baluchistan and North-West Frontier province).

In the PRC and some low- and middle-income Southeast Asian countries, the urban–rural disparity is also a major factor contributing to overall inequality. The rising disparity between cities and rural areas reflects the large initial proportion of the rural population in the total population, lower agricultural productivity growth, and relatively limited rural–urban migration opportunities. In these countries, average real consumption levels in urban areas are often about twice as high as in rural areas, and the difference in average income levels is even greater (Gill and Kharas, 2007). Urban–rural income disparity accounted for more than 40% of overall income inequality in the PRC in 2002 and 26–30% in the Philippines (Sicular et al, 2007; Shorrocks and Wan, 2005). In Viet Nam, 32% of the overall expenditure inequality in 1997/98 was attributed to the urban–rural difference (Heltberg, 2003). The low education levels of the rural labor force and institutional barriers are often major impediments to urban-rural labor mobility in these countries (Gill and Kharas, 2007).

Rapid economic growth, globalization and the nature of technological change are prime causes of growing inequality in Asia. Due to the abundance of unskilled labor and the much more rigid supply of skilled workers (which depends on medium- and long-term investment in education), rapid economic growth in Asian economies tends to raise the wage gap between skill groups. Technological change is often biased toward skilled-labor and capital, generating more demand for skills. In recent years, accelerating technological change in skill-intensive services such as information, communication, transportation, and financial services industries have contributed to higher levels and growth of wages in these sectors. Large FDI flows and the formation of regional production networks have brought about an agglomeration of economic activities surrounding populous large cities, exacerbating spatial inequality. Moreover, increasing returns to scale in new and export-oriented machinery industries operating production networks may lead to disproportional gains to owners and management of large business firms. Although increasing land and environmental pressures may eventually lead to a shift of industries to peripheral regions, so far the dominant role of agglomeration forces has been apparent.

If current trends continue, domestic inequality in developing Asia will tend to increase over the next 20 years. Chapter 9, *Global Growth and Distribution: Asia and its Progression to Developed Status* by Maurizio Bussolo, Rafael De Hoyos, Denis Medvedev, and Dominique van der Mensbrugghe, presents a baseline scenario of global growth and income distribution in 2005–2030.

Consistent with most other long-term scenarios in the volume, Chapter 9 envisages an increasingly important region with respect to world trade and income. Between 2005 and 2030, global GDP is projected to more than double, with the PRC and India accounting for a significant share. The per capita income gap between developing Asia and rich countries significantly narrows by 2030. The authors also highlight some key features of long-term global economic development: the fundamental roles of productivity and demographic change in the process of economic growth, a rather modest income convergence overall in the world economy, deepening trade integration, a more pronounced shift of production toward service activities in developing Asia, and, as a consequence, a rise in the skill premium and wage inequality within fast-growing economies.

Through combining CGE-based projections with a micro simulation based on standardized household surveys, the chapter finds, plausibly, that global economic growth will lead to a decrease in global inequality—with a decline in the global Gini index of 5 points between 2005 and 2030. This reduction is entirely explained by a reduction in disparities in average incomes across countries; moreover, 86% of the total reduction is accounted for by the difference in average income between the PRC and India versus that in the rest of the world. However, more than two thirds of low- and middle-income countries in the study sample (accounting for 86% of the population in the developing world) are projected to experience a rise in domestic inequality by 2030. Widening gaps in factor rewards, and particularly in the premium paid in for higher skills, are key driving forces behind the rise in inequality within countries.

Developing Asian economies will generally experience increases in domestic inequality due to their low initial skill premiums and high per capita growth rates. Faster growth generates more demand for skill-intensive products and requires higher rates of investment, both of which increase the returns to skilled labor. The rise in inequality is somewhat mitigated by convergence between farm and nonfarm incomes, but this effect is quite small because developing Asia's future growth is concentrated in nonagriculture sectors. Rising inequality will partly attenuate the poverty reduction effects from average income growth.

Migration of labor will rise and the global "middle class" will double in size according to the projections that link model simulations with data from expenditure surveys in the countries that account for the vast bulk of the world's population. Asia's developing economies, in particular, will experience a vast increase in middle-income populations. Yet over the next 25 years, despite the rise of an Asian middle class, the poverty challenge will still be considerable: in 2030, of the world's poor fully half will reside in developing Asia, with the vast bulk in South Asia.

Rod Tyers argues that the very rise in middle-income-driven inequality in poor and populous countries is inevitable if growth and reduction in poverty are to occur at all. His commentary on Chapter 9 reminds us that it is urbanization and industrialization that raise returns to capital (including human capital) in the first place, and that the subsequent rise in saving and the capital stock (lifting urban relative to rural labor productivity) is vital to incentives for young people to study and acquire appropriate skills. The shift of labor out of agriculture then provides the impetus for the growth accelerations seen in developing Asia—a process that is just beginning in much of South and Southeast Asia today.

As Chaudhuri and Ravallion (2006) argue in the cases of the PRC and India, some of the increased inequality may reflect the return to market-based incentives for effort, skills, investment, and entrepreneurship after the long period of government suppression of incentives for individual effort and innovation. The very removal of distortions created by state ownership and control of industry and trade, along with the freeing up of regulations and interventions that distorted labor and capital markets, undoubtedly spurred some inequality. However, at some point, even these "good" inequalities may become harmful to the economy if they become so excessive that they provoke social unrest.

Inequality in income is often associated with inequality in opportunity, and may undermine the willingness and ability of households to invest in human capital and health. Rising inequality might also be a cause of the backsliding on efficiency-enhancing reforms in developing countries. Finally, a high level of inequality can be a source of political instability and social unrest, with attendant discouragement of private investment and innovation. Given the trends toward greater inequality, Asian policy makers' actions to rebalance growth to be more inclusive could be decisive in reversing this trend. The tensions between achieving rapid economic growth and structural reforms on the one hand will have to be balanced against the forces that are leading to deteriorating income distribution on the other. Managing these tensions well will be crucial to sustaining the growth process.

1.5 CONCLUSIONS

Through sound development policies, developing Asian economies have, by and large, achieved enviable economic prosperity over the past 30 years. In recent years, the rapid emergence of the region as a major economic power has become more evident, led by the accelerating pace of economic growth in the PRC and India. But the growth acceleration in Asia has not been confined to the two regional giants. Economic growth in some of the smaller regional economies, such as Viet Nam, has also picked up strongly recently, spurred by their continuing efforts at structural reform and by the opening up of their economies. Even the economies hit by the crisis of a decade ago have rebounded into a new period of rapid development, albeit at a slightly slower pace than before the crisis.

Current superior performance is no guarantee of future success. To avoid being lulled into complacency, a clear vision of the future of these Asian economies is important for regional policy makers and markets. Will the trend of recent years continue for the next 20 years? And what are the major risks and challenges that could blight Asia's future prospects?

The preceding discussion in this chapter suggests that a window of opportunity is now open for developing Asia to adopt a more sustained and inclusive growth pattern. Regional economies are likely to maintain most of their underlying strengths, which have supported their spectacular economic performance of the past few decades, for the foreseeable future. This will enable them to continue to catch up with the advanced economies in terms of living standards. However, despite developing Asia's overall rapid growth, there are still some poor economies that have lagged behind. The large and widening gaps in income between poor and rich highlight the desirability of a shift of the pattern of growth toward greater regional convergence. As most of Asia's developing economies are progressing toward middle-income status, it is timely for them to seek to spread growth opportunities to their lower-income neighbors. The inclusion of the poorest regional economies into the growth process is a prerequisite for a stable and prosperous Asia in the long run.

This vision of Asia's future will not materialize automatically. Grounded in the strengths of regional economies, an agenda for sustained growth and regional convergence needs to be built; it must also address potential challenges. This volume suggests five key components of this agenda:

Managing Asia's trade integration. Trade has been a key driver of Asia's economic growth over the last 50 years. Intensified regional trade integration, which has been driven mainly by the rise of regional production networks and intraregional FDI flows, holds enormous promise for greater trade and growth for the region, as well as presenting great challenges for regional policy makers. Formal institutional arrangements are increasingly necessary to manage the regional production and trade systems and to ensure their smooth functioning. However, potential vulnerabilities in the international trade system and in the architecture of the region's bilateral arrangements might undermine trade dynamism in the future. The analysis in this volume suggests that the current proliferation of regional trade agreements in Asia can be remedied through ensuring the success of global multilateral trade liberalization, improving the design of such agreements, and ensuring convergence toward a single pan-Asian agreement. However, the analysis finds that although applying good practices in BTAs, such as comprehensive product and services coverage, low and symmetrical rules of origin, and transparent customs procedures, can lessen the damage that regional trade agreements are likely to cause, they can not eliminate it. In this context, the authors conclude that efforts to move toward a single harmonized trade agreement in Asia will be crucial in the absence of a successful multilateral trade round, and that an ASEAN-plus strategy may provide a promising approach to a unified Asian FTA.

Catalyzing growth and integration. Like the growth process, the development of regional integration has been uneven across Asia. The countries that have lagged in terms of economic growth have also been less engaged in the regional integration process. Adverse geographic conditions, poor infrastructure, weak institutional quality, or low levels of human capital are often major impediments to their integration into the international economy. Lagging economies' potential for fuller participation in regional integration so as to achieve rapid growth needs to be catalyzed by efforts toward structural and institutional reform aimed at removing binding constraints on growth and integration.

This volume highlights two key catalysts of growth and integration in Asia: infrastructure investment and trade facilitation. It argues that geographic reality determines that the unleashing of the full trade potential between East Asia and South Asia will depend crucially on infrastructure development. Through its facilitating effects on market access and regional integration, infrastructure development can be a potent catalyst for wider economic participation, both within and between Asian economies, and promises large benefits to the poorest regional economies. This volume suggests that the trade and growth potential in the least-developed economies can be better tapped through a broadening of the policy focus from traditional tariff reform to wider supply-side constraints. In these least-developed economies, policy makers have to make sequential reforms to address the barriers to trade both at the border and behind the border.

Addressing resource constraints. Rapid economic growth in developing Asia has raised concerns about whether available resources will be sufficient to support future growth. Chapters 6 and 7 sketch out a broad picture of the agricultural and energy future in developing Asia and investigate their implications for the overall economy. Future growth will depend critically on the region's ability to secure adequate and growing supplies of food and fuel and to ensure efficient land, water, and energy use. Increased trade with other regions of the world with abundant supplies of food and energy, as well as technological progress, will be vital for developing Asia to secure the resources it needs. However, its heavier reliance on commodity imports will impact on world commodity markets, and leave regional economies more exposed to any shocks in these markets. The region's governments and businesses need to improve substantially their ability to manage risks arising from volatile world commodity markets. Moreover, the analysis in this volume suggests that sustaining agricultural productivity growth through R&D investment and securing energy supplies through regional infrastructure investment are important policy options for overcoming potential resource constraints in the region.

Preparing for demographic transition. Low fertility and longer life expectancy will lead to an unprecedented and rapid pace of population aging in developing Asia over the next five decades. This demographic change will have implications for growth of the labor supply and may be accompanied by a decline in saving and investment, which in turn would slow the rate of economic growth. Rapidly aging populations also bring challenges in the form of public pension and health-care systems, few of which are well established in developing Asia. Faced with these challenges, the region's governments may need to respond with appropriate policy actions.

The most direct instrument is an adjustment in population policy. For example, the relaxation of the "one-child policy" in the PRC may partly offset the contraction of the labor force and help slow population aging. The modeling study given in this volume suggests that, although a two-child policy in the PRC would increase GDP and reduce the proportion of the aged population dependency ratio, it would also lead to lower per capita income growth, mainly due to the associated rise in the youth dependency ratio. Thus, it would seem that population policies leading to higher fertility rates in the PRC should be complemented with policy efforts toward mitigating the possible negative impact on per capita income growth, by, for example, raising labor market participation rates and increasing retirement ages. In addition to population policy, productivity improvements related to higher levels of education and skill formation, and application of new technologies, would also help offset some of the effects of aging on economic growth.

Making growth more inclusive. In spite of overall rapid growth and significant poverty reduction, income inequality within countries has increased sharply in developing Asia over the past two decades. This has been reflected in widening income gaps across regions and between urban and rural areas in most countries. Rapid economic growth, globalization, and the nature of technological change are prime causes of the growing inequality. If current trends continue, domestic inequality in developing Asia will tend to increase over the next 20 years. According to a baseline projection reported in Chapter 9, although global economic growth will lead to a decrease in global inequality, this reduction is entirely explained by a reduction in disparities in average incomes across countries. Most low- and middle-income countries, including those in developing Asia, are projected to experience a rise in domestic inequality by 2030, because their faster growth generates more demand for skill-intensive products and requires higher rates of investment. The widening income disparity between rich and poor may be offset by ensuring that inequalities in opportunities for education and skill acquisition are themselves reduced and that basic services such as health care and nutrition are improved for poor and low-income households. Without these moves, rising inequality may prove harmful to economic stability and growth. Given existing trends toward greater inequality, Asian policy makers' actions to rebalance growth to be more inclusive could be decisive in sustaining a rapid and equitable growth process.

To implement this agenda, bold actions by governments and societies of the region are required. The potential for a new era of more sustained and equitable Asian growth can be realized if the difficult challenges ahead are met. There is much to be done, but the rewards are tremendous.

ENDNOTES

1   According to Encyclopedia Britannica (http://www.britannica.com/eb/article-9054556/Gunnar-Myrdal): "Myrdal warned that economic development of rich and poor countries might never converge. Instead, the two might possibly diverge, with poor countries locked into producing less-profitable primary goods while rich countries reaped the profits associated with economies of scale. This pessimistic view, however, has not been borne out by events."

2   Cross-country income inequality measures of convergence/divergence in themselves are not suitable for welfare analysis because of different population sizes among countries. For developing Asia, the two data points for the PRC and India cover about 2.4 billion people, while data points for countries such as Cambodia or Lao PDR have much smaller population weights. A distinct concept of global income inequality is the inequality between individual citizens of different countries, which accounts for inequality both between and within countries (Milanovic, 2006). See, for example, Bourguignon and Morrison (2002), Milanovic (2002), and Sala-i-Martin (2006) for recent empirical work along these lines, and Chapter 9 of this volume for a discussion of Asian and global income distribution.

3   See Kim, Lim, and Park (2007) for the case of Korea. In addition to trade, advances in investment and productivity have also been key drivers of growth (Gill and Kharas 2007).

4   Sri Lanka adopted more liberal trade policies in the 1980s but the impetus to growth was reduced by the conflict that began there in 1983.

5   Broadly defined, trade costs refer to all costs incurred in delivering a good to

final users other than the cost of producing the good itself (Anderson and van Wincoop, 2004). They include transport and freight charges, local distribution costs, time in transit, the cost of information, import tariffs, nontariff barriers, and other border-related costs such as customs procedures and currency exchange transactions.

6   For example, in the case of Indonesia and the PRC, export subsidies were eliminated but at the same time the exchange rate was adjusted to compensate exporters (James and Stephenson 2002).

7   The most obvious cause of the trade frictions between East Asia and other countries may be the large trade surpluses that East Asia is running with the rest of the world, but particularly with the EU and North America. Within the region, closer trade integration and competition may also lead to increased use of trade remedies or result in use of WTO dispute-resolution mechanisms. Different standards of rules of origin often cause trade frictions between the PRC and its trade partners.

8   For a review of regionalism in Asia, see among others, ADB (2002 and 2006), Lloyd (2002), Findlay, Piei, and Pangestu (2003), Pangestu and Gooptu (2004), Kawai (2005), and Park, Urata, and Cheong (2007).

9   In new economic geography models, the agglomeration forces arise from increasing returns to scale, transport costs, interindustry linkages, and preferences for variety. Because of transportation costs and factor availability, firms like to locate production close to input suppliers (forward linkage) and output markets (backward linkage). The centripetal forces can be magnified by increasing returns to scale and preference for variety, as a greater number of suppliers means lower input prices, and larger markets means lower average costs. Simultaneously dispersion forces arising from limited supply of immobile resources (such as land) and increasing competition on labor and product markets operate in the opposite direction. The interaction of agglomeration and dispersion forces determines the dynamics of industrial clusters. See Fujita, Krugman, and Venables (1999) and Baldwin et al. (2005) about the theory of new economic geography, and World Bank (2006a) about its implications in the East Asian context.

10 There is a wide range of estimates for crude oil prices in the next 20 years, and historically prices have been highly variable and can be strongly effected by political events. Some leading energy agencies envisage a softening trend in long-term prices and project a price range of US$50–60/barrel in 2025–2030 (EIA, 2007; IEA, 2007). The leading energy agencies normally use either energy models or expert judgments in deriving their oil price projections. This approach is different from the economywide model used in Chapter 7, which considers interaction of supply and demand in the entire world economy. The energy prices in the model are determined endogenously by all economic sectors, not just energy sectors. Obviously, considerable uncertainties surround the baseline results of Chapter 7, and it is good for long-term planning to consider the

possibility of a fairly wide range of prices for the future, rather than to focus on a narrow consensus range.

11 The decline in Gini coefficients in Indonesia, Malaysia, and Thailand may reflect the fact that urban higher-income groups were adversely impacted by the collapse of asset prices, while low-income households in rural areas were better protected by their agricultural activities, which partly cushioned the shocks.

REFERENCES

Asian Development Bank. 2002. "Preferential Trade Agreements in Asia and the Pacific." In *Asian Development Outlook 2002*. Manila.

———. 2006. "Routes for Asia's Trade." In *Asian Development Outlook 2006*. Manila.

———. 2007a. "Ten Years after The Crisis: The Facts about Investment and Growth." In *Asian Development Outlook 2007*. Manila.

———. 2007b. "Growth amid Change." In *Asian Development Outlook 2007*. Manila.

———. 2007c. *Key Indicators 2007*. Manila.

Anderson, J.E., and E. van Wincoop. 2004. "Trade Costs." *Journal of Economic Literature* 42(3, September):691-751.

Baldwin, R. 2006. "Managing the Noodle Bowl: The Fragility of East Asian Regionalism." CEPR Discussion Papers 5561. Centre for Economic Policy Research, London.

Baldwin, R., R. Forslid, P. Martin, G. Ottaviano, and F. Robert-Nicoud. 2005. *Economic Geography and Public Policy*. Princeton, New Jersey: Princeton University Press.

Barro, R.J., and X. Sala-i-Martin. 1992. "Convergence." *Journal of Political Economy* 100(2, April):223-51.

Bourguignon, F., and C. Morrisson. 2002. "Inequality among World Citizens: 1820-1992." *American Economic Review* 92(4, September):727-44.

Chaudhuri, S., and M. Ravallion. 2006. "Partially Awakened Giants: Uneven Growth in China and India." In L. Alan Winters and S. Yusuf (eds.), *Dancing with Giants: China, India and the Global Economy*. Washington, DC: World Bank.

Durlauf, S.N., and P.A. Johnson. 1995. "Multiple Regimes and Cross-Country Growth Behavior." *Journal of Applied Econometrics* 10(4):365-84.

EIA (Energy Information Administration). 2007. *Annual Energy Outlook 2007 with Projections to 2030*. Washington, DC. February.

Findlay, C., H. Piei, and M. Pangestu. 2003. "Trading with Favourites: Free Trade Agreements in the Asia Pacific." Pacific Economic Papers 335. Australia-Japan Research Centre, Australian National University, Canberra.

Fujita, M., P. Krugman, and A.J. Venables. 1999. *The Spatial Economy: Cities, Regions, and International Trade*. Cambridge, Massachusetts: Massachusetts Institute of Technology Press.

Gill, I., and H. Kharas. 2007. *An East Asian Renaissance: Ideas for Economic Growth.* Washington, DC: World Bank.

Hausmann, R., L. Pritchett, and D. Rodrik. 2005. "Growth Accelerations." *Journal of Economic Growth* 10(4, December):303-29.

Heltberg, R. 2003. "Spatial Inequality in Vietnam: A Regression-based Decomposition." Unpublished manuscript.

IEA (International Energy Agency). 2007. *World Energy Outlook 2007—China and India Insights.* Paris. November.

James, W.E., and S. Stephenson. 2002. "The Evolution of Policy Reform: Determinants, Sequencing and Reasons for Success." In F. Iqbal and W.E. James (eds.), *Deregulation and Development in Indonesia.* Westport, Connecticut: Praeger Publishers.

Kanbur, R., and X. Zhang. 2005. "Fifty Years of Regional Inequality in China: A Journey through Revolution, Reform and Openness." *Review of Development Economics* 9(1):87-106.

Kawai, M. 2005. "East Asian Economic Regionalism: Progress and Challenges." *Journal of Asian Economics* 16(1, February):29-55.

Kim, S., H. Lim, and D. Park. 2007. "Can Imports Be Beneficial For Economic Growth? Some Evidence from Korea." ERD Working Paper Series No. 103. Economics and Research Department, Asian Development Bank, Manila.

Krongkaew, M., and R.H.M. Zin. 2007. "Income Distribution and Sustainable Economic Development in East Asia: A Comparative Analysis." The IDEAs Working Paper Series No. 02/2007. International Development Economics Associates, New Delhi.

Lloyd, P. 2002. "New Bilateralism in the Asia-Pacific." *The World Economy* 25(9):1279-96.

Milanovic, B. 2002. "True World Income Distribution, 1988 and 1993: First Calculation Based on Household Surveys Alone." *Economic Journal* 112(476, January):51-92.

———. 2006. "Global Income Inequality: What it is and Why it Matters." Policy Research Working Paper Series 3865. World Bank, Washington, DC.

Myrdal, G. 1968. *Asian Drama: An Inquiry into the Poverty of Nations.* Volume 3. New York: The Twentieth Century Fund.

OECD (Organisation for Economic Co-operation and Development). 2001. *Economic Survey of Korea.* Paris.

Park, Y.C., S. Urata, and I. Cheong. 2007. "The Political Economy of the Proliferation of FTAs." In S. La Croix and P.A. Petri (eds.), *Challenges to the Global Trading System: Adjustment to Globalization in the Asia Pacific Region.* Oxford: Routledge.

Pangestu, M., and S. Gooptu. 2004. "New Regionalism: Options for East Asia." Chapter 3 in *East Asia Integrates: A Trade Policy Agenda for Shared Growth.* Washington, DC: World Bank.

Petri, P. 2007. "Turning Crisis into Opportunity." Asian Development Bank, Manila. Unpublished manuscript.

Quah, D.T. 1996. "Twin Peaks: Growth and Convergence in Models of Distributional Dynamics." *Economic Journal* 106(437):1045-55.

———. 1997. "Empirics of Growth and Distribution: Stratification, Polarization, and Convergence Club." *Journal of Economic Growth*, 2(1):27-59.

Rodrik, D. 2005. "Growth Strategies." In P. Aghion and S.N. Durlauf (eds.), *Handbook of Economic Growth*. Amsterdam: Elsevier.

Roland-Holst, D., J.-P. Verbiest, and F. Zhai. 2005. "Growth and Trade Horizons for Asia: Long-term Forecasts for Regional Integration." *Asian Development Review* 22(2):108-25.

Sala-i-Martin, X. 2006. "The World Distribution of Income: Falling Poverty and … Convergence, Period." *Quarterly Journal of Economics* 121(2, May):351-97.

Shorrocks, A., and G. Wan. 2005. "Spatial Decomposition of Inequality." *Journal of Economic Geography* 5(1):59-81.

Sicular, T., Y. Ximing, B. Gustafsson, and L. Shi. 2007. "The Urban-Rural Gap and Income Inequality in China." *Review of Income and Wealth* 53(1):93-126.

Solow, R. 1956. "A Contribution to the Theory of Economic Growth." *Quarterly Journal of Economics* 70(1):65-94.

Spence, M. 2007. "Wealth of Nations: What Drives High Growth Rate." *The Wall Street Journal*. 24 January.

Temple, J. 2003. "Growing into Trouble: Indonesia after 1966." In D. Rodrik (ed.), *In Search of Prosperity: Analytic Narratives on Economic Growth*. Princeton, New Jersey: Princeton University Press.

The Competitiveness Program. 2007. "Sri Lanka's Per Capita GDP With and Without War." Colombo.

Winters, L.A. and S. Yusuf. 2007. "Introduction: Dancing with Giants." In L.A. Winters and S. Yusuf (eds.), *Dancing with Giants: China, India and the Global Economy*. Washington, DC: World Bank.

World Bank. 2000. *The Quality of Growth*. Washington, DC.

———. 2006. *Can South Asia End Poverty in a Generation?* Washington, DC.

2

Why are Bilateral Trade Agreements so Popular, and Does it Matter?

Jayant Menon

2.1 INTRODUCTION

On 15 August 2004, Mongolia signed a trade and investment framework agreement (TIFA) with the United States (US), a precursor to a bilateral trade agreement (BTA). Prior to this, Mongolia was the only country that had not signed either a TIFA or a BTA with another country, or had not joined a regional or plurilateral trade agreement (PTA). Every other country in the world today is a member of at least one BTA, and most are members of multiple BTAs.[1] If PTAs were considered the main threat to the world trade system in the 1990s, the concern has since shifted toward BTAs. BTAs have been proliferating at an astounding pace recently.

What are the underlying factors driving this proliferation? Why are Japan and the Republic of Korea (hereafter Korea), countries that had long resisted the worldwide trend to join or form PTAs, now pursuing BTAs "with a vengeance"? Can we explain why Singapore is currently negotiating a BTA with Kuwait, or why Sri Lanka has signed one with the Islamic Republic of Iran, or Taipei,China with Nicaragua, for that matter?

Indeed, what are the motivations behind the 176 BTAs currently being proposed, negotiated, or implemented involving at least one country from the Asia-Pacific region, or the 300 or so BTAs worldwide?

This chapter attempts to provide an answer to these questions by providing a taxonomy of BTAs, identifying the underlying motivations in terms of both economic and noneconomic factors. Apart from trying to understand why BTAs have been proliferating, identifying the factors driving them is important because they may reveal the impact that they are having on the world trade system. Depending on why countries form BTAs, they could be working as either building blocks or stumbling blocks on the road to a more integrated and successful international economy.

The chapter is in five parts. Section 2.2 provides some facts and figures relating to BTAs, including their proliferation, to provide the backdrop for the ensuing analysis. Section 2.3 provides a taxonomy of BTAs, identifying the different reasons that motivate countries to form them. The impact that BTAs are having on multilateralism and the world trade system is the subject of Section 2.4. A final section provides a summary of main points, and considers likely scenarios for the future landscape of world trade, and possible responses.

2.2 BILATERAL TRADE AGREEMENTS: SOME FACTS AND FIGURES

It is useful to start by defining what we mean by a BTA. In our definition, the key distinguishing feature of a BTA relates to the number of parties involved, and that number is two. A BTA can vary by the nature of the members involved and by the nature of the agreement. Most BTAs are between two countries, but a BTA can also be signed between a country and a PTA, between a BTA and a PTA, and between two BTAs or PTAs. Furthermore, one or even both parties to the BTA need not be a country, or a BTA or PTA. Several entities, such as the European Union (EU); Hong Kong, China; and Macao, China, are currently recognized as members of the World Trade Organization (WTO) but not as independent countries. Macao, China has a BTA with the People's Republic of China (PRC) and the EU, while Hong Kong, China has a BTA with the PRC and is in negotiation with New Zealand.

The most common type of bilateral agreement is a free trade agreement (FTA), although it can also take the form of a customs union (CU) or a services agreement. A bilateral CU is rare and a services agreement tends to be accompanied by an FTA.

Figure 2.1 provides a chronological summary of BTAs and PTAs involving at least one economy in the Asia-Pacific region.[2] A complete listing of such BTAs, together with their status, is provided in Appendix Table A2.1. As of October 2006, there were 176 BTAs in the region (at various stages from proposal to implementation). As Figure 2.1 highlights, the number of BTAs doubled between 1995 and 2000, but increased more than fourfold between 2000 and 2006. Every country, with the exception of Mongolia, is involved in at least one BTA. India heads the list with 22 BTAs, although most of these have yet to be implemented. The US comes in second with 20 BTAs, half of which are already under implementation. Pakistan and Singapore are tied in third place with 19 BTAs each. The latecomers to PTAs—Japan and Korea—have caught up on

Figure 2.1 BTAs and PTAs of Asia-Pacific Economies, October 2006

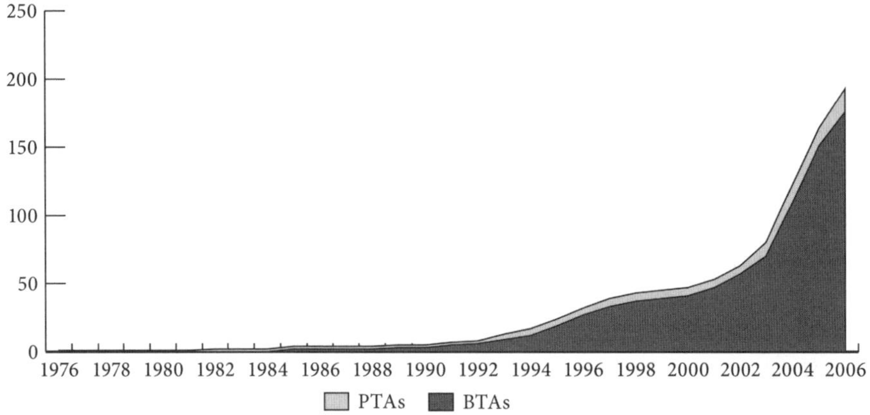

Sources: Author's compilation based on data from the following Web sites: ADB ARIC, available: aric. adb.org; Bilaterals.org, available: www.bilaterals.org; Foreign Affairs and International Trade Canada, available: www.dfait-maeci.gc.ca; Office of the US Trade Representative, available: www.ustr.gov; and World Trade Organization, available: www.wto.org.

preferential arrangements through BTAs it would seem, and are involved in 17 and 15 of them, respectively.

Out of the 176 BTAs, 155 are between countries. Two of them involve Hong Kong, China and Macao, China, and the remaining 19 involve either a PTA and/or a BTA. There are seven PTAs and a BTA that are party to at least one BTA in the Asia-Pacific region. The BTA concerned is the Australia-New Zealand Closer Economic Relations Agreement (ANZCER), which is negotiating a BTA with the Association of Southeast Asian Nations (ASEAN).

Apart from ASEAN, the other six PTAs involved in BTAs are the European Free Trade Area (EFTA); EU; Gulf Cooperation Council; MERCOSUR; North American Free Trade Agreement (NAFTA); and South African Customs Union.

Fifty-two of the 176 BTAs, or about 30%, are already being implemented. Twenty-eight BTAs have been signed but implementation has yet to commence; in some cases, legislative or executive ratification is required before this can begin. Another 30% are currently under negotiation, a quarter of which have also signed a framework agreement. A quarter of the BTAs are still at the proposal stage, where consultation and study are ongoing to determine whether the BTA should, in fact, proceed.

2.3 WHY ARE BTAS SO POPULAR?

The first thing to note when discussing the popularity of BTAs relates to possibilities, or the maximum number that are technically possible. In theory, it is possible to have many more BTAs than PTAs simply because only two entities are involved and there are no geographic (i.e., regional) restrictions on membership. With 192 United Nations (UN) member states and three members of WTO that are not UN member states (Hong Kong, China; Macao, China; and Taipei,China), it is technically possible to have up to 18,915 BTAs (195 times 194 divided by 2) between them! If we include BTAs between a country and a PTA, a BTA and a PTA, or between PTAs, then this number becomes even bigger. Adding the seven PTAs and one BTA that have already engaged in BTAs raises the maximum number to 20,301. Of course there are many more than seven PTAs and any of them could start negotiating BTAs in the future. Furthermore, the possibility exists for new PTAs to be formed in the future, which could then participate in BTAs as well, and there is nothing stopping BTAs from forming new BTAs between themselves, and so on and so forth! All of this does not explain why BTAs are popular of course, but it does suggest that if they are, they can proliferate in a dramatic and almost uncontrollable way, unlike other forms of PTAs.

So what are the factors driving the proliferation of BTAs in the world today? In answering this question, we identify a set of *general* as well as *specific* factors or motivations for the popularity of BTAs. The general motivations apply to most, if not all BTAs, but there is always at least one additional specific factor that drives the formation of a BTA. For instance, each party to the BTA may have its own motivation in pursuing the agreement, and this may not coincide with the interest of the other. It is also possible that each party has more than one motivating factor. When there are two or more factors, the impact on the world trading system will depend on a balance of forces, after netting out the individual impact of the different factors.

An important general reason for the popularity of BTAs (*general* factors are discussed in this and the following four paragraphs) is the apparent disenchantment with the pace of progress with liberalization at the multilateral level. The difficulties associated with concluding the Doha Round have simply reinforced this view. Many feel that WTO has failed to deliver and so have pursued BTAs (and PTAs) as a means of pressing ahead with their trade and liberalization agendas.[3]

A kind of snowballing or domino effect, as with PTAs in the past (Baldwin, 1996), has also been driving the growth in BTAs. In the Asia-Pacific region, interest in forming BTAs began in the late 1990s with Japan, Korea, New Zealand, and Singapore initially. By 2000, the US, Australia,

Thailand, and PRC had joined the trend, with more than 40 new BTAs being proposed or negotiated (Appendix Table A2.1). The momentum gathered over subsequent years to the point where other Asia-Pacific countries may have felt disadvantaged if they did not join the trend. The number of BTAs thus continued to grow, and almost doubled to 109 between 2002 and 2004. It is quite possible that it may double again very soon.

There is a momentum effect driving some of the growth in BTAs with countries not wanting to be left behind in this apparent race. Baldwin (2006a, p. 22) argues that it could continue to play a role in the proliferation of BTAs in the region in the coming years:

> If history is any guide, the domino effect in East Asia will spread to many, many more countries in the neighborhood. In Europe, for example, the playing out of several waves of domino effects has left the EU with preferential trade deals with every WTO member except nine. It is therefore conceivable that the 13 members of the ASEAN+3 group will end up signing a very large number of bilaterals in the coming years.

BTAs also tend to attract less attention than PTAs, including from the media. So, the pressure from opposition forces at home, such as the anti-free-trade lobby or particular "sensitive" industry groups, or from abroad, such as traditional trade partners or members of a regional grouping of which the country is a part, is likely to be low. This would facilitate not only the speed at which a BTA can be negotiated, but also the number of them. Of course there are exceptions, and these generally arise when the partner is a large country (e.g., the US) or when sensitive sectors are involved in the negotiations (e.g., rice in the Korea-Thailand BTA, now defunct as a direct result).

Finally, it is often claimed that some, if not most, BTAs are essentially politically motivated. There is no doubt that political economy considerations, and indeed political parties or politicians themselves, play a major role in driving the proliferation of BTAs. A recent example of this in the US is how the control of both houses by the Democrats has put at risk some of the BTAs that President Bush's administration had been pursuing. Although we try, in this chapter, to take into account political, strategic, and foreign policy-related issues, we focus on economic and economic-related considerations because they are easier to identify and measure. Thus, the discussion that follows is likely to understate the role that politics and politicians play in the proliferation of BTAs, simply because these influences are often difficult to measure or model, let alone classify.

There are three broad categories of *specific* factors (discussed through the end of Section 2.3) that we identify: economic, strategic, and event driven. As depicted in Figure 2.2, each of these broad categories has their subcategories, and the subcategories for economic and event-driven BTAs are each subdivided into two subcategories as well. Thus in total, we identify 11 specific factors to explain the proliferation of BTAs.

Figure 2.2 Different Motivations for Forming BTAs: Specific Factors

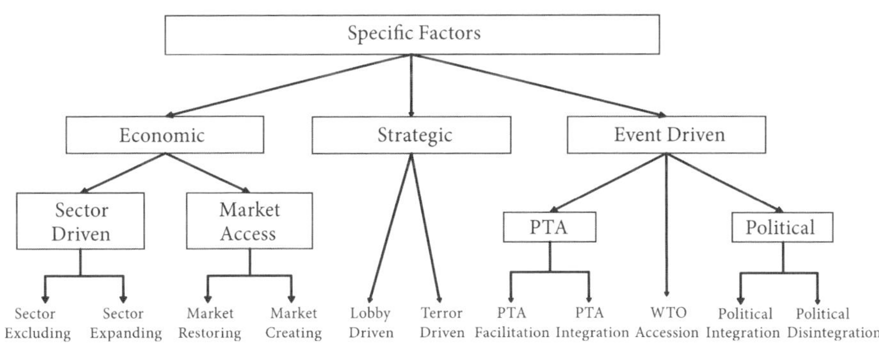

Source: Author

2.3.1 Economically Motivated BTAs

Within the economic motivation, the two subcategories are sector-driven and market-access BTAs. Sector-driven BTAs are further subdivided into sector-expanding and sector-excluding BTAs. Market-access BTAs are also divided into two groups: market-restoring and market-creating BTAs.

Sector-Driven BTAs

These BTAs are motivated mainly by one or a few key sectors. There is both a positive and a negative element to this sector-based motivation, with some BTAs designed to expand liberalization into sectors or areas that have previously been ignored at the multilateral level, while others are designed to exclude sensitive sectors or issues. We discuss them separately because their impact on the world trade system is likely to be quite different depending on whether they are sector expanding or excluding.

Sector-Expanding BTAs. It is easy to see why BTAs are easier to negotiate and conclude than PTAs or a multilateral deal: with only two parties involved, the potential for disagreement is reduced. As the focus of liberalization shifts from the relatively easier task of reducing trade taxes on industrial products, achieving agreement on a multilateral level has become more difficult as the agenda broadens to address less transparent forms of protection, more complex issues, and new sectors. By requiring only two parties to agree, a BTA could face fewer obstacles than a regional or multilateral pact. BTAs may then have the potential to achieve a deeper level of integration than possible through the multilateral approach alone. Even if they are not any deeper, it is often argued that they are faster than the multilateral approach.

In other words, both the degree and scope of liberalization policy may be enhanced in the context of only two negotiating partners, and so bilateral efforts may be able to surpass the extent of integration possible at the multilateral level. In this sense, sector-expanding BTAs are often described as "WTO-plus" or "New Age" BTAs. The US-Singapore BTA is one of the first such BTAs and is often described as a model worthy of emulation by other negotiating partners. In fact, the BTAs being pursued by the US with other ASEAN countries as part of its "Enterprise for ASEAN Initiative" are using it as a model.[4]

Of the various so-called "Singapore issues" that were raised at the WTO Ministerial Conference in Singapore in 1996, only the rather fuzzy concept of trade facilitation measures appears to have survived on the WTO agenda. Other Singapore issues, such as establishing rules for investment, competition policy, and government procurement, are being pursued in some sector-expanding BTAs. Progress with liberalization of services in general has been slow at the multilateral level and fraught with difficulties, given country-specific sensitivities, and a wide-ranging multilateral deal looks unlikely in the near future. Some sector-specific BTAs have emerged in response.

Also in this environment, BTAs have been driven by the fact that preferential access may enable a supplier to steal an irreversible march on the competition, and cement a long-term advantage in the market. Many of the US BTAs with developing countries are pursuing rules more favorable than those in PTAs or WTO in relation to investment and intellectual property rights.

Sector-Excluding BTAs. The most sensitive sector as far as liberalization is concerned is agriculture. Most sector-excluding BTAs relate, in one way or another, to agriculture. An example of the negative element would be the BTA between Japan and Singapore, known as the Japan-Singapore Economic Partnership Agreement (JSEPA). Japan has long resisted joining PTAs because of its reluctance to liberalize its agriculture sector, but the absence of any significant agriculture sector in the city-state of Singapore has facilitated the signing of this BTA. Even the few agricultural products that Singapore does export were easily excluded from the JSEPA, such as cut flowers and ornamental fish. Less than 10% of the volume of exports of agricultural products from Singapore to Japan is provided with duty-free access, and the JSEPA did not create any new preferences in the agriculture sector (Ravenhill, 2006).

A similar set of exclusions of sensitive sectors can be found in Japan's BTA with Mexico. Unlike Singapore, Mexico has a large agriculture sector and is a major exporter of meat (pork in particular) to Japan, and the exclusions have been so widespread that about 13% of Mexico's exports to Japan are excluded from the BTA. So, even when agriculture is important to one partner but sensitive in the other, it appears that BTAs can still be reached by excluding this sector. As well as exclusions, there is also greater room to manipulate rules of origin in a one-on-one setting to limit liberalization of sensitive sectors. Clearly the flexibility provided by BTAs through one-on-one negotiations allows such compromises to be made and trade agreements to be concluded when they might otherwise stall or fail.

Market-Access BTAs

As mentioned earlier, we divide market access BTAs into two groups: market restoring and market creating.

Market-Restoring BTAs. In the discussion earlier on general factors behind the popularity of BTAs, we noted that one of the reasons was the apparent disenchantment with the pace of progress in multilateral liberalization. The same disenchantment with WTO was one of many factors driving the original interest in PTAs of course. It also set off a kind of snowballing or domino effect (Baldwin, 1996). As the world trade system started being carved into blocs, countries that did not belong to a PTA felt compelled to form or join one in order to secure regional markets, or to compensate for markets in other regions that were becoming more isolated and less accessible.

Some BTAs have developed in response to such a global trading environment. The motivation behind them is to try and restore trading links that existed prior to a trading partner's joining a PTA. They generally apply to nonregional but traditional trade partners where one or both have become members of a relatively integrated PTA, which has weakened trade links between them as a result. These BTAs are designed to bypass, or at least reduce, the discriminatory treatment imposed on them as a result of the PTA. Lloyd (2002) describes this as the one factor that is common to all new PTAs and sees it as becoming more important relative to the other factors. As he puts it (p. 6), "This is the fear of exclusion from major markets. In this context, exclusion does not mean that a country is denied access to a market, that is, total exclusion. It means that it has access on terms less favorable than some other country or countries."

With the EU and NAFTA as centers of regional preferential trade, and with little or no prospect of other countries becoming members of these regional trade blocs, many of the BTAs being pursued with them (either with the EU or NAFTA or with individual member countries) would serve as examples of BTAs designed to restore market access.

The US is a major trading partner for most ASEAN countries, all of which except Myanmar have either concluded or are pursuing BTAs with that country. The ASEAN countries view BTAs as a means of restoring market access in the post-NAFTA era.

Market-Creating BTAs. These BTAs usually involve countries seeking to strengthen trade and investment relations where economic relations had been few or weak in the past. To the extent that this was due to trade barriers or other regulatory or commercial restrictions, market-creating BTAs may be successful in achieving their objective of promoting bilateral trade. For instance, it could be that both countries had relatively high trade barriers with the rest of the world, but then each removed them preferentially among regional partners in a PTA. In this case, there may be potential for boosting trade between the two countries through a BTA that opens up a conduit between the PTAs of which each country is a member.

If, however, historically weak trade relations stemmed from reasons of comparative advantage, such as competitive rather than complementary resource endowments, then such BTAs will have little, if any effect, on boosting bilateral trade, unless the preference margins are very large.

2.3.2 Strategically Motivated BTAs

BTAs that are motivated by strategic factors are classified into two groups: lobby driven and terror driven.

Lobby-Driven BTAs

The Seattle Ministerial Meeting of WTO in 1999 collapsed when developing countries opposed the push by various industrial economies, spearheaded by the US and the EU, to introduce labor standards and environmental regulations onto the WTO agenda. Critics claim that the US, having failed at WTO, is now trying to press ahead with these matters by intimidating small, weak countries into accepting them in one-on-one negotiations, while simultaneously trying to seduce them with preferential access to a large domestic market. The so-called "fair trade" push by the US and the EU is seen as nothing less than covert protectionism that penalizes exports from low-wage emerging and developing economies.[5] Bhagwati (2005) also laments the introduction onto the agenda of a trade organization of what he describes as trade-unrelated "fair trade" demands, referring not only to labor and environmental standards but also intellectual property rights protection.

The first precedent relating to labor standards was set in NAFTA, or more specifically by the North American Agreement on Labor Cooperation, which was negotiated as a side agreement to NAFTA, and which came into effect on 1 January 1994. But critics such as Bhagwati (2005) complain of a ratcheting-up effect, as these issues progress from being annexes to trade agreements and move into their text. With the US-Jordan BTA, labor standards and environmental regulations found their way into the body of an agreement for the first time. For the BTAs with Chile and Singapore, the agenda broadened to include capital controls, which are forbidden to these countries under these agreements. The precedent-setting formula is described as a blueprint pattern, whereby the "strongest" BTA to date serves as a model for negotiating the next one.

Terror-Driven BTAs
It would appear that US trade policy has not escaped President Bush's administration's apparent preoccupation with fighting the "war on terror." Some of the US BTAs are viewed as another instrument in pursuing this objective. As Tonelson (2002) notes, "trade policy as an anti-terror weapon is an understandably appealing idea. It doesn't put American soldiers in harm's way. It is nonviolent, market-friendly and holds the promise of 'draining the swamp' where terrorists are assumed to thrive. And it doesn't require a line in the federal budget." The use of trade incentives has long been a part of US foreign policy. During the Cold War in particular, trade and access to the US market was used to strengthen ties with allies such as Israel (with whom the US signed its first BTA in 1985); Korea; and Taipei,China.

There is an element of rewarding friends and forging new geopolitical links by engaging potential foes in this current pursuit. The TIFA with Pakistan and subsequent strong push to conclude a BTA is an example of rewarding an ally for continuing support in this endeavor. The Middle East Free Trade Initiative, proposed by President Bush in May 2003, has already seen BTAs concluded with Bahrain, Jordan, and Morocco, and negotiations are ongoing with Oman and the United Arab Emirates. According to FTA Watch (2006), the BTA with Morocco is designed "to 'reward' a moderate Muslim government for its support to the White House's 'war on terror' and to pull a friendly North African kingdom deeper into its sphere of influence, creating a wedge vis-à-vis the Arab world." The US strategy in the Middle East is a graduated one, negotiating BTAs country by country before moving toward a regional agreement to be completed in 2013. Strong supporters of the war on Iraq, such as Australia, are also in negotiations with the US on a BTA which would reward Australian firms with the opportunity to directly tender, for the first time, for US government contracts.

2.3.3 Event-Driven BTAs

Event-driven BTAs are divided into three subcategories: PTA, WTO accession, and political. The PTA subcategory is further divided into PTA-facilitation and PTA-integration BTAs. WTO-accession BTAs are not further subdivided. Political BTAs are divided into political integration and political disintegration BTAs.

PTA BTAs

PTA-Facilitation BTAs. These are BTAs that are designed to hasten the pace of integration between a country seeking to join a PTA of which the other country is a member. In other words, it is a BTA between a nonmember and a member of a BTA. (Although both parties are usually countries, they need not be; they can be BTAs or PTAs.) An example of this would be the India-Thailand BTA, with India looking to strengthen ties with the ASEAN Free Trade Area (AFTA). The same is true of the "Plus 3" countries of ASEAN, with PRC, Japan, and Korea pursuing individual BTAs with ASEAN members. Such BTAs can also be pursued with the PTA as a whole, and all the "Plus 3" countries are doing so with ASEAN.

PTA-Integration BTAs. These are BTAs between members of a PTA. These types of BTAs stand out because, unlike all other BTAs, the parties involved already have some form of PTA designed to promote closer economic relations. Examples of such BTAs include the Lao PDR-Viet Nam BTA and the Singapore-Thailand BTA, where all countries are also members of AFTA.

WTO-Accession BTAs

These market-accession BTAs are essentially a means to an end, and that end is WTO membership. Countries wanting to join WTO have to negotiate bilateral agreements with major economic powers (such as the US and EU) as part of their entry procedure. These bilateral negotiations lead to specific commitments, concessions, and schedules to liberalize trade in goods and services. The results of these negotiations are merged with the results of more general negotiations carried out between the candidate country and a working party of the WTO members to form an overall "accession package."

For nonmembers, WTO is the largest and most restrictive PTA in the world. It is easily the largest with 149 member countries, and it clearly is the most restrictive because the cumulative domestic content requirement to access WTO accords is effectively 100%. In this way, WTO-accession BTAs have much in common with PTA facilitation BTAs from the perspective of nonmembers. Almost all (28 out of 33) observers at WTO are currently negotiating bilateral market-accession agreements, mostly with the US.[6] When the Russian Federation, the largest nonmember of WTO, signed a BTA with the US during the 2006 Asia-Pacific Economic Cooperation (APEC) Summit in Hanoi, this was supposed to finally clear the way for its accession to WTO. Prior to 2002, almost half of the country-to-country BTAs notified to WTO involved at least one nonmember.

Political BTAs
Political-Integration BTAs. Political-integration BTAs are designed to hasten the economic integration of recent political unions. Examples of these include the BTAs between PRC and its two special administrative regions (SARs), Hong Kong, China (the first BTA for both parties); and Macao, China. As noted earlier, these entities are members of WTO in their own right but have since become SARs of the PRC. It is also interesting that Hong Kong, China's Chief Executive, Tung Chee Hwa, approached Beijing with the BTA proposal only days after the PRC announced that the SARs would not be included in the proposed PRC-ASEAN FTA (Dent, 2006).

Taipei,China is also a member of WTO but has so far rejected the PRC's offer of becoming an SAR. It does not have a BTA with the PRC nor is it pursuing one. Instead, it is actively seeking a BTA with the US, which, though, appears unlikely to be concluded as a result of political pressure from the PRC and apparent US concern over Taipei,China's poor record in protecting intellectual property rights. In the absence of such a BTA, and in order to gain access to the US market, Taipei,China is pursuing BTAs with as many Central American countries as it can, as a way of pursuing access to the US market through the back door.

Political-Disintegration BTAs. The breakup of the Soviet Union in 1991 resulted in 15 newly independent or post-Soviet States.[7] These newly independent states have been rapidly forging BTAs among themselves. In fact, it appears as if BTAs will be signed between most, if not all, of these countries. These BTAs appear to work to restore some degree of political affiliation while ensuring continued economic integration, despite political dissolution. They can work as an interim measure to secure market access for goods when market institutions, payments arrangements, and exchange rate convertibility are not yet fully functioning (Tumbarello, 2005). The strengthening of ties among each other may also be designed to counter the influence of the Russian Federation in the region, and in this way further strengthen their independence. Being newly independent states, many are not yet members of WTO. Forging alliances through BTAs or a PTA could strengthen their collective bargaining power and consolidate common positions in negotiating the most favorable deal in WTO accession.

2.4 IMPACT ON MULTILATERALISM AND THE WORLD TRADE SYSTEM

We began Section 2.3 by examining a number of general factors that were driving the proliferation of BTAs. We begin this section by examining the general impact that the overall growth in the number of BTAs is having on multilateralism and the world trade system, before turning to the effects that different types of BTAs are having.

With regard to general factors, a widespread concern relating to the explosion of BTAs is the distractive effect it is having on multilateralism. As countries devote more and more of their resources toward discussing, designing, negotiating, and implementing BTAs, fewer are available for multilateralism. This would be particularly true for smaller and poorer developing countries. Apart from detracting from the multilateral effort, interest in unilateral trade liberalization—an important but often overlooked modality in the overall liberalization effort of the past few decades—is also likely to wane in the light of the obsession with BTAs.

A related concern is that the appeal of reviving the stalled Doha Round of WTO will fade as more and more BTAs are negotiated. To the extent that BTAs are being pursued to compensate for the perceived inadequacies, or subsequent collapse, of the Doha Round, the apparent need to revive it will presumably diminish with each successive BTA. But can BTAs, if there are enough of them, substitute for a multilateral deal? In other words, does a BTA with every member of WTO sum to equal a multilateral deal, for instance? Although this could be true in theory, it is unlikely to be so in practice, for at least two reasons: (i) the products covered in each BTA are unlikely to be the same, i.e., the sets of exclusions are likely to vary depending on the partner country; and (ii) the assortment of implementing rules are likely to vary across BTAs, e.g., rules of origin, rules of cumulation, and transition periods. This being the case, the sheer number of BTAs cannot substitute for a multilateral deal and, to the extent that it reduces the likelihood of reaching such a deal, it is detrimental to the world trade system.

The fact that most BTAs and PTAs are WTO consistent does little to allay concerns relating to their potentially detrimental effects on the world trade system, either. This is because the requirements of Article XXIV and the Enabling Clause and the General Agreement on Trade in Services (GATS) are very weak and have never really been enforced. For instance, as Lloyd (2002) points out, the meaning of "substantially all trade" has never been defined and has been interpreted in many ways. The only effective restraint that GATT/WTO rules have imposed on BTAs and PTAs is that they have generally prevented trade barriers from being raised against third countries.[8]

Furthermore, almost all of the deep integration features of recent BTAs are altogether outside WTO rules.

The rest of Section 2.4 discusses the impact of specific factors.

2.4.1 Economically Motivated BTAs

Sector-Expanding BTAs

Whether sector-expanding BTAs can support multilateralism will depend on whether the accords, which apparently can be achieved at the bilateral but not multilateral level, are eventually offered on a multilateral most-favored-nation basis to nonmembers. So far, there is limited evidence of this happening, but then it might still be too soon to pass judgment.

There is also concern that if the major trading nations achieve liberalization in new sectors through bilateral or plurilateral agreements among each other, then the perceived returns from, or motivation for, a WTO-wide agreement will diminish. A WTO agreement would allow smaller developing countries to free ride on achievements made at the multilateral level. Without such a deal, and with limited multilateralization of BTA accords, these developing countries may be locked out and will not be able to participate in the benefits of liberalized markets.

Sometimes BTAs can set positive precedents and develop negotiation modalities that can be adopted later in multilateral negotiations. The Canada-US FTA is an example of this. This developed concepts and modalities in the service trade area that was important in the development of GATS. This process can serve the objectives of multilateralism by advancing the agenda in a demonstrably attainable way.

Sector-Excluding BTAs

Although sector-excluding BTAs may provide a vehicle to overcome obstacles preventing progress with liberalization in other areas, are they working to further compromise liberalization of these sectors at the multilateral level? It would seem that they are. Basically, they set a negative precedent that can be exploited. Once a country succeeds in securing exclusion, it can use the precedent set in negotiations with other countries. For example, once Japan was able to secure exclusions for certain agricultural products in the JSEPA with Singapore, it insisted on the same exclusions in negotiations with Korea and Mexico. But other countries can also refer to these precedents in their own negotiations. Korea, for instance, was reported to have cited the Japanese exclusions in agriculture to strengthen its negotiating position with Mexico (Min, 2006).

The multilateral approach is arguably the best way to deal with liberalization of these excluded sectors because it has one key advantage over the bilateral (or regional) approach in this respect. This is the ability of a country to trade concessions across disparate interests, that is, to weigh up the costs of conceding protection in sensitive sectors (such as agriculture) against the benefits from increased market access in areas in which it has a comparative advantage (e.g., through changes to rules relating to investment, intellectual property, or services).[9] Every time a BTA allows a country to bypass this trade-off simply through its choice of partner, and secure benefits without incurring costs, the task of liberalizing such sensitive sectors is made more difficult.

Market-Restoring BTAs

As members of a PTA engage in more and more BTAs with nonmembers, the PTA becomes more porous. In this way, BTAs can work to reduce the restrictiveness of existing trading blocs, and open them up to external trade, albeit in a somewhat piecemeal fashion. If a high share of members of a PTA engage in a large number of BTAs with nonmembers, this has the potential to return trade and investment patterns to a form that existed prior to the establishment of the PTA.

In this way, such BTAs can dilute preference margins and thereby reduce the trade and investment diversion induced by the PTA. If they do this, then market-restoring BTAs would complement the multilateral trading system and work as building rather than stumbling blocks toward free and open trade.

Market-Creating BTAs

The impact of market-creating BTAs on multilateralism and the world trade system depends on the type of trade that they generate. If, on the one hand, the preferences provided by the BTA serve to divert trade that was previously being conducted with a country that was a lower-cost supplier, this would be welfare reducing. If, on the other hand, the BTA works to reduce or remove trade barriers or other restrictions that have previously constrained bilateral trade between the two countries, the impact on multilateralism could be positive, even if second best.

Thus, much depends on why trade relations had been limited to begin with. If historically weak trade relations are due to resource endowments being competitive rather than complementary, then such BTAs, if they affect trade patterns, will run counter to multilateralism. Even if they do not affect trade patterns, their impact may still be negative because administering the BTA and implementing the rules associated with it will be a drain on resources. Some BTAs may be directed at increasing foreign investment flows, but the same arguments relating to trade apply equally to investment flows.

2.4.2 Strategically Motivated BTAs

Lobby-Driven and Terror-Driven BTAs
We discuss the likely impact on multilateralism of lobby-driven and terror-driven BTAs jointly because they both involve the use of trade policy to pursue non-trade-related objectives.

To the extent that BTAs, a trade policy instrument, are used to pursue non-trade-related objectives, the likelihood that the BTA is distorting is increased. If a terror-driven BTA is designed to reward allies, for instance, it cannot do so unless it provides a margin of preference sufficiently high to divert a significant amount of trade or investment. In fact, it may de designed to do so, if the objective is to reward, in a one-sided transfer, rather than to be mutually beneficial, from a gains-from-trade point of view.

The main concern relating to lobby-driven BTAs is that they may be setting precedents that run counter to multilateral principles, and may be promoting protectionism.

Furthermore, as Lloyd (2002) points out, it is useful to adopt a global-welfare point of view in evaluating such BTAs, and ask if they have a positive effect on world welfare. For lobby-driven BTAs in particular, this approach also avoids having to make value judgments associated with the objectives being pursued and focuses attention on economic effects. Prima facie, both lobby- and terror-driven BTAs appear unlikely to raise global welfare for at least two reasons.

First, the fact that such BTAs are likely to be trade distorting suggests that global welfare will be reduced as a result. This negative impact may be higher for terror-driven BTAs because they may be trade or investment diverting by design, whereas lobby-driven BTAs are trade distorting only as a consequence of using the wrong instrument to pursue a particular objective. Second, as various empirical studies have shown, BTAs and PTAs generally result in the reduction of welfare of some nonmembers, and the extent of this reduction is usually related to the extent to which trade is distorted.[10] For highly distorting BTAs, the extent of the global reduction in welfare is also likely to be high.

Apart from the effect on global welfare and the world trade system, others, such as Bhagwati (2003), are also concerned about the impact that lobby-driven BTAs are having on WTO as an institution. The concern is that WTO, a trade institution, is being politicized, and being turned into one where domestic lobbies, good or bad, can distort the working of the institution itself.

2.4.3 Event-Driven BTAs

PTA-Facilitation BTAs
Whether or not PTA-facilitation BTAs serve the interests of multilateralism depends on the PTA concerned. If the PTA is inward looking, adopts complex rules-of-origin requirements, and has a high margin of preference, the BTA may hinder multilateralism and hamper the world trade system. Conversely, if the PTA is based on open regionalism (Menon, 2005), the BTA may assist the non-PTA member to hasten its liberalization and integration with the world trade system.

PTA-Integration BTAs
A BTA between these countries suggests that they wish to pursue a level of integration that surpasses that possible with the PTA of which they are members. Often members of a PTA can only proceed as fast as its slowest or least ambitious member, especially if the decision-making process is consensus based. A BTA may then allow some of its members to pursue more ambitious liberalization programs. This should lead to a positive outcome for the world trade system if it results in a deeper level of integration.

WTO-Accession BTAs
By supporting the process of WTO accession, these BTAs serve to promote multilateralism. Sometimes, the bilateral agreements commit countries to rules on trade liberalization that exceed those of WTO. For instance, Ecuador had to renounce its status as a "developing country," based on demands from the US, and thereby implement several WTO agreements within a much shorter time frame. The PRC agreed to a range of "WTO-plus" measures pushed separately by the US and the EU, including antidumping measures and import restrictions to curtail the entry of PRC goods into their markets, prior to WTO accession.

2.5 CONCLUSIONS AND THE FUTURE LANDSCAPE OF WORLD TRADE

Interest in forming BTAs has been growing at a phenomenal rate. In the Asia-Pacific region alone, the number of BTAs has more than tripled over the past 5 years, from 57 in 2002 to 176 in October 2006. Furthermore, this interest seems to be accelerating. The key distinguishing feature of bilateralism is the amount of flexibility it provides—both in terms of process and in pursuing disparate interests. Any two countries, in any part of the world, can form a BTA simply by wanting to do so. In a one-on-one setting, just about any objective can be pursued, and trade-offs can be designed to accommodate the parties in a way that would be difficult in a multilateral setting.

In this context, it is not surprising that a wide array of both economic and noneconomic factors appears to be driving the proliferation of BTAs. We identified a set of general and specific factors. The general factors were: disenchantment with progress of WTO; snowballing and domino effects as a result of countries not wanting to be left behind; lower visibility and thus lower resistance from opposing forces; and pure politics driven by politicians and political parties. The three broad categories of specific factors were economic, strategic, and event driven. Each of these broad categories have their subcategories, and the subcategories for economic and event-driven BTAs are each subdivided into two subcategories as well. Thus, in total, we identified 11 specific factors to explain the proliferation of BTAs.

It would appear that the sheer number of BTAs and their continued rapid growth is fragmenting the world trade system. The most obvious impact is the much discussed spaghetti-bowl effect (Baldwin, 2006b). It is also distracting, drawing scarce resources away from the multilateral effort. But the story becomes less simple and straightforward once we consider specific factors. The fallacy of division applies because the motivation in pursuing a BTA can determine if its impact on the world trade system is positive or negative. Whether or not a BTA contributes to the integration or fragmentation of the world trade system can vary depending on this.

Most of the event-driven BTAs, except perhaps some PTA-facilitation agreements, appear to either support multilateralism or have a positive effect on the world trade system. All of the strategically motivated BTAs appear to have a negative effect. Of the economically motivated BTAs, sector-expanding and market-restoring BTAs have the potential to support the multilateral process, while market-creating and sector-excluding BTAs appear to threaten it.

Are BTAs likely to continue proliferating? At the moment, the answer appears to be yes, since they are increasing at a greater rate. How much longer is this likely to continue, and where is all of this likely to lead? Baldwin (2006b) is emphatic that regionalism is here to stay, but is equally sure that the motley assortment of trade deals is a poor way of organizing world trade or running the world trade system. It may be that BTAs will continue to proliferate until the world trade system is so distorted that countries will be forced to seek a remedy. This response may take several forms.

One is the consolidation of BTAs into regionwide PTAs, or blocs, where the various BTAs among members belonging to the same region become largely redundant. For instance, many if not all of the event-driven BTAs are likely to fall into this category, but there could be more. There are numerous examples of BTAs that became defunct following the establishment of the EU. In the Asia-Pacific region, the US-Canada BTA was superseded by the establishment of NAFTA, and the India-Sri Lanka BTA by SAFTA. An Asia-wide FTA would supersede a host of regional BTAs, and consolidate them into one regionwide agreement, if the rules are changed to accommodate this.

Although this consolidation may reduce the number of intraregional BTAs, it may be something of a hollow "victory" if it serves to further fragment the world trade system by carving it up into distinct regional blocs. Also, it may not always be easy to do, with serious technical and implementation problems associated with "folding several FTAs together that have different tariff rates and innumerable rules of origin (often defined differently by product) for preferences to kick in" (Bhagwati, 2006).

Furthermore, even if such consolidation were possible, it may provide fresh impetus for a new wave of market-restoring BTAs, as traditional trade partners outside the region seek to retain trade access with members of the consolidated PTA. In fact, with more countries outside the region than inside, it is possible that the total number of BTAs could rise if the reduction in the number of intraregional BTAs through a consolidated PTA is more than offset by the number of interregional market-restoring BTAs that it indirectly induces. This is hardly a remedy for the problems facing the world trade system.

The second response may come in the form of the completion of the Doha Round with minimum compromises. This would undoubtedly be the preferred response to the current chaotic environment of criss-crossing BTAs. A bona fide conclusion to the Doha Round should dilute preferences that are currently scattered around the world, and take away much of the incentive to continue pursuing BTAs. If this happens, the proliferation of BTAs would have contributed to their own eventual demise, in terms of their impact on the world trade system. This is much more like a remedy to the problems facing the world trade system.

But what if the Doha Round fails, or is concluded in such a watered-down and compromised form that its impact is minimal? Although this may provide an additional incentive to pursue more BTAs and PTAs, there may eventually come a point where countries may voluntarily seek a remedy that lies in their own best interests. One thing that is clear is that the cost of administering and implementing multiple country-specific BTAs is high. The cost to the supplying countries also rises with the number of country-specific BTAs. The cost of securing preferences or complying with rules of origin is also apparently high, and may explain why only a very small share of nonagricultural world trade is conducted under preferential terms (Grether and Olarreaga, 1998).

Once a country has concluded BTAs with most, if not all, of its major trading partners, it may then make sense for it to equalize preferences across these BTAs and then offer them to non-BTA countries on a most-favored-nation basis. This would remove the administrative burden, and eliminate distortions to country and global trade patterns. There are precedents to the voluntary multilateralization of preferential accords, and so this is not as far-fetched as it may sound. Indeed, AFTA and the actions of its original members confirm this possibility (Menon, 2005; Feridhanusetyawan, 2005).

As often is the case with reversing much of second-best policies, however, it is the actual *realized* cost of implementation rather than any potential *unrealized* benefits that usually drives the process. And there are significant unrealized benefits that will accrue to the country concerned as well as the world trade system if this process of multilateralizing preferences is pursued, irrespective of the reason for doing so. An interim (possibly definitive) measure toward full multilateralization of accords may take the form of loosening up of rules of origin. This could be done by harmonization, and expanding rules of cumulation. If these rules are sufficiently expanded and then harmonized across different agreements, the outcome could be such that formal or complete multilateralization may no longer be necessary.

ENDNOTES

1   Technically, the Vatican City (Holy See) is considered one of the 193 countries in the world, and has permanent observer status at WTO, but is not a member of the United Nations. It is not a member of any BTA or PTA and is unlikely ever to become one.

2   There are several definitions of the Asia-Pacific region. In this chapter, we use the definition employed by ADB in its ARIC Web site, aric.adb.org, which includes the Central Asian Republics, but we expand it to include the US and Canada.

3   In a paradoxical twist, it seems WTO meetings themselves are being overshadowed and provide an opportunity for members to pursue new BTAs with other member countries. In the Bangkok-based daily *The Nation* dated 17 June 2004, an item entitled "Peru seen as FTA Gateway" reported that: "In the corridors of the WTO meetings, Thai officials discussed the possibility of FTAs with Mexico, Chile and Peru." In the same vein, it is somewhat ironic that the Japan-Singapore BTA was concluded at the APEC summit meeting in Shanghai in October 2001.

4   Agreements with Lao PDR, Singapore, and Viet Nam have been concluded, and one with Thailand is in negotiation. As of October 2006, TIFAs have been signed with Brunei Darussalam, Indonesia, Malaysia, Philippines, and Thailand.

5   This view of "fair trade" is not new, however. As far back as in 1881, William Gladstone remarked: "Fair trade bears a suspicious likeness to our old friend protection. Protection was dead and buried 30 years ago, but he has come out of the grave and is walking around in the broad light of day. But after long experience underground, he endeavours to look more attractive than he used to appear ... and in consequence he found it convenient to assume a new name" (quoted in Brittan, 2005).

6   The five exceptions are: Equatorial Guinea, Islamic Republic of Iran, Iraq, São Tomé and Principe, and Vatican City.

7   Apart from the Russian Federation, the following four categories are identified: (i) Central Asia, consisting of Kazakhstan, Kyrgyz Republic, Tajikistan, Turkmenistan, and Uzbekistan; (ii) Baltic states, consisting of Estonia, Latvia, and Lithuania; (iii) Eastern European states, namely Belarus, Moldova, and Ukraine; and (iv) Transcaucasus, consisting of Armenia, Azerbaijan, and Georgia.

8   Even here there appear to be exceptions. See Panagariya (1999).

9   See Menon (1998) for more details. A recent but potent example of this trade-off was provided in the lead-up to the WTO meeting in Hong Kong, China in December 2005. Brazil and India, representing the apparent position of a majority of developing countries, proposed opening their markets further to industrial goods and services in exchange for the EU and the US dismantling the elaborate system of support to their agriculture sectors.

10 Scollay and Gilbert (2001), for instance, find that all BTAs in Asia and the Pacific have negative effects on the welfare of some outside countries, with the sole exception of the New Zealand-Singapore agreement, which has a zero effect on all countries. This exception arises because both countries have close to zero most-favored-nation tariff rates and thereby minimize the distortion that a BTA can introduce.

REFERENCES

Baldwin, Richard E. 1996. "A Domino Theory of Regionalism." In Richard E. Baldwin, P. Haaparanta, and J. Kiander (eds.), *Expanding Membership of the EU*. Cambridge: Cambridge University Press.

———. 2006a. "Managing the Noodle Bowl: The Fragility of East Asian Regionalism." CEPR Discussion Paper 5561. London: CEPR.

———. 2006b. "Multilateralising Regionalism: Spaghetti Bowls as Building Blocs on the Path to Global Free Trade." *World Economy* 29(11):1451-1518.

Bhagwati, Jagdish N. 2003. "The Singapore and Chile Free Trade Agreements." Testimony before US House of Representatives Committee on Financial Services, 1 April.

———. 2005. "From Seattle to Hong Kong." *Foreign Affairs* 84/7, (WTO Special Edition). December.

———. 2006. "Why Asia Must Opt for Open Regionalism on Trade." *The Financial Times.* 3 November.

Brittan, S. 2005. "Free Trade versus 'Fair Trade.'" Remarks at a Foreign Policy Centre meeting with Hilary Benn, 10 January 2005. Available: http://www.samuelbrittan.co.uk/spee39_p.html.

Dent, Christopher. 2006. *New Free Trade Agreements in the Asia Pacific.* Basingstoke: Palgrave-Macmillan.

Feridhanusetyawan, Tubagus. 2005. "Preferential Trading Agreements in the Asia-Pacific Region." IMF Working Paper 149. International Monetary Fund, Washington, DC.

FTA Watch 2006. "Overview of Bilateral Free Trade and Investment Agreements." Background paper prepared for the Fighting FTAs workshop, Bangkok, 27-29 July.

Grether, Jean-Marie and Marcelo Olarreaga. 1998. "Preferential and Non-preferential Trade Flows in World Trade," Staff Working Paper ERAD-98-10. WTO, Geneva.

Lloyd, Peter. 2002. *New Regionalism and New Bilateralism in the Asia-Pacific.* Singapore: Institute of Southeast Asian Studies.

Looney, Robert E. 2005. "US Middle East Economic Policy: The Use of Free Trade Areas in the War on Terrorism." *Mediterranean Quarterly* 16(3):102-117.

Menon, Jayant. 1996. *Adjusting towards AFTA: The Dynamics of Trade in ASEAN.* Singapore: Institute of Southeast Asian Studies.

———. 1998. "The Expansion of the ASEAN Free Trade Area." *Asian-Pacific Economic Literature* 12(2):10-22.

———. 2005. "Building Blocks or Stumbling Blocks: Regional Cooperation Arrangements in Southeast Asia." Discussion Paper 41. Asian Development Bank Institute, Tokyo.

Min Gyo Koo. 2006. "From Multilateralism to Bilateralism. A Shift in South Korea's Trade Strategy?" In Vinod K. Agrawal and Shujiro Urata (eds.), *Bilateral Trade Agreements in the Asia-Pacific.* London: Routledge, 140-59.

Panagariya, A. 1999. "The Regionalism Debate: An Overview." *World Economy* 22:477-511.

Ravenhill, John 2006. "The Political Economy of the New Asia-Pacific Bilateralism: Benign, Banal, or Simply Bad?" In Vinod K. Agrawal and Shujiro Urata (eds.), *Bilateral Trade Agreements in the Asia-Pacific.* London: Routledge, 27-49.

Scollay, R. and J. P. Gilbert. 2001. "New Regional Trading Arrangements in the Asia Pacific?" Institute for International Economics, Washington, DC.

Tonelson, Alan. 2002. "There's Only So Much That Foreign Trade Can Do." *Washington Post.* 2 June.

Tumbarello, Patrizia. 2005. "Regional Trade Integration and WTO Accession: Which Is the Right Sequencing? An Application to the CIS." IMF Working Paper WP/05/94. International Monetary Fund, Washington, DC.

APPENDIX

Appendix Table A2.1 BTAs of Countries in the Asia-Pacific Region, and Status (up to October 2006)

No.	Bilateral Trade Agreement (Status)
1	Armenia-Georgia Free Trade Area (Under Implementation)
2	Armenia-Kazakhstan Free Trade Agreement (Under Implementation)
3	Armenia-Kyrgyz Republic Free Trade Agreement (Under Implementation)
4	Armenia-Moldova Free Trade Agreement (Under Implementation)
5	Armenia-Russian Federation Free Trade Agreement (Under Implementation)
6	Armenia-Turkmenistan Free Trade Agreement (Under Implementation)
7	Armenia-Ukraine Free Trade Agreement (Under Implementation)
8	ASEAN-Australia and New Zealand Free Trade Agreement (Under Negotiation)
9	ASEAN-People's Republic of China Free Trade Area (Under Implementation)
10	ASEAN-EU Free Trade Agreement (Proposed/Under Consultation and Study)
11	ASEAN-India Regional Trade and Investment Area ([FA] Signed/FTA Under Negotiation)
12	ASEAN-Japan Comprehensive Economic Partnership ([FA] Signed/FTA Under Negotiation)
13	ASEAN-Republic of Korea Free Trade Area (Signed)
14	Australia-Japan Free Trade Agreement (Proposed/Under Consultation and Study)
15	Australia-Mexico Free Trade Agreement (Proposed/Under Consultation and Study)
16	Australia-New Zealand Closer Economic Relations Trade Agreement (Under Implementation)
17	Australia-United Arab Emirates Free Trade Agreement (Under Negotiation)
18	Azerbaijan-Georgia Free Trade Agreement (Under Implementation)
19	Azerbaijan-Kazakhstan Free Trade Agreement (Signed)
20	Azerbaijan-Moldova Free Trade Agreement (Signed)
21	Azerbaijan-Russian Federation Free Trade Agreement (Signed)
22	Azerbaijan-Turkmenistan Free Trade Agreement (Signed)
23	Azerbaijan-Ukraine Free Trade Agreement (Signed)
24	Azerbaijan-Uzbekistan Free Trade Agreement (Signed)
25	Canada-Chile Free Trade Agreement (Under Implementation)
26	Canada-Costa Rica Free Trade Agreement (Under Implementation)
27	Canada-Dominican Republic Free Trade Agreement (Under Negotiation)
28	Canada-Israel Free Trade Agreement (Under Implementation)
29	Canada-Singapore Free Trade Agreement (Under Negotiation)
30	Canada-United States Free Trade Agreement (Under Implementation)
31	People's Republic of China-India Regional Trading Arrangement (Proposed/Under Consultation and Study)
32	European Free Trade Area-Singapore Free Trade Agreement (Under Implementation)
33	India-Afghanistan Preferential Trading Agreement (Signed)
34	India-Australia Free Trade Agreement (Proposed/Under Consultation and Study)
35	India-Chile Preferential Trading Agreement (Signed)
36	India-Colombia Preferential Trading Arrangement (Proposed/Under Consultation and Study)

37	India-Egypt Preferential Trade Agreement (Under Negotiation)
38	India-European Union Free Trade Agreement (Proposed/Under Consultation and Study)
39	India-Gulf Cooperation Council Free Trade Area ([FA] Signed/FTA Under Negotiation)
40	India-Indonesia Comprehensive Economic Cooperation Arrangement (Proposed/Under Consultation and Study)
41	India-Israel Preferential Trade Agreement (Proposed/Under Consultation and Study)
42	India-Republic of Korea Comprehensive Economic Partnership Agreement (Under Negotiation)
43	India-Mauritius Comprehensive Economic Cooperation and Partnership Agreement (Under Negotiation)
44	India-MERCOSUR Preferential Trade Agreement (Signed)
45	India-Singapore Comprehensive Economic Cooperation Agreement (Under Implementation)
46	India-Southern African Customs Union Preferential Trade Agreement ([FA] Signed/FTA Under Negotiation)
47	India-Sri Lanka Free Trade Agreement (Under Implementation)
48	India-Thailand Free Trade Area ([FA] Signed/FTA Under Negotiation)
49	India-Uruguay Preferential Trading Arrangement (Proposed/Under Consultation and Study)
50	India-Venezuela Preferential Trading Arrangement (Proposed/Under Consultation and Study)
51	Indo-Nepal Treaty of Trade (Under Implementation)
52	Japan-Brunei Darussalam Free Trade Agreement (Under Negotiation)
53	Japan-Canada Free Trade Agreement (Proposed/Under Consultation and Study)
54	Japan-Chile Economic Partnership Agreement (Under Negotiation)
55	Japan-Gulf Cooperation Council Free Trade Agreement (Under Negotiation)
56	Japan-India Economic Partnership Agreement (Proposed/Under Consultation and Study)
57	Japan-Indonesia Economic Partnership Agreement (Under Negotiation)
58	Japan-Republic of Korea Free Trade Agreement (Under Negotiation)
59	Japan-Malaysia Economic Partnership Agreement (Under Implementation)
60	Japan-Mexico Economic Partnership Agreement (Under Implementation)
61	Japan-Philippines Economic Partnership Agreement (Signed)
62	Japan-Singapore Economic Agreement for a New-Age Partnership (Under Implementation)
63	Japan-Switzerland Free Trade Agreement (Proposed/Under Consultation and Study)
64	Japan-Thailand Economic Partnership Agreement (Under Negotiation)
65	Japan-Viet Nam Free Trade Agreement (Under Negotiation)
66	Kazakhstan-Georgia Free Trade Agreement (Under Implementation)
67	Republic of Korea-Canada Free Trade Agreement (Under Negotiation)
68	Republic of Korea-Chile Free Trade Agreement (Under Implementation)
69	Republic of Korea-European Free Trade Association Free Trade Agreement (Under Implementation)
70	Republic of Korea-MERCOSUR Preferential Trading Agreement (Proposed/Under Consultation and Study)
71	Republic of Korea-Mexico Strategic Economic Complementation Agreement (Under Negotiation)
72	Republic of Korea-Singapore Free Trade Agreement (Under Implementation)
73	Republic of Korea-South Africa Free Trade Agreement (Proposed/Under Consultation and Study)

74   Republic of Korea-United States Free Trade Agreement (Under Negotiation)

75   Kyrgyz Republic-Kazakhstan Free Trade Agreement (Under Implementation)

76   Kyrgyz Republic-Moldova Free Trade Agreement (Under Implementation)

77   Kyrgyz Republic-Russian Federation Free Trade Agreement (Under Implementation)

78   Kyrgyz Republic-Ukraine Free Trade Agreement (Under Implementation)

79   Kyrgyz Republic-Uzbekistan Free Trade Agreement (Under Implementation)

80   Lao People's Democratic Republic-Thailand Preferential Trading Arrangement (Under Implementation)

81   Malaysia-Australia Free Trade Agreement (Under Negotiation)

82   Malaysia-Chile Free Trade Agreement (Proposed/Under Consultation and Study)

83   Malaysia-India Comprehensive Economic Cooperation Agreement (Proposed/Under Consultation and Study)

84   Malaysia-Republic of Korea Free Trade Agreement (Proposed/Under Consultation and Study)

85   Malaysia-New Zealand Free Trade Agreement (Under Negotiation)

86   Malaysia-Pakistan Free Trade Agreement (Under Negotiation)

87   New Zealand-People's Republic of China Free Trade Agreement ([FA] Signed/FTA Under Negotiation)

88   New Zealand-Hong Kong, China Closer Economic Partnership (Under Negotiation)

89   New Zealand-Republic of Korea Closer Economic Partnership (Proposed/Under Consultation and Study)

90   New Zealand-Mexico Free Trade Agreement (Proposed/Under Consultation and Study)

91   New Zealand-Singapore Closer Economic Partnership (Under Implementation)

92   Pacific ACP-EU (African, Caribbean and Pacific Group of States-European Union) Economic Partnership Agreement (Under Negotiation)

93   Pakistan-Afghanistan Free Trade Agreement (Proposed/Under Consultation and Study)

94   Pakistan-Bangladesh Free Trade Agreement (Under Negotiation)

95   Pakistan-Gulf Cooperation Council Free Trade Agreement ([FA] Signed/FTA Under Negotiation)

96   Pakistan-Indonesia Free Trade Agreement ([FA] Signed/FTA Under Negotiation)

97   Pakistan-Iran Preferential Trade Agreement (Signed)

98   Pakistan-Jordan Free Trade Agreement (Proposed/Under Consultation and Study)

99   Pakistan-Kazakhstan Preferential Trade Agreement (Proposed/Under Consultation and Study)

100   Pakistan-Mauritius Preferential Trade Agreement (Under Negotiation)

101   Pakistan-MERCOSUR Preferential Trade Agreement ([FA] Signed/FTA Under Negotiation)

102   Pakistan-Morocco Preferential Trade Agreement (Under Negotiation)

103   Pakistan-Philippines Free Trade Agreement (Proposed/Under Consultation and Study)

104   Pakistan-Singapore Free Trade Agreement (Under Negotiation)

105   Pakistan-Sri Lanka Free Trade Agreement (Under Implementation)

106   Pakistan-Tajikistan Preferential Trade Agreement (Proposed/Under Consultation and Study)

107   Pakistan-Thailand Free Trade Agreement (Proposed/Under Consultation and Study)

108   Pakistan-Turkey Preferential Trade Agreement ([FA] Signed/FTA Under Negotiation)

109   Papua New Guinea-Australia Trade and Commercial Region (Under Implementation)

110   People's Republic of China-Australia Free Trade Agreement ([FA] Signed/FTA Under Negotiation)

111	People's Republic of China-Chile Free Trade Agreement (Signed)
112	People's Republic of China-Gulf Cooperation Council Free Trade Agreement (Under Negotiation)
113	People's Republic of China-Hong Kong, China Closer Economic Partnership Arrangement (Under Implementation)
114	People's Republic of China-Iceland Free Trade Agreement (Proposed/Under Consultation and Study)
115	People's Republic of China-Japan-Republic of Korea Free Trade Agreement (Proposed/ Under Consultation and Study)
116	People's Republic of China-Republic of Korea Free Trade Agreement (Proposed/Under Consultation and Study)
117	People's Republic of China-Macao,China Closer Economic Partnership Arrangement (Under Implementation)
118	People's Republic of China-Pakistan Free Trade Agreement (Under Negotiation)
119	People's Republic of China-South Africa Free Trade Agreement (Proposed/Under Consultation and Study)
120	People's Republic of China-South African Customs Union Free Trade Agreement (Under Negotiation)
121	People's Republic of China-Thailand Free Trade Agreement (Under Implementation)
122	Singapore-Australia Free Trade Agreement (Under Implementation)
123	Singapore-Bahrain Free Trade Agreement (Proposed/Under Consultation and Study)
124	Singapore-Egypt Free Trade Agreement (Under Negotiation)
125	Singapore-Jordan Free Trade Agreement (Under Implementation)
126	Singapore-Kuwait Free Trade Agreement (Under Negotiation)
127	Singapore-Mexico Free Trade Agreement (Under Negotiation)
128	Singapore-Panama Free Trade Agreement (Signed)
129	Singapore-Peru Free Trade Agreement (Under Negotiation)
130	Singapore-Qatar Free Trade Agreement (Under Negotiation)
131	Singapore-Sri Lanka Comprehensive Economic Partnership Agreement (Proposed/Under Consultation and Study)
132	Singapore-United Arab Emirates Free Trade Agreement (Proposed/Under Consultation and Study)
133	Sri Lanka-Iran Preferential Trade Agreement (Signed)
134	Taipei,China-Dominican Republic Free Trade Agreement (Proposed/Under Consultation and Study)
135	Taipei,China-El Salvador Free Trade Agreement (Under Negotiation)
136	Taipei,China-Guatemala Free Trade Agreement (Signed)
137	Taipei,China-Honduras Free Trade Agreement (Proposed/Under Consultation and Study)
138	Taipei,China-Nicaragua Free Trade Agreement (Signed)
139	Taipei,China-Panama Free Trade Agreement (Under Implementation)
140	Taipei,China-Paraguay Free Trade Agreement ([FA] Signed/FTA Under Negotiation)
141	Tajikistan-Armenia Free Trade Agreement (Signed)
142	Tajikistan-Belarus Free Trade Agreement (Signed)
143	Tajikistan-Kyrgyz Republic Free Trade Agreement (Signed)
144	Tajikistan-Russian Federation Free Trade Agreement (Signed)
145	Tajikistan-Ukraine Free Trade Agreement (Signed)
146	Tajikistan-Uzbekistan Free Trade Agreement (Signed)
147	Thailand-Australia Free Trade Agreement (Under Implementation)

148   Thailand-Bahrain Free Trade Agreement ([FA] Signed/FTA Under Negotiation)

149   Thailand-Chile Free Trade Agreement (Proposed/Under Consultation and Study)

150   Thailand-EFTA Free Trade Agreement (Under Negotiation)

151   Thailand-MERCOSUR Free Trade Agreement (Proposed/Under Consultation and Study)

152   Thailand-New Zealand Closer Economic Partnership Agreement (Under Implementation)

153   Thailand-Peru Free Trade Agreement ([FA] Signed/FTA Under Negotiation)

154   Turkmenistan-Georgia Free Trade Agreement (Under Implementation)

155   United States-Australia Free Trade Agreement (Under Implementation)

156   United States-Bahrain Free Trade Agreement (Signed)

157   United States-Brunei Darussalam Free Trade Agreement (Proposed/Under Consultation and Study)

158   United States-Chile Free Trade Agreement (Under Implementation)

159   United States-Indonesia Free Trade Agreement (Proposed/Under Consultation and Study)

160   United States-Israel Free Trade Agreement (Under Implementation)

161   United States-Hashemite Kingdom of Jordan Free Trade Agreement (Under Implementation)

162   United States-Malaysia Free Trade Agreement (Under Negotiation)

163   United States-Marshall Islands Compact of Free Association (Under Implementation)

164   United States-Federated States of Micronesia Compact of Free Association (Under Implementation)

165   United States-Morocco Free Trade Agreement (Under Implementation)

166   United States-Pakistan Free Trade Agreement (Proposed/Under Consultation and Study)

167   United States-Republic of Palau Compact of Free Association (Under Implementation)

168   United States-Philippines Free Trade Agreement (Proposed/Under Consultation and Study)

169   United States-Singapore Free Trade Agreement (Under Implementation)

170   United States-Sri Lanka Free Trade Agreement (Proposed/Under Consultation and Study)

171   United States-Taipei,China Free Trade Agreement (Proposed/Under Consultation and Study)

172   United States-Thailand Free Trade Agreement (Under Negotiation)

173   Uzbekistan-Georgia Free Trade Agreement (Signed)

174   Uzbekistan-Kazakhstan Free Trade Agreement (Signed)

175   Uzbekistan-Moldova Free Trade Agreement (Signed)

176   Uzbekistan-Russian Federation Free Trade Agreement (Signed)

ASEAN = Association of Southeast Asian Nations; FA = Framework Agreement.

Sources: Author's compilation based on data from the following Web sites: ADB ARIC, available: aric.adb.org; Bilaterals.org, available: www.bilaterals.org; Foreign Affairs and International Trade Canada, available: www.dfait-maeci.gc.ca; Office of the US Trade Representative, available: www.ustr.gov; and World Trade Organization, available: www.wto.org.

Commentary on Chapter 2

Siow Yue Chia

In reading through this chapter I am unclear whether its scope is global, Asia-Pacific, or Asia. Figure 2.1 and Appendix Table A2.1 cover Asia-Pacific, which apparently does not refer to the Asia-Pacific Economic Cooperation (APEC) group of economies, since the figure and table include South Asia and Central Asia and exclude Pacific Latin America. My comments will focus mainly on Asia, and more particularly on East Asia.

1 Proliferation of Bilateral Trade Agreements and Regional Trade Agreements

The author defines bilateral trade agreements (BTAs) to cover agreements not only between pairs of countries but also between a country and a regional trade agreement (RTA). The World Trade Organization (WTO) defines RTAs to include BTAs. RTAs notified to WTO that have been implemented or signed grew from a cumulative total of 104 in 2000 to 211 in 2005, a doubling. Every WTO member, except Mongolia, is now a member of an RTA and many have joined multiple RTAs. Departure from the most-favored-nation (MFN) principle of GATT started in Europe and spread to North America, Africa, and Latin America.

Figure 2.1 and Appendix Table A2.1 show that "Asia-Pacific" appears to be a late-comer. It had only one RTA in 1976, and only two RTAs and five BTAs in 1991. Asian catch-up and escalation took place primarily in the post-2001 period. The number of BTAs shot up from a cumulative 41 in 2000 to 151 in 2005, 3.7 times as high. By October 2006 there were cumulatively 176 BTAs and 17 RTAs. However, of these 176 BTAs, only 53 have been implemented, 28 have been signed, and 95 are still at the proposal, study, or negotiating stage.

2 Motivations for BTAs (Menon definition) and RTAs (WTO definition)

The author attempts to develop an analytical framework for studying the various types of BTAs according to their motivations and effects. He classifies motivations into general factors and specific factors, but it is unclear what their distinctive characteristics are. Under general factors are disenchantment with the pace of liberalization at the multilateral level, including difficulties with the Doha Round negotiations; the domino effect; less pressure and opposition to BTAs; and political motivations (this also appears as a specific factor). The domino effect is becoming increasingly evident as more countries participate in BTAs, putting tremendous pressure on competing economies to follow suit. With regard to less opposition to BTAs, it bears noting that many BTAs are receiving wide media coverage these days and opposition to WTO and the Doha Round appears to have spread to BTAs, as evidenced in the case of India, Republic of Korea, Malaysia, and Thailand in recent times. Also, every BTA has a political motivation, so it may not be a useful criterion for classifying BTAs.

In terms of specific factors, the author classifies them into economic, strategic, and event driven. This is a very useful classification, but some of the subclassifications appear confusing. Under economic motivation, he makes distinctions between sector excluding, sector expanding, market restricting, and market creating. It would be difficult to classify BTAs according to these criteria, as a particular BTA could be both sector excluding and sector expanding, and market restricting and market creating. Hence in evaluating the impact of any particular BTA, it would be necessary to look at the net outcome of these positive and negative effects.

The strategic factors are divided into lobby driven and terror driven, but these classifications appear too narrow and United States (US)-centric. Event-driven BTAs are divided into PTA facilitating, PTA integrating, WTO accession, political integration, and political disintegration. The distinction between facilitating and integrating PTAs is unclear and could be due to stages of development in the BTA-PTA relationship. BTAs are generally seen as distinct from the WTO process, yet the classification of "WTO accession" categorizes BTA as a preliminary step to WTO and is thus confusing. Political disintegration refers specifically to the disintegration of the former Soviet Union. However, an event-driven BTA in Asia, namely the 1997 financial crisis, has not been included, neither was the rise of the People's Republic of China (PRC).

Here I will outline the main characteristics and list the motivations for BTAs and RTAs in East Asia in order to illustrate their complexity and some of the difficulties in fitting them into the author's framework.

Characteristics of RTAs (including BTAs) in East Asia
- Japan and the Republic of Korea, which have traditionally relied on multilateral trade liberalization, are increasingly making RTAs the centerpiece of their trade policy. An increasing number of Southeast Asian economies are pursuing a multitiered trade strategy of multilateralism, regionalism, and bilateralism.
- RTAs of East Asian economies are no longer constrained by geography, but have extended beyond East Asia to the rest of the world.

- RTAs are becoming increasingly complex. The scope is "WTO-plus," including not only trade in goods and services, but also provisions on trade facilitation, investment, competition, intellectual property protection, government procurement, labor and the environment, and economic and development cooperation. Some critics argue that some of these RTAs are at the same time "WTO-minus," with large exclusion lists, particularly pertaining to agriculture, and a lack of safeguards provisions.

Driving Forces of RTAs in East Asia
Political and strategic motivations. In nearly all cases, politics plays an important role. RTAs are often one component of a larger political effort toward political and security cooperation as well as the deepening of economic relations. ASEAN was started as a regional group to secure peace and stability in Southeast Asia during the Cold War and went on to establish the ASEAN Free Trade Area in 1992. The ASEAN+1 initiatives also had political and strategic motivations, including the PRC's efforts at political confidence-building. The PRC's overtures were followed by moves from Japan, Republic of Korea, India, and Australia-New Zealand as they also sought to maintain or establish political influence in Southeast Asia. The latest efforts are by the European Union (EU) and the US. Agreements between developing countries often reflect a political desire to form or join a broadly based regional initiative. Studies show that RTAs that expand trade flows have a substantial dampening impact on conflict.

Market access and foreign direct investment (FDI) access motivations. In East Asia increasing volumes of exports are undertaken by foreign-affiliated firms. Hence export capability and competitiveness are closely linked with the ability to attract foreign investment. Enlarging the ASEAN regional market, together with ASEAN+1 FTAs and bilateral agreements between individual ASEAN countries and major trading and investing countries, helps ASEAN collectively and member countries individually attract more FDI and technology transfers.

Resource access. A major objective of RTAs with resource-rich countries is to secure access to supplies of energy, metals, and minerals. In recent years, with energy demand and prices soaring, Gulf Cooperation Council countries are being wooed into RTAs by countries the world over, including resource-poor East Asian economies. It is also an important consideration in the Japan-Indonesia FTA currently under negotiation.

Flexibility and WTO-plus. RTAs offer flexibility to pursue trade-expanding agreements beyond the WTO mandate. As border barriers (tariffs and nontariff barriers) topple under successive rounds of multilateral trade negotiations under GATT/WTO, within-border barriers such as restrictions on investment, competition, government procurement, intellectual property, customs procedures, and product standards assume added importance. In addition, some RTAs reflect a desire to deal with region-specific issues that are difficult to broach at the multilateral level, such as transit, water, energy, migration, and movement of labor. The RTAs also have flexibility provisions for less-developed economies.

Economic and development cooperation. For less-developed economies, apart from conferring market access, RTAs have the additional benefits of economic, financial, and technical assistance from more-developed and bigger partners. This is an important consideration for Cambodia, Lao People's Democratic Republic, Myanmar, and Viet Nam joining in the ASEAN+1 initiatives.

Disappointment with WTO and APEC processes. The more open and liberal economies in East Asia were disappointed with the slow and uncertain processes of liberalization in the WTO Doha Round and in APEC, and believe that RTAs could provide speedier results. Some RTAs took less than 2 years from conception to implementation, while the Uruguay Round took 7 years, and the Doha Round, launched in December 2001, is currently (March 2007) in a comatose state. RTAs provide some insurance against a Doha collapse and a future rise in protectionism. There is also growing concern over the ineffectiveness of APEC's open regionalism since the failure of Early Voluntary Sectoral Liberalization and the realization that the Bogor goals of free trade and investment for developed countries by 2010 and for developing countries by 2020 are unattainable within the previously agreed time frames.

The "domino effect" or defensive motivation. Countries in East Asia were trying to catch up with regionalism in North America and Western Europe, as they felt increasingly disadvantaged in these preferential markets. This led to the deepening and acceleration of ASEAN economic integration, and the ASEAN+1 initiatives. As individual countries such as Singapore and Thailand embarked aggressively on bilateral FTAs, other ASEAN countries tried to play catch-up for fear of losing export market share and FDI competitiveness.

Event-driven Asian financial crisis. The 1997–98 Asian financial crisis acted as a trigger for East Asian regionalism. It demonstrated the close economic and financial interdependence among those economies. There was also unease and dissatisfaction over the policies of the "Washington consensus." This led to the resolve for regional monetary and financial cooperation to help achieve regional economic stability and resilience under the ASEAN+3 initiative. The initiative also provided the forum for formal dialogue between Southeast Asia and Northeast Asia and to the emerging idea of an East Asia economic bloc.

Event-driven rise of the PRC and its WTO accession. The PRC has been enjoying rapid economic growth for over two decades. For the rest of East

Asia, there is a rising need for further cooperation and integration as well as competition with the PRC. Since WTO accession in December 2001, the PRC has shown growing interest in regional economic integration.

3 Concerns over RTA Proliferation

Theoretically, multilateralism provides the "first-best" way of liberalizing trade, and regionalism and bilateralism are second-best alternatives. However, proponents of regionalism argue that the "first-best" approach is unattainable in practical terms, particularly as WTO membership has expanded in number and diversity, and the liberalizing issues have become much more complex. In contrast, regionalism is more practicable; it also provides market access, and improves economic efficiency through economies of scale, regional competition, and the encouragement of domestic reforms and restructuring. Critics of regionalism point to the negative welfare effects of trade and investment diversion; condoning continuing protectionism of sensitive sectors; creating a "spaghetti bowl" of diverse rules of origin, standards and conformance, and time lines for liberalization, which ultimately raises transaction costs; and diverting attention and negotiating resources away from the Doha objective and undermining WTO as an international trade institution.

4 Some Possible Responses to RTA Proliferation

Ensuring the Success of the Doha Round
A successful Doha Round will help stem the tide of regionalism and the reemergence of rampant protectionism.

Improving the Design of RTAs
The World Bank (2005) notes that given the wide variety of motives that induce countries to pursue RTAs, regionalism is likely to remain popular, no matter how well the multilateral system functions. Hence the most important challenge is to seek ways to maximize RTA welfare effects and their compatibility with WTO, while minimizing their negative effects. The World Bank suggests adoption of certain principles in RTAs, which could help consolidate and build on the benefits of RTAs and promote a more effective multilateral system.

First, countries could signal their willingness by concurrently lowering MFN tariffs alongside RTA preferential tariffs, thus reducing the likelihood of trade and investment diversion. An even bolder move would be to move toward across-the-board elimination of duties on industrial products at an MFN level.

Second, countries could promote the principle of transparency by ensuring that comprehensive information on tariffs, regulations, and rules of origin of their RTAs is publicly and easily available, and that all such RTAs are notified to WTO in a timely fashion.

Third, by agreeing to a consultative system to map and monitor RTAs and by redefining, where necessary, the rules applicable to RTAs, a more effective link might be forged between regionalism and multilateralism.

Article XXIV of GATT complemented by the 1979 Enabling Clause (for developing countries) provides the legal foundation for RTAs in trade in goods, while rules covering trade in services in RTAs are set out in GATS Article V. It is widely recognized that existing RTA rules in GATT/WTO have proved inadequate in handling proliferating RTAs:

- The rules that require RTAs to be transparent and to provide for deep internal trade liberalization and neutrality vis-à-vis nonpartners have been subject to diverging interpretations and led to great ambiguity in the relationship between RTAs and the multilateral trading system.
- The task of verifying WTO compliance of RTAs notified under GATT Article XXIV and GATS Article V rests with the WTO Committee on Regional Trade Agreements. The Committee has had little success in assessing the WTO consistency of the RTAs, due to various political and legal difficulties. Another problem is the controversy about interpretation of the WTO provisions, such as "substantially all trade." Yet another arises from either absence of WTO rules or from troublesome discrepancies between existing WTO rules and those contained in some existing RTAs.
- The Doha Ministerial Conference agreed to launch negotiations aimed at clarifying and improving the relevant disciplines and procedures under existing WTO provisions.

Convergence Toward an East Asian FTA

The feasibility of an East Asian FTA comprising ASEAN plus PRC, Japan, and Republic of Korea (ASEAN+3) is under study. The political argument for this is that the experiences of the EU and ASEAN have shown that closer economic cooperation and integration help reduce political and military tensions and conflicts. In addition, with regard to economic arguments, a larger East Asian FTA can create more benefits than the smaller ASEAN+1, ASEAN, or bilateral agreements. It would contain a wider mix of economies at different levels of economic development and of industrial and technological competence, would minimize the trade and investment diversion effects, and maximize the creation effects. Complementarities and diversities would provide for an efficient regional division of labor and so facilitate the full realization of an East Asian production network.

Market consolidation is necessary to achieve economies of scale and overcome the spaghetti bowl effect. It will enable the East Asian region and individual countries to meet the challenges of globalization and the emergence of continental economic blocs in the Americas and Europe.

However, the realization of an East Asian FTA faces a number of challenges and issues. First, there is no consensus of what constitutes "East Asia." ASEAN+3 excludes several economies in Northeast Asia, notably Hong Kong, China; Democratic People's Republic of Korea; Mongolia; and Taipei,China. There is also a counter-proposal from Japan for an ASEAN+6, which in addition includes India, Australia, and New Zealand.

Second, there is as yet no common political vision for East Asia, however defined. Countries in the region need to be convinced that they have a common destiny, and that the political and economic gains of economic cooperation and integration outweigh the costs arising from the dilution of national sovereignty that is necessary for creating common institutions and common rules and disciplines. Potential PRC-Japan rivalry for regional hegemony could be problematic.

Third, the wide differences in development levels and economic competencies make consensus building difficult. Countries would want to open up at different paces and exclude different sensitive sectors, products, and services. Governments would be pressured to protect less competitive sectors, thus slowing the process of economic restructuring. Hence, hand in hand with efforts targeted at trade and investment liberalization, should be efforts aimed at trade and investment facilitation, capacity building, development cooperation, and assistance for less-developed economies.

Finally, some East Asian countries have strong external political, security, economic, and technology links with nonmembers, particularly US, EU, India, and Australia and New Zealand. Hence, an East Asian FTA should be outward looking, to engage the American and European blocs positively and to remain committed to the WTO process. East Asian regionalism should complement and not substitute for multilateralism. After all, East Asia has been a major beneficiary of an open global trading system and should continue to be so.

Reference to Commentary

World Bank. 2005. *Global Economic Prospects: Trade, Regionalism and Development.* Washington, DC.

3

Regionalizing Bilateral Free Trade Agreements in Asia

Frank Harrigan, William James, Michael Plummer, and Fan Zhai

3.1 INTRODUCTION

The trend toward bilateralism in Asia is gaining momentum and may well become the main avenue for trade negotiations in the wake of the suspension of the Doha Round negotiations. The rising tide of bilateralism is well documented and is becoming particularly notable in Asia where the former emphasis on "open regionalism" has been replaced with preferential agreements based on reciprocity enforced by rules of origin (ADB, 2006). In 1995, there were only three bilateral preferential trade agreements (PTAs) involving developing member countries (DMCs) of the Asian Development Bank (ADB) notified to the World Trade Organization (WTO). By 2006, over 40 such agreements involving DMCs had been notified and nearly 100 others were in the process of being negotiated. Moreover, research on notified agreements that are available on the WTO homepage reveals that each has distinctive product coverage and varying rules of origin (James, 2006). This means that there will be no simple process of rolling these agreements into a regionwide free trade area.

Bilateralism's key result is likely to be an unintended one, namely the probable creation of "hub-and-spoke" systems within Asia and the Pacific. The large hub economies of Japan, United States (US), Republic of Korea (hereafter Korea), People's Republic of China (PRC), and India will likely occupy central and dominant positions within such systems. However, it is also possible that ASEAN[1]-Plus agreements could supplant the individual hub-and-spoke systems, provided that ASEAN can hold itself together and advance toward an integrated single market. A complication with this ASEAN-Plus regional scenario is that individual ASEAN members, particularly Malaysia, Philippines, Singapore, and Thailand, are actively seeking their own bilateral arrangements, particularly with Japan and the US. Inconsistency in coverage, rules of origin, and emphasis in individual bilateral agreements may complicate efforts by the larger ASEAN group to develop agreements that are consistent with WTO and that can provide the basis for broader regional integration.

Section 3.2 reviews the requirements for bilateral or regional PTAs in WTO and proposes the "best practices" for limiting potential damage from PTAs. Since complex and overlapping rules of origin are a major concern in the proliferation of bilateral agreements involving DMCs, Section 3.3 evaluates the rules of origin in emerging Asian hub-and-spoke PTA configurations and their possible remedy in a regionwide free trade arrangement.

A simple model of the choices facing firms that wish to take advantage of PTAs is developed in Section 3.4, using the concept of compliance cost as a key decision factor. After illustrating the choice facing firms, alternative scenarios are created, which compare open and closed hub-and-spoke systems with a more general regionwide free trade arrangement. This exercise may provide input into the approach taken by political leaders within the Asia-Pacific region toward developing regional free-trade and related institutional arrangements.

One of the key assumptions is that trade costs matter. Trade costs are broadly defined to include all impediments to trade, including border measures (tariffs and tariff-rate quotas, quantitative restrictions); behind-the-border measures (licensing, tax and regulatory restrictions, port handling and infrastructure bottlenecks, corruption, and security); and across-the-border measures (standards, testing requirements, safety, health, and environmental standards). In *Asian Development Outlook 2006* (ADB, 2006) it was demonstrated that the main gains from trade liberalization are those realized on a *nondiscriminatory basis*, that is, through the reduction of trade costs for all agents and firms in an economy. Such gains may result from efficiency-improving trade agreements or from unilateral policy improvements that influence productivity in a positive manner.

Needless to say, bilateral trade agreements that force firms into pursuit of tariff preferences that *are applied on a discriminatory basis* and that involve substantial compliance costs may cut in the opposite direction by increasing the costs of trading. The standard technique for evaluating trade agreements (i.e., trade creation versus trade diversion) does not capture changes in trade costs and may understate the negative impact of rising trade costs for business.

3.2 BEST PRACTICES IN PREFERENTIAL TRADE AGREEMENTS

3.2.1 Second-Best Free Trade Agreements in the WTO Context

The principle of nondiscrimination is established in Article I of the General Agreement on Tariffs and Trade (GATT).[2] The principle is also referred to as most-favored-nation (MFN) treatment. The central meaning of the principle is:

> With respect to customs duties or charges of any kind imposed on or in connection with importation or exportation or imposed on the international transfer of payments for imports or exports, and with respect to the method of levying such duties and charges, and with respect to all rules and formalities in connection with importation and exportation, and with respect to all matters referred to in paragraphs 2 and 4 of Article III, any advantage, favour, privilege or immunity granted by any contracting party to any product originating in or destined for any other country shall be accorded immediately and unconditionally to the like product originating in or destined for the territories of all other contracting parties.

Exceptions to Article I are permitted under Article XXIV: Territorial Application—Frontier Traffic—Customs Unions and Free Trade Areas; under the Enabling Clause: Differential and More Favorable Treatment, Reciprocity and Fuller Participation of Developing Countries (established by the decision of Contracting Members on 28 November 1979 during the Tokyo Round Negotiations); and under the General Agreement on Trade in Services (GATS) Article V: Economic Integration as Part of the Uruguay Round Agreement.[3] Each of the three "escape routes" from the MFN principle has requirements of varying degrees.

Article XXIV specifically requires notification of customs unions or free trade agreements to the WTO Committee on Regional Trade Agreements; that such agreements cover substantially all trade in goods; that products excepted or excluded from agreements be integrated into the agreement within "a reasonable length of time" (considered to be a maximum of 10 years); and forbids such agreements to increase restrictions on the commerce of nonparties who are contracting members relative to the situation existing prior to the entry into force of such agreements. Article XXIV also requires contracting members to take measures to ensure observation of the terms of such agreements by subnational units of government and other authorities within their territories.

PTAs that cover services in addition to goods require separate notification under Article V of GATS.[4] The notification requirement is to the WTO Council for Trade in Services. Other requirements under Article V include: substantial coverage of services sectors; elimination of discriminatory measures among the members of such agreements; and prohibition of agreements from raising the overall level of barriers to commerce in services to nonpartners among contracting members compared with the situation that existed before entry into force of the preferential services agreement.

The "Decision on Differential and More Favorable Treatment, Reciprocity and Fuller Participation of Developing Countries" (1979), known as the "enabling clause," aims at encouraging developing countries to participate more fully in international trade and provides for nonreciprocal preference programs between more developed members and less developed members as well as for PTAs among developing-country members. Requirements are lighter than under GATT Article XXIV: notification of agreements to WTO including consultation with any contracting members that so request it. The enabling clause specifies that developed-country members that extend preferences (e.g., under the Generalized System of Preferences [GSP]) to developing-country members do not expect reciprocation by the developing members but also that such agreements create no impediment to elimination of tariffs and nontariff barriers to trade on an MFN basis.

Nonreciprocal agreements between developed countries on the one hand and developing or less developed countries on the other are potentially more beneficial to the latter than are reciprocal agreements between developing countries, by reason of market size and improvement in market access implied. However, the ability of developing countries to take advantage of such access under nonreciprocal preferences may be curtailed by incomplete coverage of trade in goods and by restrictive rules of origin that make compliance costly for exporters in the developing-country beneficiaries.

The proliferation of PTAs, especially free trade agreements (FTAs) that are bilateral, in the region is making MFN treatment more the exception than the rule. As stated in Consultative Board (2004, p. 1):

> . . . nearly five decades after the founding of the GATT, MFN is no longer the rule; it is almost the exception. Certainly, much trade between major economies is conducted on an MFN basis. However, what has been termed the "spaghetti bowl" of customs unions, common markets, regional and bilateral free trade areas, preferences and an endless assortment of miscellaneous trade deals has almost reached the point where MFN treatment is exceptional treatment. Certainly the term might now better be defined as LFN, Least-Favored-Nation treatment.

Recent research on PTAs has established that membership in a PTA makes members less willing to liberalize trade on an MFN basis on the subset of goods that the country imports under a PTA (so-called "PTA goods") than for non-PTA goods (Limao, 2006). MFN tariffs on PTA goods may therefore remain higher than otherwise as almost all contracting members of WTO are now party to at least one PTA. If PTA membership makes countries reluctant to engage in multilateral trade liberalization negotiations, and this can be empirically demonstrated, then PTAs violate the requirement in obtaining a waiver to Article I of GATT that such agreements must not constitute an impediment to lowering tariffs on an MFN basis.

In practice, PTAs may also divert trade away from nonmembers through use of restrictive rules of origin coupled with high margins of preference. A major difficulty presented by bilateralism is that rules of origin, used to determine which goods may receive preferential treatment and which may not, are not subject to any discipline under the WTO at present. Efforts to incorporate preferential rules of origin into the WTO have resulted merely in a nonbinding declaration, as more serious efforts to impose disciplines over rules of origin have been vetoed.[5] The lack of discipline over preferential rules of origin constitutes a major loophole in the global trading rules that protectionist interests have seized.[6]

Despite the above caveats, there are economic reasons why countries would wish to engage in FTAs (see, for example, World Bank, 2005; ADB 2002, 2006; Kreinin and Plummer, 2002; Frankel, 1997). One of the most commonly cited reasons is that FTAs allow for like-minded countries to pursue "deeper" integration than would be possible in the context of WTO with its 150 member countries. In fact, the frustration at lack of progress in the Doha Round stems in large part from the complications of diversity. Arguably this is nothing new: the GATT/WTO has often been criticized for being too restrictive in its coverage, and, coupled with the great variance across commodities in terms of tariff cuts, this partial liberalization leads to "second-best" distortions of its own. In other words, some of the negative effects associated with discrimination across *countries* (in FTAs) are applicable to discrimination across *commodities* (at the GATT/WTO).

This problem is borne out in the data. For example, in a controversial academic piece in the *American Economic Review* (but widely circulated beforehand), Andrew Rose tests the hypothesis that WTO has really made a difference in stimulating world trade (Rose, 2004). Using a gravity model of international trade, he rejects the hypothesis. In other words, over the 1948–2000 period, being a member of WTO had no statistically significant effect on influencing bilateral trade, when one controls for other relatively standard variables. One explanation for this is the fact that key sectors, such as agriculture, and textiles and clothing, as well as other protected sectors have largely remained outside the GATT/WTO liberalization process over the relevant period. Another would be that distortions in effective rates of protection caused by unbalanced, selective liberalization in the GATT/WTO have impeded trade among WTO member countries. But Subramanian and Wei (2007) criticize some methical problems in Rose (2004), such that he constrained the impact of the WTO to be same as that of the GATT, while the GATT is a much weaker agreement than the WTO. Using the same data, Subramanian and Wei (2007) find a stronger, but more uneven impact of the GATT/WTO on trade. They also find that the commodity composition of a country's trade affected the extent to which it gained from the GATT/WTO.

Thus, given the "revealed" desire to negotiate FTAs (for whatever reason) and the advantages of FTAs in terms of the possible depth of trade and investment facilitation and liberalization, it would make sense to try to ensure that preferential trading accords minimize any potential negative effects (e.g., trade and investment diversion) while at the same time maximizing the advantages of FTAs. This might be called the "best practices" approach to regionalism.

The desirability of PTAs in general and "stumbling bloc versus building bloc" considerations in particular constitute a divisive debate among mainstream international trade economists. But while there is no consensus, essentially all would agree that the relationship between regionalism and overall policy reform is of the essence. To the extent that regionalism is open and supports a market-friendly economic reform process, it would be welcomed by all. Hence, a blueprint for best practices in PTAs is desirable.

Even though a great deal has been written on this and related issues, little has been done focusing on specific components of regional trade groupings themselves and how they influence the debate. The Asia-Pacific Economic Cooperation (APEC) forum and the Pacific Economic Cooperation Council (PECC) have also taken up the issue of best practices in FTAs, and they have articulated key general principles and guidelines that the Asia-Pacific region needs to embrace in order to reduce business-related transaction costs.[7] They stress that FTAs should embrace nondiscrimination (presumably this means where possible, as FTAs are by their very nature discriminatory), comprehensiveness, flexibility, WTO-consistency, transparency, and cooperation. However, as noted by Scollay (2004), the language of related statements does not go far beyond that of the relevant clauses in the 1994 WTO Understanding on Interpretation of GATT Article XXIV.

In the Trade Facilitation Action Plan (October 2002), subsequently formalized in the 2003 "Shanghai Declaration," APEC leaders dedicated themselves to a 5% reduction in transactions costs due to red tape and other costly barriers to doing business by 2006 through trade facilitation measures.

The Action Plan articulated over 50 reforms to be undertaken in the general areas of movement of goods (including expediting customs clearance), standards (e.g., harmonization of procedures and rules in goods and services trade), business mobility, and e-commerce.[8] A midterm assessment of the Action Plan, prepared by the APEC Committee on Trade and Investment in October 2004,[9] concluded that members had made good progress in achieving the stipulated objectives. In June 2006, the APEC ministers responsible for trade considered the idea of reducing such costs by an additional 5% by 2010, though the modalities to achieve this were somewhat unclear.[10] Interestingly, they also committed themselves to work on "high-quality" regional and bilateral free-trade areas. In short, APEC gives a high priority to the adoption of "best practices," though the road to efficiency will be a long one (and full of potholes).

APEC and PECC have also been active in trying to estimate the potential benefits that might accrue from trade facilitation measures. For example, in the APEC Economic Committee's Report, *2004: Trade Facilitation and Trade Liberalization: From Shanghai to Bogor,*[11] a methodology developing proxies for the measurement of various trade facilitation policies is offered, followed by some empirical estimation comparing trade facilitation improvements to reductions in tariffs.[12] The report finds that the trade-creation effect of tariff facilitation is greater than that of trade liberalization: when APEC economies liberalize tariffs by 10%, intraregional imports rise by about 2%, but they increase by about 3.7% with a 10% improvement in the four areas of trade facilitation (customs procedures, information and communications technology, business mobility, and standards and conformity).

3.2.2 Ten Rules of Thumb

Concerns over the consistency of PTAs with WTO requirements and over the possible damage that proliferation of PTAs might create, lead us to propose 10 "rules of thumb," in terms of best practices in FTAs.[13]

1. Product Coverage: Goods
Comprehensive coverage is best, to be included within a reasonable period of time (defined as 10 years by the GATT/WTO). While, as noted above, Article XXIV of the GATT/WTO stipulates that, in an FTA or customs union, product coverage should include "substantially all goods," few FTAs cover all goods. Exclusions of individual products can be problematic on efficiency grounds, particularly when they involve products that are used as inputs in the productive supply chain. For example, duty-free inputs of steel will cause exaggerated protection of value added (the "effective rate of protection") in the automotive sector. Elimination of tariffs on imported lumber will do the same

in the furniture industry if the latter is excluded from liberalization. "Positive list" approaches tend to be the worst possible mechanisms in this regard, as items that would generate trade creation are excluded and those that would generate trade diversion (i.e., promote intraregional trade at the expense of nonpartners) would be included.

Thus, to the greatest political extent possible, the FTA should include all goods. Some will no doubt be excluded either temporarily or permanently, but such exemptions should be as few as possible and should take into account the important effects that they might have on the effective rate of protection, as well as on trade diversion.

2. Product Coverage: Services

Again, *comprehensive coverage and a reasonable time period for implementation are best* from an economic perspective, and transparency is important in some areas. Services present some special and important challenges. Certain services are fairly easy to liberalize, e.g., in terms of allowing for the movement of professional persons, tourist-related services (the most important in terms of exports for the ASEAN countries, for example), and even high-tech/knowledge-based services. Others are extremely difficult. Education services tend to be highly protected. Financial services are often the most difficult to include in any liberalization package. Even the EU, which has been a regional trading organization for almost a half century and technically completed its single market over 10 years ago, has a long way to go before incorporating financial services at the EU level, despite commitments to do so.[14] The same is true for postal services, which continue to be protected within the EU based on "universal service obligations" but in reality due to heavy unionization of the sector. Within the framework of GATS, some financial services will be included but education and postal services will be excluded for their politically sensitive nature.

Hence, if such opposition to full inclusion of services exists in advanced developed-country agreements, it is obvious that certain sectors will elicit controversy in those accords that include developing countries. Nevertheless, services should be included as much as possible. In fact, in many DMCs, this could be one of the best policies for "forced" structural policy change in the region. Telecommunications and financial services might even be highest on the list of the most productive in this sense. Development of the telecommunications sector is extremely important in the functioning of a modern economy, as it serves as a key input to knowledge-based products and services. Financial-services development is essential in modernizing the financial sector, increasing opportunities for savers and investors, and enhancing the stability of the financial system. And given the importance of education in the modernization of instruction and preparation of populations for a highly competitive global economy, greater competition in this sector is critical in achieving the development goals of many developing (and developed) Asian economies. Already liberalization is taking place; the process can be enhanced through FTAs. Liberalization of services, such as telecommunications, is highly complementary to liberalization of goods in that expansion of services within the FTA will induce greater demand for, e.g., telecommunications equipment that can benefit nonmembers as well.

3. Rules of Origin
Rules of origin should be as low as possible as well as symmetrical. "Abuses" of rules of origin in FTAs represent the most common criticism of regional agreements by economists. Existing FTAs between developed countries tend to be the most comprehensive and "deep"; however, they also have their "dark sides," and the darkest are arguably the rules-of-origin provisions. Research as to how much compliance with rules of origin taxes efficiency is difficult to find. One estimate (Estevadeordal and Suominen, 2003) puts the cost to be in the range of 3–5% of the free-on-board value of the exported goods.[15] Similar estimates have been made for the Australia-New Zealand Closer Economic Relations (CER) by Australia's Productivity Commission (2004). One way to reduce compliance costs is to provide choice to firms wishing to take advantage of tariff preferences by introduction of flexible rules of origin (Lloyd, 1993). In addition, specified processes that confer origin may be listed as an alternative to a value-added test or a change-in-tariff-heading (CTH) test. Making value-added requirements lower for less-developed members would also help poorer countries take advantage of PTAs. Allowing these countries to use nonoriginating materials and single transformation rules for clothing and textiles, as has been done in the case of Canada's GSP program and the US-Jordan FTA (James, 2006), can be especially beneficial.

Stringent rules could have important trade and investment diversion effects, with a potentially high cost to nonpartners. For example, the boom in foreign direct investment (FDI) in Mexico in the automotive industry was certainly due to the North American Free Trade Agreement (NAFTA) and no doubt came at the expense of more efficient investment elsewhere in Asia. To keep these effects to a minimum and to avoid the complicated web knit by the rules-of-origin codes, Singapore worked out with the US the "integrated sourcing initiative," in which selected products that are not made in Singapore, but exported through Singapore, are deemed of Singaporean origin and entitled to preferential treatment when exported to the US.

4. Customs Procedures

To the greatest extent possible, customs procedures should follow global best practices and GATT/WTO-consistent protocols. Customs and related procedures are at the heart of "trade facilitation," a key priority in the Doha Round. They are obviously closely related to rules of origin, as one of the key challenges of customs officials is to clear countries of origin of imports. The extent of globalization of production combines with the need for rules of origin in the context of FTAs (and, sometimes, customs unions, if the issue relates to nonreciprocal agreements such as the GSP or the EU's "Everything but Arms" initiative) to ensure that customs procedures and related regulations form an essential component of any regional accord. A key issue in the customs negotiations pertains to transparency and risk management.[16] Best practices under the WTO relate to the Agreement on Customs Valuation, which provides private-sector access to a review and appeal mechanism. Some agreements go further. For example, in the context of the US-Singapore FTA, the US import declaration is the only document necessary to prove origin.[17]

Regional trading agreements can be used as instruments to modernize customs laws, regulations, administrative guidelines, and procedures. The most basic questions being asked are (McLinden, 2005, pp. 76-77): (i) Has a process of continuous review been created? (ii) Has an official process of the review and rationalization of exemptions and concessions been developed? (iii) Is there in place an efficient cross-agency process in applying regulatory requirements? (iv) Have internationally accepted conventions and standards, including those found under the WTO Valuation Agreement, been implemented? (v) Do regional trading groups adopt internationally accepted standards and work toward regionalization of best practices? and (vi) Are the laws, regulations, procedures, and administrative guidelines transparent?

If best practices are developed, progress in this area could be an important advantage of FTAs, especially if, as part of the agreement, developed countries help modernize these procedures, build capacity, transfer related technology, and train administrators. One sees this happening in such agreements, such as the (nonpreferential) US-Viet Nam Bilateral Trade Agreement and Japan's Economic Partnership Agreements with ASEAN member countries.

5. Intellectual Property Protection

Intellectual property right (IPR) guidelines should be nondiscriminatory and consistent with the Agreement on Trade-Related Aspects of Intellectual Property Rights (TRIPS), TRIPS Plus, and related international conventions. The protection of intellectual property is one of the most sensitive issues in FTA negotiations. Developed countries, having a strong comparative advantage in IPR-intensive products, want to make sure that such rights are taken seriously both in actual fact and according to the law. In fact, many developing countries, including those that often find themselves on the US "special 301 watch list" of IPR offenders, have appropriate laws on the books, but fail to implement or enforce these laws. Developed countries have included IPR as essentially a prerequisite in bilateral FTAs.

Developing countries often criticize the IPR stance of developed countries as being too severe and overly protective of innovators at the expense of consumers, e.g., in granting patent monopolies for an exaggerated amount of time, or being too insensitive in areas such as pharmaceuticals. However, it may be that stronger, more serious IPR protection can actually be positive for the development of a country's own innovative and artistic sectors. Moreover, a new literature in the international investment area gives credence to the view that IPR protection influences not only the amount of FDI but also the distribution of FDI across industries and the degree of technology transfer (Naghavi, 2007). Countries with stronger IPR protection tend to receive more FDI in sectors in which technology transfer is more likely.

In any event, the greater the extent to which IPR-related clauses within an FTA reinforce international conventions, the more likely the accord will support multilateralism, provided, of course, that the clauses are nondiscriminatory across countries.

6. Foreign Direct Investment
Investment-related provisions should embrace national treatment and nondiscrimination, shun performance requirements, and make use of a negative-list approach that is strictly limited, as well as provide the usual protection necessary for foreign investors. Most East and Southeast Asian countries in particular place a strong emphasis on FDI, and having liberal, nondiscriminatory provisions in place tends to be less controversial than in other developing regions. Exceptions might exist with respect to FDI in state-owned enterprises and "sensitive" sectors. This is true not only for developing but also developed countries: state-owned enterprises have traditionally greatly restricted FDI penetration in areas such as defense, public morals, the media, and certain other sectors of high "national security" or "national sovereignty" importance. This will always be true with or without FTAs. Still, pacts should keep them to a minimum.

Also, it is important that the accords embrace national treatment, thereby not giving preferential treatment to local firms (relative to foreign firms). This has important implications for creating a competitive environment. Further, with respect to the "outward orientation" of the agreement, nondiscrimination vis-à-vis nonpartners is also essential in creating a level playing field.

7. Antidumping and Dispute Resolution
Antidumping procedures and dispute resolution need to be transparent and fair, and the process needs to be well specified and effective. Antidumping and countervailing duties, also known as "administrative actions," have been condemned as an important weapon in the arsenal of the "new protectionism." Antidumping duties have mainly been used by developed countries, but some developing countries have begun to use them as well. Antidumping measures may or may not be stipulated directly in an agreement; sometimes, the references may be exclusively directed to WTO dispute resolution. Antidumping clauses in an FTA might be used as a means to tighten antidumping evaluations procedures, to promote transparency, and to expedite any processes. But it is also important that dispute-settlement procedures be clearly identified and respected. Otherwise, confusion can follow. A good model for dispute settlement is the NAFTA panel approach, where five panelists are selected from lists of experts submitted by each member (two from each country in the dispute and one selected to chair the panel chosen by agreement between the two parties). The dispute-settlement procedures in NAFTA were modeled on those of the multilateral system (Trebilcock and Howse, 2005, pp. 147-148).

8. Government Procurement
Government procurement should be open and as nondiscriminatory as possible, and procedures should be clear and as open as possible. The size of the state sector varies across Asia and globally, but in most countries government procurement constitutes a significant sector. There is a WTO Agreement on Government Procurement, but not all WTO member countries are signatories. Moreover, rules on market access in this agreement are relatively limited. Chapters on government procurement in the deeper FTAs tend to go much further. Best practices would require that the arrangement produce a transparent, open, and nondiscriminatory regime granting as much national treatment as possible to partner countries, with an excluded (negative) list as short as feasible and the threshold-bid level as low as practical.[18]

9. Competition
Policies related to competition should create a level playing field for both locals and partners, and they should not put nonpartner competition at a disadvantage. Many countries in Asia do not have a competition policy as such. Even Singapore, with a relatively advanced regulatory framework, has no comprehensive competition policy or competition law, though it does have sector-specific regulatory arrangements (e.g., in utilities and telecommunications services). But trade and investment liberalization is

affected by industrial organization at the domestic level, and this becomes an especially important area in countries having active state-owned enterprises (like Singapore). Hence, it follows that "deep" FTAs should have basic rules and procedures designed to prevent anticompetitive behavior, from state-owned enterprises, parastatal firms, privately owned domestic monopolies/oligopolies, and the like, which would grant a competitive edge over foreign competition.

10. Technical Barriers to Trade

These should be kept to a minimum, harmonized in a nondiscriminatory way, and having clear and transparent mechanisms for determination of standards. The WTO Agreement on Technical Barriers to Trade attempts to "ensure that technical negotiations and standards, as well as testing and certification procedures, do not create unnecessary obstacles to trade." The Agreement takes on particular significance at the global level, as many of its aspects, including harmonizing standards, "mutual recognition," and defining what are legitimate means of protecting, for example, animal and plant life and the environment, should have global rules of conduct. International standards, however, are bound to be general. FTAs, as they only involve a few or several countries, can potentially achieve far deeper means of integration and progress in this area. What would be critical for efficiency and outward-orientation, therefore, would be that any "technical barriers to trade" clauses in FTAs should be based on international standards, have high levels of transparency, embrace best practices, and eschew discrimination against outsiders as much as possible.[19] The Uruguay round created a Code of Good Practice for the Preparation, Adoption and Application of Standards by standardizing bodies; FTAs should build on these, or at least not contradict them.

In sum, by adopting best practices, FTAs could generate significant gains in terms of economic efficiency, well beyond the effects of traditional FTAs (which can potentially be welfare inhibiting) and, arguably, beyond what any realistic multilateral approach could possibly hope to generate. How much, though, is "significant"? This would be difficult, indeed, to model. However, the EU's single market program, which did not focus entirely on best practices but is largely devoted to improving efficiency through the harmonization of the types of policies included in this section, was estimated (Cecchini et al., 1988) to increase EU GDP by up to 6.5%. Moreover, in order to compare traditional estimates—induced by liberalization of tariff and tariff-equivalent nontariff barriers—of gains due to trade liberalization in Asia (the first scenario) and more general trade-cost reduction effects such as improving customs clearance, lower transaction costs, and facilitation of international market access (the second scenario), Brooks et al. (2005) ran simulations to compare the aggregate impact on real income, exports, and terms of trade.[20] They assume that non-policy-related trade costs are around 120% and are cut by half over a 20-year period for East Asia, Southeast Asia, and South Asia.[21] The results are illuminating. Under the first scenario, real income rises in the range of 0.9–2.9% for East Asia, 1.9–6.6% for Southeast Asia, and 0.3–0.6% for South Asia. Under the second, the gains are many times as large, that is, 8.1–53.8%, 35.5–116.6%, and 10.4–22.4%, respectively.

Hertel et al. (2001) go even further in their analysis of the potential gains from the Japan-Singapore FTA. They essentially develop a dynamic GTAP-based model using an ex ante simulation but with some ex post features in estimating what were defined above as dynamic and policy relationships in the model. Thus, they add to traditional trade barrier effects the harmonization of e-commerce standards, liberalizing rules in trade in services, automating customs services in Japan (to be consistent with Singapore), and investment flows. Interestingly, given the nature of this "new age" agreement, *all* regions of the world gain, including, of course, Japan and Singapore. Fully 70% of the gains accrue to Japan (a good share of which is due to improved customs services). Hertel et al. (2001) stress that it is precisely the "new age features" that drive the positive results for all. It should also be remembered both that these are just a few of the possible areas delineated above and that the agreement is between two advanced countries with less to gain from best practices.

3.3 EVALUATION OF HUB-AND-SPOKE VS. REGIONWIDE ECONOMIC INTEGRATION IN ASIA

Rules of origin in recently notified agreements have been examined for consistency with best practices as outlined in Section 3.2 above (James, 2006). Rules of origin for primary products are based on the "wholly obtained" criterion (within the customs territory or within the legally defined territory of the originating country) and, although not free of controversy (Imagawa and Vermulst, 2005), are less complex and simpler to harmonize than rules of origin for processed and manufactured goods where value and components are sourced in more than one country. For these goods, the principle of "last substantial transformation" may be satisfied by one or more of three tests: a CTH test implemented at the six-digit harmonized system level; a specified process test (identifying which operations confer origin); a value-added or percentage test (specifying minimum regional content or maximum nonoriginating content); or a mixture of the three tests.

An examination of rules of origin in newly notified PTAs involving at least one DMC (James, 2006) revealed a lack of internal consistency in rules of origin in the region. Korea-Singapore and Korea-Chile agreements, for example, have divergent rules of origin. Rules of origin across the main hubs for PTAs in Asia (PRC, Japan, Korea, Singapore, and Thailand) are inconsistent and would be extremely difficult, if not impossible, to harmonize. For example, although Australia and New Zealand have a common FTA (the CER), the rules of origin for the CER are different from those for the Australia-Thailand, New Zealand-Thailand, Australia-Singapore, and New Zealand-Singapore FTAs. The value-added ratio required in Australia-Thailand is 55% in textiles and clothing compared with 50% in New Zealand-Thailand, for example. For most manufacturing sectors, Australia-Thailand combines a CTH rule with a value-added rule, whereas New Zealand-Thailand has only a CTH rule. The CTH rule is inappropriate for machinery sectors where assembly and testing of a product constitute a substantial transformation, however, and require supplementation by a CTSH rule (a change in tariff *sub*heading). The unwillingness of New Zealand and Australia to adopt consistent rules of origin in their bilateral agreements with Asian partners illustrates why harmonization of preferential rules of origin is an unlikely prospect.

A comparison of rules of origin in FTAs linking bilateral partners in Asia (e.g., Korea-Singapore or Japan-Singapore) and those linking bilateral partners with countries outside the region (e.g., Korea-Chile or Japan-Mexico) reveals that bilateral FTAs within Asia provide less favorable treatment in rules of origin than agreements with partners outside Asia. For example, Korea-Singapore rules of origin for manufactured goods require regional content of 55% in addition to a CTH test; those for clothing also require a strict yarn-forward test. Moreover, tariffs on clothing items are phased out gradually in even annual increments over a 10-year period in Korea-Singapore. In contrast, in Korea-Chile the regional content rule is 45% for the "build-down" method or 30% for the "build-up" method; that for clothing is waived in favor of a specified process test. Tariffs were liberalized as soon as the agreement entered into force for Korea-Chile in textiles and clothing.

The implicit discrimination within Asia found in Korea's agreements is also found in those of Japan. Japan-Singapore regional content is 60% compared with 50% for most manufactured sectors in Japan-Mexico. However, for clothing, Mexico only has to meet a CTH rule while Singapore must have 60% regional content and a CTH as well. Rules of origin have also been designed with protection of local industry in mind. For example, Japan-Mexico imposes a 65% rule for certain automotive products, reflecting the presence of a large automotive sector in Mexico. In contrast, Japan-Singapore requires only a CTH as Singapore has a negligible automotive industry.

Thus the hub-and-spoke systems emerging in Asia have different and inconsistent rules of origin for manufactured products that do not bode well for developing efficient production networks. As regards market access under rules of origin and tariff elimination schedules, Asian hubs offer less favorable terms for other Asian countries than for partners outside Asia. The complexity of the emerging systems in rules of origin is likely to confront businesses with difficult trade-offs and higher than necessary costs of compliance if they are to take advantage of available tariff preferences. The disruption of efficient sourcing in favor of preference-based sourcing could also render industries less competitive in world markets—the opposite of the intention of these agreements. These issues are examined, and a simple model and some illustrative scenarios of these issues are constructed, in Section 3.4 below.

ASEAN-Plus agreements may hold potential for overcoming hub-and-spoke marginalization of small, poor, and isolated economies as well as for providing a platform for a broader regional agreement. The key determinant for this to happen is if these agreements allow ASEAN cumulation, which could eventually be extended across all PTAs in the region—for example, to the South Asian Association for Regional Cooperation (SAARC)—in a manner similar to the EU's Pan-European Cumulation System (PECS). The ASEAN cumulation principle is observed, for example, under Japan's GSP rules of origin and is partially adopted in Japan's bilateral agreements with ASEAN members for textiles and clothing. This sets a good precedent but should be extended to as many manufacturing and processed product sectors as possible—at a minimum to the ASEAN priority sectors. These sectors have been identified for rapid integration in the effort to create an ASEAN economic community along the lines of the European Economic Community.[22]

3.4 MEASURING THE IMPACT OF GOOD-PRACTICE AGREEMENTS

The potential welfare impacts of a variety of (hypothetical) free trade arrangements are examined in ADB (2006). A global free trade "ideal"—based on the assumptions of the "GEMAT" model—lifts developing Asia's income by 1.3% by 2025. If, instead, trade is liberalized only within Asia (including Japan), but not between Asia and the rest of the world, developing Asia's income rises by 1.1%. Taken at face value, this result suggests that Asia could capture much of the gains from global free trade by liberalizing internally. But hypothetical bilateral arrangements within Asia do not look nearly as attractive. When it is assumed that an ASEAN (free trade) hub bilaterally dismantles tariff and nontariff (equivalent) barriers with all other Asian countries, benefits are cut by a quarter compared to an Asian free trade area. And if the PRC removes all tariff and nontariff barrier equivalents with its Asian trading partners, but these partners do not liberalize among themselves, benefits are nearly halved.

Recognizing that the commercial and political-economy interests that drive free trade arrangements now have considerable momentum, it is worth considering to what extent "good practices" (see Section 3.2) can deliver benefits. Any arrangement that confers preferences will entail some trade diversion, but these costs may be large or small depending on the details of the arrangement. To be set against costs are possible gains through trade creation (including in agricultural and services trade), through liberalization of investment flows, and through possible reductions in trade costs. A particularly attractive feature of measures that reduce trade costs is that they are inclusive. Improved port infrastructure or more efficient customs services benefit all who trade. Some estimates suggest that for a $1 reduction in trade costs, developing Asia could stand to gain up to $3 (including the original $1 which was originally wasted) (ADB, 2006). The additional $2 benefit derives from induced multiplier effects, scale expansion, greater variety, and accumulation.

"Good practice" FTAs are now compared with "shallower" agreements along three dimensions: the costs and restrictiveness of the agreements; the degree to which the spokes of the system are joined up; and the degree of diversity among the countries involved. The architecture of hypothetical agreements that vary in these dimensions is described in Table 3.1. Two parameters are used to characterize the nature of the FTAs: a utilization rate and a compliance cost parameter. The utilization rate measures the share of trade which is tariff and tax exempt under the agreement. Trade outside the agreement attracts tariffs and taxes as before. Compliance costs have an "iceberg" character and are the costs of qualifying for preferences in terms of satisfying rules of origin and other requirements. Compliance costs generate no benefits and are essentially waste. High compliance costs would normally entail low utilization rates.

The first hypothetical arrangement imagines a "closed" hub-and-spoke system. The hub is assumed to be India. All other developing countries in Asia are assumed to be spokes. Some simplified but characteristic features of India's existing agreements are incorporated. Textiles and apparel are assumed to be a "sensitive" sector and have a very low utilization rate (10%). More generally, high compliance costs (5% of the value of exports) lead to utilization rates for other goods of just 40%.

The second simulation considers a hub-and-spoke arrangement that has a more open character. The hub is assumed to be Japan, and other Asian countries are spokes. Exemptions under the arrangement are more limited and compliance costs are lower. As a consequence, the utilization rate for nonagricultural merchandise trade is assumed to be 70%. Agricultural trade, which is assumed to be a sensitive sector, has a much lower utilization rate of 20%.

Table 3.1 Simulation Assumptions

Simulation	Assumed FTA Architecture
1 Closed Hub and Spokes	
India Hub	India is the regional hub and has bilateral FTAs with all other Asian countries (spokes).
	Bilateral tariff and export taxes between India and its FTA spokes are removed for all merchandise sectors.
	Assumed compliance costs of utilizing preferences are 5%.
	The assumed utilization rate is 40%, but only 10% for textiles and apparel as these are assumed to be "sensitive" for India.
2 Open Hub and Spokes	
Japan Hub	Japan is the regional hub and has bilateral FTAs with all other Asian countries (spokes).
	Bilateral tariff and export taxes between Japan and its FTA spokes are removed for all merchandise sectors.
	Assumed compliance costs are 2.5%.
	The preference utilization rate is 20% for the sensitive agricultural sector and 70% for other merchandise sectors.
3 Region wide Open Integration	
ASEAN FTA	An ASEAN Free Trade Area is assumed, i.e., bilateral tariff and export taxes among ASEAN members are eliminated for all merchandise sectors.
	Given the diversity of membership, no sensitive sectors are assumed.
	Assumed compliance costs are 2.5%.
	The overall utilization rate is 70%.
ASEAN+1 FTA	Scenario ASEAN FTA plus PRC as a member of the regional FTA.
ASEAN+3 FTA	Scenario ASEAN+1 FTA plus Japan and Korea as members of the regional FTA.
ASEAN+6 FTA	Scenario ASEAN+3 FTA plus India, Australia, and New Zealand as members of the regional FTA.
4 ASEAN Hub	
ASEAN Hub + 3 spokes	Scenario ASEAN FTA plus PRC, Japan, and Korea as bilateral spokes.
	Bilateral tariff and export taxes among ASEAN members and between ASEAN and its three spokes are eliminated for all merchandise sectors.
	Assumed compliance costs are 2.5%.
	The overall utilization rate is 70%.
ASEAN Hub + 6 spokes	Scenario ASEAN FTA plus PRC, Japan, Korea, India, Australia, and New Zealand as bilateral spokes.
	Bilateral tariff and export taxes among ASEAN members and between ASEAN and its six spokes are eliminated for all merchandise sectors.
	Assumed compliance costs are 2.5%.
	The overall utilization rate is 70%.
ASEAN Hub + 3 spokes (closed hub and spokes)	Scenario ASEAN Hub + 3 spokes, except for a lower utilization rate of 40% and higher compliance costs of 5%.
ASEAN Hub + 6 spokes (closed hub and spokes)	Scenario ASEAN Hub + 6 spokes, except for a lower utilization rate of 40% and higher compliance costs of 5%.

Source: Authors.

The third simulation looks at a regional arrangement rather than a hub-and-spoke configuration. ASEAN countries are assumed to eliminate their tariffs and export taxes in all merchandise sectors. No exclusions occur in this ASEAN FTA, as it assumed these would be difficult to agree among 10 negotiating parties. Compliance costs are modest at 2.5% and there is a 70% utilization rate of preferences.

The next three experiments broaden the hypothetical ASEAN FTA. First, the FTA is expanded to include the PRC (ASEAN+1). Next, Japan and Korea are added, along with the PRC (ASEAN+3). Finally, India, Australia, and New Zealand join as full members, along with PRC, Japan, and Korea (ASEAN+6). In these extended regional arrangements, precisely the same assumptions are used as in the ASEAN simulation.

Finally, the ASEAN+3 and ASEAN+6 FTA simulations are compared with an ASEAN hub in which there are "open" and "closed" bilateral (spoke) agreements. This allows identification of the benefits of more inclusive arrangements both in terms of country coverage and the share of trade covered by preferences.

Simulation results are reported in Table 3.2. All simulations are static and exclude any changes in income that could occur through induced accumulation. In some models (e.g., ADB, 2006) dynamic gains account for as much as 50% of total income gains accruing from liberalization. As it is variations between different free trade arrangements that are of most interest here, dynamic effects are suppressed. They are unlikely to influence materially either rankings or comparative sizes of simulated income changes.

A number of points emerge quite clearly from the simulations. Most immediately, shallow FTAs yield very small gains compared with alternative arrangements that have lower transaction costs and wider coverage. In the "closed hub" simulation, total gains for developing Asia are just 0.13% of baseline GDP and the bulk of these (71%) accrue to India as the hub nation.[23] ASEAN, as an important trading partner of India, gains. But although Bangladesh and Sri Lanka are assumed to have agreements with India, they lose because they suffer from competition from more efficient producing countries in India's markets. Non-Asian countries, all of which are assumed to be outside the radius of the bilateral arrangements, lose too. This is largely a consequence of trade diversion.

The "open hub" assumptions for Japan generate gains that (as a share of GDP) are twice as large as those for the closed Indian hub. To some degree, this is because Japan is a much bigger economy and more closely integrated through trade with the rest of Asia and with the rest of the world. But it is also because the assumed bilateral agreements are deeper. At a global level, GDP gains double and within developing Asia they increase by 78% relative to the

Table 3.2 Welfare Effects of Trade Liberalization (equivalent variation as % of baseline GDP)

	India-Hub	Japan-Hub	ASEAN	ASEAN+1	ASEAN+3	ASEAN+6	ASEAN Hub+3 spokes	ASEAN Hub+6 spokes	ASEAN Hub+3 spokes (closed hub and spokes)	ASEAN Hub+6 spokes (closed hub and spokes)
East Asia	0.01	0.09	0.00	0.00	0.27	0.34	0.03	0.03	0.02	0.02
Japan	0.01	0.13	0.00	0.00	0.17	0.24	0.04	0.04	0.02	0.02
China, People's Rep. of	0.02	0.10	0.00	0.05	0.16	0.25	0.04	0.03	0.02	0.02
Korea	0.04	-0.06	-0.01	-0.06	1.94	1.97	0.03	0.02	0.02	0.01
Hong Kong, China	0.00	0.02	0.01	0.08	0.21	0.21	0.04	0.02	0.01	0.01
Taipei,China	0.04	-0.14	-0.01	-0.07	-0.26	-0.31	-0.10	-0.11	-0.04	-0.05
ASEAN	0.15	0.43	0.57	1.56	2.01	2.45	2.00	2.52	0.81	0.96
Indonesia	0.17	-0.08	0.29	0.55	0.38	0.94	0.46	1.11	0.14	0.32
Malaysia	0.34	-0.33	0.45	1.99	2.36	3.70	2.61	4.11	1.08	1.49
Philippines	0.02	-0.09	0.91	1.45	0.86	0.88	1.21	1.29	0.72	0.77
Singapore	-0.01	0.02	0.41	1.46	1.15	1.01	-0.04	-0.41	-0.11	-0.31
Thailand	0.21	2.01	0.33	1.70	3.80	4.19	4.07	4.72	1.56	1.78
Viet Nam	0.00	1.46	2.59	4.93	6.76	6.81	7.00	7.06	3.12	3.12
South Asia	0.51	-0.10	0.00	-0.01	-0.03	1.19	-0.02	1.18	-0.01	0.49
Bangladesh	-0.15	-0.04	-0.01	-0.01	0.02	0.06	-0.01	0.02	-0.01	0.00
India	0.59	-0.11	0.00	-0.01	-0.04	1.34	-0.02	1.33	-0.01	0.55
Sri Lanka	-0.01	-0.03	-0.01	-0.04	-0.06	-0.01	-0.03	0.02	-0.01	0.00
Rest of the World										
Australia and New Zealand	0.00	-0.01	-0.01	-0.01	-0.02	0.89	-0.02	-0.01	-0.01	0.00
United States	0.00	0.00	0.00	0.00	0.00	0.00	0.00	0.00	0.00	0.00
Europe	0.00	0.00	0.00	0.00	0.01	0.01	0.00	0.00	0.00	0.00
Latin America	0.00	0.00	0.00	0.00	-0.01	-0.02	0.00	-0.01	0.00	0.00
Others	0.00	-0.01	0.00	0.00	0.00	-0.01	-0.01	0.00	0.00	0.00
World	0.01	0.02	0.01	0.03	0.09	0.14	0.04	0.07	0.02	0.03

Source: GEMAT simulations.

closed hub simulation. Again, the simulation results forcefully demonstrate that the largest winner from a hub-and-spoke configuration is the hub, with Japan capturing 75% of the total gains. ASEAN and the PRC also gain. Gains within ASEAN are captured largely by Thailand and Viet Nam, with the remaining countries (other than Singapore) losing out. The estimated gains are significant. Thailand's bilateral agreement with Japan lifts its income by just over 2% and in Viet Nam the dividend is close to 1.5% of its baseline GDP. The main reason for these large impacts is that efficient agricultural producers benefit from liberalization of agricultural trade. Elsewhere, Korea and Taipei,China lose modestly as they suffer terms-of-trade losses as net importers of agricultural products and foods, whose real price rises.

The simulation results for the assumed ASEAN FTA are quite striking. Even with a high utilization rate and low compliance costs, an ASEAN regional agreement generates very few benefits outside ASEAN itself. But the benefits for ASEAN are significant, amounting to nearly 0.6% of baseline GDP. Within ASEAN, the Philippines and Viet Nam gain most. Both countries have small trade shares with the rest of ASEAN and liberalization allows them to expand without significant deterioration in their terms of trade. Also, Viet Nam's initial tariff rates are among the highest in ASEAN, and so are cut by more than others.

The gains from a regional free trade area will more closely approximate those from multilateral liberalization as its membership becomes more diverse. An obvious partner for ASEAN would be the PRC, given its central position in regional supply chains. The simulation results suggest that including the PRC to make an ASEAN+1 FTA arrangement is clearly beneficial for the PRC, lifting its income by 0.05% over baseline. But the benefits that accrue to ASEAN itself are larger still. ASEAN GDP rises by an additional 1% over the baseline. The inclusion of PRC more than triples the economic size of the free trade area and, as the PRC's initial tariff rates are higher, the implied liberalization is greater. ASEAN also benefits from terms-of-trade gains in this scenario.

In much the same way, gains rise steeply as Japan and Korea, and then India, Australia and New Zealand are added to the ASEAN FTA nucleus. At a global level, gains expand 14-fold over those observed with a narrow ASEAN FTA. Within developing Asia, gains rise 9.4 times. From an ASEAN perspective, the inclusion of the PRC generates most benefits, followed by Japan and Korea, then India, and Australia and New Zealand. Gains for ASEAN leap from 0.6% of GDP under the ASEAN FTA to 2.5% of GDP in the expanded ASEAN+6 "community". These results illustrate vividly the benefits of enlarged market size and diversity within an FTA. Also, outside the ASEAN+6 grouping, there are few losers. Notably, both Europe and the US gain, though added income is small in percentage terms.

To what extent are these gains a function of the expansive and diverse nature of the free trade area, and to what extent do they reflect the "deep" nature of the assumed regional agreement? To figure this out, the impacts are recalculated on the assumption that countries outside ASEAN are included in bilateral spoke arrangements, rather than in a full regional FTA. And within this hub-and-spoke configuration, deep and shallow arrangements are also compared.

When countries are added to the ASEAN FTA nucleus as spokes rather than FTA partners, there is very little change in the income gains for ASEAN: they are reduced, but only fractionally. But compared to an expanded FTA the benefits for spokes are greatly diminished. For the PRC, for example, benefits are slashed by a factor of four relative to an ASEAN+3 FTA, and by a factor of eight relative to an ASEAN+6 FTA. For India, and Australia and New Zealand, isolated bilateral tie-ups with ASEAN actually result in income losses, whereas each enjoys significant gains in an expanded FTA. The reason for this is that the main benefit for Australia and New Zealand of an expanded FTA lies in their trade with the other non-ASEAN members in East Asia (PRC, Japan, and Korea). Under a bilateral agreement with ASEAN alone, trade diversion occurs or the terms of trade deteriorate.

Finally, dilution of liberalization within FTA, or raising of transactions costs, has a pronounced effect on benefits. To see this most clearly, compare the results for the ASEAN Hub+3 spokes best practice arrangement versus the ASEAN Hub+3 spokes shallow agreement. In the case of the ASEAN Hub, best practice arrangements increase benefits by a factor of 2.5 over the "bad practice" arrangements. For the PRC and Korea, best practice doubles benefits. There is, however, an important rider to this result. In those cases where the hub and spoke configuration of bilateral agreements work to the detriment of a spoke, deepening the extent of liberalization and coverage within the FTA magnifies losses rather than transforming them to gains. Where the potential for trade diversion exists, a more open FTA would seem to amplify losses.

In summary, the simulations reported here confirm the benefits of good-practice, more open, FTAs. They also show the superiority of regional FTAs to hub-and-spoke arrangements. Regional FTAs with diverse members come closest to delivering the benefits that might accrue from multilateral and nondiscriminatory liberalization of trade. But sometimes good practices may be insufficient, as in cases where hub-and-spoke arrangements cause trade diversion or terms-of-trade deterioration for spoke countries. Indeed the simulations reported here seem to suggest that, in some cases, it is possible that deeper FTAs could result in more damage than shallow ones. This underlines the importance of initiatives that either open up new areas to trade or that could reduce trade costs and have unambiguously positive impacts.

3.5 CONCLUSION

Regionalism—or the creation of a wider, single FTA within Asia—is likely to generate greater benefits for developing Asian economies than bilateralism or the creation of hub-and-spoke systems that "fail to connect the spokes." In particular, remote and low-income spoke countries such as Bhutan, Lao People's Democratic Republic, and Nepal might be put at a severe disadvantage in attracting investment relative to large hub economies in these systems. Good practices in bilateral agreements can lessen the damage they are likely to do, particularly in isolating lower-income spoke countries, but they cannot eliminate the damage altogether. Linking bilateral FTAs together enhances the gains when good practices are the norm, but linking bilateral agreements that adopt bad practices could actually magnify harmful effects.

An Asia-wide FTA that adopts the good practices outlined in Section 3.2 above provides strong benefits around the globe in comparison with hub-and-spoke systems, particularly those that fail to adopt good practices. However, because of the idiosyncratic nature of the bilateral agreements that are emerging involving Asian and Pacific countries (including developed countries), such an outcome is in doubt. Divergent coverage of goods, services, and investment; tendencies to exclude "sensitive sectors"; and adoption of complex and conflicting rules of origin under pressure from protectionist lobbying—all pose difficult challenges to creating a regionwide FTA.

This chapter has shown that a possible way out of the dilemma posed by bilateralism is to route Asian FTAs through the largest existing FTA grouping—ASEAN. The creation of ASEAN-Plus agreements, which are themselves linked together with common coverage and rules of origin, would greatly enhance the beneficial effects of freeing up trade; and, by reducing trade costs, it would have substantial benefits for nonmembers. Securing this outcome is likely to be complicated, to say the least. The tendency for intra-Asian bilateral FTAs to offer less favorable treatment than extra-Asian FTAs is also a cause for concern, if not alarm. This tendency could be checked by ensuring that all Asian bilateral agreements contain a clause for cumulation across the region for as many sectors as possible. Otherwise, there is a danger that Asian bilateral agreements could interfere with development of efficient production networks and could, in effect, raise trade costs instead of lowering them.

Bilateral or regional agreements that cover least-developed and developed countries and that involve reciprocal exchange of concessions are likely to be asymmetric in the sense that the least-developed countries have far more to do in reducing border and behind-the-border barriers. To offset this asymmetry, the following could have far-reaching beneficial effects: including development cooperation clauses ("aid for trade") that build capacity in poorer countries in the areas of customs administration, enforcing intellectual property rights, meeting product standards and testing requirements, improving governance and rooting out corruption, and strengthening the ability of the private sector to reduce real costs and to adopt new technologies and management practices.

ENDNOTES

1   Association of Southeast Asian Nations.

2   This section draws on James (2006).

3   Exceptions to Article I are elaborated on in Trebilcock and Howse (2005, pp. 53-55). The full texts of these articles and agreements can be downloaded from the WTO homepage, available: http://www.wto.org.

4   The GATT and GATS are separate agreements but are both within the overarching framework of WTO. Trebilcock and Howse (2005, pp. 356-372) provide a summary of the negotiations leading to GATS and its provisions.

5   James (2005) provides a review of the nonbinding declaration on preferential rules of origin.

6   This is documented by James (2005). See Imagawa and Vermulst (2005) for a detailed account of the negotiation over nonpreferential rules of origin in WTO.

7   See, for example, PECC Trade Policy Forum (2004) and summaries in Scollay (2004).

8   Available: http://www.whitehouse.gov/news/releases/2002/10/20021027.html, accessed 20 June 2006.

9   Available: http://www.apec.org/apec/enewsletter/apr_vol5/publication. primarycontentparagraph.0003.LinkURL.Download.ver5.1.9.

10   Available: http://www.acnnewswire.net/press/en/32057/APEC.html, accessed 20 June 2006.

11   Available: http://www.apec.org/apec/enewsletter/dec_vol4/publication. primarycontentparagraph.0003.LinkURL.Download.ver5.1.9.

12   The model used, however, is a gravity model, which has numerous shortcomings in analyzing the effects of regionalism. See, for example, Frankel (1997) and Kreinin and Plummer (2002).

13   This discussion follows from Plummer (2006).

14   Foreign control of (especially retail) banking is taboo in many European countries. Foreign competition in retail banking is essentially lacking in the biggest continental European countries, i.e., France, Germany, and Italy. In 2005, a scandal broke in Italy when the Bank of Italy seemingly used illegal

means to thwart the takeover of an Italian bank (Antonveneta) by a Netherlands bank (ABN Ambro). The Italian central bank governor was eventually forced to resign.

15 This study is available on the PECC Web site: http://www.pecc.net/trade_washington.htm.

16 That is, "a systematic framework to assess the risk on goods imported which target limited resources on high risk goods and high risk traders while facilitating the clearance of legitimate cargoes through the checkpoints" (Chia, 2005). See also Liang and Lazaro (2006).

17 Chia (2005).

18 Given the nature of government procurement, political sensitivities would prevent comprehensive national treatment even in the best of circumstances.

19 As there would essentially always be trade diversion in an FTA (one way or another), the same is true of harmonization of standards within a regional group. When the EU launched its single market program in 1986, for example, one major aspect was the harmonization of standards and professional qualifications, thereby making a truly regional market. A European standard, however, cannot be a completely global one.

20 Brooks et al. (2005) model the second scenario liberalization as an "iceberg effect," in which a fraction of goods and services "melt away in transit due to the trade costs" (p. 4, fn 4).

21 It is important to note that this value is a "guesstimate" and is not derived systematically or empirically.

22 The 12 priority sectors are: agro-based products, air travel, automotive components, electronic commerce ("e-ASEAN"), electronics, fisheries, health care, logistics, rubber-based products, textiles and apparel, tourism, and wood-based products.

23 The impacts are also influenced by the overall degree of "openness" of the Indian economy. As a large economy in which international trade has a comparatively small share of GDP, the potential benefits of trade liberalization measured in units of GDP are smaller than elsewhere. A completely autarkic country would gain no benefit.

REFERENCES

Asian Development Bank (ADB). 2002. *Asian Development Outlook 2002: Preferential Trade Agreements in Asia and the Pacific*. Manila.

———. 2006. *Asian Development Outlook 2006: Routes for Asia's Trade*. Manila.

ADB and Commonwealth Secretariat. 2005. *Towards a New Pacific Regionalism*. Joint Report to the Pacific Islands Forum Secretariat, Pacific Studies Series. October.

Brenton, Paul and Hiroshi Imagawa. 2005. "Rules of Origin, Trade and Customs." Chapter 9 in Luc De Wulf and José B. Sokol, *Customs Modernization Handbook.* Washington, DC: World Bank.

Brooks, Douglas H., David Roland-Holst, and Fan Zhai. 2005. "Asia's Long-Term Growth and Integration: Reaching beyond Trade Policy Barriers." *ERD Policy Brief No. 38.* September.

Cecchini, Paolo, Michel Catinat, and Alexis Jacquemin. 1988. *The European Challenge 1992: The Benefits of a Single Market.* Aldershot, Hants: Wildwood House.

Chia, Siow Yue. 2005. "Special Issues in the EAI Bilateral FTAs: Singapore." Contribution to Chapter 4 in Seiji F. Naya and Michael G. Plummer (eds.), *Economics of the Enterprise for ASEAN Initiative.* Singapore: ISEAS.

Consultative Board (P. Sutherland, J. Bhagwati, K. Botchwey, N. FitzGerald, K. Hamada, J. Jackson, C. Lafer, and T. de Montbrial). 2004. *The Future of the WTO: Addressing Institutional Challenges in the New Millennium.* Geneva: WTO Secretariat.

Estevadeordal, Antoni and Kati Suominen. 2003. "Rules of Origin: A World Map." Paper presented at PECC/LAEBA symposium on Regional Trading Agreements in Comparative Perspective: Latin America and the Caribbean and the Asia-Pacific. Inter-American Development Bank, Washington, DC, 23 April.

Frankel, Jeffrey A. 1997. *Regional Trading Blocs in the World Trading System.* Washington, DC: Institute for International Economics.

Hertel, Thomas W., Terrie Walmsley, and Ken Itakura. 2001. "Dynamic Effects of the 'New Age' Free Trade Agreement between Japan and Singapore." GTAP Working Papers 823. Center for Global Trade Analysis, Department of Agricultural Economics, Purdue University.

Herzstein, Robert E. and Joseph P. Whitlock. 2005. "Regulating Regional Trade Agreements: A Legal Analysis." Chapter 46 in Patrick J. Macrory, Arthur E. Appleton, and Michael G. Plummer (eds.), *The World Trade Organization: Legal, Economic and Political Analysis.* New York: Springer, pp. 203-47.

Imagawa, Hiroshi and Edwin Vermulst. 2005. "The Agreement on Rules of Origin." In Patrick J. Macrory, Arthur E. Appleton, and Michael G. Plummer (eds.), *The World Trade Organization: Legal, Economic and Political Analysis* (Vol. I). New York: Springer.

James, William E. 2005. "Rules of Origin and Rules of Preference and the World Trade Organization: The Challenge to Global Liberalization of Trade." In Patrick F. J. Macrory, Arthur E. Appleton, and Michael G. Plummer (eds.), *The World Trade Organization: Legal, Economic and Political Analysis* (Vol. II). New York: Springer.

———. 2006. *Rules of Origin in Emerging Asia-Pacific Preferential Trade Agreements: Will PTAs Promote Trade and Development?* ARTNeT (Asia-Pacific Research and Training Network on Trade) Working Paper Series No. 19. August.

Kreinin, Mordechai E. and Michael G. Plummer. 2002. *Economic Integration and Development: Has Regionalism Delivered for Developing Countries?* London: Edward Elgar.

Liang, Jeffrey and Dorothea Lazaro. 2006. *Risk Management: Catalyst of Customs Reforms and Modernization.* Manila: Asian Development Bank. April.

Limão, Nuno. 2006. "Preferential Trade Agreements as Stumbling Blocks for Multilateral Trade Liberalization: Evidence for the United States." *American Economic Review* 96(3):896-914. June.

Lloyd, Peter J. 1993. "A Tariff Substitute for Rules of Origin in Free Trade Areas." *The World Economy,* 16(6):699-712. November.

McLinden, Gerard. 2005. "Integrity in Customs." Chapter 4 in Luc De Wulf and José B. Sokol, *Customs Modernization Handbook.* Washington, DC: World Bank.

Naghavi, Alireza. 2007. "Strategic Intellectual Property Rights Policy and North-South Technology Transfer." *Welfwirtschaftliches Archiv.* Vol. 143, Issue 1.

PECC Trade Policy Forum. 2004. "Asia-Pacific RTAs as Avenues for Achieving APEC's Bogor Goals." Mimeo.

Plummer, Michael G. 2006. "Toward Win-Win Regionalism in Asia: Issues and Challenges in Forming Efficient Trade Agreements." *ADB OREI Working Paper No. 5.* Available: aric.adb.org. September.

Productivity Commission. 2004. *Rules of Origin under the Australia-New Zealand CER Trade Agreement.* Research Report. Canberra. June.

Rose, Andrew. 2004. "Do We Really Know that the WTO increases Trade?" *American Economic Review* 94(1):98-114. March.

Scollay, Robert. 2004. "PTAs in the Asia-Pacific Region: An Overview." In *2004 PECC.* Available: www.pecc.org, pp. 79-104.

Subramanian, Arvind and Shang-Jin Wei. 2007. "The WTO Promotes Trade, Strongly but Unevenly." *Journal of International Economics* 72(1):151-175.

Trebilcock, Michael J. and Robert Howse. 2005. *The Regulation of International Trade.* 3rd ed. London: Routledge.

World Bank. 2005. *Global Economic Prospects: Trade, Regionalism, and Development.* Washington, DC.

Commentary on Chapter 3

Patrick Low

1 GENERAL OBSERVATIONS

I find this a useful and well conceived chapter. Four features of its analytical approach are particularly attractive. First, it is strong on policy relevance. It asks hard questions about a pressing policy issue facing the Asian region. It does so without pretending to know all the answers, but its conclusions point strongly in particular directions where governments would do well to look. While the focus is on Asia, some of the conclusions are likely to be applicable to other regions.

Second, the chapter contains a useful combination of institutional-cum-policy analysis and modeling techniques that simulate a variety of policy options. The discussion has much greater credibility because of its attempt to specify in concrete policy terms what underlies the simulated scenarios. So, for example, when it refers to "best practice" or deep regionalism, we know what policy areas are implicated. This link between the practical aspects of policy formulation and the generalization made inevitable with numerical estimation of the effects of alternative policy stances is something that is too often missing in analyses that rely on computable general equilibrium (CGE) or other modeling techniques to draw policy conclusions.

Third, the chapter is careful to draw out the key contrasts among regional trade agreements (RTAs) around which the welfare calculus revolves. Distinctions are made between the policy content of agreements, their architecture, and their geographic coverage. Each of these elements is an important determinant of the likely costs and benefits of RTAs. Policy content refers primarily to standard trade barriers that may or may not be removed under an RTA as well as elements of deeper integration and the treatment of trade costs (which include rules of origin). Section 3.2's discussion of the 10 "rules of thumb" for best-practice free trade agreements (FTAs) is a useful inventory of policy areas that primarily impact on trade costs, providing an indication of what should be done to minimize the negative effects of poorly designed policies in these areas. The work of Brooks et al. and Hertel et al., referred to in the chapter, is also a useful reminder of just how important trade costs can be. The simulations in Section 3.4 also show how important are the factors relating to trade costs in determining the size of the welfare effects of differently designed FTAs.

A key element in the architecture is whether an agreement comprises an integrated whole among its constituent parts or is a hub-and-spoke arrangement. The question of geographic coverage is simply about how welfare benefits will be affected by the number of parties to an agreement. By building scenarios that vary these features, it is possible to show what is likely to work and what carries risks of doing damage—not just to third parties, but also to members of the agreements concerned. It is an important insight, for example, that if an agreement is shallow and trade distorting, deepening the agreement can simply increase a negative welfare outcome rather than improving the situation.

Fourth, I like the way CGE techniques have been used in the analysis. We all know about the limitations of CGE simulations, relating to such matters as model assumptions, poor data, and aggregation. We also know how CGE models can lend themselves to misuse in policy and political discussions when simulation results are anointed as promises, and attention is paid only to a single, large- (or small-) sounding number. Recent work using CGEs, including that by ADB, has focused more on comparative analyses, looking at the relative size of welfare effects under alternative scenarios rather than absolute values. When this is done, one can worry less about model specifications. This chapter, for example, uses a static specification of the GEMAT model because the analysis concerns itself with a comparison of alternative scenarios and the added sophistication is redundant.

2 A NEW ASIAN PHENOMENON—WHY BURGEONING REGIONALISM?

For a long time, Asia behaved as if GATT/WTO was practically the only serious game in town. Even the Asia-Pacific Economic Cooperation forum was modest in its trade objectives and talked of nondiscriminatory regional initiatives, or open regionalism. The recent explosion of discriminatory FTAs is a dramatic shift in emphasis, which, as the chapter points out, carries considerable risk as well as potential. The discussion does not pay much attention to possible explanations for this new fascination with discriminatory regional arrangements, but it is perhaps important to understand the motivation in order to gauge the likelihood of being able to design friendly FTAs with real economic benefits. This sort of analysis is probably best undertaken by political economists and political scientists, which could be a useful complement to the economic analysis.

The end of a bipolar world, with the collapse of communism, is likely to have changed US political calculations and perhaps raised questions in Asia about US commitment to the region. This goes well beyond economics and trading arrangements, but would certainly be reflected in trade policy as well. At the same time the rise of Asia, in particular the People's Republic of China and India, changes the status quo ante in terms of relative economic power and influence. But what of political leadership at the global level? Is political authority shifting in the same way as economic power? We do not really see this yet in WTO. Perhaps part of the headlong rush into RTAs in all the major regions is partly a reflection of a leadership vacuum—the potential public good aspect of some level of consensual global leadership and initiative may be underfunded. Hence the temptation to do business at a lower level of political aggregation.

And what of WTO? Indigestion from the Uruguay Round in some parts of the world has weakened consensus in WTO. The very public disagreements at Seattle and Cancún, the difficulties of keeping the Doha Round going, and the open espousal of regionalism by the United States—as well as more recently by the EU and Asia—have all combined to raise questions about what, at least in the near term, WTO will contribute to maintain a vibrant and forward-looking trade agenda.

Part of WTO's problems may arise from historical expectations as to what WTO can deliver by way of trade liberalization. While Rose's analysis is flawed in some important respects, it touches on an intriguing question about how far GATT/WTO has contributed to market opening over the years. There is a success story to be told on industrial tariffs in industrial countries over several decades, but developing countries have liberalized little via GATT/WTO, almost nothing has been done in agriculture, and what we have to show by way of liberalization under GATS is rather modest. Yet the Doha Round is ambitious on the trade liberalization front. Despite the assertions one reads occasionally to the contrary, trade liberalization in and of itself is not a public good, and in any event regional, bilateral, and unilateral avenues have been widely used for market opening. A better defense of GATT/WTO's contribution in trade policy, it seems to me, relates to what really is a public good—the system of WTO rules. The rules base of the multilateral trading system, I would argue, has been its most valuable contribution, often overlooked in the characterization (often vilification) of GATT/WTO as a trade liberalization vehicle. The chapter recognizes this contribution when it discusses best practice regionalism, which draws on GATT disciplines in key areas.

A core question in the chapter is whether solid rules and disciplines relating to the conduct of trade—that is, norms that impact directly on trade costs—can be effectively developed and maintained at the regional level. Will

FTAs in Asia be able to do this, or will too many agreements be shallow, partial, and fractured in regulatory terms? This, indeed, is the nub of the chapter's analysis, and the conclusions do not inspire uncritical confidence in recent trade policy trends in Asia.

It seems that some FTAs in the region may reduce welfare and lessen opportunities for competitive production-sharing arrangements across the region. Some rules of origin are more generous when it comes to agreements involving countries outside the region than they are in intra-Asian agreements. And coherence around a central grouping like ASEAN may also be compromised by the tendency of individual ASEAN members to strike their own bilateral agreements with extra-ASEAN partners.

3 CAN WTO HELP TO MAKE RTAS BETTER?

My earlier remarks about GATT/WTO contributing to best practice disciplines certainly do not apply across the board. Meaningful disciplines on RTAs are conspicuous by their absence in WTO. This is not only a function of weak and partial disciplines in GATT Article XXIV, the Enabling Clause, and GATS Article V. It is also a reflection of a long-standing reluctance on the part of governments to rectify this situation. Sporadic attempts to strengthen the rules have been largely abortive, and examinations of notified customs unions and FTAs have rarely been conclusive or led to any action that would improve the quality of agreements. Moreover, governments have not always notified their regional agreements, or have been extremely slow in doing so.

The "substantially all" requirement for customs unions and FTAs under Article XXIV has been poorly defined, and often disregarded in spirit, even if we do not know exactly how the letter should be read. There is very little to go on when it comes to rules of origin. In examining agreements, preferential rules of origin have sometimes been discussed as if they were an external trade measure under Article XXIV:5(b) and at other times as if they were internal measures under Article XXIV:8(b). This is confusing at best. The jurisprudence from the 2003 India-US case on rules of origin[1] suggests that governments have wide discretion to define unilaterally their origin rules. Efforts to negotiate harmonized rules of origin have not prospered even in respect of nonpreferential rules of origin. Another weakness in the rules, brought out in the 2000 EU-Argentina footwear case,[2] is that there is no need to respect the nondiscriminatory features of safeguard actions under GATT Article XIX in relation to RTAs.

All this leads one to doubt that it is reasonable to expect any near-term action in WTO to improve the quality of RTAs. The chapter also rightly notes the imprecision of GATS Article V and Enabling Clause language, and the same observations apply here. One qualification to this rather pessimistic conclusion is that in the Doha Round a serious effort has been made to begin the process of amassing systematic, comparative information on the policy content of RTAs notified to WTO. Notwithstanding the fact that the Doha negotiations are ongoing, WTO Members agreed to give effect to the Decision on Transparency Mechanism for Regional Trade Agreements on 14 December 2006. This Decision triggers the work on gathering more systematic and analytical information in WTO on regional agreements. The analysis is to be based on Secretariat reports and improved notifications. This transparency exercise is a very positive step in laying the groundwork for looking at ways of improving the rules.

Another qualification to this pessimism relates to the Doha negotiations on trade facilitation, which are mentioned in the chapter. To the extent that such negotiations were to contribute to reducing trade costs, the nature of the measures involved would mean that the benefits would extend automatically to the regional context. The same is, of course, true in reverse.

Two minor points about the treatment of WTO rules in the chapter are perhaps worth mentioning. First, the suggestion that governments are obliged to impose RTA-related disciplines at the sub-federal level under Article XXIV:12 is overstated. This provision has tended to be treated very much as a best-endeavors undertaking, although the Uruguay Round Understanding on the Interpretation of Article XXIV of the General Agreement on Tariffs and Trade 1994 (WTO, 1999) makes it clear that members remain legally responsible in the WTO for the actions of sub-federal authorities. Second, the Limao work that shows how most-favored-nation liberalization is likely to be slowed down where regional preferences are in place would be unlikely to give grounds for legal action under WTO. The argument for such a legal complaint would have to be that an RTA has frustrated multilateral action in a manner inconsistent with the WTO rules. The relevant language in this context can be found in Paragraph 3(b) of the Enabling Clause and it is quite imprecise. Moreover, the language only applies to RTAs involving solely developing countries.

A final point regarding the WTO perspective that the chapter might have considered briefly is recent work by Richard Baldwin on "multilateralizing regionalism". The idea that Baldwin is trying to formalize to a degree is not new—it is simply that if enough RTAs become messy enough and raise trade costs enough, there could be a sufficiently energetic reaction from the business sector to overturn the current, growing mosaic of criss-crossing RTAs and move toward a more rational generalized set of arrangements that would come back into a multilateral framework. Baldwin (2006) discusses the EU's Pan-European Cumulation System (PECS) and the WTO Information Technology

Agreement as illustrations of how previously fractured arrangements in particular policy areas were "multilateralized". Such a process could be motivated through top-down action from the WTO side and bottom-up action at the regional level, converging toward coherence.

4 THE SIMULATIONS

As already noted, the opportunity to compare alternative scenarios under the CGE simulations greatly enriches the chapter. The use of the simulations is novel, I think, in allowing an analysis of both RTA architecture (hubs and spokes, RTA size) and the impact of best practice on utilization rates and compliance costs.

It would be useful, however, to know more about the GEMAT model, which is an extension of the World Bank's Linkage model. I know it is a cutting-edge simulation tool that incorporates scale and variety effects, and that it can also model dynamic effects (even if it was not used in this way in this work). But a little more on the features of the model and how these influence the results would be useful to readers who are not directly involved in this kind of analysis.

Another question is where the utilization and compliance cost estimates come from, since this is not made very clear. The assumed ASEAN utilization rate of 70% in the chapter stands in strong contrast to other literature—such as Baldwin (2006) and Teh (1999)—which suggests utilization rates of around 5%. Presumably utilization rates are a function of the rules of origin and the magnitude of preference margins. The latter, at least, are rather low because of low most-favored-nation rates among ASEAN countries. Obviously, such big differences would have strong effects on the results. In any event, perhaps some sensitivity analysis would help here. How readily would the choice of different utilization rates and compliance costs overturn the welfare ordering of the different scenarios?

A third question relates to the seeming exclusion of an important part of the Asian RTA story—namely, that many Asian players have formed, are forming, or are thinking of forming FTAs with non-Asian partners (e.g., Australia-US, India-EU, Japan-Mexico, Republic of Korea-Chile, Republic of Korea-Canada, Republic of Korea-EU, Republic of Korea-US, Malaysia-US, Singapore-US, Singapore-EFTA, and Thailand-US). Admittedly, some of these are not even on the drawing board, but how feasible would it be to take this factor into account in estimating welfare costs and benefits in the various scenarios developed in the chapter?

All said, I am fully attuned to the basic intuition of the simulation results that: (i) significant benefits accrue to "good practice" and more open FTAs;

and (ii) regional FTAs are superior to hub-and-spoke arrangements. Less intuitive, perhaps, is the very important finding that deeper FTAs can result in more damage than shallow ones where arrangements spawn trade diversion and terms-of-trade losses to the spokes in hub-and-spoke arrangements.

I also very much like the message that, when action is directed at dealing with trade costs in RTAs, it is in the nature of many of these actions that they will benefit all trade, not just trade within the region. In that sense, these are not preferential or discriminatory actions. In fact, in some cases they can be thought of as having global public good characteristics.

A final thought, of which it is useful to be reminded, only appears in the last paragraph of the conclusions. It is that progress on the trade-costs front, and presumably supply capacity generally, would be assisted by Aid for Trade infusions into the low-income countries in the region.

Endnotes to Commentary

1   United States – Rules of Origin for Textiles and Apparel Products, DS/243: http://www.wto.org/english/tratop_e/dispu_e/cases_e/ds243_e.htm

2   Argentina – Safeguard Measures on Imports of Footwear, DS/121: http://www.wto.org/english/tratop_e/dispu_e/cases_e/ds121_e.htm

References to Commentary

Baldwin, Richard. 2006. "Managing the Noodle Bowl: The Fragility of East Asian Regionalism." CEPR Discussion Paper No. 5561.

Teh, Robert. 1999. "Completing the CEPT Scheme for AFTA." Paper presented at the Hanns Seidel Foundation-Center for Research and Communications Conference, "Beyond AFTA and Towards an ASEAN Common Market", 19-20 October, Makati City, Philippines.

World Trade Organization. 1999. "The Legal Texts: The Results of the Uruguay Round of Multilateral Trade Negotiations," pp. 26-28. Cambridge University Press.

4

Infrastructure as a Catalyst for Regional Integration, Growth, and Economic Convergence: Scenario Analysis for Asia

David Roland-Holst

4.1 INTRODUCTION

Recent research at the Asian Development Bank (ADB) on Asian regional integration has highlighted the importance of structural barriers to trade (Brooks et al., 2005). Indeed, it now appears that overcoming geographic and institutional obstacles that increase trade and transport margins is a very important constraint to regional trade expansion and sustained growth. In their 2005 study of infrastructure requirements for Asia, *Connecting East Asia: A New Framework for Infrastructure*, ADB, the Japan Bank for International Cooperation, and the World Bank, present a comprehensive review of the region's infrastructure needs. These needs are substantial and particularly so in relative terms, i.e., the need is *relatively* most acute in the poorest countries. In a region that enjoys unprecedented external and domestic savings reserves, and at a time when real interest rates are as low as they have been in generations, it is surely an auspicious time to consider how large-scale regional investment could help Asia more fully realize its vast economic potential. The goal of the present chapter is to link the two elements, using rigorous empirical methods to show how a more determined commitment to creating regional infrastructure can act as a catalyst for Asian integration, facilitating more sustained and comprehensive economic growth.

In a vast literature on trade facilitation, it is doubly unfortunate that investment in infrastructure has received only scant attention. Infrastructure is one of the oldest and most decisive determinants of trade patterns. Public infrastructure also confers some of the most desirable benefits of trade facilitation, including open market access and pro-poor growth and income effects. By lowering costs of market participation in a relatively nondiscriminatory manner, improvements in infrastructure broaden the basis for growth and directly contribute to its sustainability. By reducing trade and transport margins, infrastructure promises a neat reconciliation of private interests, in the process increasing producer prices while reducing purchaser prices.

In the Asian context, the parallel emergence of the People's Republic of China (PRC) and India portend dramatic change in the economic landscape. Because of geographic realities, however, the full growth potential of these large economies, both for the region and the global economy, will depend critically on infrastructure. Although they share borders in some areas, the Himalayan plateau is unlikely to sustain more than a small fraction of their bilateral trade in the foreseeable future. A much more attractive bridge between the emerging giants is Southeast Asia, already a robust trading environment and one that could capture many of the indirect benefits of intensified trade linkages between the PRC and India. For these reasons, the entire Asian region has an important stake in an expanded Southeast Asian trade infrastructure. This is particularly true of many of the region's poorest economies, which would be directly in the path of many new transport axes under consideration. Cambodia, Lao People's Democratic Republic (Lao PDR), Myanmar, and (to a lesser extent) Viet Nam have long been at the margins of the more dynamic East and South Asian growth experience, yet they could become central pillars of any comprehensive bridging infrastructure between the PRC and India.

The research reported in this chapter is based on applications of a multicountry dynamic model that captures detailed trade and domestic market interactions within Asia and between Asia and the rest of the world. This kind of computable general equilibrium (CGE) modeling has already established itself as the preferred tool for empirical research on trade policy, and is ideally suited in the present context for demonstrating how infrastructure changes neoclassical fundamentals (market access costs) to amplify gains from trade and accelerate growth. There are relatively few examples of economywide simulation modeling being used for infrastructure assessment. This is an unfortunate, missed opportunity because this approach is well suited to capturing the kinds of neoclassical cost-price effects and extensive indirect linkages that make up infrastructure's main contribution to economic activity.[1]

This chapter studies one of the world's most dynamic multilateral trading regions, which presents an ideal application of the Global Trade Analysis Project dataset. Preliminary results indicate that determined commitment to infrastructure investment can sharply expand economic participation, and leverage the superior growth rates of Asia's largest countries for the benefit of the entire region, with large, proportionate, gains for the poorest countries. In this way, integration will accelerate as regional supply chains are consolidated, and growth externalities can be substantial for all participants. In the absence of more determined infrastructure commitment, trade will simply be intensified along established channels and its benefits diverted over more distant trade routes to traditional markets.

4.2 MOTIVATION AND BACKGROUND

In economics, both the theoretical and policy literature recognize the importance of infrastructure. In this section, the issue is reviewed from both perspectives. The next subsection provides a conceptual framework for understanding infrastructure's primary economic effects. This is followed by an overview of the available empirical literature on estimating the real impacts of infrastructure investments. In both contexts, macro- and microeconomic analyses are included.

4.2.1 Conceptual Framework

There is broad agreement on what constitutes infrastructure, yet its economic agency is quite diverse. A convenient way to understand infrastructure's role is by decomposition into three functional economic categories:

Keynesian. This refers to the pure expenditure component of infrastructure, as reflected in national, regional, and local aggregate demand and employment stimulus.

Ricardian. This relates to infrastructure's effect on the cost of transport and distribution. Reducing trade margins can have a potent effect on prices and competitiveness, intensifying comparative advantage and increasing both domestic and international trade flows.

Neoclassical. Modern economic theory recognizes infrastructure's contribution to increasing productivity, as technology embodied in transport, communications, and distribution systems increases the efficiency of search, transactions, and shipments. These are generally termed endogenous growth benefits, and are considered among the most important economic contributions of modern infrastructure investments.

Keynesian Stimulus

The direct macroeconomic benefits of public investment have long been recognized, and infrastructure spending itself is a popular means of direct medium-term or transitory employment stimulus. In many economies, programs such as the Worker Protection Act in the United States (US), work relief in the PRC, and the heavy countercyclical and recurrent fiscal commitments to public works in Japan, often have employment as their primary goal and downstream benefits as a secondary one.

Because of its generality, this kind of spending can be targeted across a wide spectrum of regions and socioeconomic groups and can be conducted at national, regional, or local level, timed to coincide with cyclical economic events. In the case of real public goods infrastructure, multiplier effects from both direct employment and downstream use can be substantial. Obviously, the latter benefits will be greater if more investment can be focused on real public goods and on widely used infrastructure capacity. In this chapter, targeted increases in investment in trade and transport infrastructure for those Asian economies considered to have the greatest unmet needs are examined.

ADB/JBIC/World Bank (2005) identified several countries that needed to maintain higher long-term infrastructure investments if they were to catch up with faster-growing or higher-income countries in the region. As Figure 4.1 indicates, Asia will need $106 billion in new infrastructure between 2006 and 2010.

Figure 4.1 ADB/JBIC/World Bank Estimates of Asia's Infrastructure Needs

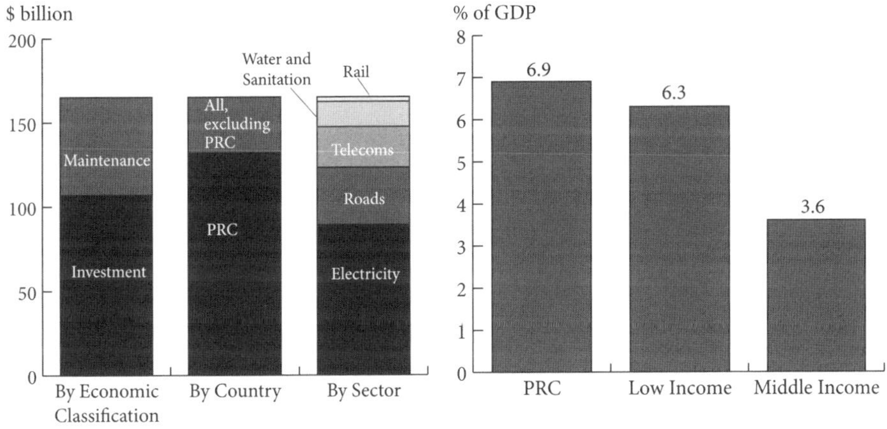

Source: Yepes (2004).

To accomplish these infrastructure development goals, it is estimated that low-income countries must sustain infrastructure investment levels at 6.3% of gross domestic product (GDP) over this period and beyond. At the moment, many of these countries have rates below 3% because of low domestic savings, weak fiscal institutions, or both. In the analysis presented below, the detailed growth and structural implications of achieving these investment objectives are examined.

Ricardian Stimulus

At the microeconomic level, the role of infrastructure in reducing distribution margins is widely acknowledged in the policy and theoretical literature, but explicit treatments are relatively few and not easy to synthesize into a general approach. Policy-oriented discussion emphasizes the obvious advantages of increased market participation, as infrastructure commitments reduce distribution margins, expanding the profitable horizon of market-oriented investments, whether private or public. This is particularly the case in emerging economic environments, where distribution costs are an important source of price distortions that significantly limit market access and reduce economic efficiency. Such access barriers are particularly important in countries with poor, rural majorities, or those between economic "zones" (e.g., South Asia and East Asia) that are separated by more remote subsistence areas. Not only does infrastructure facilitate integration between active zones, it also confers growth externalities across the networks so established. In this way, for example, the parallel emergence of the PRC and India has the potential to confer substantial growth externalities across Southeast Asia, especially among the latter's poorest countries. Cambodia, Lao PDR, and Myanmar are among the areas ideally suited to become pillars of a "growth bridge" between Asia's two emerging giants.

Empirical evidence of the significance of distribution margins is more plentiful and also quite diverse. It can generally be divided into four categories. The first deals with traditional and modern issues related to physical geography. In the second, a large volume of work relates to direct transport costs, including means as well as distance. Third, institutional economics has examined trade margins arising from administrative, regulatory, and political conditions governing transboundary and international commerce. Fourth, there is a special component of international finance that deals with exchange rate and purchasing power parity (PPP) distortions and their influence on underlying commerce.

Infrastructure reduces trade margins. This in turn has three important structural effects on the economy.

Intensification of Comparative Advantage. Classical trade theory states that price differences create incentives for international and interregional exchange of goods and specialization, which increases aggregate efficiency. Distribution margins serve to undermine these price differences, and thus the basis for trade and more efficient specialization. To see this, consider two prices *PH* and *PF* for comparable goods from two different sources (home and foreign), although they could simply be from different regions or even cities in the same country. Given that a trade margin (*M*) is generally symmetric, the ratio of these two prices, with margins taken into account, is given by the following expression, evaluated as M rises without limit. Evidently, the higher the margin, the less the degree of comparative advantage for either good across these markets.

$$\frac{P_H + M}{P_F + M} \xrightarrow[M \to \infty]{} 1$$

Improved International Terms of Trade. A second advantage of falling margins is improving international terms of trade. Consider now the domestic producer price of exports $PE = PWE - M$, where PWE denotes the international price of an export good and M the margin that must be debited against the exporter's net revenue (producer) price. Symmetrically, the domestic purchaser price of imports takes the form $PM = PWM + M$, where PWM is the corresponding international price of an imported good and the margin M must be added to the purchaser price. It can be observed that falling margins induce an increase in terms of trade PE/PM. Once again, the double virtue of falling margins and increasing producer prices alongside falling purchaser prices sharpens the incentive for trade.

$$M\!\downarrow \;\Rightarrow\; \frac{PWE - M}{P_D}\!\uparrow \text{ and } \frac{PWM + M}{P_D}\!\downarrow$$

Improved Agricultural Terms of Trade. Finally, margins are inversely related to the rural terms of trade, and thus investments that reduce distribution margins are pro-poor in most developing countries. Consider the rural terms of trade defined as follows:

$$\rho = \frac{P_R^R}{P_U^R} = \frac{P_D - M}{P_D + M}$$

where rural prices of rural products (or rural household producer prices) must be debited for distribution to the domestic market (at prices P_D) and rural prices of urban products (or rural household purchaser prices) must include shipping costs from domestic urban markets. Differentiating this ratio of rural producer prices to rural consumer prices,

$$\frac{\partial \rho}{\partial M} = -2 \frac{P_D}{(P_D + M)^2}$$

reveals that falling margins increase the rural terms of trade. Note also that, because this relationship is quadratic in margins, high initial barriers make it difficult to animate market incentives.

Neoclassical Stimulus

Modern economic theory recognizes many "endogenous growth factors," i.e., economic conditions that facilitate readiness for growth and can accelerate growth when they are present in an economic setting. Many of these are facilitated by infrastructure, including productivity enhancement, technology diffusion, information diffusion, supply chain articulation and other network externalities, and human capital development (including the effects of migration).

Many of these factors are among the most sought-after rewards of direct investment, whether domestic or foreign in origin. They are often embodied in new investment, particularly that which is technology oriented, and are thought to contribute strongly to economic and institutional modernization, so accelerating growth, increasing labor productivity and real wage potential, and ultimately contributing to higher sustainable living standards. While these characteristics are widely acknowledged and increasingly understood, many of them are notoriously difficult to measure. This chapter uses counterfactual experiments to appraise their general significance.

4.2.2 Empirical Findings on Economic Returns to Investment in Infrastructure

It is widely agreed that infrastructure makes an essential economic contribution to economic growth, but calibrating this for benefit-cost assessment is extremely difficult. As with many public goods, even directly targeted willingness-to-pay surveys are difficult because individuals cannot or will not accurately measure infrastructure's contribution to their individual balance sheets. The basic issues are summarized in Box 4.1. Much of the empirical research is confined to Organisation for Economic Co-operation and Development (OECD) countries, where growth rates are low, and infrastructure stocks, public and private investment levels, and incomes are relatively high. These characteristics may limit the relevance of these results, discussed in the rest of this section, for emerging Asian economies, particularly the poorest countries.

Results for OECD Countries

Private returns to public infrastructure investment can be decomposed into two generic categories: top-down and bottom-up approaches, which look at the role of economic returns to public investments in infrastructure. The former usually begin with macro or large-scale public investments and attempt to identify sector- or even firm-level welfare benefits; the latter generally begin with sectoral or even agent-level profit, efficiency, or some other welfare proxy, then try to associate changes in this with specific or generic public goods or infrastructure investment. Both approaches have strengths and weaknesses, and neither of them offers definitive estimates of the private value of these public investments.

Most of these studies suggest limits to the supply of projects with high economic returns, and there are serious limits to growth-rate benefits from increases in infrastructure investment, if any. Moreover, some studies recognize a crowding-out effect, where public dollars yield less than a dollar of net investment because some portion would probably have been undertaken in any case by private parties or by regional or local governments. Because these levels of government can often see what central government initiatives are in the pipeline, and so avoid spending their own resources, central government investment might even discourage other investment and reduce reliance on local knowledge for project selection. This could undermine project selection quality, reduce the incentive benefits of local ownership, and undermine the long-term sustainability of services from these public goods.

Evidence from Non-OECD Countries

Despite sparse evidence, those studies that have been carried out are positive in their findings. First, they make consistent, positive links between well-targeted infrastructure and aggregate growth, productivity improvements, and poverty reduction. Second, a range of countries presents clear evidence that basic infrastructure has the highest rates of social and private return. Finally, it is apparent from some work that returns to public investment diminish monotonically with respect to aggregate income, a result that means that weak effects observed for OECD economies do not imply low returns in low-income countries.

One study of the PRC (Fan et al., 2002) for example, finds high GDP multipliers for public investment in road systems. More strikingly, it finds that the multiples are several times higher for low-quality roads than for high-quality ones. This strongly supports the idea that the earlier the stage of development, the higher the private return to public investment in infrastructure. In contrast, Lin and Song (2002) focused on the urban sector. Using data for 189 PRC cities from 1991 to 1998, they found that an increase in paved roads is positively and significantly related to growth in per capita GDP in urban areas. Benziger (1996) provides interesting evidence on the linkages between urban and rural sectors, testing whether greater access to urban markets increases the intensity of input use and productivity in the

Box 4.1 Infrastructure and Growth

A number of studies have found empirical support for a positive impact of infrastructure on aggregate output, especially in developing countries. Overall, results suggest that the returns to infrastructure investment are probably highest during the early stages of development, when infrastructure is scarce and basic networks have not been completed. Returns to such investment tend to fall, sometimes sharply, as economies reach maturity, so that some studies of the United States have found even negative effects (Briceño-Garmendia et al., 2004).

In a seminal paper, Aschauer (1989) found that the stock of public infrastructure capital is a significant determinant of aggregate total factor productivity. However, the economic significance of his results was deemed implausibly large, and found not to be robust to the use of more sophisticated econometric techniques (Holtz-Eakin, 1994; Cashin, 1995; Baltagi and Pinnoi, 1995). Gramlich (1994) provides an overview of this literature.

More recent empirical literature, mostly in a context of cross-country panel data, has confirmed the significant output contribution of infrastructure. It relies on increasingly sophisticated econometric techniques to address reverse causation. (Infrastructure may cause growth, but growth also causes firms and people to demand more infrastructure—failure to take this into account would result in the overestimation of the contribution of infrastructure to growth.)

Notable papers include Canning (1998), using panel data for a large number of countries, and Demetriades and Mamuneas (2000), using data for the Organisation for Economic Co-operation and Development. Röller and Waverman (2001) also find large output effects of telecommunications infrastructure in industrial countries in a framework that controls for the possible endogeneity of infrastructure accumulation. Similar results for roads are reported by Fernald (1999) using industry data for the United States. Calderón and Servén (2004) present a similar empirical analysis with a focus on Latin America. They find positive and significant output contributions of three types of infrastructure assets—telecommunications, transport, and power.

A few papers go beyond measures of infrastructure spending and infrastructure stocks, and consider the issue of infrastructure efficiency or quality. Hulten (1996) finds that differences in the effective use of infrastructure resources explain one quarter of the growth differential between Africa and East Asia, and more than 40% of that between low- and high-growth countries. Esfahani and Ramirez (2002) report significant growth effects of infrastructure in a large panel dataset in which the contribution of infrastructure is affected by institutional factors. Finally, Calderón and Servén (2003b) find a robust impact of both infrastructure quantity and quality on economic growth and income distribution using a large panel dataset encompassing over 100 countries and spanning the years 1960–2000. They use a variety of specification tests to ensure that these results capture the causal impact of the exogenous component of infrastructure quantity and quality on growth and inequality.

Source: Ferranti et al. (2004).

rural sector in the province of Hebei, PRC. His econometric results show that road density and distance to the nearest city are positively correlated with the use of fertilizer per unit of land, machinery utilization per worker, and average land and labor productivity.

Many focused studies in developing countries reach similar conclusions. In the case of road investments, for example, positive links to output and productivity are reported by Ahmed and Hossain (1990) for Bangladesh; Khandker et al. (1994) for Morocco; Songco (2002) for Viet Nam; Jacoby (2000) for Nepal; and Riverson et al. (1991), who reviewed 127 World Bank–supported road projects and showed that the majority stimulated income and productivity growth. Having said this, although the effects on poverty may generally be positive, inequality is often found to increase because of road development.

International comparison studies, mostly in a cross-country panel data context, have confirmed the significant output contribution of infrastructure. For example, Canning (1998) used panel data for a large number of countries, and Demetriades and Mamuneas (2000) used OECD data. Röller and Waverman (2001) also find large output effects of telecommunications infrastructure in industrial countries in a framework that controls for the possible endogeneity of infrastructure accumulation.

Among the most comprehensive recent studies is research in the Latin American context by Calderón and Servén (2005). These authors produce generalized method of moments estimates of a hypothetical Cobb-Douglas production technology obtained from a very large (121-country) panel dataset, finding positive and significant output contributions by three types of infrastructure assets: telecommunications, transport, and power. The estimated marginal productivity of these assets significantly exceeds that of noninfrastructure capital. On the basis of those estimates, Calderón and Servén infer that a major portion of the per capita output gap that opened between Latin America and East Asia in the 1980s and 1990s can be traced to the slowdown in Latin America's infrastructure accumulation during that period.

In contrast with the relatively large literature on the output effects of infrastructure, studies of the impact of infrastructure on long-term developing-country growth are not numerous. In a study of the growth impact of government spending, Easterly and Rebelo (1993) find that public expenditure on transport and communications significantly raises growth. Also, Sanchez-Robles (1998) presents evidence that summary measures of physical infrastructure are positively and significantly correlated with growth in per capita GDP. Easterly (2001) reports that a measure of telephone density contributed significantly to growth performance of developing countries over the previous two decades, but the strict interpretation of this result is one of correlation rather than causality.

A subset of this literature extends the basic analysis of infrastructure stocks and investment to consider quality or efficiency of infrastructure. Prominent among these is Hulten (1996), who finds that differences in the effective use of infrastructure resources explain one quarter of the growth differential between African and East Asian economies, and more than 40% of that between low- and high-growth countries. In a more generic correlation exercise, Esfahani and Ramirez (2002) find significant growth links arising from infrastructure across a large panel dataset where explicit account is taken of institutional factors affecting infrastructure's growth performance.

4.3 OVERVIEW OF THE CGE MODEL

The complexities of today's global economy make it very unlikely that policy makers relying on intuition or rules of thumb will achieve anything approaching optimality in either the domestic or international arenas. Market interactions are so pervasive in determining economic outcomes that more sophisticated empirical research tools are needed to improve visibility for both public and private sector decision makers. The preferred tool for detailed empirical analysis of economic policy is now the CGE model. It is well suited to trade analysis because it can detail structural adjustments within national economies and elucidate their interactions in international markets. The model is based on a prototype global trade model developed by the World Bank and is fully documented elsewhere, but a few general comments will facilitate interpretation of the scenario results that follow.[2]

Technically, a CGE model is a system of simultaneous equations that simulate price-directed interactions between firms and households in commodity and factor markets. The roles of government, capital markets, and other trading partners are also specified, with varying degrees of detail and passivity, to close the model and account for economywide resource allocation, production, and income determination.

The role of markets is to mediate exchange, usually with a flexible system of prices (the most important endogenous variables in a typical CGE model). As in a real market economy, commodity and factor price changes induce changes in the level and composition of supply and demand, production and income, and the remaining endogenous variables in the system. In CGE models, an equation system is solved for prices that correspond to equilibrium in markets and satisfy the accounting identities governing economic behavior. If such a system is precisely specified, equilibrium always exists and such a consistent model can be calibrated to a base period dataset. The resulting CGE model is then used to simulate the economywide (and regional) effects of alternative policies or external events.

The distinguishing feature of a general equilibrium model, applied or theoretical, is its closed-form specification of all activities in the economic system under study. This can be contrasted with more traditional partial equilibrium analysis, where linkages to other domestic markets and agents are deliberately excluded from consideration. A large and growing body of evidence suggests that indirect effects (e.g., upstream and downstream production linkages) arising from policy changes are not only substantial, but may in some cases even outweigh direct effects. Only a model that consistently specifies economywide interactions can fully assess the implications of economic policies or business strategies. In a multicountry model such as the one used for this chapter, indirect effects include the trade linkages between countries and regions, which themselves can have policy implications.

4.4 OVERVIEW OF INITIAL CONDITIONS

Infrastructure conditions across Asia are highly varied, even between neighboring countries. As the following figures indicate, Asian infrastructure expansion trends have been dramatic, but only in a few locations. This diversity is addressed in detail in ADB/JBIC/World Bank (2005); the next section examines growth consequences in some detail. Before presenting these results, however, it is useful to examine initial infrastructure conditions for the region.[3]

Figures 4.2 and 4.3 present trends in installed, improved roadway over the last 45 years, expressed in two ways. The first, road length per unit of domestic national land area, gives an indication of national road density. This is a trend that should certainly rise for all countries striving for modernization, and indeed those with the fastest rising trends are among the most affluent (Japan and Singapore).

A few comments about these two figures, as well as Figures 4.4 and 4.5, are in order. First, general increases are seen over time, although at very different rates. The variance stems from three factors. The first is initial conditions and early period data availability. Some countries do not report until 1970, and even then reporting is incomplete. Second, these measures do not take into account population density on a national basis. Some countries, like the PRC, have vast unpopulated areas, and their infrastructure is allocated accordingly. In the case of roads for example, the PRC has made enormous commitments to expanding its infrastructure, but on a national land-area basis, the road surface remains small compared with, for example, metropolitan Hong Kong, China or Singapore, and with more densely populated, larger economies. Third, some

Figure 4.2 Paved Road Systems and Land Area

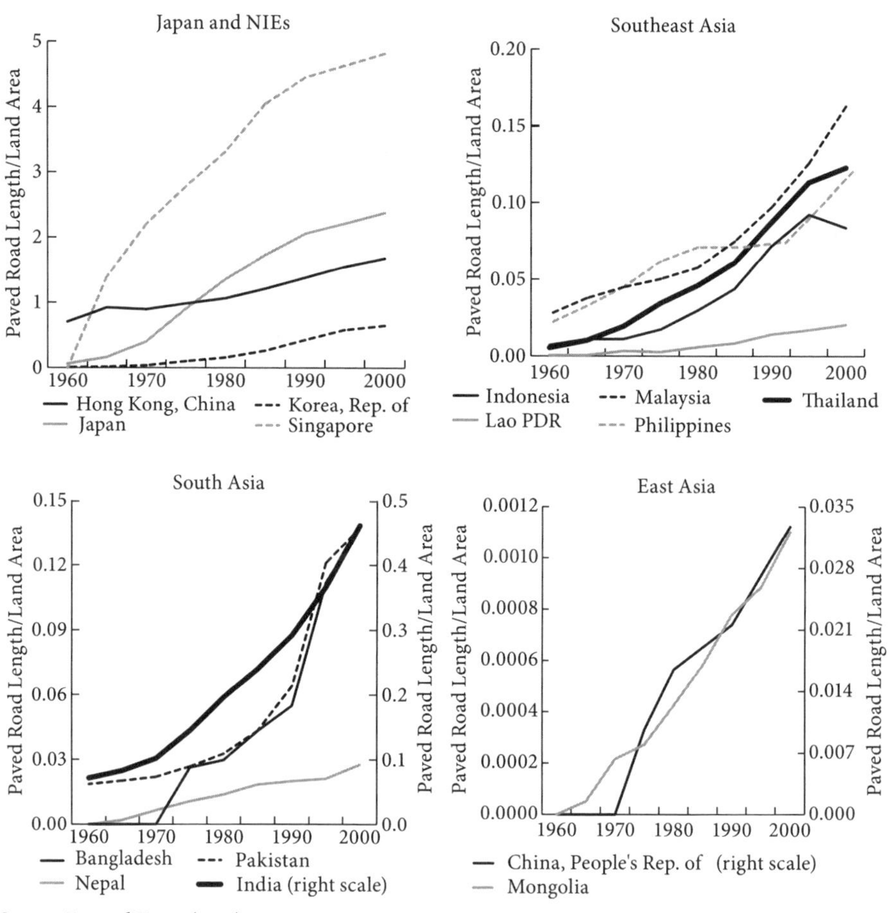

Source: Fay and Yepes (2003).

per capita measures are difficult to compare between countries with dominant urban or rural populations.

It is another matter, however, to compare this indicator across countries. For example, the PRC has been building roads faster (in length terms) for the last 10 years than the US did during its "golden age" of transport infrastructure development in the 1950s. In spite of this, vast tracts of the PRC are—and will likely remain—desolate of people, markets, and transport services. For this reason, the PRC is very difficult to discern in Figure 4.2 (or would be if it had the same scale as, say, the Republic of Korea), even though its annual growth over the last two decades has been nearly double that of the Republic of Korea, a much smaller country with advanced road networks

Figure 4.3 Paved Road Systems and Population

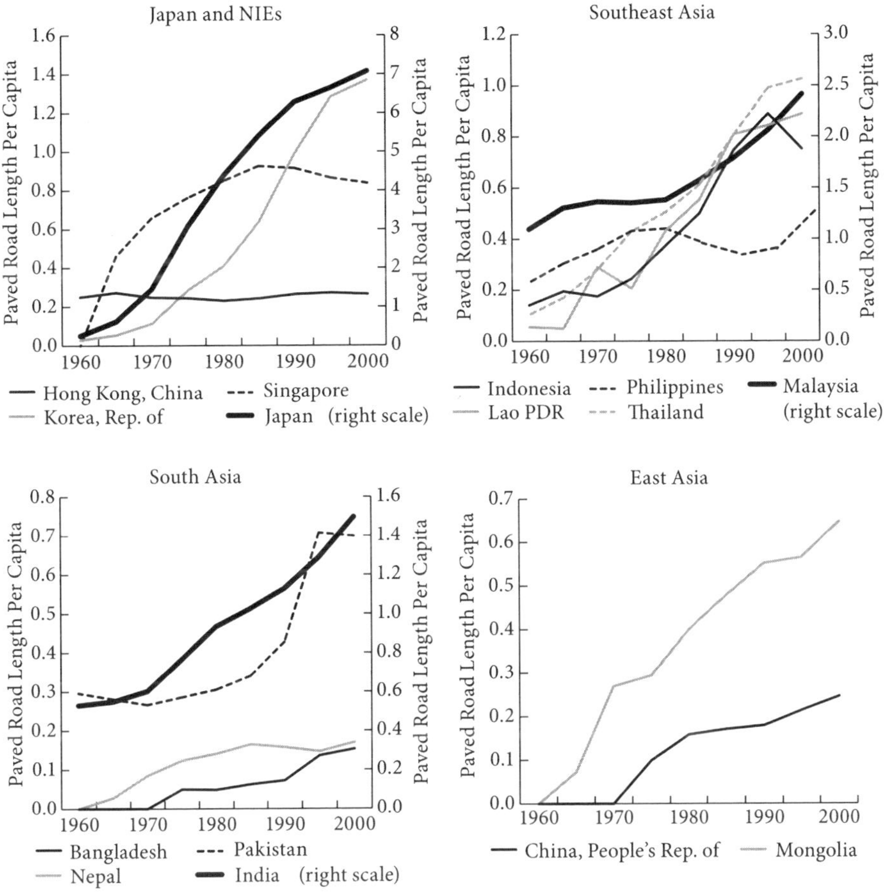

Source: Fay and Yepes (2003).

and much higher per capita income. For purposes of country comparison, the stage of infrastructure development is probably more accurately reflected in a service measure, such as total road length per capita (Figure 4.3). Here Japan and Malaysia take the lead in the region, even as public transit resources are not taken into full account, with which both Hong Kong, China and Singapore are well endowed.

Another popular measure of modernization infrastructure is electricity capacity per capita. This is depicted in Figure 4.4 and the cross-country disparities are very much in line with earlier discussion about the regional growth hierarchy. Electrification is an essential component of modernization, sustainable urban development, and higher productivity around the world, and this will clearly be a focal point for Asian infrastructure investment, particularly in countries that are late starters.

Another popular index of modernizing infrastructure is the scope of mobile telecommunications adoption, depicted for the Asian region in Figure 4.5 in per capita subscriber terms. Close examination and comparison of these trends reveal that this is indeed a good proxy for economic modernization, and the hierarchy of per capita income in Asia is almost perfectly reflected in these data. Urban density creates a slight bias for the metropolitan areas, but otherwise mobile saturation is a near-perfect proxy for per capita income. However, different kinds of infrastructure are more appropriate to facilitate growth at different stages of development. In countries with large rural poor populations, for example,

Figure 4.4 Electrification

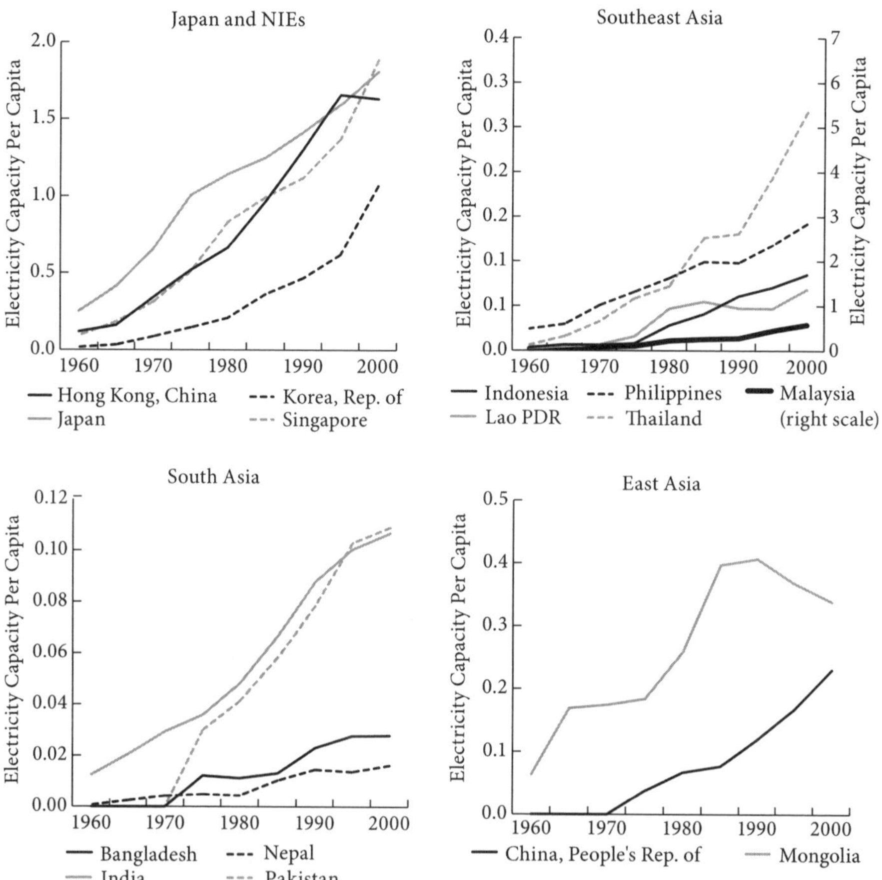

Source: Fay and Yepes (2003).

improved roads and other transport facilities are much more growth friendly and pro-poor than large investments in modern telecommunications systems.

Figure 4.6 makes clear how domestic income and savings constrain infrastructure development. Lower-income Asian countries are caught in a low-investment trap, where both domestic private and public resources are insufficient to support rapid emergence from their less-developed status. These countries might be considered fortunate in one respect, however. The developing countries are members of the Asian region, which currently enjoys the world's highest average savings rates and unprecedented stocks and inflows of external savings. ADB/JBIC/World Bank (2005) emphasizes that external partnership can play an essential role in overcoming these constraints.

Figure 4.5 Mobile Telephony

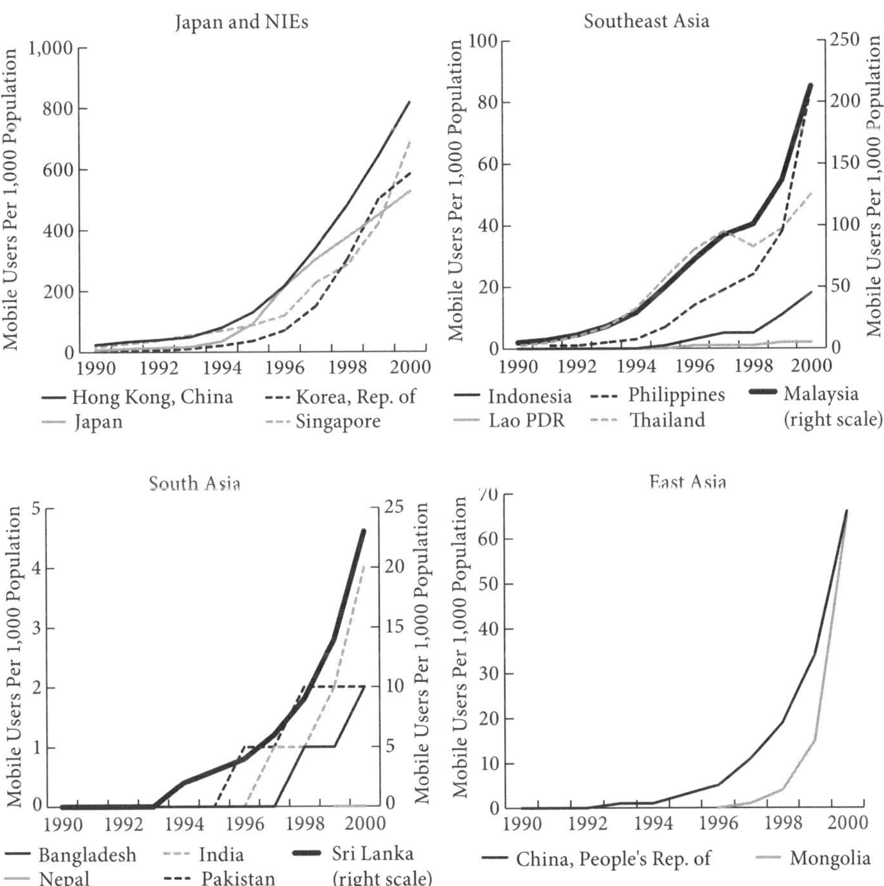

Source: Fay and Yepes (2003).

Figure 4.6 Income and Infrastructure

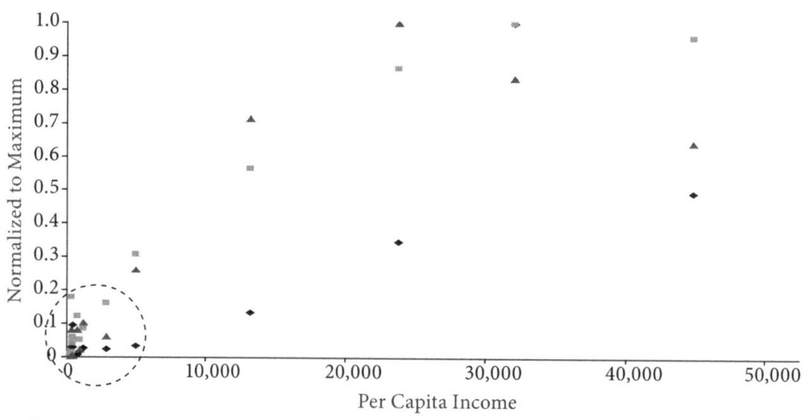

Source: Fay and Yepes (2003).

Table 4.1. and Figure 4.7 show clearly why this makes sense. Table 4.1 presents data on incomes, and aid levels for selected Asian and Pacific economies, while Figure 4.7 shows trends in private (investment) and public (aid) foreign capital inflows to Asian countries. The table and figure support a single conclusion, namely that people live in a world of complementarity where equitable growth is concerned, and therefore domestic and external partnerships as well as public-private partnerships are necessary, yet neither set of partnerships is likely to be sufficient, if the comprehensive growth needs for effective Asian economic integration are to be met.

4.5 SCENARIO ANALYSIS

As indicated in the discussion in Section 4.2 above, the basic approach is to examine the effects of infrastructure investments from three different economic perspectives: macroeconomic (Keynesian), margins/prices (Ricardian), and productivity (neoclassical). Each approach uses different estimation strategies, and sheds light on the different contributions that infrastructure can make to Asian economies. The general assumptions underlying the following scenarios are summarized in Box 4.2.

4.5.1 Macroeconomic Experiments (Keynesian)

This category of effects focuses on fiscal commitments and aggregate demand and employment linkages. At the national level, a standard macroeconomic model can capture much of this process, but for the entire region, a

Table 4.1 Aid Dependency in East Asia and the Pacific, Selected Low- and Middle-Income Countries, 2004

	Income per Capita ($)	Aid per Capita ($)	Aid as % of:	
			National Income	Gross Investment
Malaysia	4,520	11.6	0.3	1.1
Thailand	2,490	0.0	0.0	0.0
China, People's Rep. of	1,500	1.3	0.1	0.2
Philippines	1,200	5.7	0.5	3.0
Indonesia	1,130	0.4	0.0	0.1
Mongolia	600	104.1	16.4	44.3
Papua New Guinea	550	46.1	7.6	-
Viet Nam	540	22.3	4.1	11.4
Lao PDR	400	46.5	11.3	62.3
Cambodia	350	34.7	10.3	38.0
East Asia and Pacific Ave.	1,417	3.7	0.3	0.7

- = data not available.
Source: *World Development Indicators* online database.

multicountry framework and a general equilibrium model that more fully captures the myriad spillover benefits that follow from general investment projects, such as infrastructure, are needed.

To assess the potential contribution from this kind of aggregate demand stimulus, the starting point is the position set forth in ADB/JBIC/World Bank (2005): that less-developed Asian economies need to attain higher annual rates of infrastructure investment over the long term. In particular, that

Figure 4.7 Asian Inbound Aid and FDI

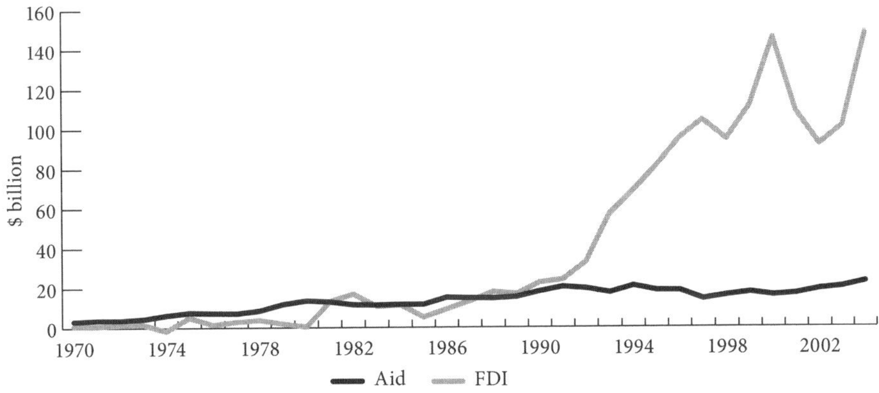

Sources: OECD aid statistics (available: www.oecd.org) and UNCTAD FDI statistics (available: http://stats.unctad.org).

work suggests that a useful focal point for this investment level over the next decade would be 6.3% of GDP. Many economies in the region are below this

---

Box 4.2 Scenario Summary

Keynesian Experiments
• Asian economies with below average baseline infrastructure accelerate investment
• New investment needs are met by a combination of higher domestic saving and external capital inflows

Ricardian Experiments
• Productivity growth in the trade and distribution sectors is assumed to occur as a result of the accelerated Keynesian investment prescribed above
• A variety of different elasticities of sectoral total factor productivity growth with respect of investment are considered (0, 0.5, 1.0, 2.0, 4.0)

Neoclassical Experiments
• Productivity growth in all sectors is assumed to occur as a result of the accelerated investment prescribed above

Source: Author.

---

level, and some significantly so, and it can be expected that stepping up their commitments will accelerate growth domestically.

Estimating Asia's unmet and prospective infrastructure needs was undertaken for ADB/JBIC/World Bank (2005) and this effort is also the subject of an extensive, diverse, and interesting research and policy literature. For this chapter, individual national needs for countries that are significantly below their infrastructure needs in terms of baseline investment and forgone growth potential are identified. From this perspective, the path-breaking work of Calderón and Servén (2003a and b) provides important guidance and data. Although their main contribution was an appraisal of Latin American infrastructure needs, they assembled a global database and estimated historical national indexes for infrastructure quantity and quality. These data include many Asian economies, and this subset is used to infer national infrastructure needs and the investment requirements to meet them.

More specifically, Calderón and Servén (2003a and b) construct a synthetic index of infrastructure from the capital stocks in essential transport, distribution, and communications sectors. Figure 4.8 describes the Calderón-Servén index (CSI) for 13 Asian economies in the last year of their sample, 1995. Also included are mean values computed with weights for GDP, population, and as a simple average.

considerations emphasized in Sections 4.2 and 4.4 above. To the Calderón-Servén database, national data on investment and capital formation are added to estimate the implied cost of bringing those countries that are below mean CSI values up to the mean. The regression details are given in the Appendix to this chapter, and Table 4.2 summarizes the estimates of the percentage increase in baseline investment that would be needed to move below-mean countries up to the mean. Depending on which averaging method is thought to represent a reasonable Asian standard for infrastructure availability, these estimates represent the corresponding unmet investment requirement for each country below that standard. For the sake of discussion, the lower (population weighted) standard is adopted as the target for the scenarios that follow.[4]

In particular, for the counterfactual experiments reported here, it is assumed that economies with above average infrastructure levels (the Republic of Korea and Singapore, for example) maintain their investment at baseline levels. Asian economies that are below average, by contrast, increase their investment along a logistic trend to reach a steady state, exceeding baseline levels by the above percentages by 2015. It is assumed that these investments are financed by a combination of higher domestic saving and external capital inflows, which of course implies requirements for a favorable investment climate that might be difficult to fulfill.

As one would expect in a finance experiment like this, substantial aggregate benefits result from diverting household gross income to investment, even before considering more complex growth linkages. Two main components drive these results, the first-round multiplier effect of government spending

Figure 4.8 Aggregate National Indexes of Infrastructure Resources, 1995

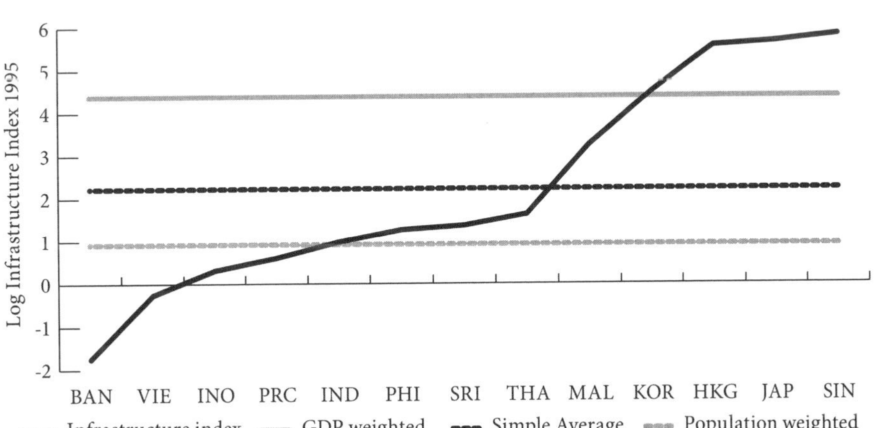

Note: See Appendix Table A4.1 for a discussion of the index and country abbreviations.
Source: Calderón and Servén (2004).

Table 4.2 Estimated Changes in Baseline Aggregate Investment, by Type of Target Mean (%)

Economy	GDP-Weighted	Simple Average	Population-Weighted
Bangladesh	613	397	267
Viet Nam	464	249	118
Indonesia	407	191	60
China, People's Rep. of	378	162	31
India	341	125	
Philippines	312	96	
Sri Lanka	302	87	
Thailand	276	60	
Malaysia	114		
Korea, Rep. of			
Hong Kong, China			
Japan			
Singapore			

Source: Author's estimates.

(particularly with high average savings rates in Asia), and the macro benefits of domestic and external capital accumulation (incremental capital output ratio and average wage effects).

For lower-income countries, and particularly for economies where capital is tightly constrained with respect to labor (Bangladesh and Viet Nam), the effects are substantial, and lift real GDP significantly. In Viet Nam, for example, cumulative GDP over the 20-year period is 40% higher, rising steadily to 65% higher in the terminal year. During the 5-year intervals considered, growth accelerates over the investment stimulus interval and then stabilizes above baseline rates (Tables 4.3 and 4.4). In Bangladesh, for example, accelerated Keynesian infrastructure stimulus adds an average of 3 percentage points to baseline annual GDP growth.

Differences in aggregate growth dividends depend on the relative commitments to accelerated infrastructure investment, and this in turn depends on initial conditions. Bangladesh was furthest behind in this sense (Figure 4.8 above), thus it experiences both the biggest percentage investment stimulus and highest Keynesian growth dividend. Viet Nam is second in this sequence, followed by Indonesia and the PRC. With more up-to-date data, the PRC might not even be in the infrastructure-deficient group by the population-weighted standard, having already enjoyed much of the estimated Keynesian stimulus from voluntary acceleration of domestic investment over the period 1995–2005.

These macroeconomic results clearly bear out the importance of the Asian infrastructure initiative (ADB/JBIC/World Bank, 2005) advanced jointly by ADB, Japan Bank for International Cooperation, and the World Bank. While higher-income countries in the region have the means to meet their own infrastructure requirements, the overall regional gains from further integration will depend for all economies on the capacity of less-developed Asian

Table 4.3 Macroeconomic Results: Annual and Cumulative Real GDP, 2005–2025 (% changes from baseline)

	2010	2015	2020	2025	Cumulative
Bangladesh	5	26	53	74	47
China, People's Rep. of	1	6	11	15	10
Indonesia	2	15	32	46	28
Viet Nam	3	21	44	65	40

Source: Author's estimates.

Table 4.4 Annualized Growth Rate of Real GDP (percentage point premium over baseline)

	2010	2015	2020	2025	Average
Bangladesh	1.0	4.0	4.1	2.9	3.0
China, People's Rep. of	0.3	1.0	1.0	0.7	0.7
Indonesia	0.5	2.5	2.9	2.1	2.0
Viet Nam	0.6	3.5	3.9	2.8	2.7

Source: Author's estimates.

economies to facilitate trade and domestic commerce. The dual challenge of more sustainable and inclusive regional growth can be significantly advanced by accelerated infrastructure investment in these less-developed economies.

4.5.2 Margin/Price Experiments (Ricardian)

In what this chapter has termed the Ricardian context, infrastructure is seen as reducing transport, trade, and other distribution margins to facilitate broader market participation. As already emphasized, this aspect of public investment is particularly appealing because it facilitates individual private agency and promotes self-directed poverty reduction. Given the remoteness of marginalized communities in some parts of Asia, such indirect commitments can be much more cost effective than targeted transfer schemes or more direct interventions for poverty reduction.

If one were to assess such policies without a CGE framework, however, many indirect effects could be omitted because of the complex behavioral and structural linkages between reducing trade costs and growth. A survey of the economic literature indicates three main ways in which these effects are propagated. First, by reducing commercial margins, infrastructure can narrow the gap between producer and purchaser prices in the domestic economy. The direct effect of this is to benefit domestic agents, particularly those in proximity to improved infrastructure. Indirect effects extend well beyond this however, as narrower margins between producer and purchaser prices increase the scope of profitable commerce and investment, enlarging the domestic market.

A second category of indirect benefits relates to international trade. Border prices coming closer to import purchaser prices and to export producer prices implies net price reductions for the former and increases for the latter. In both cases, terms of trade improve and trade is facilitated, expanding both domestic absorption and supply to export markets.

Finally, a third effect of falling margins relates to domestic returns to scale. Trade and transport margins are an important component of marginal cost, and reducing these will shift the minimum efficient scale of production to higher output levels, allowing firms to increase supply and domestic employment while realizing greater scale economies.

The CGE experiments conducted here are designed to model margin reduction by increasing total factor productivity (TFP) in the sectors that provide distribution services, i.e., trade, transport, and communications. Productivity growth in these sectors, which arises from infrastructure improvements, will translate directly into reduced costs for the services provided by these sectors, thereby making market access less expensive for all. In this set of experiments, the spirit (if not the letter) of an extensive literature is followed, linking infrastructure and productivity of distribution services (e.g., in Aschauer, 1989). Aschauer found with US data that an additional dollar invested in public capital yields a much higher economic payoff than another dollar of private capital. Significantly, the main driver of his conclusion was a high temporal correlation between productivity and the stock of public infrastructure. As discussed in Box 4.1, his results were controversial and propagated an extensive literature.

For this chapter's purposes, in the absence of any independent evidence estimating the direct infrastructure-margin cost effect, general inferences from productivity studies are used. All those surveys acknowledge the agency of infrastructure on margins, and all studies agree on the underlying productivity relationship, i.e., that the infrastructure-GDP linkage is positive, but in elasticity terms this effect varies across the literature by two orders of magnitude (from about 10% to 0.1%). However, the vast majority of these studies rely on data for OECD economies, and those estimates that exist for developing countries are higher and more uniform, suggesting a natural diminishing-returns relationship. For the present study, the important thing is to use a calibrated simulation model to estimate the economic potential of reduced distribution margins. Individual infrastructure investments and local conditions affecting them will vary, but policy makers need to know how the economy as a whole can respond to improved market access.

For this reason, the following experiments are based on indicative productivity gains that can be seen to span a set of reasonable expectations. This counterfactual exercise is coupled to the last, with the same logistic

Table 4.5 Margin/Price Results: Cumulative Real GDP, 2006–2025 (% changes from baseline)

	ε				
	0.0	0.5	1.0	2.0	4.0
Bangladesh	47	52	56	65	94
China, People's Rep. of	10	11	12	14	20
Hong Kong, China	0	2	3	6	14
India	0	1	3	5	12
Indonesia	28	29	29	31	35
Japan	0	1	1	2	5
Korea, Rep. of	0	1	1	3	6
Malaysia	0	2	3	5	14
Philippines	-1	0	0	1	3
Singapore	1	2	2	4	8
Sri Lanka	0	2	4	8	26
Taipei,China	0	1	2	4	9
Thailand	0	1	1	3	6
Viet Nam	40	41	42	43	48

Source: Author's estimates.

Table 4.6 Margin/Price Results: Annualized Growth Rate of Real GDP (percentage point premium over baseline)

	ε				
	0.0	0.5	1.0	2.0	4.0
Bangladesh	3.0	3.2	3.4	3.7	4.9
China, People's Rep. of	0.7	0.8	0.9	1.0	1.2
Hong Kong, China	0.0	0.1	0.2	0.3	0.8
India	0.0	0.1	0.2	0.3	0.8
Indonesia	2.0	2.0	2.1	2.1	2.3
Japan	0.0	0.0	0.1	0.1	0.3
Korea, Rep. of	0.0	0.1	0.1	0.2	0.4
Malaysia	0.0	0.1	0.2	0.4	0.9
Philippines	-0.1	0.0	0.0	0.0	0.2
Singapore	0.1	0.1	0.2	0.3	0.5
Sri Lanka	0.0	0.1	0.3	0.6	1.7
Taipei,China	0.0	0.1	0.2	0.3	0.6
Thailand	0.0	0.1	0.1	0.2	0.4
Viet Nam	2.7	2.7	2.8	2.8	3.0

Source: Author's estimates.

profile of accelerated infrastructure investment. In addition, it is assumed that productivity in the distribution sectors increases with four alternative elasticity values—$\varepsilon=(0.5, 1.0, 2.0, 4.0)$—with respect to changes in sectoral investment. Thus a 1% increase in infrastructure investment would increase distribution service productivity by ε%. Note that the first data column in these results (Tables 4.5 and 4.6, and Figure 4.9), for $\varepsilon=0$, corresponds to the Keynesian experiment of the previous subsection.

Aggregate results in Table 4.5 clearly demonstrate the potential of reduced market-access costs to stimulate economic growth and development. To the extent that infrastructure can lower these costs for all market participants, the benefits will be greater, the larger the investment relative to the initial stock of infrastructure. For this reason, the poorer countries, with lower levels of initial stocks and concomitantly high internal trade margins, are the greatest relative beneficiaries in the base case ($\varepsilon=0$) and all others. These are precisely the economies identified for accelerated investment by ADB/JBIC/World Bank (2005), and include Bangladesh, Indonesia, Sri Lanka, and Viet Nam. Had the Philippines also been targeted for accelerated investment, it would probably have been in the same category.

Note that in this set of experiments, however, the gains are not restricted to these economies alone. This is because it is assumed that trade and transport productivity effects occur in all countries experiencing new investment, not just those with accelerating investment. There is no productivity growth in the baseline. Taking account of that, even relatively mature economies such as Japan can increase cumulative GDP (for 2005–2025) by up to 5%.

4.5.3 Endogenous Growth Effects (Neoclassical)

One of the most important insights to emerge from neoclassical studies of trade and development is the notion of endogenous growth effects. As explained above, they refer to a wide array of economic factors that have the potential to accelerate growth, are endemic to the economic environment, and are activated by individual incentives arising from either markets or

Figure 4.9 Margin/Price Results: Cumulative Real GDP, 2006–2025

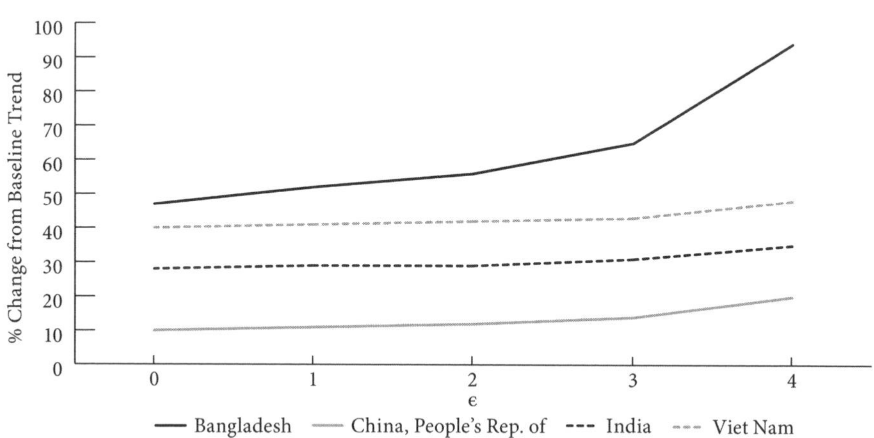

Source: Model simulations.

policy interventions. They include, for example, such things as human capital formation (the individual pursuit of education/training), technology transfer from foreign direct investment or direct external assistance, interindustry or intra-industry spillovers, and positive network externalities.

Obviously, the diversity of these growth effects and the complexity of their economic agency make them difficult to study empirically. However, they are believed to be among the most potent stimuli for economic growth and modernization, and as such cannot be ignored. On the contrary, endogenous growth factors like technology transfer and high-skill job creation are among the most sought-after elements in multilateral trade and investment negotiations, both public and private. Infrastructure investment is considered one of the most important enabling policies to promote endogenous growth processes. For all these reasons, the links between infrastructure and growth through this channel need to be better understood.

As in the previous experiments, productivity is used as a proxy variable for endogenous growth factors. This is appropriate in the present context since productivity (individually and for all factors) is one of the most common metrics for assessing an economy's capacity for accelerating growth by internal (endogenous) means. To get a tangible sense of how these factors can contribute to growth in the context of Asian regional integration, an extension of the previous two scenarios is considered. In particular, infrastructure trends are assumed to follow those of the first two experiments, but productivity dividends from infrastructure are assumed to be more widely distributed across the economy. This extensive productivity view is universally supported in the empirical literature, although its exact magnitude is still a subject of empirical study.

More specifically, in the work discussed at the beginning of this section, Calderón and Servén (2005) construct a synthetic index of infrastructure from the capital stocks in essential transport, distribution, and communications sectors. After extensive econometric specification testing, they obtain results showing that the productivity impact of infrastructure stock on growth is positive and significant, and varies inversely with the prior level of the stock. In other words, economies with smaller initial stocks are more growth sensitive to the same absolute and relative quantity of new infrastructure investment. In particular, these authors find that investments that achieve 5-year movements of two standard deviations in the initial sample distribution of infrastructure stocks would add 1.7–3.1% to the growth rate of bottom quartile economies.

The present experiments proxy a low-end 2.0% growth dividend with TFP growth of the same amount in all sectors, assuming that this arises from the patterns of investment acceleration used in the last two scenarios. In other words, the growth dividend is not uniform, but depends on the movement of each economy with respect to the initial distribution of infrastructure. Lower-income countries that catch up with higher rates of investment will enjoy higher dividends (up to a maximum of 2 percentage points higher real GDP growth). Of course, compounding TFP growth can make average or cumulative growth rates much higher.

Therefore in this context, infrastructure improvements not only lower transaction costs, but also increase individual and total factor productivity. For example, a worker who can drive to work on an improved road saves money and time, increasing both purchasing power and productivity.

The experiment reported next assumes the same scenario as the previous sections, but applies infrastructure-induced productivity growth to all sectors in each economy. As earlier, the main empirical guidance for this experiment is the exhaustive Latin American survey by Calderón and Servén (2003a and b; 2005), who explicitly estimate the composite growth and implied TFP effects of infrastructure across an extensive and diverse panel dataset. This work established a nearly definitive standard for econometric estimation in this area, and the results are extended to the Asian context in the absence of anything approaching this statistical quality for Asia.

The macroeconomic results in Table 4.6 are predictably higher than in the case where productivity growth is confined to distribution sectors. The empirical literature on infrastructure and productivity offers a clear consensus that productivity gains from extensive public goods infrastructure are widely dispersed across economic activities. The extent of this dispersal is an empirical question, but a spectrum of productivity (aggregate investment) elasticities is examined as in the previous experiments. Even in this case, a doubling of GDP growth rates (Tables 4.7 and 4.8, and Figure 4.10) is possible for the economies with lowest prior infrastructure stocks. Other economies in the region are assumed to experience the same productivity benefits from their baseline investment commitments, and their growth premiums are a reminder of the importance of capital accumulation in the dynamic Asian development story.

Among the accelerated investment countries, an interesting case is provided by the PRC's "overtaking" of Bangladesh at higher elasticity levels. The reason for this lies in the PRC's high baseline investment levels. In addition to assuming investment acceleration to close the infrastructure gap, these scenarios assume that productivity benefits accrue from baseline investment trends. Because of its very high baseline savings-investment rate, the PRC's growth accelerates rapidly when productivity benefits accompany this investment acceleration. Indeed, the PRC is placed high in the Asian "league table" of growth economies.

Table 4.7 Endogenous Growth Results: Cumulative Real GDP, 2006–2025 (% changes from baseline)

	ε				
	0.0	0.5	1.0	2.0	4.0
Bangladesh	47	58	68	92	187
China, People's Rep. of	10	21	33	61	185
Hong Kong, China	0	3	6	13	33
India	0	7	15	32	101
Indonesia	28	35	43	61	126
Japan	0	2	4	7	19
Korea, Rep. of	0	4	8	17	46
Malaysia	0	8	17	36	111
Philippines	-1	2	5	12	36
Singapore	1	5	8	16	42
Sri Lanka	0	5	11	23	71
Taipei,China	0	4	9	18	49
Thailand	0	4	8	17	49
Viet Nam	40	49	58	78	156

Source: Author's estimates.

Table 4.8 Endogenous Growth Results: Annualized Growth Rate of Real GDP (percentage point premium over baseline)

	ε				
	0.0	0.5	1.0	2.0	4.0
Bangladesh	3.0	3.4	3.9	4.7	7.3
China, People's Rep. of	0.7	1.4	2.0	3.2	6.9
Hong Kong, China	0.0	0.2	0.4	0.8	1.8
India	0.0	0.5	1.0	1.9	4.7
Indonesia	2.0	2.4	2.8	3.5	5.8
Japan	0.0	0.1	0.3	0.5	1.3
Korea, Rep. of	0.0	0.3	0.5	1.1	2.6
Malaysia	0.0	0.6	1.1	2.1	5.1
Philippines	-0.1	0.1	0.3	0.7	2.0
Singapore	0.1	0.3	0.6	1.0	2.3
Sri Lanka	0.0	0.3	0.7	1.4	3.6
Taipei,China	0.0	0.3	0.6	1.1	2.7
Thailand	0.0	0.3	0.6	1.1	2.8
Viet Nam	2.7	3.0	3.4	4.1	6.4

Source: Author's estimates.

These endogenous growth results are not at all hypothetical in qualitative terms, as can be made apparent with an important example of Asian regional development, namely, supply networks. One of the more dramatic modern manifestations of reduced trade costs and productivity growth is the regional and global decomposition of supply chains. Foreign direct investment and contractual linkages are distributing production tasks, employment, and income around the world for myriad reasons. These include factor price

Figure 4.10 Endogenous Growth Results: Cumulative Real GDP, 2006–2025

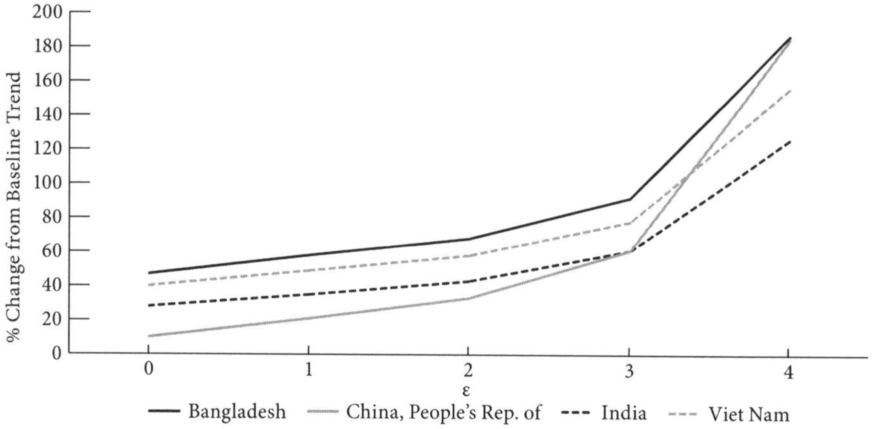

Source: Model simulations.

differences, local and regional market access, and simple diversification strategies, but in all cases, the result is an ever-growing web of regional trade linkages.

This trend has been greatly facilitated in the Asian region by infrastructure investment, which reduces network management and integration costs and sharpens the differentials between costs and prices in different locales. As this process evolves, the emergence of mature industries is seen, where once was only a primary product or component producer. Each time this happens, the individual locality migrates up the value-added ladder and local resources command higher premiums in the global marketplace. In this way, supply chain decomposition and the infrastructure that makes it possible contribute to ever-wider networks of value creation, and to more stable and widely dispersed regional growth.

In East Asia, this process has advanced very quickly and pervasively, facilitated by both industrial-country foreign direct investment and a "stepladder effect" where more advanced Asian economies reallocate production to less advanced ones. In the process of distributing supply chains, foreign investors in the region create new nodes of production in different localities, and another indirect phenomenon emerges. In this process, fully autonomous enterprises and markets sprout from the nodes of a "root system" of global intermediate supply. This process is long established in the newly industrialized economies and can be seen to emerge now in the PRC and other emerging Asian economies. The result is replication of industries and markets at an exponential rate. Infrastructure, whether publicly or privately financed, is a prerequisite for effective participation in this regional production sharing.

4.6 INFRASTRUCTURE DEVELOPMENT GOALS

One of the most important contributions infrastructure can make to economic progress is improving the living standards of the poor. Improved living standards can take many forms, from increased market access to better quality of and access to essential public goods. As part of its broad-based commitment to advancing infrastructure's contribution to Asian regional integration and growth, ADB has placed high priority on poverty reduction. In this chapter, the many facets of infrastructure's contribution to economic growth have been discussed. This section proposes a concrete set of development goals that explicitly recognize these contributions (compare, e.g., Canning, 1998).

Formally, these objectives are called the infrastructure development goals to evoke their close relationship with the United Nations' more general Millennium Development Goals (MDGs) that assess progress in global living standards. While the infrastructure development goals are of independent interest, their conformity with the MDGs recognizes the usefulness of the latter in the international development dialogue, and is also intended to emphasize the integral contribution of infrastructure to improving the livelihoods of the majority of the world's poor.

The 2005 publication of ADB/JBIC/World Bank emphasized the importance of infrastructure's contribution to the MDGs. Here that linkage is made more explicit by setting forth eight infrastructure development goals that can be used to measure the performance and progress of public and private development participation in poor countries. The goals cover direct economic contributions from infrastructure, but also include a variety of other welfare criteria associated with economic activity, education, health, environment, and sustainability. Establishing specific, transparent standards and metrics to measure infrastructure's contribution to improved standards of living, as well as a policy dialogue to support this process, can support more effective development strategies for development and emerging economy growth policy.

Box 4.3 proposes eight infrastructure development goals for use in publicly and privately financed evaluation.

Box 4.3 Infrastructure Development Goals

Goal 1: Eradicate Infrastructure Poverty. Halve, between 1990 and 2015, the proportion of people who lack access to basic infrastructure services.

Goal 2: Achieve Universal Access to Primary Education. Ensure that, by 2015, children everywhere, boys and girls alike, have local access to full-time primary educational resources.

Goal 3: Improve Access to Information and Communication Technology. Reduce by three quarters, by 2015, the number of households without local and affordable access to telecommunication and digital information services.

Goal 4: Improve Electrification. Reduce by two thirds the number of households without access to in-home electricity.

Goal 5: Improve Market Access. Promote investment in transport infrastructure that can reduce average domestic seller and worker travel times by two thirds, preferably by 2015.

Goal 6: Improve Public Health Access. Promote more extensive investment in public health resources, increasing local access for urban and rural populations generally and for the poor in particular. Reduce by three quarters, preferably by 2015, the average combined travel and queuing time for access to licensed health care services.

Goal 7: Promote Environmental Sustainability. Integrate the principles of sustainable development into infrastructure policies and programs, and reverse the losses of environmental resources.

Reduce by three quarters, by 2015, the proportion of people without sustainable access to safe drinking water.

Reduce by three quarters, by 2015, the proportion of people without sustainable access to sanitation services.

Goal 8: Develop a Global Partnership for Infrastructure. Establish the institutional framework needed to facilitate coherent multilateral approaches to infrastructure development, including regional policy coordination, financial market integration, and standards and technology sharing.

4.7 CONCLUDING REMARKS

Infrastructure can play a significant role in promoting regional integration and with it more rapid and sustained growth in Asia. Using a global CGE model, it is found that infrastructure can be a potent catalyst for wider economic participation, both within and between Asian economies, and that it can promote private, individual agency as a means of poverty reduction and more rapid growth among the poorest regional economies. The basic approach elucidates the role of infrastructure as a demand stimulus, a means of reducing trade costs, and as an agent of productivity growth. In the first case, significant economywide multiplier effects accelerate growth, particularly in less developed regional economies whose initial conditions require faster investment rates to upgrade their infrastructure.

A series of simulations focusing on trade cost reduction indicate that infrastructure investment can facilitate domestic market access and regional integration, sharply increasing economic growth, but its effects vary significantly between economies. Two types of countries are most likely to gain: those with very high prior domestic margins, and those with high prior levels of external trade dependence. Investment in domestic infrastructure is especially important for less open low-income countries. In these cases, external partnerships could be an important source of investment leverage to overcome domestic savings constraints, and the results indicate these initiatives would be rewarded with superior regional growth rates and improvements in regional equity via economic convergence.

Multilateral strategies of this kind are indeed essential to make regional growth and integration opportunities more inclusive. The estimates reinforce the importance of infrastructure to overcoming bottlenecks to growth, particularly in terms of broader regional market participation. These general conclusions could be refined with more intensive local empirical work, but they are unlikely to be contradicted.

Finally, appealing to an extensive theoretical literature on endogenous growth effects, but a fairly narrow basis of prior empirical work, indicative results are given about how infrastructure-induced productivity growth can stimulate regional integration and convergence. These results need refinement with more localized data on the infrastructure–growth–productivity nexus. Despite this caveat, however, the results can faithfully illustrate infrastructure's potential as a catalyst for growth and regional poverty reduction, and it is believed that qualitative results obtained here will also prove robust to more localized calibration.

Extensions of the present work could shed much new light on the more detailed effects of infrastructure commitments at every stage, including financial/fiscal sourcing; domestic, bilateral, and multilateral project implementation; and myriad downstream assessments including economic facilitation (as studied here), productivity spillovers and other growth externalities, income growth, and distributional outcomes. Given the importance of these issues to development in general and ADB's mission in particular, and in recognition of the capacity of general equilibrium models to account for these complex effects, the present approach can support a broad agenda of policy research with more detailed empirical study.

As a final observation, it is worth noting that the current experiments have not addressed trade policy directly. To clearly identify the role of infrastructure in domestic economic growth, the experiments are not compounded with scenarios, for example, for regional or global trade liberalization. This would be a natural extension of the present work, and would in all likelihood demonstrate strong complementarity between Asian regional policy agendas for economic integration, trade, and investment.

ENDNOTES

1   One exception is Agénor et al. (2005) who apply a different but related approach.

2   See van der Mensbrugghe (2005) for complete model documentation.

3   For more extensive discussion of infrastructure assessment and proxies for quality and performance criteria, see for example, Estache and Goicoechea (2005).

4   For reference, the population-weighted standard yields additional investment needs of $157 billion per year, compared with the ADB/JBIC/World Bank (2005) estimate of $200 billion for Asia's unmet growth needs. For the simple average and GDP-weighted standards, the shortfalls are $816 billion and $2 trillion, respectively.

REFERENCES

Agénor, P-R., N. Bayraktar, and K. E. Aynaoui. 2005. "Roads out of Poverty? Assessing the Links between Aid, Public Investment, Growth, and Poverty Reduction." World Bank Policy Research Working Paper 3490, Washington, DC.

Ahmed, R., and M. Hossain. 1990. "Developmental Impact of Rural Infrastructure in Bangladesh." IFPRI Research Report 83, International Food Policy Research Institute, Washington, DC.

Aschauer, D. A. 1989. "Is Public Expenditure Productive?" *Journal of Monetary Economics* 23:177–200.

ADB/JBIC/World Bank. 2005. *Connecting East Asia: A New Framework for Infrastructure.* Asian Development Bank, Japan Bank for International Cooperation, and World Bank. Manila.

Baltagi, H., and N. Pinnoi 1995. "Public Capital Stock and State Productivity Growth: Further Evidence from an Error Components Model." *Empirical Economics* 20:351–9.

Benziger, V. 1996. "Urban Access and Rural Productivity Growth in Post-Mao China." *Economic Development and Cultural Change* 44:539–70.

Boarnet, M. G. 1997. "Highways and Economic Productivity: Interpreting Recent Evidence." *Journal of Planning Literature* 11(4):476–86.

Briceño-Garmendia, C., A. Estache, and N. Shafik. 2004. "Infrastructure Services in Developing Countries: Access, Quality, Costs, and Policy Reform." World Bank Policy Research Working Paper 3468, Washington, DC.

Brooks, D., D. Roland-Holst, and F. Zhai. 2005. "Asia's Long Term Growth and Integration: Reaching Beyond Policy Barriers." ERD Policy Brief 38, Asian Development Bank, Manila.

Calderón, C., and L. Servén. 2003a. "Macroeconomic Dimensions of Infrastructure in Latin America." Paper presented at the Fourth Annual Stanford Conference on Latin American Economic Development, 13–15 November, Stanford Center for International Development, Stanford University, Palo Alto.

———. 2003b. "The Output Cost of Latin America's Infrastructure Gap." In W. Easterly and L. Servén (eds.), *The Limits of Stabilization: Infrastructure, Public Deficits, and Growth in Latin America.* Palo Alto: Stanford University Press and the World Bank.

———. 2004. "The Effects of Infrastructure Development on Growth and Income Distribution." World Bank Policy Research Working Paper 3400. Washington, DC.

Canning, D. 1998. "The Contribution of Infrastructure to Aggregate Output." World Bank Policy Research Working Paper 2246, Washington, DC.

Cashin, P. 1995. Government Spending, Taxes, and Economic Growth. *IMF Staff Papers* 42(2):237–69.

Demetriades, P., and T. Mamuneas. 2000. "Intertemporal Output and Employment Effects of Public Infrastructure Capital: Evidence from 12 OECD Economies." *The Economic Journal* 110:687–712.

Easterly, W. 2001. "The Lost Decade: Developing Countries' Stagnation in Spite of Policy Reform." World Bank, Washington, DC. Unpublished manuscript.

Easterly, W., and S. Rebelo. 1993. "Fiscal Policy and Economic Growth: An Empirical Investigation." *Journal of Monetary Economics* 32:417–58.

Esfahani, H., and M. T. Ramirez. 2002. "Institutions, Infrastructure and Economic Growth." *Journal of Development Economics* 70:443–77.

Estache, A., and A. Goicoechea. 2005. A "Research Database on Infrastructure Economic Performance." World Bank Policy Research Working Paper 3643, Washington, DC.

Fan, S., L. Zhang, and X. Zhang. 2002. "Growth, Inequality, and Poverty in Rural China: The Role of Public Investments." IFPRI Research Report 125, International Food Policy Research Institute, Washington, DC.

Fay, M., and T. Yepes. 2003. "Investing in Infrastructure: What is needed from 2000 to 2010?" World Bank Policy Research Working Paper 3102, Washingon, DC.

Ferranti, D. de, G. E. Perry, F. Ferreira, and M. Walton (eds.). 2004. *Inequality in Latin America and the Caribbean: Breaking with History?* World Bank, Washington, DC.

Fernald, J. G. 1999. "Roads to Prosperity? Assessing the Link Between Public Capital and Productivity." *The American Economic Review* 89:619–38.

Florio, M. 1997. "The Economic Rate of Return of Infrastructures and Regional Policy in the European Union." *Annals of Public and Cooperative Economics* 68(1):39–64.

Fisher, R. C. 1997. "The Effects of State and Local Public Services on Economic Development." *New England Economic Review* March/April:53–67.

Garcia-Mila, T., T. J. McGuire, and R. H. Porter. 1996. "The Effect of Public Capital in State-Level Production Functions Reconsidered." *Review of Economics and Statistics* 88(1):177–80.

Gramlich, E. M. 1994. "Infrastructure Investment: A Review Essay." *Journal of Economic Literature* 32(September):1176–96.

Hines, J. R., Jr., and R. H. Thaler. 1995. "Anomalies: The Flypaper Effect." *Journal of Economic Perspectives* 9(4):217–26.

Holtz-Eakin, D. 1994. "Public Sector Capital and the Productivity Puzzle." *The Review of Economics and Statistics* 76(1):12–21.

Holtz-Eakin, D., and A. E. Schwartz. 1994. "Spatial Productivity Spillovers from Public Infrastructure: Evidence from State Highways." *International and Public Finance* 2(3):459–68.

Hulten, C. 1996. "Infrastructure Capital and Economic Growth: How Well You Use It May Be More Important than How Much You Have." NBER Working Paper 5847, National Bureau of Economic Research, Massachusetts.

Jacoby, H. 2000. "Access to Rural Markets and the Benefits of Rural Roads." *The Economic Journal* 110:713– 37.

Khandker, S., V. Lavy, and D. Filmer. 1994. "Schooling and Cognitive Achievements of Children in Morocco." World Bank Discussion Paper 264, Washington, DC.

Lin, S., and S. Song. 2002. "Urban Economic Growth in China: Theory and evidence." *Urban Studies* 39(12):2251–66.

Morrison, C. J., and A. E. Schwartz. 1996. "State Infrastructure and Productive Performance." *American Economic Review* 86(5):1095–111.

Munnell, A. H. 1992. "Infrastructure Investment and Economic Growth." *Journal of Economic Perspectives* 6(4):189–98.

Nadiri, M. I., and T. P. Mamuneas. 1996. "Contribution of Highway Capital to Industry and National Productivity Growth." Report submitted by Apogee Research, Inc., Bethesda, Md., to the Federal Highway Administration, Office of Policy Development, September. Available: http://www.fhwa.dot.gov/pubstats.html.

OECD. 2006. *International Development Statistics.* Development Assistance Committee, Organisation for Economic Co-operation and Development, Paris.

Riverson, J., J. Gaviria, and S. Thriscutt. 1991. "Rural Roads in Sub-Saharan Africa—Lessons from World Bank Experience." World Bank Technical Paper 141, Africa Technical Department Series, Washington, DC.

Röller, L-H., and L. Waverman. 2001. "Telecommunications Infrastructure and Economic Development: A Simultaneous Approach." *American Economic Review* 91:909–23.

Sanchez-Robles, B. 1998. "Infrastructure Investment and Growth: Some Empirical Evidence." *Contemporary Economic Policy* 16:98–108.

Songco, J. A. 2002. "Do Rural Infrastructure Investments Benefit the Poor? Evaluating Linkages: A Global View, A Focus on Vietnam." World Bank Policy Research Working Paper 2796, Washington, DC.

Sturm, J. E., and J. de Haan. 1995. "Is Public Expenditure Really Productive? New Evidence for the USA and the Netherlands." *Economic Modeling* 12(1):60–72.

Tatom, J. A. 1993. "Paved with Good Intentions: The Mythical National Infrastructure Crisis." Policy Analysis 196, Cato Institute, Washington, DC.

UNCTAD. 2006. "FDI from Developing and Transition Economies: Implications for Development." In *World Investment Report.* United Nations Conference on Trade and Development, Geneva.

van der Mensbrugghe, D. 2005. "LINKAGE Technical Reference Document." Development Prospects Group, World Bank, Washington, DC. Processed.

Winston, C., and B. Bosworth. 1992. "Public Infrastructure." In H. J. Aaron and C. L. Schultze (eds.), *Setting Domestic Priorities: What Can Government Do?* Brookings Institution, Washington, DC.

World Bank. 1994. *World Development Report.* Washington, DC.

Yepes, T. 2004. "Expenditure on Infrastructure in East Asia Region, 2006–2010." Background paper prepared for the ADB/JBIC/World Bank Report on Asia's Infrastructure Needs. Asian Development Bank, Manila.

APPENDIX

Regression Results for Asian Infrastructure Needs

Calderón and Servén (2005) report estimates for an index of infrastructure availability obtained for a global database of over 100 countries covering the period 1960–1995. The index was constructed to measure availability of three categories of infrastructure: telecommunications, electric power, and road/rail networks. (See Calderón and Servén (2005) for details about the dataset, indicator definitions, and their own extensive estimation of infrastructure productivity effects.)

The three variables are stocks measured with respect to population (L) or total national surface area (A) as follows:

$$CSI_{it} = 0.6159\ \ln\left(\frac{Z_1}{L}\right)_{it} + 0.6075\ \ln\left(\frac{Z_2}{L}\right)_{it} + 0.5015\ \ln\left(\frac{Z_3}{A}\right)_{it}$$

This variable is depicted in Figure 4.8 in the chapter proper and provided the basis for the regression estimates of unmet investment needs shown in Appendix Table A4.1.

The results are based on a 13 country Asian subsample of the Calderón and Servén database, consisting of 85 observations pooled in 5-year intervals from 1960 to 1995. Some countries were not reporting until the 1970s and the last decade has been very important to infrastructure development in the PRC and a few other rapidly emerging economies. Nonetheless, the results are very robust in terms of overall goodness of fit and individual significance of the main explanatory variable (CSI) and the country dummies (defined in Appendix Table A4.1). Japan is the omitted country, so levels of infrastructure density are defined with respect to this economy (i.e., Hong Kong, China and Singapore above and the rest below the Japanese intercept; see Figure 4.8).

These results indicate that infrastructure development in Asia is highly correlated with overall investment; indeed in the 5-year intervals, an elasticity of just over unity between aggregate capital formation and the Calderón-Servén index is seen. The strength of this relationship will vary between countries, but it indicates that high rates of domestic capital formation in Asia contribute strongly to the national commons of productive infrastructure.

Appendix Table A4.1 Regression Results for Infrastructure Investment Requirements

Source	SS	df	MS		Number of obs = 85
					F(13,72) = 183.93
Model	740.238122	13	56.941394		Prob>F = 0.0000
Residual	22.2897486	72	.309579841		R-squared = 0.9708
Total	762.527871	85	8.97091612		AdjR-squared = 0.9655
					Root MSE .5564

linv	Coef.	Std. Err.	t	P>|t|	[95% Conf. Interval]	
CSI	1.125155	.0349089	32.23	0.000	1.055566	1.194745
BAN	3.928857	.2292571	17.14	0.000	3.471841	4.385873
PRC	6.404122	.2345318	27.31	0.000	5.936592	6.871653
HKG	-2.797971	.3680138	-7.60	0.000	-3.531593	-2.064349
IND	4.160417	.2115945	19.66	0.000	3.738611	4.582223
INO	4.349985	.2208816	19.69	0.000	3.909665	4.790304
KOR	.2854137	.2238050	1.28	0.206	-.1607334	.7315608
MAL	.0844627	.2142628	0.39	0.695	-.3426624	.5115878
PAK	2.726337	.2288788	11.91	0.000	2.270075	3.182598
PHI	1.839141	.2104679	8.74	0.000	1.419581	2.258701
SIN	-3.870027	.2649475	-14.61	0.000	-4.398190	-3.341864
SRI	.2580208	.2104293	1.23	0.224	-.1614623	.677504
THA	2.838656	.2114507	13.42	0.000	2.417137	3.260175

Variable Definitions:

Dependent variable: linv = Logarithm of aggregate domestic investment.

Independent variable: CSI = Calderón-Servén index of infrastructure availability.

Country-specific fixed-effect variables: BAN = Bangladesh; PRC = People's Republic of China; HKG = Hong Kong, China; IND = India; INO = Indonesia; KOR = Republic of Korea; MAL = Malaysia; PAK = Pakistan; PHI = Philippines; SIN = Singapore; SRI = Sri Lanka; THA = Thailand.

Commentary on Chapter 4

David Canning

This chapter begins by discussing the theoretical basis of the different mechanisms that can lead us to expect infrastructure to have a large impact on economic development in Asia. It then considers the evidence base for the size of these effects, and examines various scenarios for infrastructure's contribution to economic development, on the basis of likely elasticities of response to infrastructure investments.

In terms of theory and the mechanisms through which infrastructure can operate, we can organize our thinking on the complex issues involved around a few distinct principles. Theoretically, the public sector is interested in infrastructure because there is a divergence between marginal social benefit and marginal social cost if infrastructure is left entirely to the market. There are three potential mechanisms for this. The first occurs if infrastructure is a public good, either due to being a non-rival (so that one person's use does not diminish the amount available for someone else's use) or non-excludable (so that access cannot be control-priced). The second occurs if infrastructure has externalities, either in consumption or production. The third possibility is market failure due to monopoly power that generates a divergence between price and the marginal cost of production.

All these issues arise with infrastructure, but to a greater or lesser extent depending on whether we are considering roads, electricity, or telephones. In addition to these different types of infrastructure having different economic characteristics, in some cases recent technological advances have changed their characteristics.

In the case of roads, we have a non-rival public good when there is no congestion (as is usually the case with rural roads). However, on urban roads and major intercity routes there is often congestion, which makes these roads rival commodities. Pricing for roads has historically been difficult, with toll systems being expensive and themselves causing congestion. Modern technological advances have, though, made roads more excludable. Low-cost electronic pricing systems that can vary with the time of day as congestion changes allow roads to take on the characteristics of a private good.

Large externalities associated with roads are likely, though hard to measure. Trade increases the extent of the market, allowing economies of scale. More important perhaps, roads allow for many specialized small firms to be linked through rich intermediate goods markets. Roads can increase competition, and reduce markups and monopoly power throughout the economy. A road can make firms lower prices due to competitive pressure, even though in equilibrium there is no trade between locations along the road—the potential competition is sufficient to moderate prices. Lower trade costs from roads can be viewed as technological progress. Trade is an input-output machine where we put in our "exports" and produce our "imports." By making trade cheaper, the rate at which our exports can be transformed into imports improves, which to the individual looks like technological progress.

Electricity is quite different from roads. It is a private good being both excludable and rival. While there is little evidence of externalities, the electricity distribution system is a natural monopoly requiring government control or regulation. Historically, power generation has had large fixed costs, which can cause financing problems, and can create a natural monopoly in small countries. However fairly small-scale gas turbine plants are now economical, making the possibility of competition in power generation more realistic. Perhaps more important, however, than monopoly issues is that electricity is a critical input for modern economic activity—there is a real fear of supply interruptions and shortages that can undermine output. There is a role for government to ensure planning to prevent supply shortages through lack of investment and supply interruption at peak loads due to lack of reserve capacity. Note that competitive providers will prefer a situation of low capacity since it gives them pricing power.

Telephone systems are both rival and excludable. Historically, though, landline systems have been natural monopolies, but this has changed with the adaptation of mobile phones, which still have a large fixed-cost element but clearly allow entry of multiple firms and a high degree of competition. Telephones may have large externalities, similar to roads, in that they increase the extent of the market, allow for increased competition, and aid the organization of production across several locations.

The public good and monopoly power arguments for public intervention are quite clear. The real problem is with externalities. While we may expect these to be present, measuring their size is exceptionally difficult. One approach is to estimate the marginal product of infrastructure using an aggregate production function and compare this product with the cost of infrastructure building. As noted in the chapter, this approach has produced a wide variety of estimates, and, though this approach has many problems in estimation conceptually, it should capture any externalities that add to aggregate output. Another approach is to use a cost-benefit method, based on specific infrastructure projects. While it may be simpler, it is likely to miss significant externalities.

While conceptually appealing, the aggregate production function approach suffers from several specific problems. The value of infrastructure investment may not be a good guide to physical infrastructure due to wide variation in the price of infrastructure across countries. Rising output creates a demand for infrastructure and may lead to infrastructure construction. Separating out this demand-side reverse causality from the supply-side externalities of infrastructure on aggregate output is always difficult. Omitted variable bias poses a significant problem. In particular, it is difficult in aggregate production function models to accurately measure total factor productivity. This is likely to be positively correlated with infrastructure (for example through demand) tending to bias the estimated effect of infrastructure upward. The usual aggregate production function models have output responding smoothly to infrastructure, but there may be threshold effects where infrastructure is critical up to the threshold but thereafter has low productivity.

Most aggregate studies focus on estimating the productivity of infrastructure, but as said, the cost of infrastructure varies widely across countries. The cost of roads is steep in high-income countries and in low-income countries, but low in middle-income countries (Figure C.4.1). Low-income countries need to import materials, equipment, and expertise, while middle-income countries can produce these intermediate goods cheaply. The cost of electricity-generating capacity is very high in some low- and middle-income countries, which is perhaps evidence of inefficient construction (Figure C.4.2).

Given the problems associated with both the aggregate production function approach and the cost-benefit approach to looking for externalities to infrastructure, there is a need for new approaches. For example, instead of

Figure C.4.1 Cost of Paved Roads

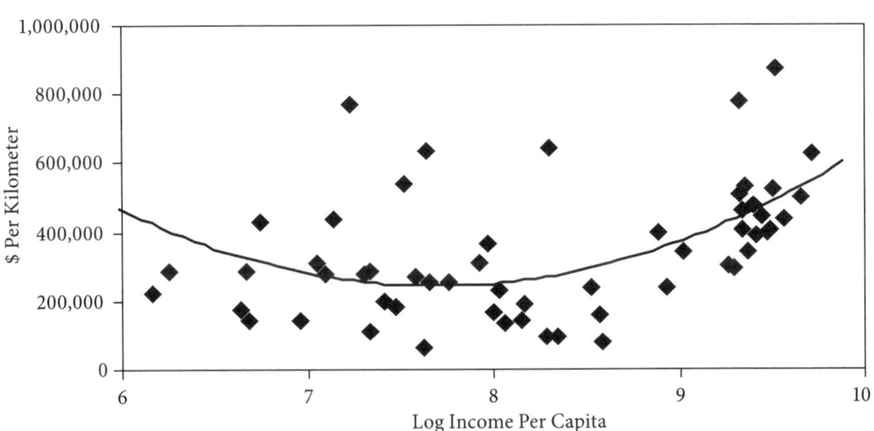

Source: Data from Canning and Bennathan (2000).

Figure C.4.2 Cost of Electricity Generating Capacity

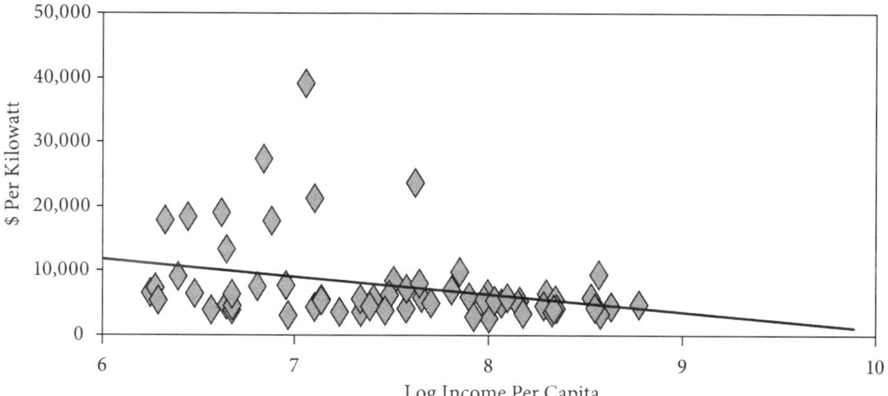

Source: Data from Canning and Bennathan (2000).

focusing on aggregate output, the spillovers of infrastructure may be seen in the volume of foreign direct investment. Foreign investors will be attracted by such spillovers even if we cannot see these externalities directly. We can also look at the effect of infrastructure on the poor. In this case public transport, which is vital for the poor to have access to road and railway infrastructure, might be considered as a type of infrastructure in its own right. Another issue that might be addressed is to look at how firm size and the degree of specialization, as well as the dearth of intermediate goods markets, vary with infrastructure provision.

In conclusion, there is a clear case for public intervention in infrastructure provision when there are public good or monopoly issues. However, technological progress has tended to weaken this case by allowing excludability and by reducing monopoly power. The key issue, though, is the magnitude of the externalities to infrastructure, and it is exactly on this point that our evidence base is weak.

Reference to Commentary

Canning, David and Esra Bennathan. 2000. "The Social Rate of Return on Infrastructure Investments." World Bank Policy Research Working Paper 2390, Washington, DC.

5

Unlocking the Trade Potential in Least-Developed Countries: A CGE Investigation for Bangladesh

Fan Zhai

5.1 INTRODUCTION

During the past four decades, the region of developing Asia has significantly increased its trade with the rest of the world and within itself. This trend was led by the newly industrialized economies (NIEs)—Hong Kong, China; Republic of Korea (hereafter Korea); Singapore; and Taipei,China—and Southeast Asian countries in the 1960s and 1970s. The People's Republic of China (PRC) caught up with them in the 1980s and 1990s. More recently, India and Viet Nam have also seen their trade shares rising. The overall share of developing Asia in world trade rose from 4.1% in 1965 to 16.6% in 2005. The region's dependence on trade, measured by the sum of exports and imports as a share of gross domestic product (GDP), increased from 11.6% to 83.1% over the same period. This expansion of international trade in developing Asia has been accompanied by rapid economic growth and substantial poverty reduction. Despite the controversial results from the trade and growth literature,[1] the growth story of developing Asia in the past few decades clearly demonstrates the vital role of trade in development.

But there is another side to the story. Trade performance is not uniform across the region. Some poor, low-income countries remain closed to trade and lag behind in growth and poverty reduction. These countries' shares in world trade have declined in the past few decades, and they risk further marginalization if no steps are taken to strengthen their competitiveness in the international market. This group includes some South Asian countries. In addition, many poor landlocked countries, such as Lao People's Democratic Republic (Lao PDR), Mongolia, Nepal, and those in Central Asia, fit this description. So while some developing Asian countries, such as the PRC and India, are becoming increasingly important players in world production and trade, making most of their people better off, the above least-developed Asian countries are being left far behind.

The reasons for these countries' weak trade performance are complex, including restrictive trade policies, geographic location, high transportation and operating costs, and poor institutions. South Asian countries typically impose high tariff rates and other controls on imports to protect their domestic industries. This import-substitution strategy undermines the competitiveness of exporting sectors, discouraging both imports and exports. Geography, too, is an important factor that weakens export performance in landlocked countries, because their remoteness to major markets and lack of access to seaports are likely to reduce export competitiveness considerably. A study by Limão and Venables (2001) shows that the median landlocked country has transport costs 50% higher and trade volumes 60% lower than the median coastal economy.

Transport costs can also increase as a result of weak transportation services and infrastructure. Low-income countries typically lack adequate infrastructure and this often acts as a major bottleneck for them to integrate into the global market. By studying Sub-Saharan African trade, both internally and with the rest of the world, Limão and Venables (2001) find that infrastructure problems largely explain the relatively low levels of African trade. Finally, the quality of institutions and governance has been taken to be an important determinant of trade performance in recent literature (e.g., Levchenko, 2007). Poor contract enforcement, weak investor protection, excessive rules and regulations, and widespread corruption can impose significant costs on international (and domestic) business.

The future growth of least-developed Asian countries will depend critically on the full realization of their potential in expanding international trade. In a world increasingly integrated through commodity, capital, and technology flows, it is hard to imagine that lagging countries can achieve rapid economic catch-up without intensifying their trade linkages with the world economy. Some questions arise: How much can their trade expand if the major obstacles to trade are removed? What is the relative importance of the determinants of trade potential? And, how may policy be reformed to facilitate the trade expansion in these least-developed countries? This chapter attempts to answer some of these questions with reference to Bangladesh.

Bangladesh is a developing country with a per capita GDP of $420 and a population of over 140 million. Exports accounted for 16% of its GDP in 2005, but were concentrated heavily in a few sectors and markets. Using a global computable general equilibrium (CGE) model with firm heterogeneity in productivity, the chapter investigates the trade expansion and welfare effects of alternative policy reform options, including trade liberalization, improvement in domestic productivity, and trade facilitation. The simulation results highlight the important role of the "extensive margin"—i.e., new exporting firms and goods—in the trade expansion of developing countries.

The rest of the chapter is organized as follows. Section 5.2 reviews trade liberalization and performance in Bangladesh. The CGE model used is introduced in Section 5.3. Section 5.4 discusses the nonpolicy trade barriers of Bangladesh, calibrated from bilateral trade-flow data. Section 5.5 presents simulation results. Some concluding remarks are given in Section 5.6.

5.2 TRADE LIBERALIZATION AND TRADE PERFORMANCE IN BANGLADESH

In the early 1990s, Bangladesh pursued wide-ranging trade liberalization reforms to reduce policy-induced distortions and to improve export competitiveness. The reforms were comprehensive and systematic, including substantial reduction and rationalization of tariffs, removal of quantitative restrictions, unification of exchange rates, and moves to a more flexible exchange rate system and to current-account convertibility. However, the reforms stalled in the mid-1990s, and even reversed somewhat toward the end of the decade, on the popular notion that earlier reforms had been "too much and too fast" (Ahmed and Sattar, 2004).

Even with these liberalization reforms, Bangladesh is still one of the most highly protected developing countries. The average customs duty is 15.5%, the top rate is 25%, with three non-zero duty slabs of 6%, 13%, and 25%. However, customs duty rates alone give a misleading impression of actual levels of protection. The authorities use various other import taxes to raise these rates, including the "Infrastructure Development Surcharge," "regulatory" duties, "supplementary" duties, and value-added taxes under which domestically produced goods are either exempt or taxable at a lower rate. These para-tariffs were modest in the early 1990s, but have been going up since fiscal year 1995/96. Between that year and 2003/04, average customs duties fell by 9.9 percentage points, but about half of this reduction was offset by an increase in average para-tariffs of approximately 5 percentage points. In the agriculture sector, the rise of protection from para-tariffs was even more evident. Average agricultural customs duties were cut during the same period by 7.6 percentage points, but this reduction was more than offset by an increase in average para-tariffs of approximately 14.9 percentage points. Consequently, more than 30% of average protection came from these para-tariffs in 2003/04.

Taking MFN (most-favored-nation) customs duties and para-tariffs

Figure 5.1 Average Protective Tariffs in Selected Asian Developing Countries

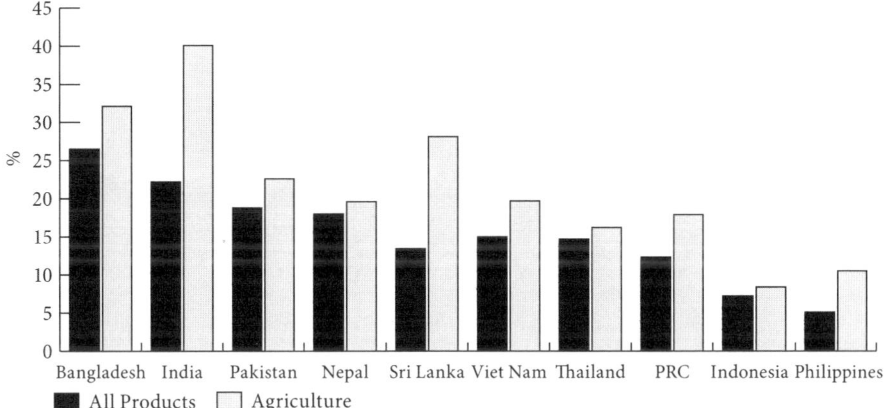

Source: World Bank (2004).

together, the average protective tariffs for Bangladesh currently stand at 26.5%—25.4% for industry and 32.1% for agriculture. These rates are not only higher than those in other East and Southeast Asian developing countries, but are also the highest in South Asia (Figure 5.1).

Bangladesh maintained many protective quantitative restrictions until fairly recently. These restrictions applied primarily to three categories: agricultural products (namely eggs, poultry, and salt), packaging materials, and textile products. In January 2005, they were finally removed (with the exception of the three agricultural products).

Partly as a result of trade liberalization reform, the country's trade-to-GDP ratio rose from 18% in 1990 to 38% in 2005. During the period 1990–2005, the average annual growth rate of exports was 12.0%, rising from only 8.2% in the 1980s. Export growth has been accompanied by changes in export composition, which has shifted away from primary commodities to manufacturing goods. However, the overall competitiveness of Bangladesh's exports is quite weak. Knitwear and hosiery products, and readymade garments account for three fourths of total exports, while four fifths of total exports go to the United States (US) and European Union (EU) (Figures 5.2 and 5.3). This high degree of product- and market-concentration makes the export sector very vulnerable to external shocks in specific goods or destinations. The weak export performance is also reflected in the country's persistent trade deficits. Despite rapid export growth, these have remained at about 6% of GDP in recent years, reflecting the high import content of exports (Figure 5.4).

It should be noted that Bangladesh's exporters enjoy preferential access to most developed-country markets. Under the "Everything but Arms" initiative

Figure 5.2 Exports by Main Product Categories, Bangladesh, 1999/2000–2003/04

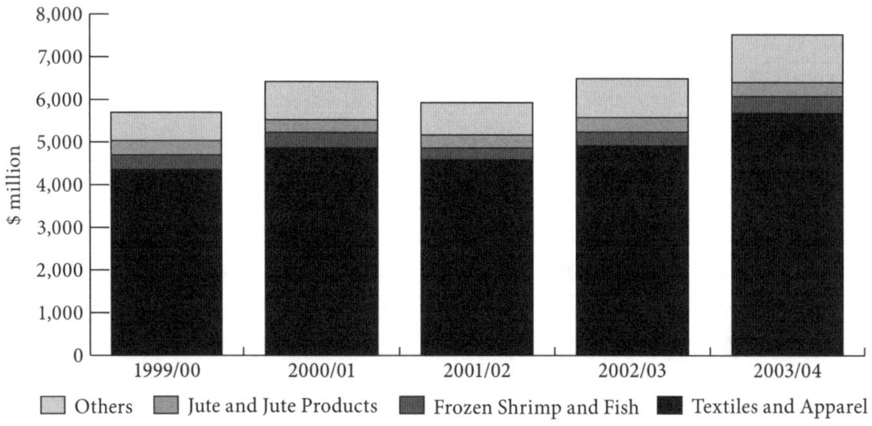

Source: IMF (2005).

Figure 5.3 Exports by Main Destination, Bangladesh, 2000–2005

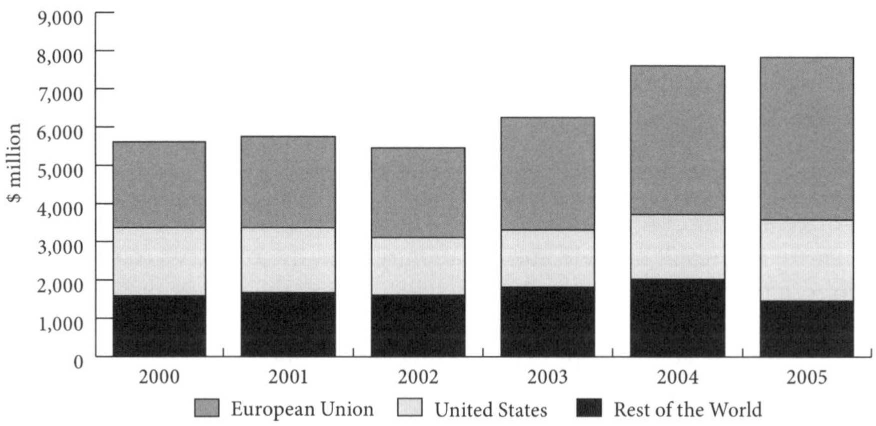

Source: IMF (2005).

of the EU, Bangladesh, along with 49 other least-developed countries, receives duty- and quota-free access for all products except arms, provided that EU rules of origin are satisfied. Among others, Australia, Canada, New Zealand, Norway, and Switzerland provide attractive market-access opportunities for least-developed countries, including Bangladesh (but the country continues to face quotas and tariffs in the US market). These preferential market access arrangements give to Bangladesh certain competitive advantages over its competitors, although the benefits are often partly offset by rules of origin.[2]

Figure 5.4 Trade Deficits, Bangladesh, 1980–2005

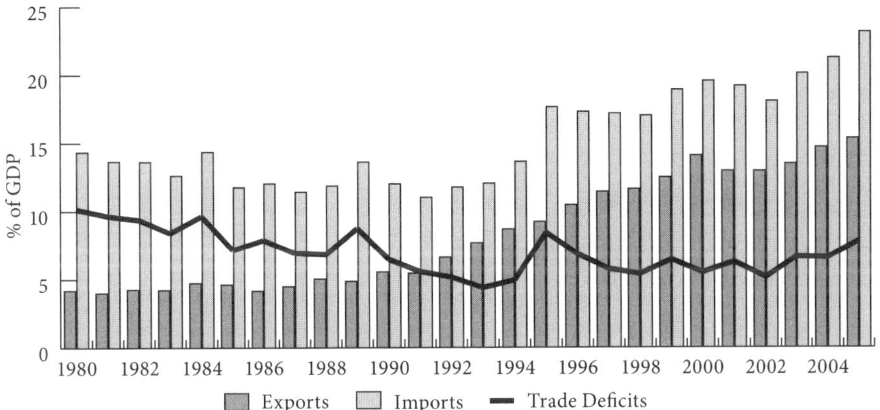

Source: World Bank, *World Development Indicators.*

Some domestic supply-side constraints heavily limit the country's export competitiveness. Weak governance is a major one. Inefficiency of government bureaucracy, pervasiveness of corruption and rent-seeking behavior, and the complex regulatory environment significantly raise business costs, and constitute major bottlenecks for international trade. According to the World Bank, on average, eight procedures are involved in starting a business in Bangladesh. It takes 37 days to complete these procedures and the associated cost is as high as 87.6% of per capita national income (Table 5.1). Enforcing a contract averages nearly 4 years. Overall, the business environment performs relatively poorly on various indicators of governance, with an overall ranking of 88 among the 175 sample countries in 2006 (Table 5.2).

Poor infrastructure is another important aspect constraining trade in Bangladesh. Weak domestic infrastructure in transportation, power, and telecommunications raises overall business operating costs. Moreover, the country suffers from a lack of adequate infrastructure at ports, leading to longer lead times. The World Bank *Enterprise Surveys* data indicate that Bangladesh significantly lags behind in infrastructure development, and this may contribute to the lengthy customs clearance procedures (Table 5.3).

5.3 THE MODEL

The model used here is a static, CGE model of the global economy. It is built on the Linkage model developed at the World Bank by van der Mensbrugghe (2005), and has its intellectual roots in a group of multicountry applied general equilibrium models used over the past two decades to analyze the impact

Table 5.1 Comparison of Costs of Doing Business

Location	Starting a Business				Enforcing a Contract		
	Procedures (number)	Duration (days)	Cost (%)[a]	Min. Capital (%)[a]	Procedures (number)	Time (days)	Cost (% of debt)
East Asia and the Pacific	8.2	46.3	42.8	60.3	31.5	477.3	52.7
OECD	6.2	16.6	5.3	36.1	22.2	351.2	11.2
South Asia	7.9	32.5	46.6	0.8	38.7	968.9	26.4
Bangladesh	8.0	37.0	87.6	0	50.0	1,442.0	45.7

a As a share of per capita national income

Source: World Bank *Doing Business* database.

Table 5.2 Business Environment Rank, Bangladesh

Ease of...	Rank in 2006	Rank in 2005
Doing Business	88	81
Starting a Business	68	63
Dealing with Licenses	67	64
Employing Workers	75	75
Registering Property	167	167
Getting Credit	48	41
Protecting Investors	15	15
Paying Taxes	72	69
Trading Across Borders	134	132
Enforcing Contracts	174	174
Closing a Business	93	87

Source: World Bank *Doing Business* database.

of trade policy reform (e.g., Shoven and Whalley, 1992; Hertel, 1997). The multicountry CGE model has increasingly become a standard tool for trade analysis because it can detail structural adjustments within national economies and elucidate their interactions in international markets.

One novel feature of the model used here is its incorporation of firm heterogeneity in productivity and fixed costs of exporting. This enables endogenization of the extensive margin of trade in the model. Recent empirical literature has emphasized the importance of the extensive margin in trade expansion and economic growth.[3] However, as Hummels and Klenow (2005) argue, neither the traditional CGE model with a representative firm and Armington national product differentiation, nor the "new trade theory" model with monopolistic competition and firm-level product differentiation, can match the facts about extensive and intensive export margins.[4]

The absence of the extensive margin in Armington-type CGE models makes

Table 5.3 Comparison of Infrastructure and Customs Clearance Indicators

	East Asia and Pacific	OECD	South Asia	Bangla-desh
Infrastructure				
Delay in obtaining an electrical connection (days)	12.02	8.32	55.23	66.29
Number of electrical outages (days)	7.04	1.14	130.22	248.96
Value lost due to electrical outages (% of sales)	2.39	2.25	5.21	2.76
Number of water supply failures (days)	1.86	0.18	9.62	17.59
Delay in obtaining a mainline telephone connection (days)	9.32	7.91	64.98	125.97
Firms using the Web in interaction with clients/ suppliers (%)	25.15	80.2	28.67	31.12
Customs clearance (days)				
Average time to clear direct exports through customs	3.71	4.63	6.25	8.27
Longest time to clear direct exports through customs	5.98	8.33	10.49	12.78
Average time to claim imports from customs	4.89	5.28	9.46	10.56
Longest time to claim imports from customs	8.98	9.40	17.28	21.39

Source: World Bank *Enterprise Surveys* database.

them especially inappropriate for least-developed countries, which usually have only limited trade with the rest of the world. As Kehoe (2005) argues, the Armington specification has the effect of locking in preexisting trade patterns and prevents the models from generating large changes in trade in sectors where there is little or no trade. Under this specification, if a country's imports of a product from another country are zero initially they will always be zero, even after significant reductions of trade barriers. If imports are not zero but small, they will remain small even if there are large changes in prices. The "stuck on zero trade" problem in CGE models may lead them to significantly underestimate the trade potential of least-developed countries.

In recent years, several new heterogeneous-firm models of international trade by Bernard et al. (2003), Melitz (2003), and Yeaple (2005) have introduced the extensive margin as a result of the firms' self-selection in export markets. They emphasize the interaction of trade costs and productivity differences across firms operating in imperfectly competitive industries. When trade costs decrease, new firms with lower productivity enter export markets in response to the potential higher profits. Empirical evidence has largely supported the predictions of these new models.

The model used in this chapter has a structure of production similar to that in Melitz (2003), which incorporates firm productivity heterogeneity in the Krugman (1979) monopolistic competition model. Within the 15 sectors of the model, the sectors of agriculture, mining, and public administration are assumed to be in perfect competition. In each of them, a representative firm operates under constant returns-to-scale technology. The other 12 sectors of manufacturing and services are characterized by monopolistic competition. Each of the 12 sectors consists of a continuum of firms differentiated by the varieties they produce and by their productivity. Firms face fixed production costs, resulting in increasing returns to scale. There are also fixed and variable costs associated with exporting activities.

On the demand side, the agents are assumed to have Dixit-Stiglitz preferences over the continuum of varieties. As each firm is a monopolist for the variety it produces, it sets the price of its product at a constant markup over its marginal cost. Firms enter domestic or export markets if—and only if—the net profits generated from its domestic sales or exports in a given country are sufficient to cover its fixed costs. This zero cutoff profit condition defines the productivity threshold for firms entering domestic and export markets, and in turn determines the equilibrium distribution of nonexporting and exporting firms, as well as their average productivities.

Usually, the combination of fixed and variable export costs ensures that the exporting productivity threshold is higher than that for the domestic market, i.e., only a small fraction of firms that have high productivity engages in export markets. These exporting firms supply both domestic and export markets. The CGE model abstracts from the dynamic parts of the Melitz model, assuming no free entry, no sunk entry costs, and no uncertainty about productivity before entry. In this way, the CGE model characterizes a static, not steady-state, equilibrium.[5]

The model is calibrated to the Global Trade Analysis Project (GTAP) version 6.2 global database. However, some information that is central to this study's model, such as the degree of returns to scale, the shape of productivity distribution, and the magnitude of the fixed and variable trade costs, is not available in the GTAP database. These parameters are set mainly on the basis of a search of the relevant literature. Table 5.4 reports some major parameters used in the model. The markup ratios are set equal to 20–25% for manufacturing sectors and 30% for services sectors. The choice of markup ratios, together with the optimal pricing rule of monopolistic firms, implies that the substitution elasticity between differentiated varieties is 5.0–6.0 for manufacturing and 4.3 for services. Firm productivity is assumed to follow a Pareto distribution. The shape parameters of the Pareto distribution are selected to match the assumed 50% profit ratio in total markup.

In each sector, the mass of potential firms is assumed proportional to the sectoral output. Eighty percent of these firms are assumed to produce and sell in the domestic market. The possibility of firms exporting to other regions' markets is calibrated to base-year bilateral trade flows. Then the fixed production costs, fixed exporting costs, and iceberg variable trade costs are

Table 5.4 Major Parameters in the Model

	Markup Ratio (%)	Substitution Elasticity between Varieties	Shape Parameter in Productivity Distribution
Processed food	20	6.0	10.0
Textile	20	6.0	10.0
Apparels	20	6.0	10.0
Chemical	25	5.0	8.0
Materials[a]	25	5.0	8.0
Electronics and Electrical Equipment	25	5.0	8.0
Vehicles	25	5.0	8.0
Machinery	25	5.0	8.0
Other Manufacturing	25	5.0	8.0
Trade	30	4.3	6.7
Transportation and Communications	30	4.3	6.7
Other Services	30	4.3	6.7

a Building materials, mineral products, metals and metal products.

Source: Author's assumptions.

calibrated from the shares of producing firms and exporting firms in the total mass of potential firms. The next section details the calibration of these fixed and variable trade costs for Bangladesh's trade.

5.4 AN ESTIMATION OF BANGLADESH'S TRADE COSTS

Broadly defined trade costs include all costs incurred in getting a good to a final user, other than the production cost of the good itself (Anderson and van Wincoop, 2004). Besides policy barriers such as tariffs and quotas, important components of the broad trade costs often include those relating to logistics, information, contract enforcement, language translation, and currency conversion. With the substantial decline in global tariff levels over the last two decades, nonpolicy barriers are increasingly becoming the major impediments in world trade. For most developing countries, these nonpolicy trade costs are significantly high, because of relatively poor infrastructure, incomplete domestic insurance and logistics services markets, and a weak institutional environment. In the Asian context, De (2006) econometrically estimates the trade costs for 10 Asian countries and finds that infrastructure quality, tariff costs, and transportation costs are the three main determinants of trade costs.

In this analysis, the trade costs of Bangladesh are calibrated from a gravity equation obtained from the CGE model using base-year bilateral trade data. In the Melitz-type firm heterogeneity model, bilateral trade flows are determined by the following gravity equation:

$$X_{ij} = (P_j D_j)^{\gamma/(\sigma-1)} \cdot N_i \cdot \left(\frac{P_j}{(1+t_{ij})\,\tau_{ij}\,V_i} \frac{\sigma-1}{\sigma} \right)^{\gamma} \cdot (f_{ij}\,(1+t_{ij})\sigma)^{1-\gamma/(\sigma-1)} \cdot \frac{\gamma}{\gamma-\sigma+1} \quad (1)$$

where X_{ij} is the value of exports from country i to county j. D_j is the volume of demand in country j and P_j represents its corresponding price. N_j is the number of potential firms. V_j is the marginal production cost in country i. t_{ij}, τ_{ij}, and f_{ij} are tariff costs, variable trade costs, and fixed exporting costs, respectively. σ is the substitution elasticity across varieties and γ is the shape parameter of the distribution of firm productivity. The condition $\gamma>\sigma\text{-}1$ is assumed to hold to ensure the size distribution of firms has a finite mean. This equation reflects the combined effects of market size $(P_j D_j)$, stiffness of market competition (reflected in P_j), technology (V_i), number of potential firms (N_i), and trade barriers $(t_{ij}$, τ_{ij}, and $f_{ij})$ on bilateral trade patterns.

The extensive margin of trade flows is reflected in the share of exporting firms, S_{ij}.

$$S_{ij} = \left(\frac{P_j D_j}{f_{ij}\,(1+t_{ij})\,\sigma} \right)^{\gamma/(\sigma-1)} \cdot \left(\frac{P_j}{(1+t_{ij})\tau_{ij}\,V_i} \frac{\sigma-1}{\sigma} \right)^{\gamma} \quad (2)$$

As the data for variable and fixed trade costs are not available, they have to be obtained through calibration. A constant elasticity function between the share of exporting firms and variable trade costs is assumed:

$$S_{ij} = a\,\tau_{ij}^{-\beta} \quad (3)$$

where β is the elasticity of the share of exporting firms with respect to variable trade costs. Using (2) and (3), (1) can be rewritten:

$$X_{if} = (P_j D_j) \cdot N_i \cdot \left(\frac{P_j}{(1+t_{if})\tau_{if}\,V_i} \frac{\sigma-1}{\sigma} \right)^{\sigma-1} \cdot (S_{if})^{1-(\sigma-1)/\gamma} \cdot \frac{\gamma}{\gamma-\sigma+1}$$

$$= (P_j D_j) \cdot N_i \cdot \left(\frac{P_j}{(1+t_{if})\tau\,V_i} \frac{\sigma-1}{\sigma} \right)^{\sigma-1} \cdot (a\,\tau_{if}^{-\beta})^{1-(\sigma-1)/\gamma} \cdot \frac{\gamma}{\gamma-\sigma+1} \quad (4)$$

The elasticity of the share of exporting firms with respect to variable trade costs, β, is assumed to equal the shape parameter of firm productivity distribution, γ. This assumption leads to a unity elasticity of trade flows X_{ij} with respect to the share of exporting firms S_{ij}. Domestic trade is assumed to incur no costs, i.e., τ_{ii} equals 1. Then from (4), the variable trade costs and share of exporting firms can be calculated using the base-year trade flows and domestic sales data. Table 5.5 presents the variable trade costs and shares of exporting firms of Bangladesh in 2001 calibrated from the GTAP database. The corresponding trade flows and tariff data are reported in Table 5.6.

The export matrix by commodity and destination in Table 5.6 clearly shows Bangladesh's commodity- and region-concentration. Most exports are textiles and apparel destined for the US and EU. It also exports some processed food and chemical products to those two economies. In Asia, Japan and Hong Kong, China are major export markets. Bangladesh exports some nongrain crops to some South Asian countries, such as India and Pakistan. It has few exports of electronics, vehicles, and machinery and almost none of grains. It is worth noting that in manufacturing sectors, the export matrix has six zero cells—electronics, vehicles, machinery, and other manufacturing exports to Viet Nam; processed food to Sri Lanka; and vehicles to Australia and New Zealand.

The large concentration of exports to the US and EU reflects these economies' larger market size, lower tariff rates on Bangladesh's products, and lower trade costs of delivering products from Bangladesh to these regions. Bangladesh exports to the EU at almost zero tariffs for all manufacturing sectors. The tariff rates imposed by the US are also relatively modest. Bangladesh's exporters face much higher tariffs in some Asian countries, such as India, Malaysia, Pakistan, Thailand, and Viet Nam. Although Hong Kong, China; Japan; and Singapore impose no tariffs, Bangladesh has only limited exports to these economies. This reflects the relatively smaller market size in Hong Kong, China and Singapore, as well as high nonpolicy barriers for Bangladesh's firms to export to these markets.

The calibrated variable trade costs are in a range of 1–2 in most sectors for Bangladesh's exports to the US, EU, and India, but in a range of 2–4 for exports to most East and Southeast Asian economies. The variable trade costs are even higher in the markets of Pakistan, Sri Lanka, and Viet Nam. Higher trade costs result in fewer firms exporting to these markets. The lower panel of Table 5.5 shows that more than 40% of Bangladesh's apparel firms and 20% of textile firms export to the EU market. The share of apparel firms exporting to the US market is even higher. But in Asian markets, the corresponding shares are generally less than 1%, except for apparel exports to Japan and Hong Kong, China. In electronics, vehicles, and machinery, the shares of exporting firms are much smaller, as only tiny numbers of firms in Bangladesh can export in these sectors.

Table 5.5 Variable Trade Costs and Shares of Exporting Firms for Exports from Bangladesh

	JPN	KOR	PRC	HKG	TAP	INO	MAL	PHI	SIN	THA	VIE	IND	PAK	SRI	US	EUR	ANZ	LAC	ROW
Variable Trade Costs																			
Processed Food	1.8	2.3	1.9	3.0	2.9	3.6	2.4	4.1	2.1	1.4	2.5	2.4	3.2	5.4	1.6	1.5	2.9	2.2	1.8
Textiles	1.8	2.0	2.2	2.0	2.1	1.8	1.9	2.6	1.7	1.8	3.0	1.8	2.4	2.1	1.2	1.1	1.7	1.6	1.3
Apparel	1.5	1.8	1.3	1.6	1.7	2.1	1.9	2.0	1.6	2.0	1.5	1.7	2.5	1.9	1.0	1.1	1.8	1.4	1.3
Chemical	2.4	3.2	3.1	2.2	2.1	4.9	3.0	2.0	2.3	1.7	2.1	1.8	2.2	2.7	1.3	1.7	1.8	2.0	1.8
Materials	2.0	2.4	2.5	2.1	2.1	2.8	3.0	2.0	2.5	2.0	3.0	1.7	3.3	2.6	1.7	1.4	2.2	2.1	1.3
Electronics and Electrical Equip.	1.5	1.9	2.1	2.2	3.1	2.3	1.9	2.8	1.9	2.8	4.1	1.9	3.3	3.2	2.1	1.5	3.3	3.0	2.3
Vehicles	2.7	2.1	3.4	2.2	3.0	3.8	2.9	3.0	2.2	2.2	5.7	1.8	2.4	2.2	2.4	1.5	5.7	3.3	2.3
Machinery	1.5	2.1	2.2	2.0	2.2	1.6	1.6	2.8	1.5	2.1	5.3	1.9	2.1	2.3	2.0	1.7	3.0	2.5	1.8
Other Manufact.	2.2	2.8	3.7	2.7	2.8	3.2	2.8	2.8	2.9	2.6	6.7	2.8	3.3	3.4	1.6	2.0	3.5	2.5	2.0
Share of Exporting Firms	(%)																		
Processed Food	0.23	0.02	0.13	0.00	0.00	0.00	0.01	0.00	0.06	2.39	0.01	0.01	0.00	—	0.81	1.48	0.00	0.03	0.19
Textiles	0.28	0.07	0.03	0.10	0.06	0.18	0.13	0.01	0.43	0.19	0.00	0.22	0.01	0.05	14.18	21.17	0.38	0.90	6.87
Apparel	1.49	0.29	7.20	0.60	0.52	0.05	0.15	0.08	0.77	0.08	1.13	0.45	0.01	0.11	78.40	44.00	0.18	3.19	6.34
Chemical	0.07	0.01	0.01	0.13	0.24	0.00	0.01	0.29	0.09	0.92	0.18	0.88	0.13	0.03	10.38	0.98	0.67	0.34	0.63
Materials	0.28	0.08	0.06	0.19	0.19	0.02	0.01	0.27	0.06	0.28	0.01	0.93	0.01	0.04	1.25	4.78	0.12	0.24	9.63
Electronics and Electrical Equip.	3.60	0.40	0.22	0.14	0.01	0.09	0.41	0.02	0.46	0.02	—	0.52	0.01	0.01	0.23	3.53	0.01	0.01	0.11
Vehicles	0.03	0.24	0.00	0.16	0.01	0.00	0.02	0.01	0.14	0.16	—	0.83	0.07	0.17	0.08	3.42		0.01	0.11
Machinery	3.36	0.23	0.16	0.26	0.13	2.04	1.84	0.02	3.62	0.19	—	0.53	0.21	0.11	0.36	1.09	0.01	0.06	0.74
Other Manufact.	0.13	0.02	0.00	0.03	0.02	0.01	0.02	0.02	0.01	0.04	—	0.02	0.01	0.00	1.58	0.34	0.00	0.06	0.26

JPN = Japan; KOR = Korea, Rep. of; PRC = China, People's Rep. of; HKG = Hong Kong, China; TAP = Taipei,China; INO = Indonesia; MAL = Malaysia; PHI = Philippines; SIN = Singapore; THA = Thailand; VIE = Viet Nam; IND = India; PAK = Pakistan; SRI = Sri Lanka; US = United States; EUR = EU25 plus European Free Trade Association; ANZ = Australia and New Zealand; LAC = Latin America and the Caribbean; ROW = rest of the world; – = not available.

Source: Author's calculations.

Table 5.6 Exports and Tariff Rates Faced by Exporters in Bangladesh

	JPN	KOR	PRC	HKG	TAP	INO	MAL	PHI	SIN	THA	VIE	IND	PAK	SRI	US	EUR	ANZ	LAC	ROW
Value of Exports ($ million)																			
Grain	—	—	—	—	—	—	—	—	—	—	—	0.1	—	—	—	0.0	—	—	0.0
Other Crops	0.1	0.1	1.8	0.0	0.1	0.5	0.3	0.1	0.2	8.5	0.3	18.4	24.0	0.2	0.4	19.5	0.7	3.5	26.1
Other Agriculture	1.2	0.1	0.2	1.0	0.3	0.0	0.5	0.0	0.2	0.2	0.0	5.1	0.0	—	0.9	0.7	0.0	0.1	1.0
Processed Food	20.2	0.1	0.7	6.9	0.2	0.0	0.3	0.0	0.9	7.0	0.2	1.0	0.0	—	83.8	148.2	0.1	1.0	9.1
Textiles	12.4	1.9	1.9	1.5	0.9	5.8	2.5	0.1	18.2	2.3	0.0	3.8	0.2	1.8	388.8	1156.6	11.5	16.0	139.2
Apparel	50.3	17.7	6.3	67.8	13.3	0.2	0.8	0.1	24.1	0.9	6.6	2.3	0.1	0.1	1751.0	1635.7	3.7	39.9	91.5
Chemical	1.3	1.4	0.1	0.2	3.0	0.0	0.1	4.4	1.5	9.5	1.9	10.0	1.2	0.5	175.3	14.5	10.9	4.0	10.0
Materials	4.0	1.7	0.5	0.9	2.4	0.3	0.1	4.4	1.2	2.4	0.0	9.2	0.0	0.1	10.5	52.8	1.4	1.3	44.9
Electronics and Electrical Equip.	2.5	0.1	0.2	0.0	0.0	0.1	0.1	0.0	0.2	0.0	—	0.2	0.0	0.0	0.2	2.6	0.0	0.0	0.1
Vehicles	0.2	0.6	0.2	0.0	0.0	0.0	0.1	0.0	0.8	0.6	—	1.3	0.0	0.7	0.4	16.6		0.0	0.4
Machinery	14.4	0.9	0.7	0.3	0.5	7.6	8.7	0.1	12.6	0.5	—	0.8	0.4	0.2	1.4	4.6	0.0	0.2	2.8
Other Manufact.	2.3	0.3	0.2	0.0	0.3	0.1	0.2	0.3	0.3	0.3	—	0.2	0.0	0.1	22.1	5.6	0.1	0.5	3.6
Tariff Rates (%)																			
Grain	—	—	—	—	—	—	—	—	—	—	—	79.7	—	—	0.0	21.5	—	—	—
Other Crops	1.3	2.0	8.0	—	—	0.7	—	3.0	0.0	5.1	3.3	18.4	10.9	4.5	3.4	2.1	—	9.3	5.5
Other Agriculture	—	5.4	7.0	0.0	10.4	0.0	3.8	—	—	7.0	—	1.0	4.4	—	0.8	0.0	—	0.0	7.5
Processed Food	3.5	11.5	16.1	—	4.1	12.6	2.4	4.1	6.9	59.9	40.2	17.7	17.1	—	0.0	0.2	1.5	21.7	9.9
Textiles	0.8	7.0	13.6	—	9.7	5.5	16.5	6.8	—	15.7	28.9	13.8	18.0	2.8	11.2	—	1.7	18.1	12.8
Apparel	—	4.1	6.9	—	5.7	4.2	18.2	6.5	—	20.5	9.7	18.1	19.4	9.1	11.7	—	10.4	19.7	16.8
Chemical	—	8.0	5.8	—	5.5	6.2	16.9	1.1	0.0	9.6	10.0	5.9	17.1	—	1.2	1.8	0.1	9.4	2.0
Materials	0.0	5.1	14.1	—	9.6	8.6	17.5	9.3	—	21.5	40.0	18.9	17.2	24.1	7.6	0.3	3.7	12.6	15.6
Electronics and Electrical Equip.	—	—	11.2	—	3.5	—	3.3	—	0.0	7.0	—	15.4	10.0	2.1	0.2	—	1.0	7.5	1.8
Vehicles	—	8.0	56.7	—	17.3	5.8	2.8	23.8	—	12.7	—	3.3	96.0	7.0	1.1	0.0	—	9.8	10.5
Machinery	—	2.4	10.3	—	4.0	2.7	—	4.9	0.0	3.7	—	19.1	14.2	11.3	0.8	0.0	1.6	9.1	2.7
Other Manufact.	—	6.2	14.9	—	4.6	8.5	9.8	6.6	0.0	15.1	—	14.1	15.8	9.3	3.8	—	1.9	15.2	3.7

JPN = Japan; KOR = Korea, Rep. of; PRC = China, People's Rep. of; HKG = Hong Kong, China; TAP = Taipei,China; INO = Indonesia; MAL = Malaysia; PHI = Philippines; SIN = Singapore; THA = Thailand; VIE = Viet Nam; IND = India; PAK = Pakistan; SRI = Sri Lanka; US = United States; EUR = EU25 plus European Free Trade Association; ANZ = Australia and New Zealand; LAC = Latin America and the Caribbean; ROW = rest of the world; – = not available.

Source: GTAP database V6.2.

5.5 SIMULATIONS

Three sets of simulations are run to explore the trade potential of Bangladesh under various policy reform measures. This first set looks at the effects of trade liberalization. It has three "subsimulations," namely, unilateral trade liberalization (*UNI*), regional free trade agreement in South Asia (*SAFTA*), and global multilateral trade liberalization (*GTL*). Under these three subsimulations, merchandise tariffs and export taxes are cut by 50% in the respective liberalizing regions.

The second set of simulations focuses on reforms to enhance national technology, in which the domestic productivity levels of Bangladesh's firms in all merchandise sectors are raised by 5% (*TECH*). The last set of simulations considers the reduction of nonpolicy barriers on Bangladesh's exports (*TF*). It assumes a broad trade-facilitation reform through which both fixed exporting costs of manufacturing sectors and variable trade costs of the country's manufacturing exports and imports are reduced by 30%.[6,7] Table 5.7 summarizes these simulations.

Table 5.8 shows the effects of these assumed policy reforms on major macroeconomic variables in Bangladesh. These are deviations from the baseline. They show that economic efficiency could be improved under all these simulations. However, the magnitude of the efficiency gains varies across different reform scenarios. Under *SAFTA*, aggregate welfare, which is measured by the household equivalent variation (EV) and reported as a share of GDP, would increase by only 0.1%. Under the *TECH* and *TF* scenarios, welfare would increase significantly, by 6.8% and 12.9%, respectively. In all these simulations, real consumption and investment would also rise, as income increases and prices of imported goods fall.

The impacts on trade are large. The expansion of Bangladesh's exports range from 11.7% under the *SAFTA* simulation to 121.3% in the *TF* simulation, indicating a huge trade potential in Bangladesh that is severely constrained by policy and structural barriers. Under the *TF* simulation, the trade-to-GDP ratio would more than double from 36.8% in the base year to 75.2% (Figure 5.5). The changes in factor prices show that trade liberalization reform in Bangladesh generally favors capital and skilled labor over unskilled labor, because the country's current tariff structure offers higher protection to the textile and apparel sectors, which use unskilled labor more intensively.

Consistent with theoretical predictions, the simulation results show that falling tariff and other trade costs would drive out the least productive firms, reducing the number of firms producing only for the domestic market. Conversely, the number of exporting firms could increase, along with the lowering of the exporting productivity threshold. Given the low share of

Table 5.7 Summary of Simulations

	Description
Set 1: Trade Liberalization	
Unilateral Trade Liberalization (UNI)	Bangladesh's import tariff rates are cut by 50%.
South Asian Free Trade Area (SAFTA)	Bilateral tariff rates and export taxes among Bangladesh, India, Pakistan, and Sri Lanka are cut by 50%.
Global Trade Liberalization (GTL)	Tariff rates and export taxes are cut by 50% in all regions.
Set 2: Technology Enhancement	
Raised Productivity Levels (TECH)	Total factor productivity of Bangladesh's firms in merchandise sectors is raised by 5%.
Set 3: Reduction of Nonpolicy Trade Barriers	
Broad Trade-facilitation Reform (TF)	Fixed costs of Bangladesh's manufacturing exports, and variable trade costs of Bangladesh's manufacturing exports and imports, are reduced by 30%.

Table 5.8 Aggregate Impacts under Various Scenarios, Bangladesh (% changes relative to baseline)

	UNI	SAFTA	GTL	TECH	TF
Equivalent Variation as % of GDP	1.7	0.1	2.1	6.8	12.9
Consumption	2.0	0.1	2.5	7.9	15.2
Investment	0.6	0.1	0.7	0.4	5.0
Exports[a]	69.7	11.7	75.9	23.8	121.3
Imports[a]	44.0	7.3	48.7	15.4	93.8
Number of Exporting Firms	73.4	15.3	77.1	27.8	202.6
Number of Nonexporting Firms	-11.7	-1.1	-13.7	7.1	-38.0
Average Manufacturing Productivity	0.4	0.1	0.7	4.0	5.8
Factor Price					
Capital	1.1	0.1	1.6	14.3	18.1
Skilled Labor	0.8	0.0	1.2	10.2	15.8
Unskilled Labor	0.3	0.1	0.6	12.6	12.3

a Measured as the sum of each firm's exports.

Note: See Table 5.7 for a summary of simulations.

Source: Model simulations.

exporting firms in total firms in Bangladesh, the increase in the number of exporsting firms is much larger than the reduction in the number of nonexporting firms. In the cases of unilateral (*UNI*) and global trade (*GTL*) liberalization, the number of exporting firms in the country is more than 70%

Figure 5.5 Trade Dependence under Various Scenarios, Bangladesh

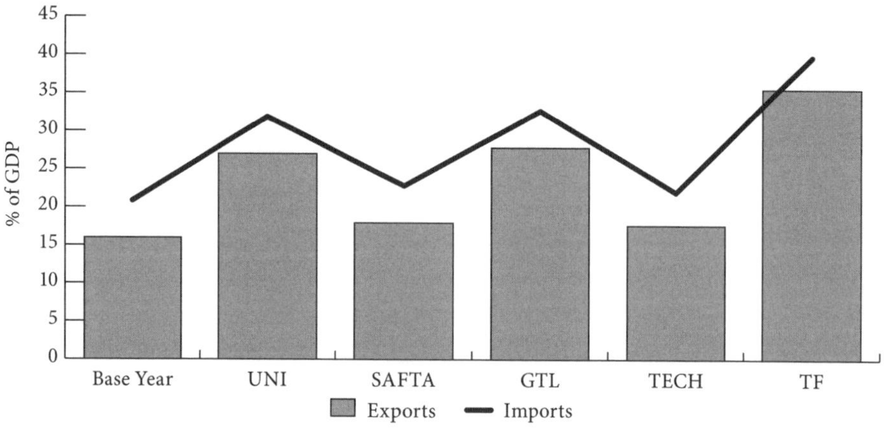

Source: Model simulations.

higher than in the baseline, while under the trade-facilitation scenario (*TF*), that number is more than 200% higher. This result demonstrates the significant role of the extensive margin in Bangladesh's trade expansion.

The simulation results also confirm that the intra-industry resource reallocation following trade liberalization increases aggregate productivity of economies that liberalize. This aggregate productivity gain comes from the exit of the least productive nonexporting firms, the entry of more productive new exporters, and the reallocation of market shares toward exporting firms (Melitz, 2003). Table 5.8 above shows that average manufacturing productivity in Bangladesh would improve modestly by less than 1% under the three trade liberalization scenarios (*UNI, SAFTA, GTL*). However, under the trade-facilitation scenario (*TF*), the intra-industry adjustment would be much more significant, and average manufacturing productivity could show a substantial rise of 5.8%.

Comparing the results from the three trade liberalization simulations, it is clear that the South Asian Free Trade Area could bring only very small benefits to Bangladesh. This is not surprising given the current limited intraregional trade flows in South Asia. Yet, because of Bangladesh's high rates of import protection, unilateral trade liberalization would promise large gains to the country. Given the high import content in Bangladesh's exports, the export sectors would benefit greatly from tariff reduction through lower costs of intermediate imports. [8] Moreover, real depreciation following unilateral trade liberalization could also boost exports. In short, Bangladesh could capture the bulk of benefits accruing from global trade liberalization through unilateral trade liberalization. Under the *GTL* scenario, enhanced market access for Bangladesh's exports is partly offset by the preference erosion in developed markets, resulting in only small additional gains obtained from the three trade liberalization scenarios.

In the domestic productivity improvement scenario (*TECH*), higher productivity lowers production costs, raising the price competitiveness of exports. As a result, Bangladesh's exports expand by 23.8%. The resulting welfare gains account for 6.8% of GDP, 1.8 percentage points more than the assumed exogenous productivity improvement and reflecting the additional benefits from expanded trade. As all firms increase their productivity levels in this scenario, a larger proportion of firms meets the productivity cut-off condition in either domestic or export markets. This leads to increased numbers of both exporting and nonexporting firms. As the new entrants of nonexporting firms are the least productive, aggregate manufacturing production increases by only 4%, or 1 percentage point lower than the exogenous productivity improvement at the firm level.

If broad trade-facilitation reform is undertaken and it leads to a 30% reduction in Bangladesh's variable trade costs and fixed exporting costs, exports would be boosted by 121.3%. This larger trade expansion effect from trade-facilitation reform reflects the higher trade costs that impede Bangladesh's exports. Under the trade-facilitation scenario (*TF)*, welfare gains reach 12.9% of GDP, much higher than those obtained from trade liberalization. This reflects the different natures of fixed and iceberg trade costs on the one hand and tariffs on the other. As the former burn up real resources, their reduction can bring direct efficiency gains. Moreover, the combined reduction in fixed exporting costs and variable trade costs induces larger growth in the extensive margin. This thereby yields stronger welfare impacts, through enhanced aggregate productivity and greater product variety enjoyed by domestic consumers.

To further investigate the export structure of Bangladesh under various policy reform scenarios, changes in exports by sector are reported in Table 5.9. Under the three trade liberalization scenarios (*UNI, SAFTA, GTL*) and the domestic productivity improvement scenario (*TECH*), the export expansion is concentrated in Bangladesh's traditional sectors of comparative advantage. In general, apparel, textiles, and processed food would experience the largest gains in exports. In the *SAFTA* and *GTL* scenarios, some sectors that are most protected in other regions, such as grain and materials, would also enjoy high export growth. Overall, the commodity structure of exports would become more concentrated under these scenarios. However, if nonpolicy trade costs are lowered by efficient trade-facilitation measures, Bangladesh's exports would effectively diversify away from textiles and apparel. Other manufacturing, processed food, chemicals, vehicles, and materials are the major winners of broad trade-facilitation reform (*TF*).

The changes in regional distribution of Bangladesh's exports under various reform scenarios indicate huge potential for Bangladesh to expand its exports to Asia. As shown in Figure 5.6, if overall trade costs are lowered, the share of exports to Asia (including Japan) in Bangladesh's total exports would nearly triple from less than 8% in the base case to 23% in the *TF* scenario. At the same time, the relative importance of its traditional export markets—the US and EU—would decline, although the value of exports to these markets would still increase by more than 60%. With reduced trade costs, the trade linkages between Bangladesh and East and Southeast Asian economies would significantly intensify. This result underlines the importance of broad trade-facilitation reform to enable Bangladesh to take full advantage of the trade and growth opportunities spilling over from dynamic regional economies.

Figure 5.6 Regional Distribution of Exports under Various Scenarios, Bangladesh

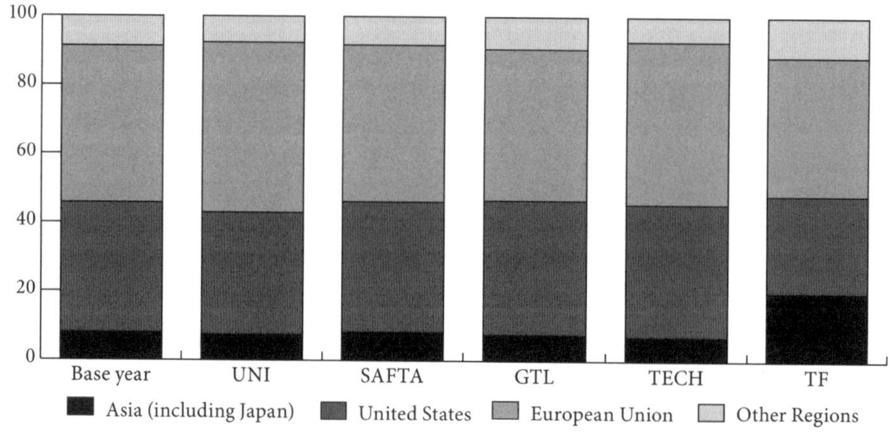

Source: Model simulations.

5.6 CONCLUSIONS

The engine of growth in least-developed countries will largely lie in the realization of their potential for expanding their trade with the rest of the world. This trade potential is often constrained by restrictive trade policies, geographic location, high transportation and operating costs, and poor institutions. Using a global CGE model with heterogeneous firms, this chapter has investigated various scenarios of unlocking the trade potential of Bangladesh through trade liberalization, domestic technology promotion, and

Table 5.9 Impacts on Sectoral Exports[a] under Various Scenarios, Bangladesh (% changes relative to baseline)

	UNI	SAFTA	GTL	TECH	TF
Sector					
Grains	22	205	164	-10	19
Other Crops	16	16	18	-12	3
Other Agriculture	4	2	0	-14	-24
Processed Food	28	4	33	4	442
Textiles	62	9	68	8	122
Apparel	100	16	107	51	102
Chemicals	19	5	21	-3	327
Materials[b]	15	10	48	-12	312
Electronics and Electrical Equipment	7	4	20	-27	217
Vehicles	8	4	7	-25	313
Machinery	8	4	8	-25	234
Other Manufacturing	19	3	30	-5	744

a Measured as the sum of each firm's exports. b Building materials, mineral products, metals and metal products.

Note: See Table 5.7 for a summary of simulations.

Source: Model simulations.

comprehensive trade-facilitation reform. The simulation results demonstrate that, given its current high tariff rates, Bangladesh can achieve important gains in terms of exports and welfare from unilateral trade liberalization. However, to fully tap its trade potential, the country needs to address some important supply-side constraints through effective and comprehensive trade-facilitation reform. Such reform would significantly boost export competitiveness, diversify the country's export structure, and bring much larger welfare gains than would trade liberalization alone.

Generalizing to developing countries beyond Bangladesh, the results suggest that the policy focus should not be confined to traditional tariff and nontariff barriers. Infrastructure, ports and customs efficiency, simplification and coherence of rules, and the investment climate are, in most developing countries, at least equally important to trade development. Policy makers should take a comprehensive and ambitious approach to dismantling all barriers to trade. However, the reduction in broad trade costs does not come without its own costs. Given the resource constraints faced by least-developed countries, it is important to identify priority areas for action. To better inform the policy-making process, future research should be undertaken to assess the contribution of the various components to broad trade costs, identify the binding constraints to trade development, and conduct cost-benefit analysis in these least-developed countries.

ENDNOTES

1   Although most of the empirical studies find a positive relationship between trade and economic growth, the methodologies applied and the causality revealed by these studies are controversial. See, for example, Dollar (1992), Sachs and Warner (1995), Edwards (1998), Frankel and Romer (1999), and Dollar and Kraay (2003) for evidence that trade promotes growth; and Rodriguez and Rodrik (2001) for a criticism of such studies.

2   Between 1995 and 2000, rules of origin for garment imports under the EU Generalized System of Preferences scheme were changed often, and resulted in volatile utilization rates for Bangladesh garment exporters (UNCTAD, 2001). In the case of the "Everything but Arms" initiative, Bangladesh's woven garments, which rely heavily on imported inputs, can hardly meet the requirement of 51% domestic and regional value-added content (Mlachila and Yang, 2004).

3   See, for example, Kehoe and Ruhl (2003); Hummels and Klenow (2005); and Eaton, Kortum, and Kramarz (2004).

4   Intensive margin refers to the expansion of existing exported products.

5   See Zhai (2007) for details of the model's structure.

6   The trade facilitation discussed here is more expansive than that defined by WTO, which refers to "the simplification and harmonization of international trade procedures, including the activities, practices and formalities involved in collecting, presenting, communicating and processing data required for the movement of goods in international trade." But it is similar in scope to that of the International Chamber of Commerce (ICC), which "focuses on improvements in the efficiency of the processes associated with trading in goods across national borders." This broadly defined trade facilitation "requires the adoption of a comprehensive and integrated approach to simplifying and reducing the cost of international trade transactions, and ensuring that all relevant activities take place in an efficient, transparent, and predictable manner, based on internationally accepted norms, standards and best practices." See "ICC recommendations for a WTO agreement on trade facilitation," a policy statement of the ICC's commission on Customs and Trade Regulation (available: http://www.iccwbo.org/policy/customs/id557/index.html).

7   In this simulation, the postreform variable trade cost is equal to $1+(\tau_{ij}-1)/2$.

8   Bangladesh's readymade garments sector is allowed duty-free import of raw materials under bonded warehouse system and duty drawback facilities. Without explicitly modeling the duty drawback schemes in Bangladesh, the model used here may overestimate the reductions in input costs resulting from the removal of tariffs on intermediate imports in the garments sector.

REFERENCES

Ahmed, Sadiq and Zaidi Sattar. 2004. *Trade Liberalization, Growth and Poverty Reduction: The Case of Bangladesh.* Washington, DC: World Bank.

Anderson, James E. and Eric van Wincoop. 2004. "Trade Costs." *Journal of Economic Literature* 42:691-751.

Armington, Paul S. 1969. "A Theory of Demand for Products Distinguished by Place of Production." *IMF Staff Papers* 16(1):159-78.

Bernard, Andrew, Jonathan Eaton, J. Bradford Jensen, and Samuel Kortum. 2003. "Plants and Productivity in International Trade." *American Economic Review* 93(4):1268-90.

De, Prabir. 2006. "Empirical Estimates of Trade Costs for Asia." Paper presented at LAEBA 2006 Third Annual Conference on Regional Integration and Regional Cooperation in Asia and Latin America: The Role of Regional Infrastructure, Seoul, 16–17 November.

Dollar, David. 1992. "Outward-oriented developing countries really grow more rapidly: Evidence from 95 LDCs 1876–1985." *Economic Development and Culture Change* 40(3):523-44.

Dollar, David and Aart Kraay. 2003. "Institutions, Trade, and Growth: Revisiting the Evidence." World Bank Policy Research Working Paper 3004, Washington, DC.

Eaton, Jonathan, Samuel Kortum, and Francis Kramarz. 2004. "Dissecting Trade: Firms, Industries, and Export Destinations." *American Economic Review* 94(2):150-4. May.

Edwards, Sebastian. 1998. "Openness, Productivity and Growth: What Do We Really Know?" *Economic Journal* 108(447):383-98, March.

Frankel, Jeffrey and David Romer. 1999. "Does Trade Cause Growth?" *American Economic Review* 89(3):379-99.

Hertel, Thomas W. (ed.). 1997. *Global Trade Analysis: Modeling and Applications.* New York, NY: Cambridge University Press.

Hummels, David and Peter J. Klenow. 2005. "The Variety and Quality of a Nation's Exports." *American Economic Review* 95(3):704-23.

International Monetary Fund. 2005. "Bangladesh: Statistical Appendix." *IMF Country Report* 05/243, July.

Kehoe, Timothy J. 2005. "An Evaluation of the Performance of Applied General Equilibrium Models on the Impact of NAFTA." In *Frontiers in Applied General Equilibrium Modeling: In Honor of Herbert Scarf.* Edited by T.J. Kehoe, T.N. Srinivasan, and J. Whalley, pp. 341-77. Cambridge, UK: Cambridge University Press.

Kehoe, Timothy J. and Kim J. Ruhl. 2003. "How Important Is the New Goods Margin in International Trade?" *Staff Report* 324, Federal Reserve Bank of Minneapolis.

Krugman, Paul. 1979. "Increasing Returns, Monopolistic Competition and International Trade." *Journal of International Economics* 9(4):469-79.

Levchenko, Andrei A. 2004. "Institutional Quality and International Trade." *Review of Economic Studies*, 74(3):791-819.

Limão, Nuno and Anthony J. Venables. 2001. "Infrastructure, Geographical Disadvantage, Transport Costs, and Trade." *World Bank Economic Review* 15(3):451-79.

Melitz, Marc J. 2003. "The Impact of Trade on Intra-Industry Reallocations and Aggregate Industry Productivity." *Econometrica* 71(6):1695-1725.

Mlachila, Montfort, and Yongzheng Yang. 2004. "The End of Textiles Quotas: A Case Study of the Impact on Bangladesh." *IMF Working Paper* 04/108, Washington, DC.

Rodriguez, Francisco and Dani Rodrik. 2001. "Trade Policy and Economic Growth: A Skeptic's Guide to the Cross-national Evidence." In B. Bernanke and K.S. Rogoff (eds.), *NBER Macroeconomics Annual 2000*, 261-324. Cambridge, MA: MIT Press.

Sachs, Jeffrey D. and Andrew M. Warner. 1995. "Economic Reform and the Process of Global Integration." *Brookings Papers on Economic Activity* 1:1-118.

Shoven John B. and John Whalley. 1992. *Applying General Equilibrium*. Cambridge, UK: Cambridge University Press.

UNCTAD. 2001. "Duty and Quota Free Market Access for LDCs: An Analysis of Quad Initiatives." UNCTAD and Commonwealth Secretariat, Geneva.

van der Mensbrugghe, Dominique. 2005. "LINKAGE Technical Reference Document." Development Prospects Group, World Bank. Processed.

World Bank. 2004. *Trade Policies in South Asia: An Overview*. Report 29949.

Yeaple, Stephen Ross. 2005. "A Simple Model of Firm Heterogeneity, International Trade, and Wages." *Journal of International Economics* 65(1):1-20.

Zhai, Fan. 2007. "Armington Meets Melitz: : Introducing Firm Heterogeneity in a Global CGE Model of Trade." Paper presented in the Tenth Annual Conference on Global Economic Analysis, 7–10 June, Purdue University.

Commentary on Chapter 5

Richard Pomfret

Asian economic development over the last quarter century has been driven by outward-oriented growth as the People's Republic of China and then Viet Nam and India followed earlier generations of newly industrialized economies. Bangladesh looked as though it might do this when reforms were introduced in the early 1990s, but it did not, in fact, turn into a "Bengal tiger."

Fan Zhai establishes first of all that, despite trade liberalization and an increase in the trade-to-GDP ratio from 18% in 1990 to 38% in 2005, producers in Bangladesh remain protected from foreign competition. Many quantitative restrictions continued to exist until January 2005, when the number was reduced to three (on eggs, poultry, and salt). More important are the large number of para-tariffs (regulatory or supplementary taxes for which domestic products are exempt or are taxed at a lower rate than imports), which, when added to formal tariffs, amount to an average nominal rate of protection of 26.5%, which is higher than in other South Asian countries and much higher than in the NIEs.

The export growth that has occurred in Bangladesh is heavily concentrated in textiles and clothing, and there is a suspicion that the country has only been competitive when country-specific quotas have hampered the country's competitors. With the ending of the Multifibre Arrangement at end-2004 and termination of temporary controls by end-2008, Bangladesh will face stiffer competition in the European Union and United States markets.

The main reasons given by Fan Zhai for the economy's disappointing performance and future vulnerability are domestic supply constraints, of which weak governance is a major one. Tables 5.1 and 5.2 in the chapter provide support for this argument, although it is more nuanced than the accompanying text implies. Bangladesh receives an average ranking for its business environment and starting a business is not especially slow, but the cost of starting a business is relatively high. Much worse is the situation with respect to registering property and enforcing contracts. According to the World Bank's *Doing Business* database, it takes on average 4 years to enforce a contract (compared with an East Asian average of 16 months and an OECD average of under a year). The evidence on poor infrastructure in Table 5.3 shows a consistently poor picture of supply failure and lengthy customs delays.

The main and most original contribution of this chapter is the use of a computable general equilibrium (CGE) model, based on the World Bank's

Linkage model and incorporating firm heterogeneity in productivity and fixed costs of exporting. Three sets of simulations are run to explore the country's trade potential. The first involves a 50% tariff cut unilaterally by Bangladesh or plurilaterally among the major South Asian Free Trade Area (SAFTA) countries or globally. The striking conclusion is that almost all the benefits to Bangladesh from global trade liberalization result from reductions in its own tariffs (Table 5.8), and that trade liberalization within SAFTA yields far smaller gains than either of the other two options (a 0.1% increase in equivalent variation relative to the baseline, while unilateral tariff cuts increase equivalent variation by 1.7% and multilateral cuts by 2.1%). This is strong confirmation of what we would expect from trade theory: for a country with relatively high trade barriers, many of the gains from trade liberalization arise from reductions in own-country tariffs. The conclusion also suggests that regionalism has little to offer, at least if it is limited to SAFTA.

The two other scenarios concern technological enhancement (a 5% increase in total factor productivity in Bangladesh's tradables sector) and trade facilitation (a 30% reduction in trade costs for the manufacturing sector). Both of these scenarios yield larger welfare gains than any of the three tariff-reduction scenarios. These are powerful results that support the chapter's conclusion that "the policy focus should not be confined to traditional tariff and nontariff barriers." However, they do raise questions about how to realize these gains.

Increasing total factor productivity has been recognized as the key to economic growth, at least since the revival of neoclassical growth theory in the 1960s and 1970s. Trade facilitation is also a desirable goal whose effective implementation is an uncertain process. Trade facilitation has been brought into the Doha Round and is part of many regional agreements, but remains difficult to define precisely and even more difficult to implement. At the Asia-Pacific Economic Cooperation (APEC) Shanghai summit in 2001, member countries agreed on the desirability of trade facilitation and set a target of a 5% reduction in trade costs by 2006, but the target proved difficult to achieve in a verifiable manner. This in turn raises the question of whether a 30% cut in trade costs is a plausible scenario for Bangladesh. Clearly with a smaller reduction, the third scenario would give less dramatic results from trade facilitation.

In sum, this chapter provides a counterweight to the frequent and upbeat analyses of Asian success stories. Bangladesh has lagged behind, despite a trade liberalization effort almost contemporaneous with the crucial Indian reforms of the early 1990s. Fan Zhai shows that this is associated both with failures to truly liberalize and with high trade and behind-the-border costs. The CGE results confirm that the remedies for unlocking the country's trade potential are domestic—including reducing trade barriers and trade costs—rather than concerning obstacles to entering other countries' markets.

6

Economic Growth, Technological Change, and the Patterns of Food and Agricultural Trade in Asia

Thomas W. Hertel, Carlos E. Ludena, and Alla A. Golub

6.1 MOTIVATION AND OVERVIEW

As growth in Asia continues to outpace that in the rest of the world, attention has once again focused on primary commodity markets. Rapidly growing demand, coupled with relatively inelastic supply, have been boosting prices for agricultural, energy, and mineral products. This chapter projects potential outcomes in this footrace between supply and demand for the year 2025, with a particular emphasis on food markets. It begins with an in-depth analysis of the fundamental drivers of change, including per capita consumer demand, population growth, accumulation of capital and labor, endowments of land by agro-ecological zone, as well as technological change. The last is found to be the critical factor in determining whether or not food prices will reverse their long-run downward trend, as well as determining the likely patterns of trade and structural change. Yet this aspect of economic growth is still not well understood.

Consequently, the chapter focuses attention on the measurement and forecasting of worldwide technological progress in agriculture. It emphasizes total factor productivity (TFP) growth, which behaves very differently from the widely used partial factor productivity measures of output per hectare and output per head of livestock. The estimates used in this chapter are based on the work of Ludena et al. (2007). Historical rates of TFP growth are shown to vary widely across countries and across subsectors within agriculture (e.g., crops vs. livestock). TFP growth is decomposed into one component that comes from "catching up" with the current technology frontier, and one that comes from an outward movement in the frontier. In projecting future

TFP growth, these components are separately modeled, which makes a big difference for Asia, where much of the past TFP growth has been fueled by catching up. This will not continue indefinitely, and it accounts for the eventual slowing of TFP growth in agriculture in the People's Republic of China (PRC), in particular.

The relative rates of TFP growth between agriculture, manufacturing, and services also play an important role in projections of structural change. Here, we draw heavily on the work of Kets and Lejour (2003) who examine sector growth rates in the Organisation for Economic Co-operation and Development (OECD) over the past two decades. They find that TFP has grown fastest in agriculture, followed by manufacturing, and then services. However, they also find a great deal of variation within the services sector, with transportation and communications growing exceptionally fast; TFP in nontraded services grows much more slowly. These relative rates of TFP growth across sectors are taken into account in our projections to 2025. Building on aggregate growth projections from the World Bank, we divide regions of the world into five overall TFP growth rates, giving rise to a set of real gross domestic product (GDP) forecasts that are broadly in line with World Bank projections, but that differ in particular cases due to the fact that we explicitly model the international movement of capital.

Discussion of the baseline results focuses on structural change in the global economy, with a particular emphasis on the region of developing Asia. Patterns of consumption and production, as well as changes in self-sufficiency ratios and net trade positions, are examined. We also consider the impact of such growth and structural change on factor markets, including the likely sources of sector employment for factors of production, in addition to factor returns.

6.2 DRIVERS OF CHANGE: INCOME AND POPULATION

There is a long tradition of forecasting demand for commodities based on per capita income and population. At constant per capita income, and unchanging prices, uniform population growth worldwide simply translates into uniform growth in the demand for all goods and services. However, population growth tends to be higher in countries with lower per capita income, and, since poorer households tend to spend a higher portion of their income on food, population growth tends to boost the relative importance of food consumption worldwide. Growth in per capita income has the opposite effect: as households become richer, their expenditure share on food tends to fall. In addition, the composition of food expenditures shifts from staple products, aimed at fulfilling caloric requirements, to animal protein, edible oils, fruits, and vegetables as consumer incomes rise above the poverty line.

Figure 6.1 Spending Patterns across the Income Spectrum in ASEAN

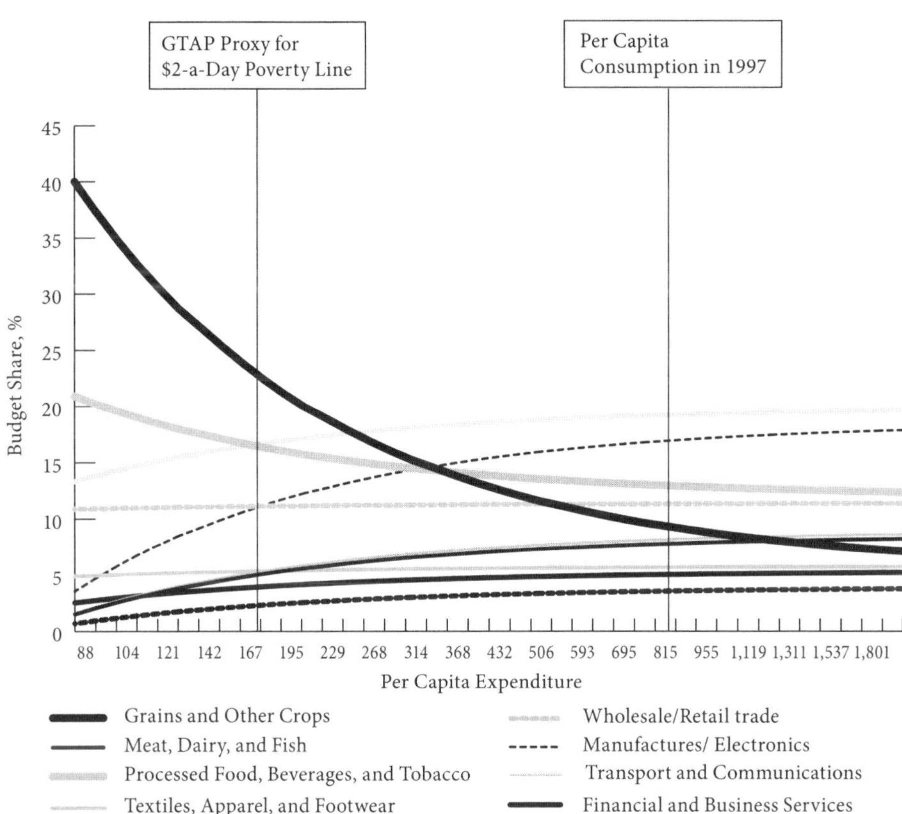

Source: Authors' calculations.

These points are illustrated in Figure 6.1, which shows the predicted expenditure shares on an exhaustive grouping of commodities and services for the Association of Southeast Asian Nations (ASEAN) region as a whole, in 1997. The horizontal axis shows per capita incomes in US dollars. (These need to be multiplied by a factor of nearly four to get to purchasing power parity [PPP] international dollars.) The first vertical line in this figure shows the $2-a-day (PPP basis) poverty line. At this per capita income level, the largest expenditure item is staple grains; followed by processed food, beverages, and tobacco; and housing. Expenditure on meat, dairy, and fish is much lower. The total food expenditure share at this level of income is estimated to be about 45%. Clearly, population growth in this income class translates into a strong increase in food demand, relative to other goods and services.

The second vertical line in the figure shows the expenditure shares for individuals at the 1997 average income level in the ASEAN region. At this point, staple grains expenditures have fallen below many other items in the budget, and the total expenditure share on food is now well under one third of the total household budget, and this is continuing to fall at the margin. Also at this point, housing, health, and education services, and manufactured items dominate the budget. So, overall income growth (i.e., rising per capita income) in ASEAN fuels a *relative* decline in the demand for food.

The predicted budget shares in Figure 6.1 above are based on an econometrically estimated *demand system*. The system approach is much preferable to the estimation of individual demand equations—particularly in an economywide projections approach such as that used in this paper. In the single equation approach, there is no guarantee that households will remain on their budget constraint—expenditures for all goods could increase without a corresponding rise in income. This is not possible in the systemwide approach. In addition, the system approach also takes account of the full range of substitution possibilities among goods and services.

The estimates used in this paper are based on the work of Reimer and Hertel (2004). Those authors estimate the demand system using the GTAP version 5.0 global database.[1] This has the great advantage of making the estimates directly usable in the projections model used in this paper. Those authors also show that the behavior of demand in their estimated model follows closely that in a model estimated on the basis of the widely used International Comparisons Project data. However, mapping the latter to the GTAP database is highly problematic. So they prefer to use the estimates obtained directly from the GTAP database.

With a complete demand system in hand, we are in a position to project the pattern of national consumer demand in 2025. The rate of demand growth in the model regions over the projections period (at constant prices) is reported in the first two sets of rows in Table 6.1 (Dmd Only).[2] This demand-side growth has been decomposed into the contribution stemming from population growth, at constant per capita income,[3] and that from both population growth and per capita income growth. When population grows but per capita income does not (i.e., income growth just keeps pace with population), per capita demand for each product category is unchanged, and aggregate demand grows at the rate of population growth in each region. This growth is highest in Sub-Saharan Africa (SSA) and Middle East and North Africa (MENA) regions and lowest in Economies in Transition (EIT) of Eastern Europe and the former Soviet Union, and Western European Union (WEU).

When per capita income is also permitted to grow, the cumulative growth in demand by sector is much larger for all of the aggregate consumption

Table 6.1 Impact of Population and Income Growth on Consumer Demand: Cumulative Growth, 1997–2025 (%)

Sector			Australia-New Zealand	China, People's Rep. of	High-Income Asia	ASEAN	South Asia	North America	Latin America	Western European Union	Economies in Transition	Middle East and North Africa	Sub-Saharan Africa
Crops	Dmd Only	Pop	23	20	3	40	46	23	41	-1	-3	59	79
		Pop&inc	88	515	19	117	278	74	161	52	128	157	154
	DmdSupply		21	192	25	68	122	17	58	31	93	138	106
Meat, Dairy, Fish	Dmd Only	Pop	23	20	3	40	46	23	41	-1	-3	59	79
		Pop&inc	130	3165	97	241	514	151	198	89	247	168	256
	DmdSupply		1	404	0	2	111	87	39	9	142	88	22
Other Food, Beverages, and Tobacco	Dmd Only	Pop	23	20	3	40	46	23	41	-1	-3	59	79
		Pop&inc	115	883	84	172	124	99	143	73	170	164	192
	DmdSupply		64	434	62	103	96	74	67	59	142	185	138
Textiles and Apparel	Dmd Only	Pop	23	20	3	40	46	23	41	-1	-3	59	79
		Pop&inc	250	2040	198	307	464	223	221	175	256	274	318
	DmdSupply		135	1263	159	223	473	125	120	110	242	229	225
Utilities/ Household Services	Dmd Only	Pop	23	20	3	40	46	23	41	-1	-3	59	79
		Pop&inc	103	1611	67	159	323	89	139	79	149	150	170
	DmdSupply		126	855	103	202	538	93	103	88	126	152	204
Wholesale and Retail Trade	Dmd Only	Pop	23	20	3	40	46	23	41	-1	-3	59	79
		Pop&inc	128	1633	81	157	272	97	150	86	175	154	159
	DmdSupply		126	778	110	296	495	90	152	91	150	215	216
Manufacturing	Dmd Only	Pop	23	20	3	40	46	23	41	-1	-3	59	79
		Pop&inc	191	2226	133	275	481	169	189	138	205	230	270
	DmdSupply		126	1329	134	216	401	104	110	93	200	203	206
Transport and Communications	Dmd Only	Pop	23	20	3	40	46	23	41	-1	-3	59	79
		Pop&inc	162	2055	118	221	475	149	176	115	243	199	235
	DmdSupply		53	816	104	112	274	56	48	20	158	117	127
Financial Services	Dmd Only	Pop	23	20	3	40	46	23	41	-1	-3	59	79
		Pop&inc	131	2756	82	208	343	95	171	87	215	181	173
	DmdSupply		145	1380	122	311	619	113	196	111	224	263	254
Housing, Education, and Health	Dmd Only	Pop	23	20	3	40	46	23	41	-1	-3	59	79
		Pop&inc	132	1974	77	200	266	97	175	90	215	188	162
	DmdSupply		133	894	115	277	598	98	152	96	168	256	208

Notes: Population only involves fixing per capita income as well. In the "demand only" scenarios, prices are fixed exogenously and endowments are in perfect supply.
See Appendix Table A6.1 for a full listing of countries in each region.

Source: Authors' simulations.

categories, but particularly so for those with higher income elasticities of demand. Meat, dairy, fish products; manufactured goods; and most of the services categories all show very strong growth under this demand-side scenario. In contrast, the staple grains/crops category shows the lowest cumulative growth rates over this 28-year period.

The final row (DmdSupply) in Table 6.1 shows the cumulative growth in consumption, by demand category, when supply-side constraints are brought to bear. In this case, prices adjust to clear the factor and commodity markets, and this tends to reduce the demand growth in many cases. This is most striking in the case of the PRC, where supply-side constraints result in significantly lower demand growth than what would be predicted from the demand side alone. More discussion of this case will be provided below, once we have discussed the supply-side determinants in our projections scenario.

6.3 DRIVERS OF CHANGE: ENDOWMENTS

Of course it is unrealistic to assume that prices will not change, and changing prices will also affect the pattern of demand (as noted in Table 6.1), as well as patterns of trade and production. So we must bring in the supply side of the picture to permit us to endogenously determine these important variables. This involves projecting changes in labor supply, both for skilled and unskilled workers. (Investment and hence capital stock are determined endogenously in the model, as discussed below.) The cumulative growth rates in skilled and unskilled labor supplies have been obtained from the GTAP v.5 baseline (Walmsley et al., 2000) and are reported in the first two columns of Table 6.2. Note that there is substantial variation within regions, as well as internationally. Cumulative growth in the unskilled workforce over this period ranges from -2% in EIT to nearly 100% in Sub-Saharan Africa. Projected growth in the skilled labor force is particularly strong in the PRC, ASEAN, and South Asia, as well as Latin America.

In addition to the labor force, it is important to think about land and natural resource endowments as well. We assume that these factors are in fixed aggregate supply. For example, barring a substantial rise in the sea level in the next two decades, it seems reasonable to assume that the total stock of land is in fixed supply. However, the quality of land varies widely across countries as well as within countries, and this will constrain the kinds of activities that can be undertaken on the land. For this reason, we incorporate the recently developed GTAP land use database into our analysis (Lee et al., 2005). This database builds on the pioneering work of the Food and Agriculture Organization of the United Nations (FAO) and the International Institute for Applied Systems Analysis (IIASA) in which they create the concept of agro-

Table 6.2 Cumulative Growth Rates in Endowments and GDP, by Region, 1997–2025 (%)

Region	Unskilled Labor	Skilled Labor	Productivity (growth rate per year)	Endogenous Variables Capital	GDP	World Bank Capital	World Bank GDP
	1	2	3	4	5	6	7
Australia-New Zealand	55	26	1	250	148	213	145
China, People's Rep. of	26	173	5	553	607	958	629
High-Income Asia	16	26	1.5	51	64	130	103
ASEAN	68	260	2	534	275	263	215
South Asia	66	222	3.5	731	413	368	326
North America	49	28	1	239	132	117	163
Latin America	43	206	1	286	172	197	114
Western European Union	26	10	1	114	82	121	100
Economies in Transition	-2	13	3	96	152	151	151
Middle East and North Africa	69	178	1	126	143	141	148
Sub-Saharan Africa	96	146	1	376	225	202	176

Sources: For skilled and unskilled labor growth the source is Walmsley et al. (2000); productivity projections are discussed in the text. Capital stocks and GDP are endogenously determined. World Bank data are obtained from the World Bank baseline.

ecological zones (AEZs). These are homogeneous units of land that exhibit similar growing conditions as determined by temperature, precipitation, soil, and topography. When combined with a model of crop-growing requirements, we can predict the length of growing period for each parcel of land, and the AEZs are grouped according to six 60-day intervals.

Once we overlay a climate map and distinguish boreal, temperate, and tropical climates we obtain a total of 18 AEZs. A critical part of using these AEZs for projections purposes hinges on knowing what activities can be undertaken on each AEZ, and the relative productivity of the different land types in each crop, livestock, or forestry enterprise. This is where most of the work has been required in building the GTAP-AEZ database. The model that we will use for projections purposes replaces the single set of market-clearing conditions for land (standard GTAP model) with six different sets of market-clearing conditions—one for each AEZ/growing period (we abstract from climatic differences here). The participation of each activity in these different land markets will be dictated by the GTAP-AEZ database. This information will also shape the ability of agriculture and forestry to respond to the changing composition of demands as the global economy grows to the year 2025.

For longer-run simulations, it is possible to use climate change forecasts to revise the global distribution of AEZs. Thus, for example, with global warming, the temperate zone would move northward in America, Asia, and Europe, as growing periods become longer. In this way, changes in the natural endowments of an economy over time can be reflected in the projections.

6.4 DRIVERS OF CHANGE: TECHNOLOGICAL PROGRESS

As we will see below, the most important piece of our projections will relate to the rate of technological progress on a sector, region, and global basis. Unlike the labor force and land endowments, technological progress is not directly observable. So understanding how it has evolved in the past—a key requisite for making projections into the future—is itself a challenging task. Furthermore, there are many competing definitions of technological progress, and each of these has quite different implications for projections. In keeping with the emphasis on structural change in food, most of the attention will be devoted to agriculture. However, competition for finite endowments between agriculture and nonagriculture will be driven in part by relative rates of TFP growth. In addition, overall TFP growth will drive economic growth, capital accumulation, and national income, therefore stimulating demand as well, so we will also discuss TFP growth in manufacturing and services in our projections.

6.4.1 Historical Analysis of Agricultural Productivity Growth

Productivity measurement in agriculture has captured the interest of economists for a long time. Most of the studies on productivity growth in agriculture have focused on sectorwide productivity measurement, with less attention to the estimation of subsector productivity. The latter has usually been assessed using partial factor productivity measures such as "output per head of livestock" and "output per hectare of land," which are an imperfect measure of productivity where factor substitution can lead to a misleading picture of performance (Capalbo and Antle, 1988).

A more accurate measure of productivity growth must account for all relevant inputs, hence the name: *total* factor productivity (TFP). However, TFP measurement requires a complete allocation of inputs to specific agricultural subsectors. The most important contribution, from the standpoint of this paper, is that of Nin et al. (2003) who propose a directional Malmquist index that finesses unobserved input allocations across agricultural subsectors. They use this methodology to generate a multifactor productivity measure for crops and livestock sectors. This technique forms the basis for the analysis presented in Ludena et al. (2007) from which we draw our projections in this paper. Ludena et al. (2007) decompose productivity growth into two components: technical change, or movement in the technology frontier for a given subsector, and catching up, which represents improvements in productivity that serve to bring the country in question closer to the existing, global frontier (Färe et al., 1994). Their forecasts distinguish between these two elements of technical progress, and this is reflected in their approach to forecasting future technology.

The historical and projected TFP growth rates by subsector and by region estimated by Ludena et al. (2007) are reported in Table 6.3 for eight broad regions of the world. The three agricultural subsectors for which directional TFP measures are available are crops, ruminants, and nonruminants, and for each of these Table 6.3 reports the average change in TFP, as well as the change in efficiency (EFF = catching up) and technical change (TCH = outward movement in the technology frontier) derived from the directional Malmquist index, both for the 36-year historical period and for the 28-year projections period 1997–2025.[4]

The results from Ludena et al. (2007) suggest that global agricultural TFP grew over the 1961–1996 period at an annual rate of 0.97% (top right-hand corner in Table 6.3). TFP growth may be decomposed into that portion stemming from an outward shift in the production possibilities frontier and that from the average degree of catching up of individual regions to this dynamic frontier. From the entries in the top right-hand corner of Table 6.3, it is clear that the frontier in agriculture advanced more rapidly (1.24% a year) than individual regions' average TFP, thereby leading to negative technical efficiency growth (-0.26% a year). World average TFP growth has been increasing from the 1970s to the 1990s, due to accelerating productivity growth in those developing regions where substantial economic reforms have taken place since 1980: PRC, Eastern Europe and the former Soviet Union, Sub-Saharan Africa, and Latin America. (See Ludena et al., 2006 for a detailed decade-by-decade discussion.)

At the subsector level, we find that global nonruminant productivity growth (2.24% a year) far outstripped that in the other subsectors. This high rate of TFP growth has been fueled by a rapidly advancing frontier, with technological change estimated to be 3.55% a year over this 40-year period. As a consequence, virtually all regions have fallen further away from the frontier (showing negative technical efficiency growth rates averaging -1.25% a year) over this period.

In the case of ruminants, the same general pattern as with nonruminant livestock productivity growth exists, although growth in the frontier has been much slower, and the industrialized countries have, as a group, been marginally increasing their technical efficiency, while other regions have been falling back from the frontier. Overall TFP growth in ruminants has been about 0.64% per year. For crops, TFP growth has been about 0.72% per year,

Table 6.3 Historical and Projected Average Total Factor Productivity Growth Rates by Region and Sector (%)

Regions/ Sectors	Period	Crops			Ruminants			Nonruminants			Weighted Average		
		TFP	EFF	TCH	TFP	EFF	TCH	TFP	EFF	TCH	TFP	EFF	TCH
World	1961–1996	0.72	-0.06	0.78	0.64	-0.03	0.66	2.24	-1.25	3.55	0.97	-0.26	1.24
	1997–2025	1.02	0.33	0.69	1.22	0.58	0.64	3.14	0.89	2.21	1.43	0.47	0.96
China, People's Rep. of	1961–1996	0.88	0.00	0.88	3.17	2.09	1.06	3.69	-2.11	5.92	1.89	-0.48	2.41
	1997–2025	1.41	0.71	0.70	3.42	2.58	0.82	6.47	2.75	3.62	3.07	1.46	1.59
East & South-east Asia	1961–1996	-0.07	-0.51	0.45	-0.36	-1.09	0.74	1.38	-1.68	3.13	0.12	-0.70	0.83
	1997–2025	-0.39	-0.74	0.35	-0.90	-1.50	0.62	3.23	0.75	2.45	0.09	-0.56	0.66
South Asia	1961–1996	0.13	-0.28	0.41	0.35	-0.14	0.49	2.06	-0.87	2.97	0.24	-0.27	0.51
	1997–2025	0.95	0.58	0.37	1.40	0.95	0.44	3.13	0.89	2.21	1.12	0.67	0.44
Economies in Transition	1961–1996	1.00	-0.33	1.35	0.28	-0.12	0.40	0.97	-0.88	1.90	0.79	-0.35	1.15
	1997–2025	1.75	0.65	1.08	0.51	-0.05	0.56	2.41	0.75	1.62	1.48	0.46	1.01
Middle East & North Africa	1961–1996	-0.02	-0.24	0.22	0.02	-0.51	0.54	0.73	-0.11	0.85	0.06	-0.29	0.35
	1997–2025	0.38	0.18	0.20	-0.29	-0.78	0.50	-0.22	-1.08	0.89	0.19	-0.14	0.33
Sub-Saharan Africa	1961–1996	0.06	-0.15	0.21	0.33	-0.10	0.43	0.51	-0.32	0.84	0.14	-0.15	0.29
	1997–2025	0.99	0.74	0.25	0.58	0.23	0.35	0.03	-0.62	0.66	0.85	0.56	0.29
Latin America & Caribbean	1961–1996	0.62	-0.46	1.08	0.09	-0.86	0.96	1.93	-1.15	3.13	0.67	-0.66	1.35
	1997–2025	0.83	-0.28	1.12	1.35	0.58	0.76	4.66	2.08	2.51	1.52	0.28	1.23
Industrialized Countries	1961–1996	1.53	0.56	0.96	0.70	0.04	0.66	1.26	-0.45	1.72	1.22	0.19	1.03
	1997–2025	1.21	0.31	0.89	0.39	-0.28	0.67	0.75	-0.69	1.46	0.87	-0.07	0.94

Notes: EFF relates to catching up; TCH to the outward movement in the technology frontier. See Appendix Table A6.2 for a detailed list of countries in each region. Productivity growth rates for agriculture as a whole are estimated 2001 output-weighted shares of each subsector in agriculture in each period.

Source: Ludena et al. (2007).

with a somewhat more rapid growth in the frontier than for ruminants. Once again, all of the developing country regions have been falling away from the frontier, with the rate of catch-up in industrialized countries offsetting this so that the world average efficiency growth is almost zero.

At the regional level, Ludena et al. (2007) find that the TFP performance of agriculture in the PRC has been strengthening since the late 1970s, when reforms were first implemented. This improvement is particularly striking in the case of livestock production, where productivity growth in the 1980s and 1990s was extraordinarily high. In the case of ruminant production, most of this TFP growth is due to catching up with the technological frontier. On the other hand, growth in nonruminant productivity in the PRC appears to have been driven by outward movement in the technological possibilities facing this sector. For East and Southeast Asia, which comprises the six largest countries in ASEAN (see Appendix Table A6.1) as well as the Republic of Korea and the Democratic People's Republic of Korea, we estimate a very modest (weighted) TFP growth rate. Here, in contrast to other regions, crop TFP appears to have fallen over the last four decades. Nonruminant productivity growth is the only bright spot for East and Southeast Asia, with a 1.38% annual growth rate. In South Asia, we find slow but positive productivity growth in crops and ruminant livestock, with faster growth in nonruminants.

The economies in transition have undergone very substantial changes in the past decade and a half, and their TFP growth record reflects this. Indeed, the decade of the 1970s shows negative TFP growth in this region (Ludena et al., 2007). This is followed by some improvement in the 1980s and rapidly accelerating productivity growth in the 1990s, following the collapse of the Soviet Union and the opening up of the Eastern Bloc. This acceleration is particularly striking in the case of crops and nonruminant livestock production. In contrast, in the Middle East and North Africa region, a lack of growth in crop and ruminant TFP leads to negligible aggregate productivity growth, with nonruminants being the only subsector with a reasonably strong performance over the historical period. In comparison, Sub-Saharan Africa shows modest TFP growth across all three subsectors, with a marked improvement in crops productivity since the structural adjustment reforms of the 1980s. In fact, the overall weighted average rate of productivity growth for this region over the 1990s is 0.79% per year. The Latin America and Caribbean region also shows accelerating growth in TFP, especially in the 1990s when Brazil in particular undertook major rural sector reforms. This jump in TFP growth is most noticeable in crops and nonruminants.

Finally, it is quite striking that in the industrialized countries, where the share of consumer expenditure on food is relatively low and where only a small portion of the labor force is employed in agriculture, productivity growth rates are much higher—indeed 40% above the world average for the historical period. This higher growth rate is fueled strongly by high TFP growth in the crops subsector, followed by nonruminants, although that rate of TFP growth is lower than the world average. Ruminants, despite being the slowest sector for this region, has, over this 40-year period, a TFP growth rate higher than in all other regions, apart from the PRC.

6.4.2 Forecasts of Agricultural Productivity Growth

In constructing forecasts of future productivity levels in agriculture, Ludena et al. (2007) depart in two significant ways from the current "state of the art" in agricultural commodity forecasts (Rosegrant et al., 2001; USDA, 2005; OECD, 2005). First of all, rather than forecasting partial factor productivity (e.g., output per hectare), they forecast TFP, building on the historical measures of TFP by the eight major regions of the world previously identified. Second, rather than simply extrapolating past trends, they recognize that there are two important contributors to historical productivity growth—technical change and technical efficiency—and that these may behave quite differently over the forecast period.

To project changes in the technical efficiency component of TFP growth, Ludena et al. (2007) assume that technological catch-up can be modeled as a diffusion process of new technologies, where the cumulative adoption path follows an S-shaped curve (Griliches, 1957; Jarvis, 1981). This curve denotes that the efficiency change at the beginning changes slowly because new technologies take some time to be adopted. As technology becomes more widely accepted, a period of rapid growth follows until growth slows again and reaches a stable ceiling. In this case, we assume that efficiency levels for all regions will eventually reach the production possibility frontier and become fully efficient (see Ludena et al., 2006, for more details).

To project the contribution to future TFP growth of the rate of technical change, Ludena et al. (2007) simply assume that countries grow at their historical trends. However, in the case of those regions with average growth rates higher than industrialized countries, the rate of future technical change is assumed to erode (linearly) over time so that it eventually falls to the rich country growth rate. In particular, it is assumed that, after 20 years, the regions with initial rates of technical change above those of the industrialized countries will be growing at the same rate as the industrialized countries (otherwise, they would eventually exceed those countries' productivity levels).

The lower portion of each regional panel in Table 6.3 contains the TFP, efficiency, and technical change projections for each subsector in each region over the projections period 1997–2025. The first thing to note is that the weighted average for the world is higher in the projections period than in the historical period for TFP (1.43% a year vs. 0.97% a year) and for all three agricultural subsectors. When we compare the component parts of TFP, we see that this difference is entirely due to the projected increase in technical efficiency over the next two decades. This reflects a continuation of the improvements in efficiency observed between the 1980s and the 1990s (Ludena et al., 2007). On the other hand, technical change is actually projected to be lower in the projections period—despite the fact that we are projecting this on the basis of historical trends. This difference between the historical period and the projections period is due to the anticipated slowing of the very high rate of technological change in a few key developing countries in the future, as discussed in the preceding paragraph.

As we move to the left in the top panel of Table 6.3, we see which subsectors contribute the most to this higher rate of average TFP growth for agriculture. The overall average TFP growth rate for crops and ruminants is lower in the historical and projections period, with nonruminants showing much higher TFP growth rates over the projections period. And, as anticipated above, this is fueled by high rates of catching up as predicted by our logistic model of technical efficiency.

The PRC's TFP growth rate in the projections period is higher for all subsectors than for the historical period. Although, with the exception of nonruminants, TFP growth for the next two decades is lower than that for the decade of the 1990s. Again, the main difference is the projected rate of growth in technical efficiency, which is extremely high for ruminants (a very small sector in the PRC, accounting for just 7% of total output). It is also high for nonruminants where TFP growth over the past two decades has been in excess of 4%, as the PRC makes the transition from backyard pig and poultry production systems to modern, industrial production.

In East and Southeast Asia, the projected weighted average productivity growth for all three subsectors is 0.09%, with higher productivity growth rates (3.23%) for nonruminants. The projections for South Asia, which, for technical reasons (see Ludena et al., 2006), are based on the entire Developing Asia region, are higher than the historical estimates, with the highest growth rates for nonruminant livestock. In the case of the economies in transition, much of the historical TFP growth was attributed to technological progress. For Middle East and North Africa, TFP for all three subsectors is projected to be 0.19%, with higher growth in crops (0.38%). In Sub-Saharan Africa, average agricultural TFP growth over the next two decades is projected to be 0.85%, fueled by both outward shifts in the frontier and by improved efficiency. For Latin America, average agricultural TFP growth is projected to be higher than historically, with the difference largely driven by livestock productivity growth. Finally, TFP forecasts for industrialized countries are quite a bit lower than in the historical period (0.87% vs. 1.22%), a consequence of a slower rate of technical efficiency growth. All three agricultural subsectors show somewhat lower TFP growth in the industrialized countries over the forecast period.

6.4.3 Total Factor Productivity Growth in Manufacturing and Services

As noted previously, while our focus in this paper is on food and agriculture, the evolution of TFP in the nonfarm sectors is also critical—both from the supply side (evolving comparative advantage) and from the demand side (fueling income growth). In order to construct these forecasts, we draw heavily on the work of Kets and Lejour (2003) as well as the economic growth forecasts of the World Bank.

In their historical study of TFP by sector in OECD, Kets and Lejour (2003) compute the increase in output per unit of value added for agriculture, manufacturing, services, and raw materials over the period 1970–1990, assuming a Cobb-Douglas production function. (Note that the agricultural TFP growth rates discussed above also reflect intermediate inputs, in addition to value added.) Simple average growth rates reported in Kets and Lejour (2003) (which are preferable to weighted average rates due to the high weight/questionable nature of some of the US estimates), are in the range of 0.42% a year for services to 2.68% a year for agriculture, with the economywide average at 0.87% a year. Their disaggregated estimates for manufactures and services show considerable variation, particularly in services, with communications (3.38% a year) and transportation (1.38% a year) above average.

Using these estimates as a guide, we have computed the ratio of TFP growth in agriculture, manufacturing, and services to the economywide average. These are reported in Table 6.4, and, with the exception of agriculture, these differentials are applied to the underlying labor productivity growth rates reported in Table 6.2 (discussed below). It should be noted at this point that, while Kets and Lejour (2003) measured productivity growth rates over all of value-added (labor and capital), in economic growth models (their model included) it is customary to implement productivity growth as applying to labor productivity only.[5] Thus, productivity growth for the nonagriculture sectors is expressed in terms of labor productivity growth only.

In the case of agriculture, we have independent estimates of the rate of technical change, worldwide (Table 6.3). We prefer to use these directly in the model, rather than treat them in the same manner as TFP for the other sectors, since the measurement concepts in the Ludena et al. (2006) TFP study are quite different from those in the Kets and Lejour (2003) study. The former considers

Table 6.4 Labor Productivity Differentials: Sectoral Value-Added Productivity Growth Relative to the Economywide Average, 1970–1990

Sector	Annual Growth (%)
Agriculture[a]	3.08
Energy Extraction	0.78
Manufactures	2.24
Services (general)	0.48
Transportation and Communications	2.24

a Agriculture differential is not used in this study.

Source: Kets and Lejour (2003).

the productivity of all inputs, not just value added. So agriculture is treated differently here.

We have also wrestled with the question of overall productivity growth in agriculture, relative to the rate of population and income growth. History suggests that, despite occasional spikes in the price of farm commodities, the long-run trend for these products is downward. So in our baseline, we augment agricultural productivity growth *in all regions* by a common factor, *tfp-agriculture*, which is chosen to ensure that global crops prices fall at the same rate as the average price for all traded goods. Were this not the case, even with the relatively high rates of TFP growth shown in Table 6.3, farm prices would rise by an implausible amount over the projections period. Despite our targeting overall TFP growth in this way, the regional and subsector variations evident in Table 6.3 result in considerable variation in prices across subsectors and across regions in the baseline forecast.

Finally, we turn to the overall growth rates of labor productivity in the 11 regions in our model. These are reported in the third column of Table 6.2. They are the base to which the productivity growth differentials for the nonagriculture sectors in Table 6.4 are applied. So, for example, the annual rate of labor productivity growth in North America is 2.24 * 1.0 = 2.24% in manufactures, transportation, and communications, but just 0.78 * 1.0 = 0.78% in energy extraction. In ASEAN, by contrast, the labor productivity growth rate in manufactures is assumed to be 2.24 * 2 = 4.48% a year.

6.5 IMPLICATIONS FOR INTERNATIONAL INVESTMENT AND ECONOMIC GROWTH

Having specified the growth rates for exogenous endowments and technological progress, we are now in a position to use the model to predict international capital accumulation and economic growth. In these projections, we use a modified version of the Dynamic GTAP model (Ianchovichina and McDougall, 2000), nicknamed GTAP-Dyn. This is a recursive dynamic model, built on the static GTAP model, which adds a sophisticated specification of international capital mobility, in addition to tracking foreign and domestic ownership of capital stock. The latter feature permits the model to track foreign income payments, which become an increasingly important feature of the balance of payments over the long run. The model permits capital to be imperfectly mobile in the near term, but allows risk-adjusted rates of return to converge in the long run, when capital is perfectly mobile. The speed of convergence in rates of return in the model, 9% a year, is based on the econometric work of Golub (2006) for a sample of OECD countries.[6]

Based on the newly parameterized GTAP-Dyn model, we can estimate the expected rate of capital accumulation, and hence GDP in each region over the baseline period. These are reported in the fourth and fifth data columns of Table 6.2, under the heading "endogenous variables." The highest rate of cumulative capital accumulation is in South Asia, where labor force growth and productivity growth are both very high. The PRC, with higher productivity growth but lesser labor force growth, has a lower rate of total capital accumulation. This contrasts sharply with the World Bank projections for capital accumulation in the PRC (second to last column of Table 6.2), which are much higher for that country and only half as great for South Asia. The GTAP-Dyn model predicts a slowing of investment in the PRC as growth in the labor force slows later in the forecast period.

As a consequence of the slower capital accumulation, the projected GDP growth in the PRC in our baseline is also lower than the World Bank forecasts, though not that much. Conversely, our cumulative GDP forecast for South Asia is considerably higher (413% vs. 326% over this 28-year projections period). Our GTAP-Dyn-based GDP projections are lower for high-income Asia, which experiences only modest labor force growth, and higher than the World Bank's projection for ASEAN.

Based on our projections for net national savings and investment as well as foreign income payments (which are faithfully tracked by GTAP-Dyn over the projections period), we obtain a baseline path for the trade balance for each region. Dividing the latter by net national income, we obtain the ratio that is plotted in Figure 6.2 for the four Asian country groupings.

Over the historical part of our projections period, the PRC and high-income Asia have been running trade surpluses, while South Asia and ASEAN have been running trade deficits. Our projections suggest that these roles will be reversed by the end of our projections period, due both to a slowing of savings in the PRC [7] and to the increased importance of income receipts from foreign assets, which come to dominate the balance of payments for high-income Asia. Indeed, by 2016, the latter region is projected to move into trade deficit as a consequence of these factors. In the case of South Asia, the opposite is true. Current investment inflows increase the stock of foreign-owned capital in the region, and eventually, foreign income payments on these new investments force South Asia to run a trade surplus.

Figure 6.2 Evolution of the Trade Balance, Relative to Net National Income, over the Projections Period

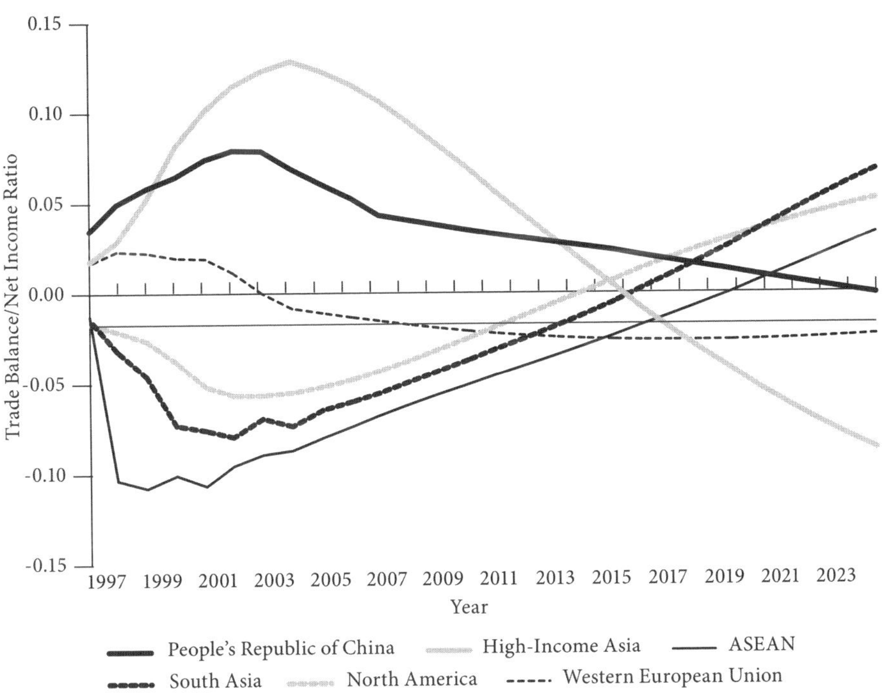

Source: Authors' simulations.

6.6 IMPLICATIONS FOR STRUCTURAL CHANGE AND FUTURE PATTERNS OF TRADE

Table 6.5 provides a useful overview of structural change in the baseline scenario. Individual sectors have been aggregated into five broad categories: Agriculture, Processed Food, Manufactures, Services, and Natural Resources. For each of these sectors, we report the change in composition of output (percentage change in sectoral output relative to real GDP) and consumption (percentage change in sectoral consumption relative to real GDP). The first thing to note is that the share of the food sector in overall real production and consumption falls sharply across the board, [8] with consumption falling more rapidly than production in the economies of Australia and New Zealand (ANZ), the Americas, and Western Europe. In contrast, the share of production falls more sharply than consumption in Asia, EIT, and MENA. Manufactures' share in real output rises strongly in the PRC and South Asia. This share also rises in SSA and North America—the latter being somewhat

Table 6.5 Relative Supply and Demand: Cumulative 1997–2025 change (%)

Sector	Ratio	Australia-New Zealand	China, People's Rep. of	High-Income Asia	ASEAN	South Asia	North America	Latin America	Western European Union	Economies in Transition	Middle East and North Africa	Sub-Saharan Africa
Agriculture	Output/GDP	-18	-53	-40	-69	-61	-14	14	-16	-30	-40	-43
	Consumption/GDP	-52	-48	-25	-58	-57	-45	-43	-30	-14	-8	-43
Processed Food	Output/GDP	-34	-52	-41	-70	-62	0	-11	-14	-22	-43	-42
	Consumption/GDP	-40	-25	-7	-52	-61	-23	-42	-24	-4	7	-35
Manuf-acturing	Output/GDP	11	37	-35	4	60	22	5	-9	-4	-6	28
	Consumption/GDP	-8	99	46	-15	6	-10	-22	8	23	28	-4
Services	Output/GDP	1	1	4	30	32	-4	8	3	-5	11	12
	Consumption/GDP	-10	43	29	-4	16	-16	-16	4	4	28	-7
Natural Resources	Output/GDP	-13	-28	232	-49	-30	-4	-30	14	21	-14	-29
	Consumption/GDP	-41	-5	15	-57	-28	-32	-44	-35	2	-10	-34

Source: Authors' simulations.

Table 6.6 Change in Trade Balance, by Sector, 1997–2025 ($ billion)

Sector	Australia-New Zealand	China, People's Rep. of	High-Income Asia	ASEAN	South Asia	North America	Latin America	Western European Union	Economies in Transition	Middle East and North Africa	Sub-Saharan Africa	Total
Agriculture	27.1	-224.1	-18.3	-47.7	-97.2	99.2	144.6	75.9	-5.2	-37.6	24.5	-58.8
Processed Food	9.3	-198.2	-209.9	-70.2	-13.6	326.6	70.0	145.7	-21.7	-95.2	-17.6	-74.9
Manufacturing	-24.5	990.3	-799.0	-146.1	261.3	439.3	-120.3	-668.2	-105.4	-287.9	-17.1	-477.6
Transport and Communications	8.0	187.4	-13.0	-22.6	95.9	169.1	7.9	87.5	209.3	-9.8	-12.1	707.7
Other Services	41.7	-320.4	-368.8	471.3	152.0	231.3	236.0	-120.8	-304.3	-111.4	72.1	-21.3
Natural Resources	-1.6	-483.1	154.2	-112.9	-234.6	-278.2	1.0	17.2	222.2	594.6	46.0	-75.1
Total	59.9	-48.1	-1254.8	71.9	163.8	987.4	339.2	-462.7	-5.1	52.8	95.8	0.0

Source: Authors' simulations.

surprising, given the share's recent, downward trend in North America. This rise in manufactures production is driven by a real depreciation in North America (predominantly the US), which is forced to run a trade surplus by the end of the projections period in order to repay foreign investors. Manufactures' share in real consumption rises in many regions, with the strongest increases arising in PRC, high-income Asia, EIT, and MENA.

Table 6.5 also shows that services' share in real output rises in all regions, excepting North America and EIT, with the rise being particularly sharp in South Asia, followed by ASEAN. The slight decline in North American services output is driven by the nontraded services sectors, and it follows from the strong expansion in the more heavily traded sectors—again due to the requirement for the region to run a trade surplus by the end of the projections period. Natural resources' share in output and consumption is driven strongly by the rapidly rising prices for these products (fisheries, forestry, and petroleum output) over the baseline period (see below for details). This constrains real consumption relative to real GDP, and results in an increase in output in some of the regions. The strong increase in petroleum output in high-income Asia results from massive capital investment. Unfortunately, the model does not take into account petroleum reserves and the potential for their development, and therefore this outcome does not appear to be realistic.

Table 6.6 reports the change in the trade balance (in billion US dollars) over the baseline period. The first thing to look at in this table is the row labeled "Total," which reports the change in the trade balance from 1997 to 2025, for each region in the model. The sum of these totals equals zero, as must be the case in a global model (zero world trade balance). As noted previously, these regional trade balances are largely driven by the changes in savings, investment, and foreign income payments. High-income Asia moves from a trade surplus at the beginning of the period to a trade deficit at the end, due to declining savings and rising foreign income payments from abroad. North America moves in the opposite direction by a comparable magnitude, as it is required to move from a trade deficit to a surplus. As a consequence of these macroeconomic aggregates, the sectoral trade balances for high-income Asia deteriorate for nearly all sectors, while those for North America improve for all sectors (except natural resources).

Turning to the column labeled "Total" in Table 6.6, we note that the row sums for the change in world sectoral trade balances are not equal to zero. They are negative for goods trade and positive for transport services. This is because the trade balance is evaluated by deducting free on board (FOB) exports from cost, insurance, freight (CIF) imports. The difference comprises the international trade and transport margins, which are recorded as services exports. This gives rise to a positive row sum for this sector, separated from other services in Table 6.6.

Now consider individual entries in Table 6.6 on a sector-by-sector basis. The entries in the second column of this table show that the PRC is expected to lift its annual net imports of farm and food products combined by more than $400 billion by the end of the projections period. The largest portion of this increase comes in the imports of (land-intensive) agricultural products—crops and ruminant meats, while the PRC actually increases its net exports of nonruminant meats for which it has a continued high rate of TFP growth, and which is unconstrained by land availability. ASEAN and South Asia also increase their net imports of total food products, with the net change in their food trade balance amounting to more than $230 billion relative to the 1997 benchmark.

The global imbalance in food trade caused by the growth in developing Asia's net imports is made up by a surplus from the rest of the world. The largest share of this increase is supplied by North America and Europe—two regions with high rates of technological progress in agriculture, low population growth rates, relatively low per capita income growth rates, low income elasticities of demand for food, and strong positions in the production and export of high value-added food products. The importance of trade in processed food products for these two regions may be seen by a comparison of the agriculture and processed food rows. In the case of Western Europe, the increase in net processed food exports is double that for agriculture. In North America, it is more than three times as large. ANZ and Latin America also play an important role in the increase in net exports of food products to the world market.

The global manufacturing trade balance is dominated by the PRC, which shows a net increase of $990.3 billion over the projections period. North America and South Asia also show increases in net exports of manufactures. In North America, this is driven by the need to improve its overall trade balance by nearly $1 trillion by 2025. The largest negative changes in the manufactures trade balance are for high-income Asia and Western Europe, both of which are expected to show strong deterioration in their aggregate trade balance by the end of the projections period.

Most of the economies show a positive trade balance in transport and communications services. This is because increased global trade requires rising use of trade and transport services, to the tune of $707.7 billion annually by the end of the projections period. Exceptions are high-income Asia and ASEAN, as well as MENA and SSA. Net exports of other services rise for ANZ, ASEAN, South Asia, the Americas, and SSA.

Finally, in the case of natural resources (dominated by petroleum), the big story is the strong increase in net imports by the PRC, and, to a lesser degree, South Asia and North America. This change is largely accommodated by increased net exports of natural resource-based products from the Middle East and North Africa, Russian Federation and the former Soviet Republics, and to a lesser degree, Sub-Saharan Africa.

In addition to viewing these changes through the trade balance, we can also analyze them through regional self-sufficiency ratios—defined simply as the ratio of the value of production, at domestic market prices, to the value of domestic absorption, again at market prices. When this ratio is equal to one, the region is deemed to be "self-sufficient." Of course even self-sufficient regions are likely to be exporting and importing the product in question, due to the prevalence of intra-industry trade, as well as the strong taste for variety in most regions. When the ratio is in excess of one, it means that the value of what a given region produces exceeds the value of what it consumes in this particular sector. When the ratio is less than one, it means that the region consumes more than it produces, measured in values at domestic market prices.

Table 6.7 reports self-sufficiency ratios for the years 1997 and 2025 for each sector/region in the model. Not surprisingly, there are some dramatic changes in these values. The PRC's self-sufficiency ratio falls sharply for all food products, excepting nonruminants and processed nonruminants. The same is true for most of Asia. On the other hand, ANZ, North America, and Western Europe (except nonruminants and nonruminants products) become far more than self-sufficient in food products, with the exception of nonruminants, where rapid productivity growth in the developing countries (including the PRC) results in increased self-sufficiency ratios. Such dramatic changes in regional self-sufficiency ratios for food will only occur in the absence of substantial changes in trade policy. However, in the absence of World Trade Organization discipline, we can expect rising protection in Asia, while budget constraints may eventually translate into reduced farm subsidies in North America and Western Europe. Both of these factors would lessen the shift portrayed in this baseline.

In the case of textiles and apparel, the PRC and South Asia strengthen their positions as surplus producers, with all other regions (except EIT) reducing their self-sufficiency ratios. In the case of other manufactures too, the PRC and South Asia enhance their positions, while North America and Europe reverse positions: the former now becomes more than self-sufficient and the latter falls below self-sufficiency, as it experiences a real appreciation and an increased trade deficit. The PRC and South Asia also experience big boosts in transportation and communications services, as their economies grow rapidly over this period, and as these services are required for increased international trade.

The change in economic structure portrayed in Tables 6.5–6.7 are driven by a combination of supply and demand forces. The forces driving the demand side were discussed at length above. However, on the supply side, there are

Table 6.7 Self-Sufficiency Ratio in 1997 and 2025

Self-Sufficiency Ratio	Year	Australia-New Zealand	China, People's Rep. of	High-Income Asia	ASEAN	South Asia	North America	Latin America	Western European Union	Economies in Transition	Middle East and North Africa	Sub-Saharan Africa
1 Crops	1997	1.43	0.99	0.79	0.95	1.01	1.12	1.07	0.80	0.96	0.87	1.08
	2025	2.46	0.71	0.76	0.74	0.84	1.42	1.27	1.29	1.02	0.78	1.21
2 Ruminants	1997	1.05	1.01	0.97	0.92	1.00	1.00	1.00	0.99	1.01	0.97	1.00
	2025	1.17	0.98	1.00	0.66	1.00	1.01	1.06	1.01	1.03	0.82	1.00
3 Nonruminants	1997	1.45	1.01	0.87	1.00	1.00	1.06	1.00	0.98	1.00	0.94	1.01
	2025	0.81	1.03	0.62	0.90	0.92	0.43	6.08	0.25	0.58	0.12	0.52
4 Processed Ruminants	1997	1.83	0.87	0.79	0.80	0.95	1.01	0.97	1.01	0.92	0.78	0.91
	2025	2.06	0.68	0.77	0.74	0.67	1.03	1.09	1.06	0.90	0.45	0.93
5 Processed Nonruminants	1997	1.08	1.01	0.70	1.01	1.00	1.05	1.02	1.00	0.89	0.53	0.94
	2025	0.93	2.08	0.36	0.71	0.76	0.98	1.17	0.75	0.71	0.25	0.81
6 Processed Food	1997	1.05	0.96	0.90	1.09	1.01	0.98	1.06	1.00	0.90	0.84	0.97
	2025	1.09	0.51	0.64	0.68	0.86	1.40	1.14	1.18	0.92	0.54	0.91
7 Textiles and Apparel	1997	0.93	1.21	0.99	1.23	1.32	0.75	1.01	0.87	0.86	0.96	0.93
	2025	0.64	1.26	0.66	1.09	1.35	0.57	0.92	0.47	0.87	0.83	0.77
8 Manufactures	1997	0.85	0.97	1.08	0.90	0.87	0.95	0.91	1.03	0.89	0.72	0.87
	2025	0.90	1.10	0.88	0.88	1.09	1.05	0.92	0.95	0.87	0.64	0.95
9 Wholesale and Retail Trade	1997	1.00	1.00	1.01	0.98	1.00	1.00	0.99	1.00	0.99	0.99	0.94
	2025	1.01	0.88	0.99	1.58	1.07	1.00	1.06	1.00	0.94	0.98	1.00
10 Transport and Communications	1997	1.02	1.03	1.03	1.11	1.02	1.06	0.99	1.07	1.14	1.05	0.98
	2025	1.06	1.27	1.01	0.96	1.26	1.10	1.00	1.09	1.61	1.00	0.95
11 Financial Services	1997	0.99	0.98	0.99	1.04	1.01	1.01	0.98	1.00	0.96	0.96	0.97
	2025	0.98	0.94	0.95	1.48	1.16	1.01	1.19	0.97	0.77	0.83	1.06
12 Household and Other Services	1997	1.01	0.99	0.99	0.99	1.00	1.01	0.99	1.00	1.00	0.96	0.99
	2025	1.01	0.98	0.98	1.03	1.18	1.02	1.04	1.00	0.95	0.96	1.03
13 Forestry	1997	1.23	0.94	0.60	1.11	0.97	1.06	1.03	0.90	1.20	0.96	1.25
	2025	1.33	0.73	0.87	0.79	0.82	1.08	1.50	1.39	1.57	0.90	1.33
14 Fishery	1997	1.21	1.02	0.89	1.03	1.01	0.93	1.05	0.98	1.05	1.03	1.04
	2025	1.19	0.89	1.35	1.08	1.02	0.64	0.82	1.12	1.18	0.97	0.98
15 Utilities	1997	1.20	1.02	0.94	1.09	0.98	1.00	0.97	0.98	1.03	1.05	1.04
	2025	1.50	0.94	0.87	1.15	1.02	1.04	1.08	1.03	0.85	0.90	1.16
16 Petroleum	1997	0.86	0.90	0.59	0.85	0.60	0.82	1.22	0.76	1.16	2.20	1.66
	2025	0.87	0.73	0.98	0.69	0.47	0.84	1.09	0.90	1.33	2.21	1.29
17 Construction	1997	1.00	1.00	1.00	0.99	1.00	1.00	1.00	1.00	0.99	1.01	1.00
	2025	1.00	0.99	0.99	1.00	1.00	1.00	1.00	1.00	0.97	1.01	1.01

Source: Authors' simulations.

also strong forces at work. Strong growth in unskilled labor in an economy favors expansion of labor-intensive activities—the so-called Rybczynski Effect. Similarly, expansion of the capital stock favors growth in the capital-intensive sectors. Of course, the question of where the additional endowments end up being employed also depends on the current employment rates for these factors of production.

Table 6.8 sheds some light on this issue by reporting the cumulative expansion in capital and labor endowments over the projections period, and where these factors end up being employed in 2025. For example, in the case of the PRC, the capital stock expands more than fivefold over the 1997–2025 period (553%). The capital services entries in the PRC column indicate that the majority of capital is absorbed in the tertiary (services) sector where capital expands by 993% over the projections period. This is followed by natural resource production, manufactures, and finally, the food sector (51% growth in capital usage). Perusal of Table 6.8 indicates that in most economies the highest rates of employment increase are in services and natural resources. However, the latter is a relatively small sector and the increase in labor and capital in these sectors is in response to dramatic price increases (see below). On the other hand, the combined food and agriculture sector continues to shed at least some factors of production in many regions.

Given the differential rates of factor accumulation, as well as differential productivity growth rates, it is hardly surprising that changes in factor prices vary widely across factors and across regions over the projections period (Table 6.9). For example, in ANZ, unskilled labor is projected to grow at twice the rate of skilled labor, and the relatively stronger growth in skilled wages reflects this fact. In the PRC, conversely, unskilled labor grows very slowly, and skilled labor quite rapidly, so unskilled wages grow much faster in the baseline. Of course, this analysis abstracts from the pool of underemployed and unskilled labor in rural PRC that might conceivably serve as a reservoir for additional workers, at least in the medium term. Perhaps more importantly, we assume in the baseline that productivity growth rates are equal for both unskilled and skilled labor. However, this is unlikely to be true. We expect future technologies to favor skilled labor, and this will serve to dampen relative wage growth for unskilled labor in most regions.

The other key factor market assumption is that of international capital mobility. We assume that, in the long run, rates of return to capital converge. This drives much of the long-run change in capital returns, which also fall on average, relative to wages, as a result of capital accumulation. We see such declines in all regions, except high-income Asia and EIT. Labor, though, is assumed to be immobile internationally. This is something of an extreme assumption, but it appears unlikely that sufficient mobility

Table 6.8 Change in Factor Usage by Sector, as Percentage of 1997 Levels, 1997–2025

Sector		Australia-New Zealand	China, People's Rep. of	High-Income Asia	ASEAN	South Asia	North America	Latin America	Western European Union	Economies in Transition	Middle East and North Africa	Sub-Saharan Africa
Food and Agriculture	Unskilled	25	-2	-32	-18	31	35	37	7	-26	8	31
	Skilled	-15	-8	-43	-14	-10	22	99	-12	-40	14	30
	Capital	76	51	-29	38	88	149	120	45	-4	9	100
Manufacturing	Unskilled	47	-12	-40	72	84	51	55	-1	-47	34	135
	Skilled	19	28	-37	222	201	36	240	-16	-50	89	176
	Capital	193	202	-35	472	604	217	322	44	-28	48	408
Services	Unskilled	57	68	33	91	63	47	38	39	19	85	93
	Skilled	28	224	41	269	203	26	194	18	24	182	137
	Capital	253	993	74	599	852	235	278	125	127	134	391
Natural Resources	Unskilled	122	120	231	151	208	168	148	109	101	150	179
	Skilled	142	204	420	233	328	185	223	144	106	184	201
	Capital	253	851	440	261	403	311	231	207	317	230	272
Total	Unskilled	55	26	16	68	66	49	43	26	-2	69	96
	Skilled	26	173	26	260	222	28	206	10	13	178	146
	Capital	250	553	51	534	731	239	286	114	96	126	376

Source: Authors' simulations.

Table 6.9 Cumulative Changes in Factor Prices over the Baseline Period, 1997–2025 (%)

Factor	Australia-New Zealand	China, People's Rep. of	High-Income Asia	ASEAN	South Asia	North America	Latin America	Western European Union	Economies in Transition	Middle East and North Africa	Sub-Saharan Africa
Unskilled	34	241	36	36	47	43	40	26	143	27	18
Skilled	62	149	30	-17	-1	58	-25	47	154	-4	4
Capital	-31	-33	8	-50	-63	-29	-37	-17	23	0	-40

Note: Price changes are relative to the global factor price index.

Source: Authors' simulations.

will be permitted over this baseline period to have a substantial impact on international wage differentials.

6.7 SUMMARY AND CONCLUSIONS

This chapter has projected potential outcomes in the footrace between supply and demand to the year 2025, with a particular emphasis on food markets in the Asian region. It began with an in-depth analysis of the fundamental drivers of change, including per capita consumer demand, population growth, accumulation of capital and labor, endowments of land by agro-ecological zone, and, particularly, technological change.

The baseline scenario was heavily influenced by our macroeconomic projections for 2025. We used the Dynamic GTAP model, which accounts for foreign ownership and the associated foreign income payments. Over time, these come to dominate the balance of payments for the regions of high-income Asia and North America. Whereas North America is at present running a trade deficit, we project that it will be running a substantial trade surplus in 2025; the opposite is true for high-income Asia. These macroeconomic changes shape the trade environment for these two regions, with North America requiring a substantial real depreciation in order to boost net exports across the board. High-income Asia increases its net imports of most products and services, as its savings rate falls and it repatriates its foreign profits.

Our base case projections show evidence of continued structural change in the global economy, with developing Asia increasing its net imports of food and natural resource-based products significantly by the year 2025. The PRC and South Asia increase their net exports of manufactures over this baseline, with other regions absorbing these increased supplies to the world market. Services exports also increase for ASEAN and South Asia. Growth in services production absorbs the bulk of the projected growth in labor and capital endowments worldwide. Asia is no exception, although manufactures play an important role in increased employment in developing Asia.

The baseline scenario is potentially quite favorable for poverty reduction, as unskilled wages rise relative to food prices throughout developing Asia. However, it is possible that this picture is overly optimistic for the poor. First of all, we have ignored the potential for surplus unskilled workers to depress wage growth. A second assumption is skill-neutral labor productivity growth, yet if technical change favors skilled, relative to unskilled labor, the poverty outcome will be less favorable. Finally, we have calibrated aggregate agricultural productivity growth rates worldwide to ensure stable crops prices. If this is not done, agricultural prices rise strongly under the baseline, and this would have a significantly adverse impact on the majority of the region's poor.

ENDNOTES

1   Before they are incorporated in the current model, the estimates must be calibrated to eliminate the error term for each country. The calibration procedure is described in Golub (2006).

2   Specifically, we have provided the regions with perfectly elastic factor supplies at constant prices to accommodate the growth in demand.

3   Technically, we have fixed per capita utility for the representative regional household over the projections period.

4   The historical estimates are from the period 1961–2000, including part of the projections estimates for 1997–2000. This is because in the GTAP database v5.4, used in this work, base year is 1997, and all other projections were based on that year.

5   This is because the availability of capital is naturally enhanced through investment and capital accumulation.

6   For purposes of this study, the GTAP-Dyn model has been modified to incorporate the AIDADS demand system from Reimer and Hertel (2004). In addition, the sectoral production functions have been altered to accommodate the differentiation of land use by AEZ, following the work of Golub (2006).

7   In the standard GTAP-Dyn model saving is a fixed proportion of income in each region. There are two unwelcome implications of this. First, net foreign positions grow without bound in GTAP-Dyn simulations. The second problem is that as economies with high savings rates, like PRC, grow, there is a glut of global savings and, as a result, of investment and capital in the world. In order to facilitate long-run projections in this work, we adopt a new approach to the evolution of savings over time (Golub and McDougall, 2006), in which the theoretical structure of GTAP-Dyn is modified such that the wealth to income ratio in each region is stabilized at region-specific level. Thus, the savings rate becomes an endogenous function of the ratio of wealth to income.

8   Initially we projected agricultural TFP growth in high-income Asia based on a sample of high income economies, including North America and Western Europe. This likely leads to an overstatement of TFP growth, particularly in the crops sector. For this reason, the annual TFP growth rate in crops in high-income Asia is set equal to annual average TFP growth rate in crops in ASEAN.

REFERENCES

Capalbo, S.M. and J.M. Antle. 1988. "Agricultural Productivity: Measurement and Explanation." Resources for the Future, Washington, DC.

Färe, R., S. Grosskopf, M. Norris, and Z. Zhang. 1994. "Productivity Growth, Technical Progress and Efficiency Change in Industrialized Countries." *American Economic Review* 84:66-83.

Golub, A. 2006. "Projecting the Global Economy in the Long Run: A Dynamic General Equilibrium Approach." Ph.D. dissertation, Center for Global Trade Analysis, Purdue University.

Golub, A. and R. McDougall. 2006. "New Household Saving Behavior in the Dynamic GTAP Model." Paper prepared for presentation at the Ninth Annual Conference on Global Economic Analysis. Addis Ababa, Ethiopia. 15-17 June.

Griliches, Z. 1957. "Hybrid Corn: An Exploration in the Economics of Technological Change." *Econometrica* 25:501–522.

Ianchovichina, E. I. and R. McDougall. 2000. *Structure of Dynamic GTAP*. GTAP Technical Paper 17, Center for Global Trade Analysis, Purdue University. Available: https://www.gtap.agecon.purdue.edu/resources/download/160.pdf.

Jarvis, L.S. 1981. "Predicting the Diffusion of Improved Pastures in Uruguay." *American Journal of Agricultural Economics*, 63:495–502.

Kets, W. and A.M. Lejour. 2003. "Sectoral TFP growth in the OECD." CPB Memorandum 58. Netherlands Bureau for Economic Policy Analysis.

Lee, H.L., T.W. Hertel, B. Sohngen, and N. Ramankutty. 2005. "Towards An Integrated Land Use Database for Assessing the Potential for Greenhouse Gas Mitigation." GTAP Technical Paper 25. Center for Global Trade Analysis, Purdue University.

Ludena, C.E., T.W. Hertel, P.V. Preckel, K. Foster, and A. Nin. 2006. "Productivity Growth and Convergence in Crop, Ruminant and Non-Ruminant Production: Measurement and Forecasts." GTAP Working Paper 35. Center for Global Trade Analysis, Purdue University.

———. 2007. "Productivity Growth and Convergence in Crop, Ruminant and Non-Ruminant Production: Measurement and Forecasts." *Agricultural Economics*, 37:1-17.

Nin, A., C. Arndt, T.W. Hertel, and P.V. Preckel. 2003. "Bridging the Gap between Partial and Total Factor Productivity Measures using Directional Distance Functions." *American Journal of Agricultural Economics*, 85:928-942.

Organisation for Economic Co-operation and Development (OECD). 2005. *OECD-FAO Agricultural Outlook 2005–2014*. Paris: OECD Press.

Reimer, J.J. and T.W. Hertel. 2004. "Estimation of International Demand Behavior for Use with Input-Output Based Data." *Economic Systems Research* 16(4):347-366.

Rosegrant, M.W., M.S. Paisner, S. Meijer, and J. Witcover. 2001. *Global Food Projections to 2020: Emerging Trends and Alternative Futures*. 2020 Vision Food Policy Report. Washington D.C., International Food Policy Research Institute.

US Department of Agriculture (USDA). 2005. "USDA Agricultural Baseline Projections to 2014." Economic Research Service, Baseline Report OCE-2005-1.

Walmsley, T., B. Dimaranan, and R.A. McDougall. 2000. "A Base Case Scenario for the Dynamic GTAP Model." GTAP Resource #417, Center for Global Trade Analysis, Purdue University. Available: https://www.gtap.agecon.purdue.edu/resources/res_display.asp?RecordID=417.

APPENDIX

Appendix Table A6.1 Aggregation of GTAP Regions

Region	GTAP Region
Australia and New Zealand (ANZ)	Australia, New Zealand
People's Republic of China (CHN)	People's Republic of China
High Income Asia (HYAsia)	Hong Kong, China; Japan; Republic of Korea; Taipei,China
Association of Southeast Asian Nations (ASEAN)	Indonesia, Malaysia, Philippines, Singapore, Thailand, Viet Nam
South Asia (SAsia)	Bangladesh, India, Sri Lanka, and rest of South Asia
North America (NAM)	Canada, United States
Latin America (LAM)	Mexico, Central America and Caribbean, Colombia, Peru, Argentina, Brazil, Chile, Uruguay, Venezuela, and rest of the Andean Pact countries
Western European Union (WEU) except Turkey	Austria, Belgium, Denmark, Finland, France, Germany, United Kingdom, Greece, Ireland, Italy, Luxembourg, Netherlands, Portugal, Spain, Sweden, Switzerland, and rest of EFTA
Economies in Transition (EIT)	Albania, Bulgaria, Croatia, Czech Republic, Hungary, Malta, Poland, Romania, Slovakia, Slovenia, Estonia, Latvia, Lithuania, Cyprus, Russian Federation, and rest of the former Soviet Union
Middle East and North Africa (MENA)	Turkey, the rest of Middle East, Morocco, and rest of North Africa
Rest of the World (ROW)	Botswana, the rest of SACU, Malawi, Mozambique, Zambia, Zimbabwe, the rest of Southern Africa, United Republic of Tanzania, Uganda, rest of Sub-Saharan Africa, and rest of the world

Source: Authors.

Appendix Table A6.2 Economies in Data of the Food and Agriculture Organization of the United Nations

1. Industrialized Countries	Australia, Austria, Benelux, Canada, Denmark, Finland, France, Germany, Greece, Iceland, Ireland, Israel, Italy, Japan, Netherlands, New Zealand, Norway, Portugal, South Africa, Spain, Sweden, Switzerland, United Kingdom, United States
2. Economies in Transition	Albania, Bulgaria, Czech Republic, Slovakia, Hungary, Poland, Romania, former Soviet Union, former Yugoslav SFR
3. People's Republic of China	People's Republic of China
4. East and Southeast Asia	Cambodia, Indonesia, Democratic People's Republic of Korea, Republic of Korea, Lao People's Democratic Republic, Malaysia, Mongolia, Myanmar, Philippines, Singapore, Thailand, Viet Nam
5. Developing Asia	Bangladesh, Bhutan, Cambodia, People's Republic of China, India, Indonesia, Islamic Republic of Iran, Iraq, Jordan, Democratic People's Republic of Korea, Republic of Korea, Lao People's Democratic Republic, Lebanon, Malaysia, Mongolia, Myanmar, Nepal, Pakistan, Philippines, Saudi Arabia, Singapore, Sri Lanka, Syrian Arab Republic, Thailand, Turkey, Viet Nam, Yemen
6. Middle East and North Africa	Algeria, Egypt, Islamic Republic of Iran, Iraq, Jordan, Lebanon, Libyan Arab Jamahiriya, Morocco, Saudi Arabia, Sudan, Syrian Arab Republic, Tunisia, Turkey, Yemen
7. Sub-Saharan Africa	Angola, Benin, Botswana, Burkina Faso, Burundi, Cameroon, Cape Verde, Central African Republic, Chad, Republic of the Congo, Democratic Republic of the Congo, Côte d'Ivoire, Ethiopia, Gabon, Gambia, Ghana, Guinea, Guinea-Bissau, Kenya, Lesotho, Liberia, Madagascar, Malawi, Mali, Mauritania, Mozambique, Namibia Niger, Nigeria, Rwanda, Senegal, Sierra Leone, Somalia, Sudan, Swaziland, United Republic of Tanzania, Togo, Uganda, Zambia, Zimbabwe
8. Latin America and Caribbean	Argentina, Belize, Bolivia, Brazil, Chile, Colombia, Costa Rica, Cuba, Dominican Republic, Ecuador, El Salvador, Guatemala, Guyana, Haiti, Honduras, Jamaica, Mexico, Nicaragua, Panama, Paraguay, Peru, Puerto Rico, Suriname, Trinidad and Tobago, Uruguay, Venezuela

Source: Authors.

Commentary on Chapter 6

Allan Rae

This excellent chapter addresses the footrace between demand and supply growth in agricultural and food markets in Asia. I find little to criticize, but try to offer a few ideas that might be useful to those interested in further pursuing this approach to researching future prospects for Asian agriculture. Dr. Hertel's chapter discusses some major drivers of demand and supply growth, and a major focus is on the measurement of agricultural productivity growth and its contribution (through applied general equilibrium analysis) to projected market outcomes.

The two demand drivers recognized in the chapter are per capita incomes and population size. A demand systems model is estimated that produces plausible results in terms of past and projected trends in consumption patterns. Two other important demand drivers, that are not incorporated in this projections model, include urbanization and population demographics. It is well known that urbanization growth is rapid in many developing countries, especially in Sub-Saharan Africa, the People's Republic of China (PRC), and other Asian countries. The movement of people from rural to urban areas encourages changes in consumption levels and budget shares, and average per capita consumption for many foods can differ greatly between rural and urban populations. There exist several reasons for this, including the earning of higher incomes and greater shopping opportunities via supermarkets, etc. Hence there is some relationship between growth in per capita incomes and urbanization growth, and the income elasticity estimates may incorporate some of this urbanization effect.

Should past trends in the ratio of income to urbanization growth change in future, however, biases in the elasticities used in this chapter may become an issue. Another important driver of projected food demands is the structure of the national population, especially its age and ethnic composition—the structure of diets can differ between younger and older people and between ethnic groups within the population. These structural parameters could change significantly over the medium term in some Asian countries, in which case their omission may also cause bias in projected consumption levels and patterns. In the PRC for example, the share of the population over the age of 60 is expected to increase from 10% in 2000 to 30% by 2050.

On the agricultural supply side, the chapter recognizes resource endowments and productivity growth as major drivers. Important innovations in the chapter are the approach taken to estimate and project productivity growth, and the separation of different classes of farmland according to agro-ecological zones (AEZs). The latter recognizes the distribution of production of any crop or livestock activity in a given country across AEZs, and the relative productivity of that activity in each AEZ. The total supply of farmland, however, is held fixed. This assumption is probably reasonable in many regions of the world, but elsewhere, countries in their efforts to increase food production are facing tightening land constraints that could easily be incorporated into the modeling framework. In Thailand, Japan, and the Republic of Korea, for example, the total agricultural area declined by between 9% and 14% from 1990 to 2003 (FAOSTAT). The use of nonparametric distance functions and Malmquist indexes to measure productivity and its decomposition into efficiency and technical change components has now become standard practice. Here, this approach is enhanced by allowing estimation of separate productivity indexes for crops and livestock through its approach to input allocation across crop and livestock sectors. It can be noted that total factor productivity (TFP) is measured at the country or regional level, and not for individual AEZs within countries or regions. This could be a significant shortcoming when TFP growth is driven by technologies that are specific to certain agro-environmental zones—irrigated crop land, for example.

Notwithstanding the authors' important methodological contribution, this general approach to measuring productivity indexes has some well-known deficiencies. First, like all frontier methods, it makes the restrictive assumption that a common technological frontier envelopes all cross-section observations. Can a common crop-livestock production possibility frontier be assumed across industrial countries and the poorest developing countries? Or across countries with grain-based intensive livestock systems and those where pasture systems predominate? Or across countries with primarily smallholder agriculture and those where commercial systems are dominant? I wonder how sensitive would be the productivity estimates to different poolings of the country data.

Second, the adopted approach does not incorporate random variation, or "noise," in the data—all of the distance between a country observation and the production frontier is assumed to be inefficiency, whereas that distance could have a random component. One specific cause of such noise is environmental conditions—for any year, some countries in the sample may have suffered serious drought for example, and ignoring this may bias upward their estimated inefficiency. One could also note that technical change is assumed to be neutral, therefore denying any biases toward one input or another. But will technical change in livestock production in Asia be labor-saving and feed-using, for example? There is some evidence from the PRC that technical change in the hog sector has actually resulted in a significant saving in the quantity of grain used for feed.

It is probably not useful to compare these productivity growth rates with those obtained in other studies, since TFP growth rates are known to be sensitive to choice of estimation methodology and data. In this study over the 1961–2000 period, average TFP growth in Asia was found to be fastest in the PRC (1.67%) compared with 0.27% in South Asia (including India) and 0.18% in East and Southeast Asia. The last was even lower than estimated productivity growth in Sub-Saharan Africa (0.21%). In the PRC, productivity growth is shown to have been negative around the 1970s, but grew at an increasingly faster rate during the 1980s and 1990s. A somewhat similar pattern was found for South Asia, whereas productivity growth was negative during the 1980s and 1990s in East and Southeast Asia. For each region over 1961–2000, TFP growth was faster in nonruminant livestock production than in ruminant, which is unsurprising.

The chapter is also innovative in the manner in which TFP growth rates are projected into the future. Efficiency growth ("catching up") is projected using an S-shaped adoption curve. This was first used by Griliches in relation to adoption of a specific technology (hybrid corn). But at the aggregate crop (or livestock) level, the productivity growth data for any country reflects the impacts of several specific technologies, whose adoption may have begun at different times. It is not immediately clear to me that the aggregation of adoption rates across such technologies might also be expected to follow the same S-curve logic, but that functional form may well provide a good fit to the data.

Technical change is projected along historical trends. The authors argue that developing countries whose historical growth in technical change exceeds that of the industrial countries will see their rate of technical change eventually fall to that of the industrial countries. But is it not possible that some developing countries (which may have become "industrialized" over a 25-year projection period) might continue to invest productively in agricultural research and development (R&D) and eventually become important movers of the frontier? In other words, the set of technically advanced countries that were responsible for outward shifts of the frontier in the past, may not be the same as the technically advanced set in the future.

Productivity gains, due to both technical change and efficiency improvements, result from many factors, including investments in own and foreign agricultural R&D, and there is an extensive body of empirical evidence in support of this. The Asia-Pacific region accounted for 20% of global public agricultural R&D spending in 1981, rising to 33% in 2000. However, the PRC and India accounted for two thirds of the Asia-Pacific total in 2000, indicating a wide disparity in agricultural R&D investments and intensities across countries in the region. This contributes to the wide range of productivity estimates derived in the chapter. Private R&D spending was 36% of global agricultural R&D in 2000, but 93% of that was performed in rich countries (Pardey et al., 2006a).

It can be useful to have a clear picture of the relationships between R&D and productivity growth for at least three reasons: (i) estimated historical TFP growth rates can be set alongside known R&D expenditures and policies so as to assist in the validation of those TFP estimates; (ii) knowledge of the underlying relationships will be useful in assessing the feasibility of projected productivity pathways, and will also be useful for helping shape future R&D policies and priorities to target specific productivity growth rates; and (iii) knowing about the R&D and productivity relationship would be essential should one wish to consider endogenizing some aspects of TFP growth within the trade model.

The chapter treats productivity improvements as exogenous—as "manna from heaven." This raises the question as to whether the analysis could be enhanced by endogenizing the process. If past trends in agricultural R&D continue unchanged, exogenous specification of productivity growth may be appropriate. Endogenizing productivity growth into the CGE model requires at least some of the more important productivity drivers also to be endogenous to the model. Can the level of R&D investment be linked to growth in national incomes? Spillovers of foreign R&D into developing countries have been shown to be related to a country's openness and trading partners, both of which are endogenous to the CGE model. The extent of spill-ins might also be related to a country's endowments of land in the various AEZs, since some technologies may be AEZ specific, for example to temperate zones. This might be a worthwhile area for future research, especially where projections are made over a relatively long time period.

Looking at the trade results for agriculture and food, I do not see too many surprises. All Asian regions are projected to face declining trade balances in agricultural and processed food products in the aggregate. These increasing import demands are export opportunities for industrial countries and Latin America. The projected self-sufficiency ratios indicate falling sufficiency across Asia in crops and processed foods excluding meats, in all but high-income Asia in ruminant-based products, and in all but the PRC in nonruminant products. The chapter does not give a breakdown of trade changes by crop type, so it is unclear whether the PRC is projected to become a net importer of maize (however, it is projected to increase its net exports of nonruminant meats). This issue is of considerable importance, as several earlier projections (summarized in Fan and Agcaoili-Sombilla, 1997) indicated that the PRC would be a net importer of maize by 2000 and 2005, when in fact it remains a net exporter. Will growing demand for, especially, nonruminant products in Asia be met by increased imports of maize, along with soybeans, to feed domestic animals, or through imports of the final product? Northeast Asia and the PRC provide two contrasting developments.

In the former, maize imports increased to supply local livestock production through the 1980s, after which imports of meats expanded rapidly. In the PRC since the mid-1980s, maize exports have fluctuated around a rising trend at the same time as the country remained a net exporter of meats. The research methods and data presented in the chapter form a valuable resource that could be used to further enlighten policy makers and others interested in Asia's evolving role in world grains and livestock trade.

The contrasting nonruminant results between the PRC and the rest of Asia are influenced by projected relative productivity growth rates. For the PRC, this rate was 6.47%, well above the historical rates of the 1980s and 1990s, and reversing the decline in productivity growth from the 1980s to the 1990s. In the other Asian regions, the projected rate was just over 3%, which, like the PRC, was also greater than recent growth rates and represents reversals of recent nonruminant productivity growth trends. Whether the PRC and East and Southeast Asia will be able to reach TFP growth of 6% and 3% respectively for nonruminants is unknown. While the chapter made an alternative projection based on faster productivity growth in ASEAN *crop* production, it would be of interest to explore the sensitivity of projected outcomes to alternative livestock TFP growth scenarios, and to project the latter on to R&D needs.

Of course, the chapter was not required to incorporate trade and other policy changes into its projections, and other chapters address these topics. It is left to the reader to wonder how projected outcomes might be influenced by an eventual World Trade Organization (WTO) multilateral trade agreement; what impact Viet Nam's recent WTO membership might have on regional trade patterns; and how the growing number of preferential trading agreements in the Asia-Pacific region (should they seriously attempt to free agricultural trade), might impact on regional trade and growth. Such trade and investment policy developments might also affect productivity growth.

Finally, I think that there is an obvious policy implication to be drawn from the chapter, and that concerns national and international agricultural R&D policies. The chapter clearly demonstrates how technical change impacts on trade patterns, the structure of economies, and poverty reduction. For the PRC and East and Southeast Asia, the chapter projects agricultural TFP growth to be higher than rates experienced over at least the past 20 years. Are these trends consistent with current and anticipated developments in R&D investments in these regions and the expected spill-ins from foreign R&D? If not, what are the implications for national and international R&D priorities and investment levels if those growth rates are to be achieved?

In East and Southeast Asia, the projected agricultural TFP growth rate is a paltry 0.09%, which masks much variation across countries in this region. What will be required of R&D efforts in these countries, as well as of international research organizations and donors, to target more substantial growth? Increased agricultural R&D investments in developing countries can be expected to improve the low productivity rates that are projected for some commodities and regions in this study. On the other hand, a slowdown in rich-country spending on agricultural R&D, changing research priorities, or increased emphasis on private R&D may curtail future spillovers from rich to poor countries. This may be exacerbated by strengthened intellectual property rights regimes and the switching of rich-country research away from staple crops to environmental issues and food attributes such as quality, safety, and convenience and reoriented to types of technologies less easily adopted and adapted by developing countries. This may lead to a slowdown in agricultural productivity growth in many developing countries (Pardey et al., 2006b), in contrast to the increasing rates of productivity growth projected for several regions in the chapter.

References to Commentary

FAOSTAT. Food and Agriculture Organization of the United Nations database. Available: http://faostat.fao.org/default.aspx.

Fan, S. and M. Agcaoili-Sombilla. 1997. "Why Projections on China's Future Food Supply and Demand Differ." *Australian Journal of Agricultural and Resource Economics* 41:169-90.

Pardey, P.G., N. Beintema, S. Dehmer, and S. Wood. 2006a. *Agricultural Research: A Growing Divide?* Washington, DC: International Food Policy Research Institute.

Pardey, P.G., J.M. Alston, and R.R. Piggott (eds.). 2006b. *Agricultural R&D in the Developing World: Too Little Too Late?* Washington, DC: International Food Policy Research Institute.

7

Energy Scenarios for East Asia, 2005–2025

Sergey Paltsev and John Reilly

7.1 INTRODUCTION

The East Asian region is among the fastest-growing regions of the world and its share of the global economy and of energy use has increased substantially over the past 30 years. Thus, continued economic growth in East Asia will strongly affect the world demand for energy. The goal of this chapter is to provide several illustrative scenarios of economic development and energy use in the region. For this purpose the MIT Emissions Prediction and Policy Analysis (EPPA) model (Paltsev et al., 2005) is used. It is a computable general equilibrium (CGE) model of the global economy, and has been widely used to study climate change policy and its implications for energy system and technology development.

East Asia, based on the regional disaggregation in the EPPA model, is defined to comprise People's Republic of China (PRC); India; Indonesia; Japan; and the dynamic Asian economies of Republic of Korea; Malaysia; Philippines; Singapore; Taipei,China; and Thailand. This definition excludes some countries that are obviously in East Asia, such as Cambodia and Viet Nam. India, which is generally considered as South Asia, is also included, since this regional grouping contains the countries in the region that dominate its energy use and account for most of the region's gross domestic product (GDP).

The PRC's economy is the fastest-growing economy in the region. The phenomenon of fast growth in that country and its implications for energy demand have attracted considerable attention from researchers (see, for example, Adams and Shachmurove, 2007; Winters and Yusuf, 2007; Zhao and Wu, 2007). There is substantial disagreement on how fast the PRC will grow in the next 10 to 30 years. As pointed out by Altman (2007), some experts predict sustained fast growth. Others appeal to an economic convergence theory, which would have growth slowing in developing economies as they catch up with industrial economies, and face diminishing returns as they adopt the most advanced technologies available. At that point, they would need to start to innovate themselves, move to advanced product markets, and compete with industrial countries in these markets. Still other observers wonder whether the political situation in the PRC will remain stable and whether the stresses of rapid growth on the environment and on natural resources there might not undermine growth.

The chapter is organized in the following way. In the next section recent trends in economic performance and energy use in the East Asian region are described. Section 7.3 presents the EPPA model, which is used for scenario development. In Section 7.4 the baseline scenario is considered. Section 7.5 then examines several alternative scenarios, where different assumptions about growth rates, energy efficiency, and energy prices are considered. Section 7.6 concludes.

7.2 ECONOMIC AND ENERGY INDICATORS, 1970–2000

Since 1970 the economies of the region have more than tripled in size, and fossil-energy use has increased some 3.5 times as shown in Tables 7.1 and 7.2. As a result, the region's share of global fossil-energy use doubled from about 13% in 1970 to about 26% in 2005. The data in Table 7.1 are used in the regional disaggregation of the EPPA model. (The complete list of countries in other regions is provided in Paltsev et al., 2005. The data are in 1990 international Geary-Khamis dollars, a conversion from market exchange rates to one corrected to reflect differences in international purchasing power.[1]) The share of East Asia in the world economy rose from 19% to about 32% between 1970 and 2000.

While similar data are unavailable for more recent years, continued rapid growth, especially in the PRC and India, means that the region's share of the world economy has likely continued to increase. Within East Asia, the PRC accounted for 38% of GDP in 2000, Japan 23%, India 17%, Other Asia[2] 16%, and Indonesia 6% when GDP is corrected for international purchasing power (Table 7.1 and Figure 7.1, panel a).

The economic shares of the four economies and one subregion ("five locations") within East Asia change when a different exchange rate convention is used, as illustrated in Figure 7.1, panel b, where GDPs for 2001 are reported at market exchange rates (MERs) based on data from the Global Trade Analysis Project (GTAP) dataset (Dimaranan, 2006). MER-based

Table 7.1 Gross Domestic Product Adjusted for International Purchasing Power

Location	1970	1980	1990	2000
China, People's Rep. of	663	1,100	2,209	4,483
India	470	637	1,098	1,924
Japan	1,014	1,568	2,321	2,669
Indonesia	139	276	451	676
Other Asia[a]	269	575	1,106	1,896
Total East Asia	2,555	4,156	7,185	11,648
World	13,583	19,767	27,058	36,406
East Asian Share (%)	19	21	27	32

a "Other Asia" unless otherwise listed consists of Republic of Korea; Malaysia; Philippines; Singapore; Taipei,China; and Thailand.

Note: Data are in billion 1990 international Geary-Khamis dollars.

Source: Maddison (2001).

comparisons result in a different ranking with Japan dominating the region (58%); the PRC and Other Asia are of a comparable economic size (18% and 15%); India's share (7%) is only half that of Other Asia (they are about the same size when adjusted for international purchasing power); and Indonesia's share is only 2%.

Figure 7.1 GDP Shares in East Asia

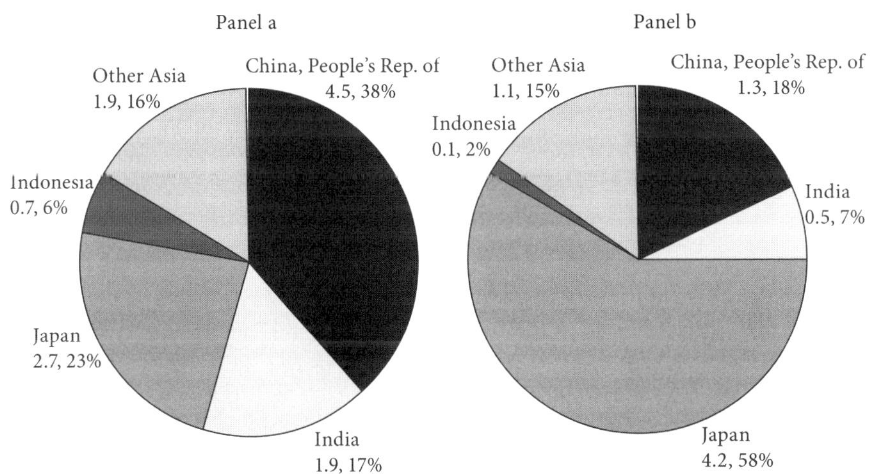

Notes: Panel a: GDP in 2000 adjusted for international purchasing power (in trillions of 1990 international Geary-Khamis dollars) and their shares in East Asia. Panel b: GDP in 2001 at market exchange rates (in trillions of 2001 US dollars) and their shares in East Asia.
Sources: Panel a: Authors' calculations based on Maddison (2001). Panel b: Authors' calculations based on Dimaranan (2006).

Table 7.2 Fossil-Fuel Energy Production and Use (exajoules)

Location	1970		1980		1990		2000	
	Prod.	Use	Prod.	Use	Prod.	Use	Prod.	Use
China, People's Rep. of	9.9	9.4	18.0	16.5	28.9	26.5	36.4	34.9
India	1.9	2.5	2.9	3.4	6.3	7.1	9.0	12.6
Japan	1.3	9.9	0.6	12.4	0.3	13.1	0.2	15.9
Indonesia	1.9	0.4	4.0	0.9	5.0	2.0	7.5	3.4
Other Asia	0.3	1.9	1.2	5.0	2.8	8.1	4.3	17.7
Total East Asia	15.3	24.0	26.7	38.2	43.3	56.7	57.4	84.4
World	197.1	187.1	254.8	247.5	292.6	284.7	329.4	323.5
East Asian Share (%)	8	13	10	15	15	20	17	26

Source: Calculated from IEA (2005).

Annual production and consumption numbers for fossil fuels for 1970–2000 are provided in Table 7.2. Fossil-fuel energy production in East Asia increased from 15 to 57 exajoules (EJ), with most of the additional production in the PRC. At the same time fossil-fuel use increased from 24 to 84 EJ. Only the PRC and Indonesia produce more fossil fuels than they consume. The PRC's production is dominated by coal, whereas Indonesia is a large oil and gas producer. Japan and Other Asia depend heavily on imports. The global share of fossil-fuel use by East Asia also increased, from 13% in 1970 to 26% in 2000. These aggregate data for fossil fuels do not show the fact that most of the increase in production has been in coal, at a time when Asia imported more and more oil.

The change in fossil-fuel energy intensity shows very different patterns among the region's economies (Table 7.3). The PRC's fossil energy intensity fell by about 45% in 1970–2000, and Japan's by 39%. However, in India, Indonesia, and Other Asia energy intensity rose.

Many of the industrial regions of the world have shown a long-term decline in energy intensity, but that pattern is not as consistent in other countries. Various factors likely affect these trends. Through at least some period of development, growth is likely to become more energy intensive as it involves rapid growth of energy-intensive industry such as steel and cement. In addition, the

Table 7.3 Fossil-Fuel Energy Intensity Index (1970 = 1.00)

Location	1980	1990	2000
China, People's Rep. of	1.06	0.85	0.55
India	1.03	1.23	1.25
Japan	0.81	0.58	0.61
Indonesia	1.12	1.59	1.78
Other Asia	1.24	1.04	1.33
World	0.91	0.76	0.64

Note: Fossil-fuel energy intensity is a ratio of fossil-fuel use to GDP. For comparability, it is indexed to the 1970 level.

Sources: GDP: Maddison (2001); fossil-fuel use: IEA (2005).

shift from non-commercial fuels during the development process shows up as an increase in measures of commercial energy intensity, even though total energy use may not be rising as rapidly. Non-commercial fuels are often used very inefficiently. Also, their use is often underreported, and so if energy use were fully accounted, the shift to commercial fuels would likely result in falling energy intensity.

Another important factor in increasing energy use is that as income increases, household demand for energy for, e.g., appliances, air conditioning, and transportation also likely contributes to increasing energy intensity. Energy pricing and industrial policy can also play an important role. Some of the most energy-intensive industries (iron ore, aluminum) have moved from industrial countries to developing countries, especially to those with lower energy prices.

In sum, though, the intensity of fossil-fuel use is the relevant measure in terms of the region's impact on fossil-fuel markets.

In recent years, various observers have attempted to explain the underlying causes of energy efficiency changes, with a particular focus on the PRC. Zhang (2003) concludes that the PRC's decline in energy intensity between 1980 and 2000 is due to an increase in energy efficiency rather than a structural economic shift. Crompton and Wu (2005) identify technical and structural changes as the main cause for this decline in the PRC. Fisher-Vanden et al. (2004, 2006) show a similar decline in energy intensity in the PRC (considering data up to 2000). Hang and Tu (2007) provide data for the PRC up to 2004 and show that aggregate energy intensity reversed its trend and has been increasing since 2001. In their analysis, they consider coal, oil, and electricity intensities, in addition to aggregate energy intensity. Electricity intensity was relatively stable from 1985 to 2004 (with some reduction from 1990 to 1999 and a relatively small increase from 1999 to 2004). Oil intensity shows only a very slight decline, while aggregate energy intensity is mainly driven by the changes in coal intensity.

Figure 7.2 illustrates the data for the PRC's energy intensity from different studies. The original units have been indexed relative to 1985. All studies agree on an impressive decline in the PRC's energy intensity between 1995 and 2000, but between 2000 and 2004 the increase in energy consumption was faster than the increase in GDP. Underlying the structural and technological changes in the PRC were large shifts in the organization of the economy as the country moved from a planned economy to one that was more driven by market forces, including adjustments to energy pricing.

A significant problem, though, in any analysis of the PRC's energy situation is data quality. Large changes in reported energy use and production in some years may reflect both changed reporting approaches rather than

Figure 7.2 Energy Intensity Index in the People's Republic of China (1985 = 1.00)

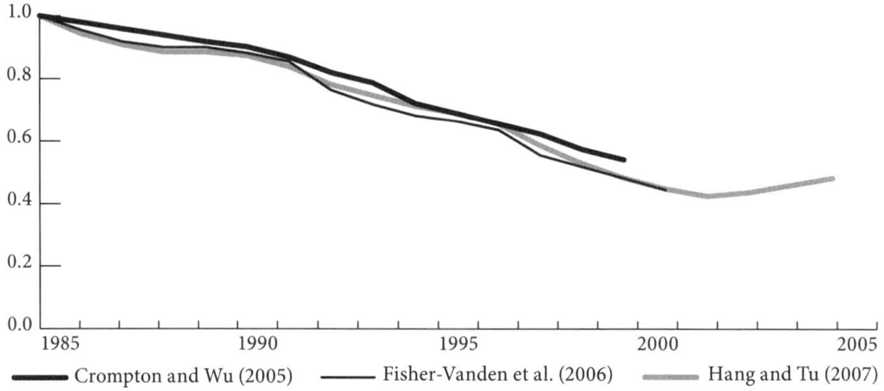

actual changes in use, and concerns about black markets in fuels that are not reported at all.

For other countries in the region, Crompton and Wu (2005) show that from 1980 to 1999 energy intensity in Indonesia, Japan, and Thailand was constant while that in the Republic of Korea increased slightly from the mid-1980s to the mid-1990s. Kasahara et al. (2007) provide historical data for energy intensity in Japan and discuss the potential future paths for energy and carbon intensities. They discuss three hypotheses: further increases in energy and carbon efficiency stemming from rising energy prices, efficiency improvements resulting from high economic growth and structural change in the economy, and exhaustion of the immediate sources of energy improvements.

As one looks forward, the outlook for energy-intensity change in the region is far from clear. The two countries that at one stage had contributed most to improving regional energy intensity, the PRC and Japan, appear to have reversed that trend, or at least stagnated. Technologically, Japan has been at the forefront of energy efficiency. The stagnation in overall intensity appears to stem from growing use of energy in households and for transportation, with slowing improvement in energy efficiency in basic industrial processes. The great improvement in energy intensity in the PRC was likely related to economic reform, whose effect may have run its course, or at least depends on how reforms will continue in the future. Energy intensity in other countries in East Asia continues to increase, although the intensity increase in India from 1990 to 2000 was very low, and so perhaps the structural transition from increasing to falling energy intensity (assuming such a pattern exists) is near. Similarly, the income level of Other Asia is fairly high, and its energy intensity increase may slow.

7.3 THE EPPA MODEL

To create illustrative scenarios of the future development of energy use in East Asia, the EPPA model is used. It is a recursive-dynamic multiregional CGE model of the world economy (Paltsev et al., 2005). EPPA is built on the GTAP dataset, which accommodates a consistent representation of energy markets in physical units as well as detailed data on regional production and bilateral trade flows (Hertel, 1997; Dimaranan and McDougall, 2002). Besides the GTAP dataset, EPPA uses additional data for emissions of greenhouse gases[3] and air pollutants[4] based on United States Environmental Protection Agency inventory data and projects.

For use in EPPA, the GTAP dataset is aggregated into 16 regions and 21 sectors (the sectors are shown in Table 7.4). Much of the sectoral detail is focused on energy production to better represent different technological alternatives in electricity generation. The base year of the EPPA model is 1997. From 2000 it is solved recursively at 5-year intervals. The EPPA model production and consumption sectors are represented by nested Constant Elasticity of Substitution (CES) production functions (or the Cobb-Douglas and Leontief special cases of the CES). The model is written in the GAMS software system and solved using MPSGE modeling language (Rutherford, 1995). EPPA has been used in a wide variety of policy applications (e.g., Jacoby et al., 1997; Reilly et al., 1999; Babiker et al., 2003; Reilly and Paltsev, 2006; CCSP, 2007; Paltsev et al., 2007).

Table 7.4 Sectors in the Emissions Prediction and Policy Analysis Model

Non-Energy
Agriculture
Services
Energy-Intensive Products
Manufacturing
Industrial Transportation
Household Transportation

Energy
Coal
Crude Oil
Refined Oil
Natural Gas
Electric: Fossil
Electric: Hydro
Electric: Nuclear
Electric: Solar and Wind
Electric: Biomass
Electric: Natural Gas Combined Cycle
Electric: Natural Gas Combined Cycle with CO_2 Capture and Storage
Electric: Integrated Coal Gasification with CO_2 Capture and Storage
Synthetic Gas from Coal
Oil from Shale
Liquid Fuel from Biomass

Note: Agriculture, services, energy-intensive products, manufacturing, coal, crude oil, refined oil, and natural gas sectors are aggregated from GTAP data; industrial transportation and household transportation sectors are disaggregated as documented in Paltsev et al. (2004); Hydropower and nuclear power and fossil-fuel electricity are disaggregated from the electricity sector (ELY) of the GTAP dataset; solar and wind power, biomass, natural gas combined cycle, natural gas combined cycle with CO_2 capture and storage, integrated coal gasification with CO_2 capture and storage, synthetic gas from coal, oil from shale, and liquid fuel from biomass sectors are advanced technology sectors that do not exist explicitly in the GTAP dataset.

Because of the focus on climate and energy policy, the model further disaggregates the GTAP data for transportation and existing energy supply technologies and includes a number of alternative energy supply technologies that were not in widespread use in 1997 but could take market share in the future under changed energy price or climate policy conditions. Bottom-up engineering details are incorporated in EPPA in the representation of these alternative energy supply technologies. Advanced technologies endogenously enter only when they become economically competitive with existing technologies. Competitiveness of different technologies depends on the endogenously determined prices for all inputs, as those prices depend on depletion of resources, economic policy, and other forces driving economic growth such as savings, investment, energy-efficiency improvements, and productivity of labor. (Additional information on the model's structure can be found in Paltsev et al., 2005.)

7.4 BASELINE SCENARIO

A key input in the baseline scenario is population, and for this purpose population projections of the United Nations (UN, 2001) are used, as shown in Table 7.5. The PRC and India are the two most populous countries in the world, and as a result nearly one half of the world's population lives in East Asia (according to the above definition). The UN projects greater slowing of population growth in East Asia compared with other regions, resulting in a decrease in East Asia's share in the total world population by 2050. India is projected to surpass the PRC as the country with the largest population by 2050.

Table 7.5 East Asian and World Population through 2025 (millions)

Location	2000	2025
China, People's Rep. of	1,282.0	1,479.5
India	1,008.9	1,351.8
Japan	127.1	123.8
Indonesia	212.8	274.1
Other Asia	211.4	272.9
Total East Asia	2,842.2	3,502.1
World	6,056.7	7,936.7
East Asian Share (%)	47	44

Source: UN (2001).

Another key element in scenario projections is the development of nuclear power and hydropower. Because of the political nature of expansion of these energy sources, the growth path of capacity for them is specified exogenously in EPPA, but in the case of hydropower it is based on an assessment of unexploited resources. As mentioned, the EPPA base year is 1997; to be consistent with recent expansion of nuclear power and hydropower, the growth of these sources through 2005 is benchmarked to IEA (2006) data. The

Table 7.6 Nuclear Power and Hydropower Production in 2005 (exajoules)

Location	Nuclear Power	Hydro-power
China, People's Rep. of	0.18	0.74
India	0.06	0.21
Japan	1.08	0.20
Indonesia	0.00	0.00
Other Asia	0.50	0.08
Total East Asia	1.83	1.23
World	9.39	7.18
East Asian Share (%)	19	17

Source: Emissions Prediction and Policy Analysis model's reference projections based on EIA (2006).

levels of production of both types of power shown in Table 7.6 are those projected by EPPA including this benchmarking.

Both types play a role in Asia (especially nuclear power in Japan and hydropower in the PRC) but they are still a small part of total energy use. Combined, these sources for the region amount to about 3 EJ compared with 84 EJ of fossil energy. To better compare electricity and fossil fuels, electricity sources such as nuclear and hydro are often reported in primary equivalent—the amount of fuel (coal, oil, gas) that would have been required to produce the same amount of electricity for a given conversion efficiency. Electricity conversion efficiencies are on average for most countries in the order of 30–35%. Thus, the primary equivalent of non-fossil sources is about three times that of electricity production. On this basis the region produced about 9 EJ of primary equivalent of nuclear power and hydropower, or still only about 10% of the fossil energy used.

The discussion of energy scenarios for East Asia begins with the baseline scenario. To perform a sensitivity analysis of the baseline results, several alternative scenarios are examined, where different assumptions about growth rates, energy efficiency, and energy prices are considered. As mentioned above, there is a substantial difference in opinion about future economic growth in Asia. In the EPPA model, GDP growth depends on population growth, labor productivity, capital accumulation, economic behavior of the agents, and other parameters of the model. Population growth and labor productivity are exogenous parameters, while decisions about production, consumption, and investment are based on economic optimization. Investments become capital in the next period.

Annual real GDP growth rates for the five locations, as well as aggregated growth rates in non-Asian regions, of the EPPA model and the total world growth rates for the baseline scenario are presented in Table 7.7. As with other components of EPPA, the period 1997–2005 is benchmarked to historical data or to short-term projections where data are not yet available. The baseline has GDP growth slowing in the PRC and India, while recovering from recent slow growth in Indonesia, Japan, and Other Asia. Annual performance of countries

Table 7.7 Annual Real GDP Growth Rates in the Baseline Scenario (%)

Year	China, People's Rep. of	India	Japan	Indonesia	Other Asia	Other Regions	World
1997–1999	6.4	6.1	0.9	1.7	2.4	3.5	3.2
2000–2004	9.6	5.0	1.1	2.4	3.3	2.3	2.5
2005–2009	5.4	4.1	3.2	3.4	3.3	3.4	3.5
2010–2014	5.0	3.8	3.3	3.7	3.4	3.4	3.5
2015–2019	4.6	3.3	3.2	3.6	3.2	3.2	3.3
2020–2024	4.3	2.8	3.2	3.7	3.0	2.9	3.1

Source: Authors' assumptions.

Table 7.8 Recent Annual Real GDP Growth Rates in the People's Republic of China, India, Indonesia, and Japan (%)

Year	China, People's Rep. of	India	Indonesia	Japan
1997	6.9	7.8	4.7	0.6
1998	6.0	4.9	-13.1	-1.0
1999	6.2	6.6	0.8	0.9
2000	8.6	5.4	5.4	3.0
2001	8.1	4.4	3.8	-1.2
2002	8.9	5.8	4.5	0.1
2003	10.4	3.8	4.8	1.8
2004	12.7	8.5	5.1	2.3
2005	10.2	7.5	5.6	2.6

Note: The PRC's growth reported by NBSC (2005) is 10.4% in 2003 and 12.7% in 2004, compared with 10.0% in 2003 and 10.1% in 2004 reported by IMF (2006a).

Sources: Data for PRC for 1997–2004: NBSC (2005); data for PRC for 2005: IMF (2006a); data for India: IMF (2007); data for Indonesia: IMF (2005, 2006b); data for Japan for 1997–2002: IEE (2004); data for Japan for 2003–2005: IMF (2006c).

in the region for 1997–2000 has been quite varied (Table 7.8), and this is clearly a large uncertainty into the future. If economic performance of the period 2000–2005 were sustained over the longer term, economic growth would be much more rapid than in the baseline case.

Figure 7.3 (panels a–f) shows the resulting energy consumption by fuel type for the East Asian region in total and for the five locations separately. Renewables include hydropower, solar and wind, and electricity from biomass and biomass liquids. Much non-commercial biomass currently used in many of these countries for cooking and home heating is not reported. Additional biofuels that are simulated in EPPA are commercial biofuels, primarily ethanol-based fuels that compete with petroleum products. Through the time horizon of this analysis (i.e., 2025), hydropower is the most significant renewable energy form, accounting for all renewables in 2000–2005 and around three quarters in 2010–2020. Some advanced biofuels begin to appear toward 2025

Figure 7.3 Energy Use in Baseline Scenario in East Asia (exajoules)

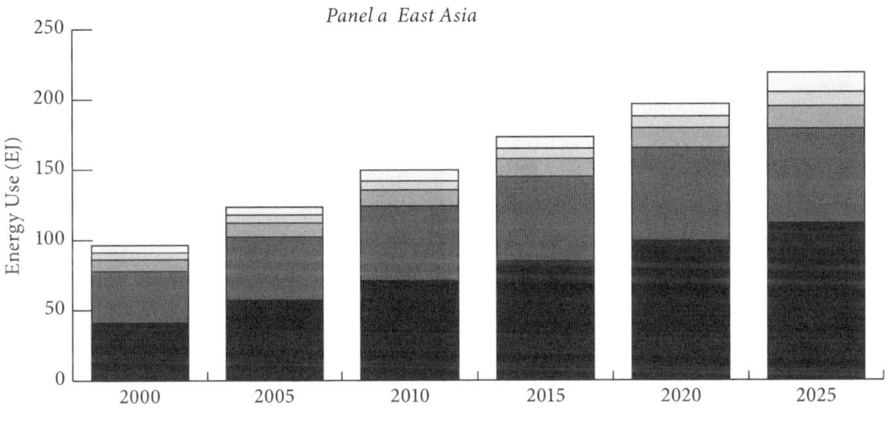

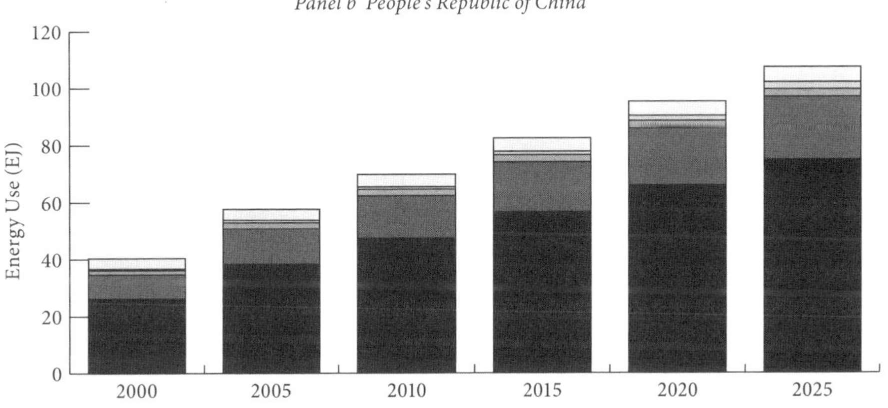

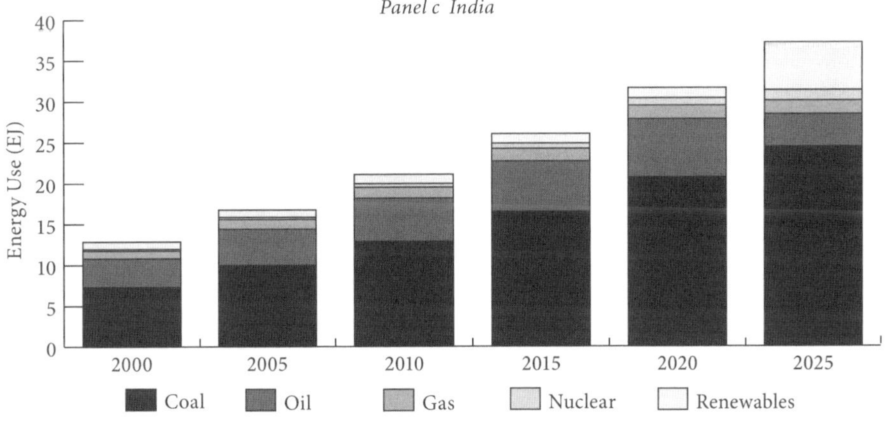

Figure 7.3 (continued)

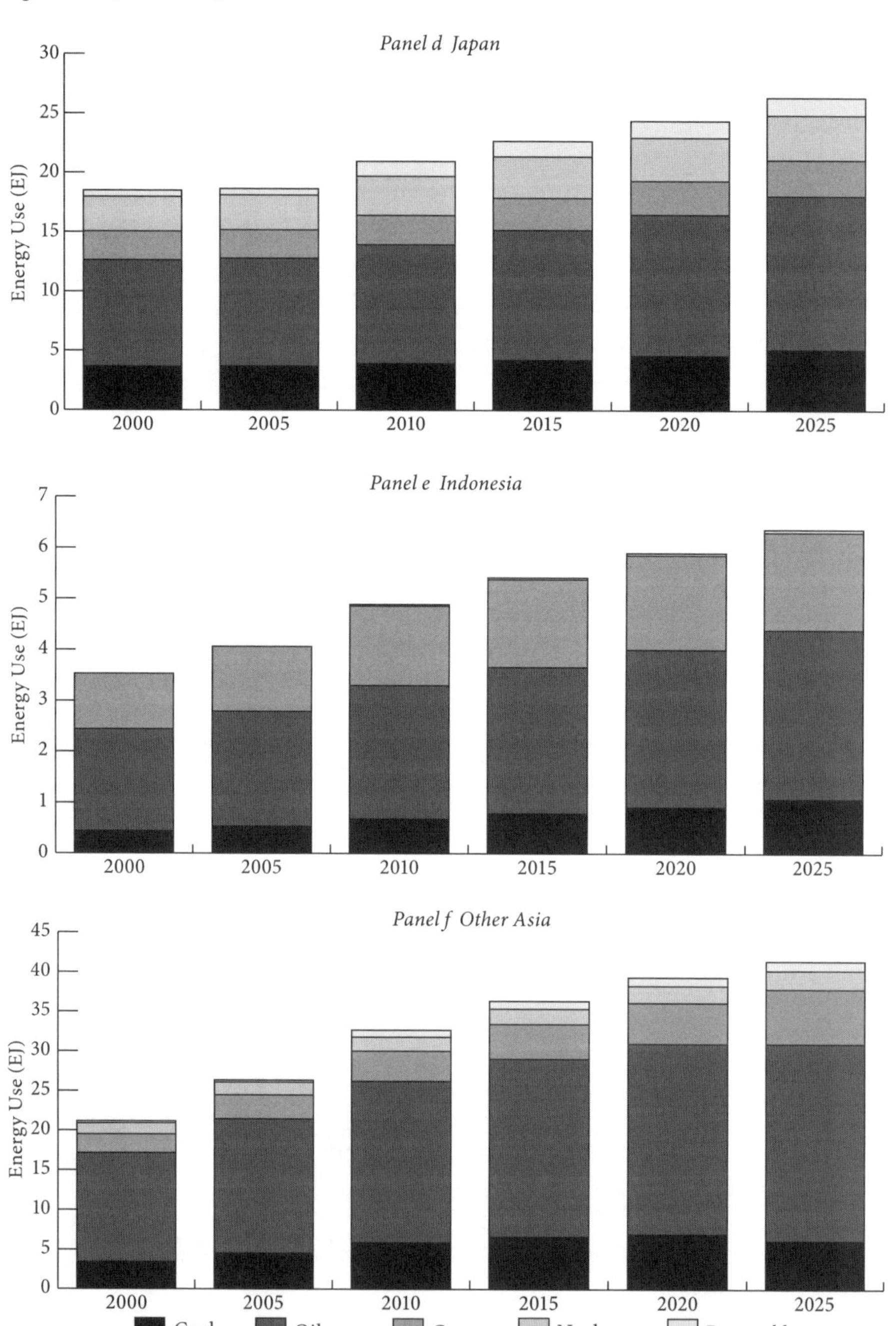

Source: Model simulations.

as oil prices rise.[5] Primary electricity (nuclear, hydro, and other renewable electricity) is reported in primary equivalent.

In the baseline, total energy use in the East Asian region is projected to increase from 124 to 219 EJ between 2005 and 2025, a 77% rise in 20 years. Of course, in the 20 years from 1980 to 2000, the region's energy use increased by 120% and so this is actually a slowing rate of growth. East Asian GDP is projected to grow by 105% in the baseline between 2005 and 2025. From these figures can be derived an implied aggregate energy-use elasticity for East Asia with respect to GDP, which is 0.74.

In this projection, energy use grows most rapidly in the PRC and India, where it triples (or nearly so). In Indonesia and Other Asia, energy use doubles over the period. In Japan it rises by only about 45%. Given this increase in energy use and GDP growth, the income elasticity of energy demand across the East Asian region varies from 0.47 in Japan, 0.55 in the PRC and Indonesia, 0.64 in Other Asia, to 1.23 in India. Adams and Shachmurove (2007) point out that a typical expectation is that energy elasticity in developing countries exceeds unity, in other words, energy consumption rises proportionately more rapidly than GDP. Of course, the actual experience of developing countries has varied as reflected in the historical changes in energy intensity discussed previously. In particular, until 5 years ago, the income elasticity of energy was considerably less than 1.0 in the PRC.

With regard to fuels, all fuel use grows rapidly in the PRC and India, whereas in the other locations oil and gas use grow more rapidly, as shown in Figure 7.3 (panels b–f). For the region as a whole, coal use expands more quickly because the PRC and India are large coal users, and rapid growth there drives the overall regional pattern. One result is that the region's share of world coal consumption rises from 48% to 53% between 2005 and 2025, and of total energy from 28% to 32%, even as its share of oil and gas changes little (Table 7.9).

Among the forces in EPPA that affect overall energy efficiency and fuel demand are the sectoral composition and non-price changes in fuel demand. A leading influence on sectoral composition is the change in patterns of

Table 7.9 Energy Use in East Asia as a Share of World Energy Use (%)

Energy	2005	2010	2015	2020	2025
Coal	48	50	53	53	53
Oil	26	27	28	28	27
Gas	11	11	11	11	12
Total Energy	28	29	31	32	32

Note: Nuclear, hydro, biomass, solar, and wind use are included in the total energy figures.

Source: Model simulations.

consumer demand with economic development. These sectoral shares are determined by many factors, including changes in relative factor prices, intermediate demand, final demand, and international trade. A CGE model like EPPA, which is based on CES functions, tends to be share preserving. As noted in Paltsev et al. (2005), additional adjustments are made from period to period to reflect the way that consumption is expected to change as per capita income increases. In addition, fuel shares for PRC households, which now often use much coal, are adjusted over time to switch to other fuels as incomes rise. In terms of production sectors, a vintaging structure in EPPA keeps some portion of capital fixed in a particular technology.

Fossil-fuel price indexes for the baseline scenario are given in Table 7.10, where 2005 is equal to 1.00. These are producer prices absent any excise taxes or trade and transport margins. The EPPA model determines relative prices, and the price projection for any particular year is most appropriately viewed as a 5-year average because the model simulates the economy in 5-year time steps. The EPPA model includes a sub-model for depletion of natural gas, oil, and coal on the basis of supply and demand conditions, and so prices are endogenously determined as an interaction of demand and supply in regional and world

Table 7.10 Fossil-Fuel Price Indexes (2005 = 1.00)

Location	Fuel	2010	2015	2020	2025
China, People's Rep. of	Coal	1.05	1.10	1.15	1.21
	Gas	1.17	1.41	1.70	2.04
India	Coal	1.07	1.16	1.26	1.33
	Gas	1.25	1.62	2.13	2.58
Japan	Coal	1.05	1.09	1.14	1.18
	Gas	1.14	1.30	1.49	1.78
Indonesia	Coal	1.05	1.09	1.14	1.17
	Gas	1.16	1.34	1.59	2.05
Other Asia	Coal	1.04	1.08	1.12	1.16
	Gas	1.19	1.39	1.67	2.18
World	Crude Oil	1.21	1.45	1.74	2.00

Note: The prices of coal and gas differ by country. Crude oil is a homogeneous good and so has a single world price.

Source: Model simulations.

markets. Coal and gas, as is the case with most goods in EPPA, are modeled as "Armington" goods, where domestic and imported goods are not perfect substitutes (Armington, 1969), and thus prices differ by country. However, crude oil is modeled as a homogenous good, giving a single world price.

Coal prices are projected to rise by about 20% by 2025, with the exception of India where prices are set to rise by 33%. The natural gas price increase is also the biggest in India, where it is projected to rise by nearly 150% compared with about 100% in the other locations in East Asia. Crude oil prices are projected to double. For a sense of actual fuel prices, the index values can be multiplied by the average 2002–2006 base prices ($40/barrel for oil, $5.40/ thousand cubic feet for natural gas, $26.70/short ton for coal).[6] In this regard, the crude oil price is already substantially higher than the recent 5-year average.

Net imports of fossil fuels (in US dollars) by the five East Asian locations increase substantially in the projections. Coal and oil imports double, while natural gas imports triple, in 2000–2025 in dollar terms. But if one looks at them as energy trade deficits as a share of GDP, the model does not predict big changes. They amount to less than 1% of GDP in 2005–2025, except for oil imports to India (around 1.5% of GDP) and oil imports to Other Asia (around 3–4% of GDP). At the same time in the baseline scenario, the EPPA model projects that the net export surplus in manufacturing and services as a share of GDP will increase in 2005–2025 from 6.5% to 7.4% in the PRC, from 3.7% to 4.9% in India, and from 7.7% to 12.8% in Other Asia. The net export surplus in these sectors in Japan is falling, but still outweighs an energy trade deficit there, while Indonesia continues to be an energy exporter over the period.

7.5 ALTERNATIVE SCENARIOS

The baseline scenario is one possible realization of future East Asian economic growth and energy use, and clearly such projections hold uncertainties. Several alternative scenarios are therefore constructed to represent these uncertainties and to help understand better how energy markets might affect energy use

Table 7.11 Illustrative Scenarios

Name	Description
Baseline	Emissions Prediction and Policy Analysis model's reference
High growth	High economic growth in all East Asia
Low growth	Low economic growth in all East Asia
High growth, PRC alone	High economic growth in PRC only
Low growth, PRC alone	Low economic growth in PRC only
No energy efficiency gain, PRC	No improvement in energy efficiency in PRC
Low energy prices	Low energy (coal, oil and gas) prices
Gas trade markets	Regional trade in gas in three markets: Asia (Asia, former Soviet Union, Middle East, Australia), Europe (Europe and Africa), Americas (North and South America)

Source: Authors.

and economic growth in the region. An outline of the alternative scenarios is provided in Table 7.11 above with shorthand scenario titles.

Economic growth is clearly one of the major drivers of energy demand and is an important uncertainty. Therefore, high and low economic growth scenarios are considered. Also, since the PRC is emerging as such a large force in the region and the world, it is interesting to ask how different prospects there could affect the region. Consequently, two scenarios are created with different economic growth assumptions in the PRC. In addition, as already noted, the last 5 years of the PRC's experience show a switch to an increase in energy intensity. To consider this effect, a scenario is built in which the non-price-induced energy efficiency improvement in EPPA (which in the baseline was improving at 1% a year) is eliminated.

A scenario is considered where energy prices return to their approximate 2000 levels and are held there. Perhaps such lower energy prices are possible, but a major purpose of this scenario is to understand whether projected rising energy prices slow economic growth in the region.

Finally, a gas market scenario (in which a fully integrated regional gas market emerges) is motivated by the fact that the region has substantial gas resources, but its lack of pipelines and liquefied natural gas (LNG) facilities currently limits use, especially in countries like the PRC and India. In this scenario it is assumed that broader regional markets in natural gas develop, implying that infrastructure impediments are overcome, and the large resources of gas in the region and from surrounding areas are made available for use in the PRC, India, and other import-dependent countries in East Asia.

7.5.1 Effects of Economic Growth in East Asia and the PRC, and of PRC Energy Efficiency, on East Asian Energy Use

To construct different scenarios of GDP growth, ranges of historical growth are considered. With regard to the PRC, the range of recent growth as shown in Table 7.8 has been wide, but for the last 5 years it has exceeded 10% per year. Some researchers question PRC national statistics (see, for example, Zhang, 2003; Adams and Shachmurove, 2007) and note that PRC statistics might have underestimated GDP in the past, and that the reported economic growth (NBSC, 2005) in recent years might be higher than actual growth as the statistics catch up with the previous underreporting (Zhang, 2003). This claim is rejected by PRC authorities on the basis that high economic growth in the PRC has been sustained for more than a decade. In recent years, India and Indonesia also have shown high economic growth rates. The International Monetary Fund (IMF) (2006b, 2007) projects sustained future economic growth in India and Indonesia of 6–7% a year. Japan has also shown an improved economic situation since 2003 and growth of more than 2%, which is slower than other dynamic Asian economies but a substantial improvement from its recent history.

The evidence would seem to suggest mostly higher economic growth than in the baseline; however, high- and low-growth cases are considered. In the high-growth case it is assumed that the PRC grows at an annual average of 9.8% over 2005–2025, India at 8%, Indonesia and Other Asia grow at 6%, and Japan at 3.5%. In the low-growth case, the PRC and India grow at an annual average of 3%, Indonesia and Other Asia at 2%, and Japan at 1%.

High growth in all East Asian locations lifts energy use to 430 EJ in 2025, while slow growth lifts it to 170 EJ, compared with the baseline of about 220 EJ (Figure 7.4, panels a and b). The 430 EJ level is about 3.5 times as high as 2005 levels whereas the 170 EJ is about a two-fifths increase. Coal and oil use both

Figure 7.4 Energy Use in East Asia under Scenarios of High and Low Growth, and No Energy Efficiency Gain in the People's Republic of China (exajoules)

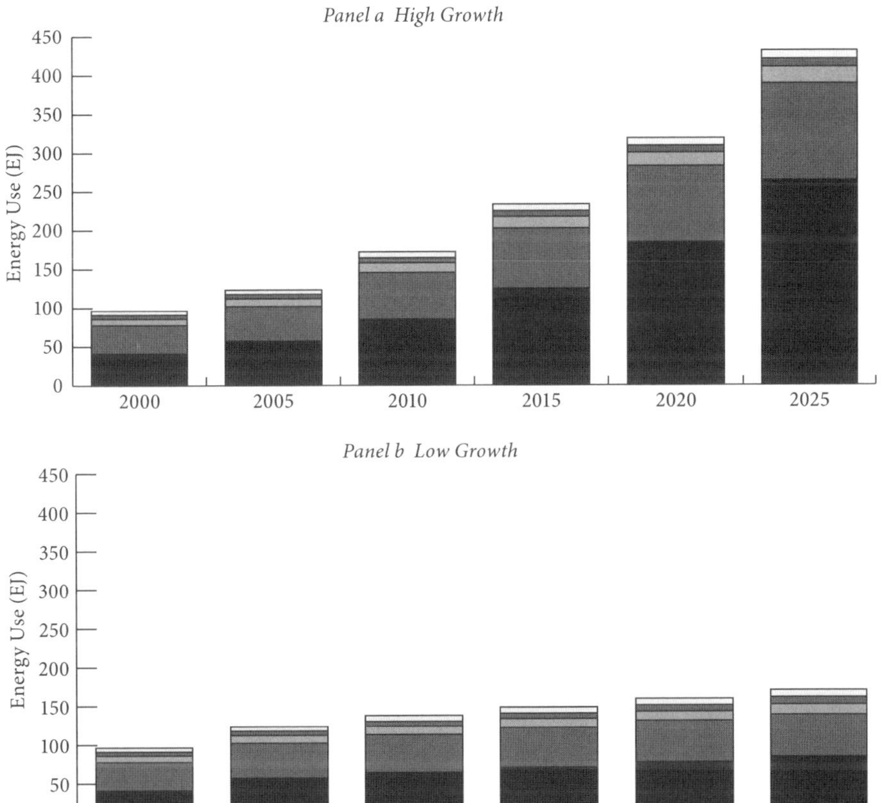

Figure 7.4 (continued)

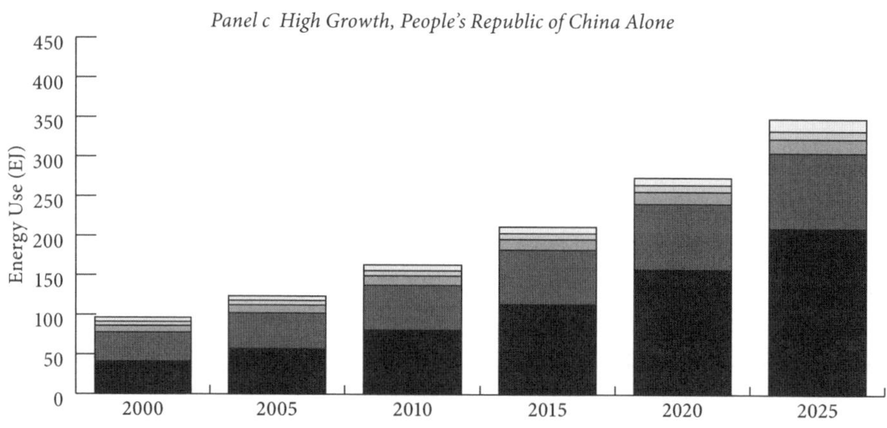

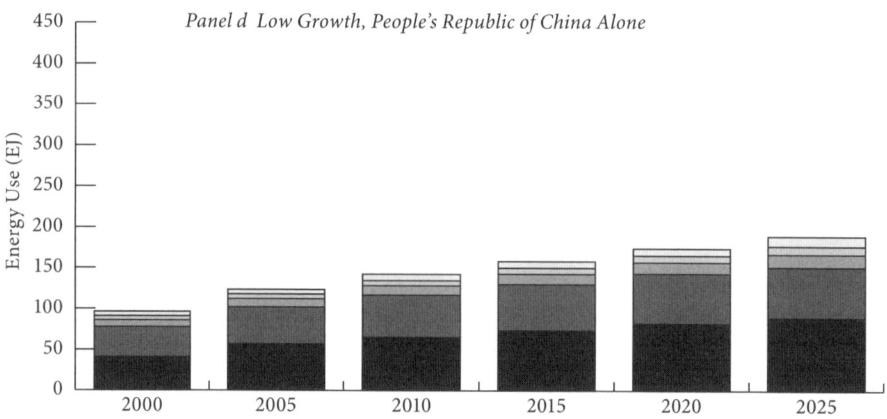

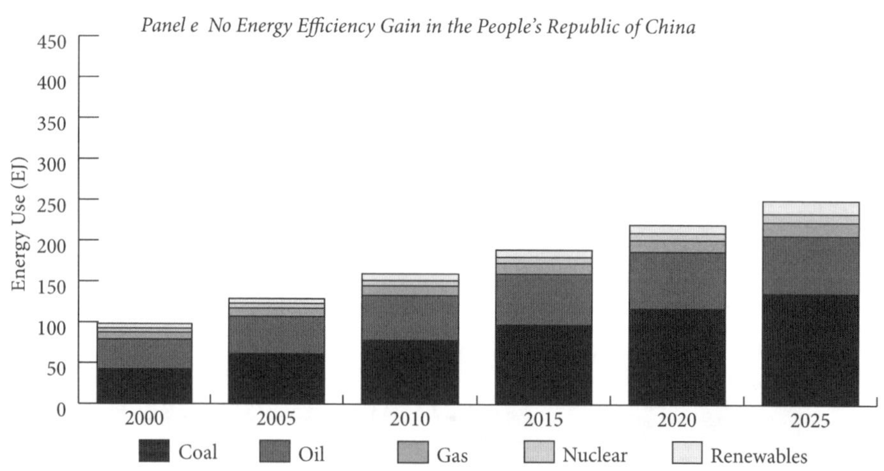

Source: Model simulations.

grow substantially. The PRC alone is a major factor in these differences. When varying GDP growth in the PRC alone is simulated, energy use in 2025 for the entire region ranges from 350 EJ (high growth, PRC alone) to about 180 EJ (low growth, PRC alone) as shown in Figure 7.4, panels c and d. High growth in the PRC alone would increase energy use by 140 EJ in 2025, nearly two thirds of the increase seen if all countries grow at the more rapid pace of the high-growth scenario.

Section 7.2 described historic trends for energy intensity in the PRC and Other Asia. There are two factors that primarily affect energy intensity in the EPPA model. The first is an exogenous factor conventionally referred to as Autonomous Energy Efficiency Improvement (AEEI). AEEI reduces the energy required in each sector to produce the same amount of output, assuming that other things (such as energy prices) are unchanged. In an actual forward simulation of the model, "other things" change endogenously, and these changes also affect energy efficiency. Actual energy efficiency of production of each sector in forward simulations is thus a combination of the exogenous AEEI factor, and endogenous effects through changes in fuel and other prices. AEEI can thus be seen as a reduced-form parameterization of the evolution of non-price-induced changes in energy demand. It is often assumed that AEEI represents technical change, but it should be seen as broadly representing other changes, such as in the structure of production within the aggregate sectors. (For more discussion about AEEI in the EPPA model, see Paltsev et al., 2005 and Kasahara et al., 2007.)

As shown in Figure 7.4, panel e, with none of the energy efficiency gain in the PRC, energy use in the region increases to 250 EJ, a 30 EJ increase from the baseline. While not as dramatic as the high-growth effect, this scenario may not provide a high bound on the energy-intensity effect. Even when the energy efficiency improvement is removed in the PRC, energy intensity still falls by around 0.5% annually over the period because of price and structural changes (compared with an annual average reduction in energy intensity in 2005–2025 of around 1.5% in the baseline scenario). The effect on energy use is not as strong as if intensity actually rises, as has occurred over the past 5 years.

7.5.2 Effects of Low Energy Prices and Gas Trade Markets on Energy Use in East Asia

While EPPA simulates fuel prices as an interaction of supply and demand, it is structured such that one can set a price path and examine the implications for energy demand. To set the prices in this way, the model ignores resource constraints and assumes that all the fuel demanded at the given price is forthcoming. As a result, the regional energy supply projections and energy trade are not particularly meaningful because they may imply large fuel resources, even though few resources are believed to exist. Thus this exercise is more useful for examining energy demand and the implications for economic growth of rising energy prices. If lower prices materialized, this would more likely result from some combination of reduced energy demand elsewhere in the world (perhaps in part because of stringent policies on greenhouse gas emissions reducing demand) or greater expansion of production in regions that are known to have large fuel resources (such as the Middle East, Russian Federation, or other countries of the former Soviet Union).

In any case, as shown in Figure 7.5, panel a, if energy prices are stable rather than rising, total energy demand in East Asia is projected to increase to almost 250 EJ, whereas in the baseline, rising prices keep use to about 220 EJ. Since the baseline has oil and gas prices rising faster than coal, it is not surprising to see more of the increase in oil and gas use.

While the fact that economic growth leads to higher energy use is generally well recognized, the potential effect of energy prices on economic growth is not often modeled. The general equilibrium structure of the EPPA model provides a consistent framework for assessing these effects. Table 7.12 shows that the energy price increases projected in the baseline would substantially slow economic growth compared with a case where fuel prices did not rise. The growth penalty is as much as 0.6% per year in India, about 0.4% per year in Other Asia, and about 0.2% per year in PRC, Indonesia, and Japan.[7]

As discussed above, natural gas markets in the baseline scenario are modeled such that international prices do not fully equalize, and therefore changes in domestic demand can have a larger effect on domestic prices. In the gas trade markets scenario the Armington specifications for natural gas are relaxed. The trade in gas is modeled in a similar fashion to trade in crude oil (which is a homogenous product with perfect substitution for imports across different regions of the world). In this scenario three regional markets are in fact assumed for natural gas, in each of which gas is a homogenous product: Asia (Asia, former Soviet Union, Middle East, Australia and New Zealand), Europe (Europe and Africa), and Americas (North and South America). "Armington-type" trade between the three regional gas markets remains. The motivation for the regional markets is that pipelines can serve to link markets that are geographically close. Whether this result accurately describes emerging global gas markets depends on how fast LNG infrastructure and pipelines can be developed (especially whether terminals and pipelines will be built to keep pace with demand), and how fast LNG production facilities can expand.

The main implication of a developing regional gas trade is that East Asia's gas use in 2025 expands from about 16 EJ in the baseline to about 28 EJ in the gas trade markets scenario. Most of this expansion displaces coal use, which

Figure 7.5 Energy Use in East Asia in Scenarios of Low Energy Prices and Expanded Regional Gas Trade (exajoules)

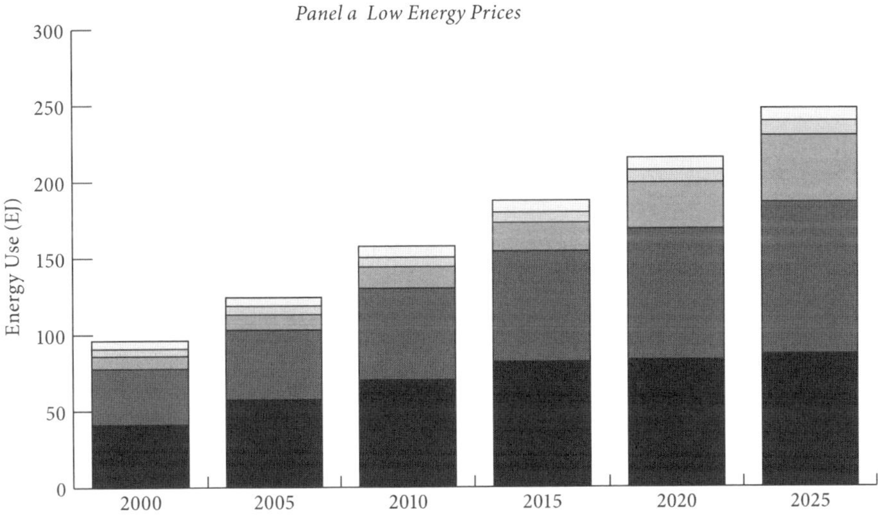

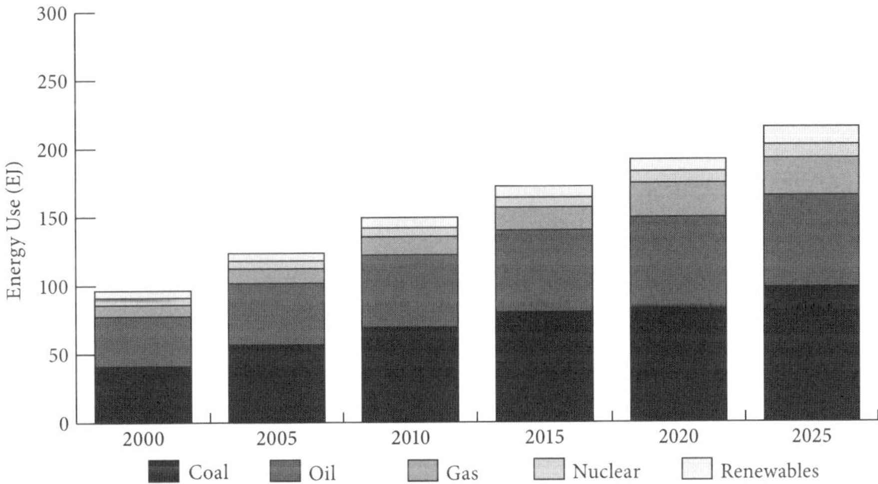

Source: Model simulations.

falls from about 110 EJ to 100 EJ in 2025. Thus, it appears that gas penetration is somewhat limited by the Armington assumption and, if this is realistic, by limits on transportation. A more fully integrated regional gas market would lead to much more gas use in the region. However, even with this significant

Table 7.12 Annual Real GDP Growth in Baseline and Low-Energy Price Scenarios (%)

	China, People's Rep. of	India	Japan	Indonesia	Other Asia
Baseline					
2010	5.4	4.1	3.2	3.4	3.3
2015	5.0	3.8	3.3	3.7	3.4
2020	4.6	3.3	3.2	3.6	3.2
2025	4.3	2.8	3.2	3.7	3.0
Low Energy Prices					
2010	5.7	4.7	3.4	3.5	3.8
2015	5.2	4.3	3.4	3.8	3.8
2020	4.8	3.8	3.3	3.7	3.6
2025	4.5	3.4	3.4	3.9	3.4

Source: Model simulations.

expansion of gas use, coal retains the largest share (by energy content) of energy used in East Asia.

7.5.3 Energy Prices in Alternative Scenarios

At the outset it was argued that as the East Asian region was large and rapidly growing, prospects there could affect energy markets globally. One way to measure East Asia's impact on energy markets is to examine energy prices. As noted previously, EPPA models a single world market for oil but national/regional markets for other fuels. Therefore, the impact on the world oil price is one direct measure of the region's effects on global energy markets. For coal and gas a stronger effect is expected within the region, but a more limited transmission of the effect is likely to other regions. Table 7.13 gives prices for coal and gas in the PRC and the world oil price under the alternative scenarios outlined above.

Taking first the world oil price in Table 7.13, the price index for crude oil reaches 2.4 in the high-growth scenario, compared with 1.89 in the low-growth scenario, and 2.00 in the baseline. Crude oil has been selling in the $60–70 range in 2006 and 2007. The baseline has it falling back from that level in the near term but rising to $80 by 2025, given a base year crude price of $40 per barrel. With high growth in East Asia, the price in 2025 is projected to approach $100 a barrel; with low growth in East Asia, the price might reach only $75. Thus in these simulations, growth prospects in East Asia could lead to a near $25 swing in the world oil price. Growth prospects in the PRC alone could lead to about a $10 swing in the global oil price. With no energy efficiency gain in the PRC, the effect on oil prices is smaller. The low-price scenario arbitrarily sets energy prices at a low level by assumption.

Table 7.13 Effects on Fossil-Fuel Prices in the People's Republic of China of Economic Growth, Energy Prices, Gas Markets, and Energy Efficiency (2005 = 1.00)

| | Baseline | People's Rep. of China Alone | | | East Asia | | | |
		High Growth	Low Growth	No Energy Efficiency	High Growth	Low Growth	Low Energy Prices	Gas Trade
Coal Price Index								
2005	1.00	1.00	1.00	1.00	1.00	1.00	1.00	1.00
2010	1.05	1.08	1.03	1.06	1.08	1.03	0.98	1.04
2015	1.10	1.19	1.06	1.13	1.20	1.05	0.98	1.08
2020	1.15	1.37	1.09	1.20	1.39	1.08	0.98	1.09
2025	1.21	1.71	1.12	1.29	1.74	1.1	0.98	1.16
Gas Price Index								
2005	1.00	1.00	1.00	1.00	1.00	1.00	1.00	1.00
2010	1.17	1.40	1.07	1.22	1.41	1.07	0.82	1.13
2015	1.41	2.08	1.18	1.54	2.1	1.17	0.82	1.28
2020	1.70	2.86	1.31	1.94	2.88	1.3	0.82	1.46
2025	2.04	3.26	1.47	2.43	3.29	1.46	0.82	1.65
Oil Price Index								
2005	1.00	1.00	1.00	1.00	1.00	1.00	1.00	1.00
2010	1.21	1.24	1.20	1.22	1.26	1.18	0.82	1.21
2015	1.45	1.53	1.43	1.46	1.60	1.39	0.82	1.45
2020	1.74	1.90	1.69	1.76	2.04	1.62	0.82	1.73
2025	2.00	2.23	1.96	2.02	2.4	1.89	0.82	2.00

Source: Model simulations.

Turning to the effects of alternative scenarios on coal and gas prices in the PRC, also shown in Table 7.13, in general the impacts are larger than on the world oil price. This is expected because the Armington trade assumption means that the ability to substitute imported fuels for domestic production is limited. Thus, much more of the increased demand pressure falls on domestic markets. There is some spillover on prices in the PRC as a result of varying conditions elsewhere in East Asia. For example, with high growth in the PRC alone, the PRC coal price index is 1.71 in 2025, but with high growth throughout East Asia, the coal price index in the PRC rises to 1.74. These spillovers can result directly from effects in the own-fuel market (the coal price is affected by increased demand for coal due to higher economic growth) and from interactions among markets (the higher price of imported gas or oil may lead to a shift to greater use of domestic coal and an increase in the domestic price).

The effects of varying scenarios of East Asia and PRC growth on coal and gas markets outside East Asia are much smaller. For example, for most of the scenarios, the EPPA model projects no substantial effects on the European or US coal price indexes. The greatest impact on energy demand is the high-growth scenario, which sees about a 1% increase in coal prices in Europe and the US, and an increase in gas prices of 6% in Europe and about 4% in the US, relative to the baseline in 2025. Effects are much smaller in other cases.

Thus, if this Armington representation of the fuel markets is realistic, the transmission of changes in East Asia to other regional markets is limited, with the major effect occurring in the crude oil market.

Also shown in Table 7.13 is the effect on prices of the development of regional gas trade markets. As expected, this reduces the price of gas in the PRC fairly substantially because it makes available to the PRC less expensive resources in the Russian Federation, other countries of the former Soviet Union, the Middle East, and Indonesia. The effect also spills over into the coal market, with the price index declining from 1.21 in the baseline to 1.16. Increased gas trade has almost no effect on the price of crude oil. The price effects are not surprising given that the main effect of regional gas trade markets is to increase gas use at the expense of coal—and less coal demand means a lower price.

Not shown in the table but of some interest is the fact that the development of regional gas trade markets results in an increased price of gas in Europe of about 7%. If gas in the Middle East, Russian Federation, and other countries of the former Soviet Union is readily accessible to East Asia, this increases competition for the fuel and makes it less available to Europe, which has developed an extensive gas transportation network.

7.6 CONCLUSIONS

The economies of East Asia are growing rapidly and energy use in the region is becoming a substantial share of world energy demand. In the baseline scenario, energy use increases in East Asia from around 120 EJ in 2005 to around 220 EJ in 2025. Coal continues to play a leading role as an energy source in the region, especially in the PRC and India, while oil and gas use is accelerated under different scenarios. For the region as a whole, coal use grows as a share of fuel use, but this is because the PRC and India are growing more rapidly, and so their fuel consumption patterns increasingly dominate the regional pattern.[8]

Alternative scenarios were developed to consider several specific questions including: How fast might energy demand grow in the East Asian region and how does such growth depend on key uncertainties? Do rising prices for energy affect growth in the region? Would growth in East Asia have a substantial effect on world energy markets? And, Would development of regional gas markets have large effects on energy use and gas markets in other regions?

With regard to future energy demand growth, the most important single factor is the rate of economic growth. In the baseline scenario, annual GDP growth rates in 2005–2025 were approximately as follows: PRC 5%, India 3.5%,

Indonesia 3.6%, Japan 3.2 %, and Other Asia 3.3%. In the high-growth scenario that extended rates seen in recent history, growth was substantially higher: PRC 9.8%, India 8%, Indonesia 6%, Japan 3.5%, and Other Asia 6%. In this scenario, energy demand rises to 430 EJ in 2025. In the low-growth scenario, it rises to only 170 EJ, compared with 220 EJ in the baseline. High growth in the PRC alone could account for about two thirds of the increase.

The effects of higher energy prices on growth in the region were found to be substantial. If, instead of rising at the rates projected in the baseline, prices were to fall back to year 2000 levels, annual average growth rates in the region would be 0.2–0.6% a year higher. The biggest growth impact is on India, and the smallest on PRC, Japan, and Indonesia.

A substantial impact of East Asia's energy demand growth on world oil markets was seen. Among scenarios of low and high demand growth in East Asia, the world oil price varied from about $75 to nearly $100 a barrel in 2025. Different growth prospects in the PRC alone could cause a swing in the world oil price in 2025 of about $10 a barrel. The effects on other fuel markets were considerably less, reflecting the lack of complete integration of these markets, at least as seen in the EPPA model.

Finally, it was found that if regional gas markets developed better links between East Asia on the one hand and the Russian Federation and the Middle East on the other, gas use in the region could grow substantially more than in the baseline, possibly increasing by about 75%. This would occur mainly through switching of gas for coal. An interesting side effect of the development of gas markets is that they could lead to higher gas prices in Europe. In the simulation, European gas prices increased by about 7% with the development of regional trade, because East Asian demand more effectively competed with that from Europe.

The above results depend on several aspects of the EPPA model structure, and on particular input assumptions that greatly simplify the representation of economic structure and decision making. The EPPA model draws heavily on neoclassical economic theory. While this underpinning is a strength in some regards, the model fails to capture many economic rigidities that could lead to unemployment or misallocation of resources; nor does it capture regulatory and policy detail. Still, given the many assumptions that are necessary to model national and global economic systems, the precise numerical results are not as important as the insights into the general direction of changes in the economy, the components of the energy system, and the approximate magnitude of the price effects seen under alternative assumptions.

ENDNOTES

1 Several methods can be used to generate economic accounts adjusted to measure "true" relative incomes and outputs of different countries. The well-known purchasing power parity indexes can be constructed in several ways and they produce somewhat different results. In this chapter the Maddison (2001) approach is followed, as are his data when the numbers adjusted for international purchasing power are reported.

2 "Other Asia" unless otherwise listed consists of Republic of Korea; Malaysia; Philippines; Singapore; Taipei,China; and Thailand. Regional aggregations are those used in the EPPA model. Detail on the regional composition is provided in Paltsev et al. (2005).

3 Carbon dioxide (CO_2), methane (CH_4), nitrous oxide (N_2O), hydrofluorocarbons (HFCs), perfluorocarbons (PFCs), and sulfur hexafluoride (SF_6).

4 Sulfur dioxide (SO_2), nitrogen oxides (NO_x), black carbon (BC), organic carbon (OC), ammonia (NH_3), carbon monoxide (CO), and non-methane volatile organic compounds (VOC).

5 The EPPA model was designed to be simulated over 100 years with a focus on greenhouse gas mitigation. In the longer term and under stringent climate policies, other renewables, especially biofuels, play a larger role.

6 These are US average prices for 2002–2006 computed from Department of Energy, Energy Information Administration price data.

7 Some caution is warranted in these calculations because of possible terms-of-trade effects that might stem from the location of the energy source, which, as discussed in the text, is not well resolved given the nature of the fuel price override in EPPA.

8 This chapter has focused on energy scenarios with no particular attention to an increase in emissions of greenhouse gases and other pollutants. The environmental consequences of rapid economic and energy demand growth, while an important topic, is beyond its scope.

REFERENCES

Adams, F.G. and Y. Shachmurove. 2007. "Modeling and Forecasting Energy Consumption in China: Implications for Chinese Energy Demand and Imports in 2020." *Energy Economics* (in press).

Altman, D. 2007. "China Growth Challenges the World's Ability to Adapt." *International Herald Tribune*, 7 March.

Armington, P.S. 1969. "A Theory of Demand for Products Distinguished by Place of Production." *International Monetary Fund Staff Papers* 16:159-76.

Babiker, M.H., G.E. Metcalf, and J. Reilly. 2003. "Tax Distortions and Global Climate Policy." *Journal of Environmental Economics and Management* 46:269-87.

Climate Change Science Program (CCSP). 2007. *CCSP Synthesis and Assessment Product 2.1, Part A: Scenarios of Greenhouse Gas Emissions and Atmospheric Concentrations.* L. Clarke et al., US CCSP, US Department of Energy, Washington, DC. Available: http://www.climatescience.gov/Library/sap/sap2-1/finalreport/default.htm.

Crompton, P. and Y. Wu. 2005. "Energy Consumption in China: Past Trends and Future Directions." *Energy Economics* 27:195-208.

Dimaranan, B. and R. McDougall. 2002. *Global Trade, Assistance, and Production: The GTAP 5 Data Base.* Center for Global Trade Analysis, Purdue University, West Lafayette, Indiana.

Dimaranan, B. 2006. *Global Trade, Assistance, and Production: The GTAP 6 Data Base.* Center for Global Trade Analysis, Purdue University, West Lafayette, Indiana.

Energy Information Administration (EIA). 2006. *International Energy Outlook 2006.* Energy Information Administration, US Department of Energy, Washington, DC.

Fisher-Vanden, K., G. Jefferson, H. Liu, and Q. Tao. 2004. "What is Driving China's Decline in Energy Intensity?" *Resource and Energy Economics* 26:77-97.

Fisher-Vanden, K., G. Jefferson, M. Jingkui, and X. Jianyi. 2006. "Technology Development and Energy Productivity in China." *Energy Economics* 28:690-705.

Hang, L. and M. Tu. 2007. "The Impacts of Energy Prices on Energy Intensity: Evidence from China." *Energy Policy* 35:2978-88.

Hertel, T. 1997. *Global Trade Analysis: Modeling and Applications.* Cambridge, UK: Cambridge University Press.

Institute of Energy Economics (IEE). 2004. *Handbook of Energy and Economics in Japan.* Tokyo.

International Energy Agency (IEA). 2005. *Energy Balances of Non-OECD Countries (2005 edition).* OECD/IEA, Paris.

International Monetary Fund (IMF). 2005. *Indonesia: Selected Issues.* IMF Staff Country Report 05/327. Washington, DC. Available: http://www.imf.org/external/pubs/ft/scr/2005/cr05327.pdf.

———. 2006a. IMF Survey. Vol. 35, 22. 11 December 2006. Washington, DC. Available: http://www.imf.org/external/pubs/ft/survey/2006/121106.pdf.

———. 2006b. Indonesia: 2006 Article IV Consultations. IMF Country Report 06/319. Washington, DC. Available: http://www.imf.org/external/pubs/ft/scr/2006/cr06319.pdf.

———. 2006c. Japan: 2006 Article IV Consultations. IMF Country Report 06/275. Washington, DC. Available: http://www.imf.org/external/pubs/ft/scr/2006/cr06275.pdf.

————. 2007. India: Staff report for the Article IV Consultations. IMF Country Report 07/63. Washington, DC. Available: http://www.imf.org/external/pubs/ft/scr/2007/cr0763.pdf.

Jacoby, H.D., R.S. Eckhaus, A.D. Ellerman, R.G. Prinn, D.M. Reiner, and Z. Yang. 1997. "CO_2 Emissions Limits: Economic Adjustments and the Distribution of Burdens." *The Energy Journal* 18(3):31-58.

Kasahara, S., S. Paltsev, J. Reilly, H. Jacoby, and A.D. Ellerman. 2007. "Climate Change Taxes and Energy Efficiency in Japan." *Environmental and Resource Economics*, 37(2):377-410, available as MIT Joint Program Report 121 at: http://web.mit.edu/globalchange/www/MITJPSPGC_Rpt121.pdf.

Maddison, A. 2001. *The World Economy: A Millennial Perspective*. Paris: OECD.

National Bureau of Statistics of China (NBSC). 2005. *China Statistical Yearbook 2005*. Beijing: China Statistics Press.

Paltsev, S., H. Jacoby, J. Reilly, L. Viguier, and M. Babiker. 2004. *Modeling the Transport Sector: The Role of Existing Fuel Taxes in Climate Policy*, MIT Joint Program on the Science and Policy of Global Change, Report 117, Cambridge, MA. Available: http://web.mit.edu/globalchange/www/MITJPSPGC_Rpt117.pdf.

Paltsev, S., J. Reilly, H. Jacoby, R. Eckaus, J. McFarland, M. Sarofim, M. Asadoorian, and M. Babiker. 2005. *The MIT Emissions Prediction and Policy Analysis (EPPA) Model: Version 4*, MIT Joint Program on the Science and Policy of Global Change, Report 125, Cambridge, MA. Available: http://web.mit.edu/globalchange/www/MITJPSPGC_Rpt125.pdf.

Paltsev, S., J. Reilly, H. Jacoby, A. Gurgel, G. Metcalf, A. Sokolov, and J. Holak. 2007. *Assessment of US Cap-and-Trade Proposals*. MIT Joint Program on the Science and Policy of Global Change, Report 146, Cambridge, MA. Available: http://web.mit.edu/globalchange/www/MITJPSPGC_Rpt146.pdf.

Reilly, J., Prinn, R.,J. Harnisch, J. Fitzmaurice, H. Jacoby, D. Kicklighter, J. Melillo, P. Stone, A. Sokolov, and C. Wang. 1999. "Multi-gas assessment of the Kyoto Protocol." *Nature* 401:549-55.

Reilly, J. and S. Paltsev. 2006. "European Greenhouse Gas Emissions Trading: A System in Transition." In M. De Miguel, X. Labandeira, and B. Manzano (eds.), *Economic Modeling of Climate Change and Energy Policies*. Edward Elgar Publishing, 45-64.

Rutherford, T. 1995. Demand Theory and General Equilibrium: An Intermediate Level Introduction to MPSGE, GAMS Development Corporation, Washington, DC. Available: http://www.gams.com/solvers/mpsge/gentle.htm.

United Nations (UN). 2001. *World Population Prospects: The 2000 Revision, Data in digital form*. Population Division, Department of Economic and Social Affairs.

Winters, L.A. and S. Yusuf. 2007. *Dancing with Giants: China, India, and the Global Economy*. World Bank: Washington, DC and The Institute of Policy Studies: Singapore.

Zhang, Z. 2003. "Why did the Energy Intensity Fall in China's Industrial Sector in the 1990s? The Relative Importance of Structural Change and intensity change." *Energy Economics* 25:625-38.

Zhao, X. and Y. Wu. 2007. "Determinants of China's Energy Imports: An Empirical Analysis." *Energy Policy* (in press).

Commentary on Chapter 7

David Roland-Holst

The dramatic and now established phenomenon of rapid Asian economic growth has global implications for resource use, and energy resources are among the most prominent of these in the minds of policy makers. Complex interactions between patterns of national growth, energy intensity, and resource development will ultimately determine the shared destiny of the world's economies, but we are clearly entering a new era of energy awareness and competition. In East Asia, economic dynamism over the past three decades has been accompanied by sharp increases in energy needs. The sustainability of Asia's growth experience will depend critically on how the region's governments manage their growth and technological progress.

Like the broader Asian economic picture, recent attention to East Asian energy demand has centered on the People's Republic of China (PRC), where explosive growth and its induced energy requirements have forced the country to look abroad to secure energy supplies. Between 1993 and 2004, the PRC moved from being a small net exporter of oil to the world's second-largest importer. Given the country's limited natural gas reserves, increasing the share of natural gas in its energy mix to lessen its predominant reliance on coal will require a heavy dependence on imports from the Russian Federation, Central Asia, Indonesia, and Australia. The PRC's coal resources, too, are affected by physical and economic constraints. Despite a 200-plus year reserve of this carbon fuel, the PRC became a net coal importer in early 2007.

The PRC's electric power expansion provides a useful case in point. Figure C.7.1 shows the PRC's capacity up to 2020, expanding sixfold over two 15-year intervals. The incremental increase in the latter period alone (shaded black) is larger than the entire installed capacity of the European Union in 2005.

As East Asian countries further integrate into the global economy, the region's energy supply-demand dynamics become increasingly implicated in global energy markets and spill over to far-away economies. Competition for scarce fossil-fuel resources has the potential to drive up energy prices across continents in world oil markets, regional natural gas markets, and potentially even coal markets. More indirectly, higher energy prices in East Asia could pose a risk to global economic stability via transmission along global supply chains that are increasingly dependent on Asian linkages. For these reasons, better visibility regarding East Asian energy trends has become ever more

Figure C.7.1 Estimated Share of the People's Republic of China's Coal-Fired Generation Capacity (gigawatts) Built by 1990, 2004, and to be Built by 2020

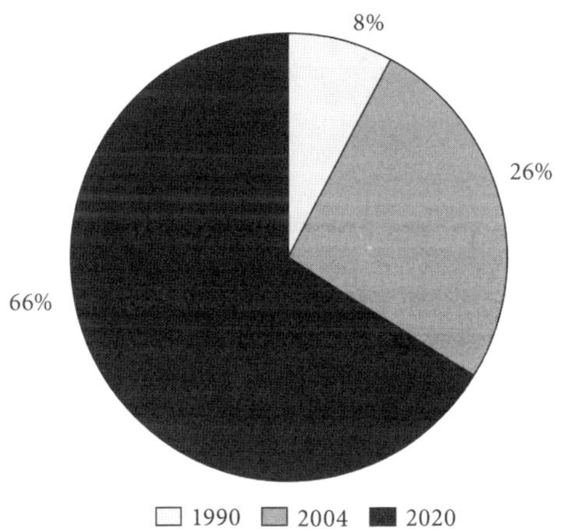

Note: Percentages are shares of an estimated 800 gigawatts of 2020 coal-fired generation capacity. For example, 26% of this capacity had been built by 2004. This assumes that targets for alternative generation sources and coal-fired power plant efficiency are met, and electricity demand grows as fast as GDP growth.
Source: Kahrl and Roland-Holst (2006).

important within the region and elsewhere.

This chapter examines the regional and global implications of East Asia's future energy demand growth. Using the MIT Emissions Prediction and Policy Analysis (EPPA) model, a multiregional computable general equilibrium model, the authors analyze the effects of a range of economic growth, energy price, and energy efficiency scenarios on East Asia's energy demand growth and economic growth. In addition, they consider the effects of East Asian energy demand growth and energy price shocks on world energy markets, particularly on natural gas markets.

The authors rightly conclude that East Asian energy needs over the next two decades are highly uncertain, varying by as much as a factor of two from their own baseline to their high-growth scenario. They also evaluate the adverse regional growth effects that would come from rising energy prices, estimating potential growth reductions of up to 0.6% a year. Internationally, the spillover effects of growth in East Asian energy demand on regional and global energy markets could be considerable. The authors estimate an East Asian "growth premium" on world oil markets that could be as high as $25 a barrel by 2025. Additionally, the dynamic demand growth in Asian regional gas markets could increase gas prices in Europe.

These are very important trends for regional policy makers and their multilateral counterparts. To a significant extent, markets will regulate scarcity through price increases, and the attendant adjustments will vary significantly across the globe. Countries with high levels of initial capital and technology will be more adaptable, while less advanced economies may experience unwelcome trade-offs between energy and other essential commodities or energy and economic growth. By historical standards, both the price and growth effects that the authors offer seem moderate. If the global economy were to experience higher price trajectories and volatility, the economic impact would be at once more dramatic and more complex. For example, sustained recessions in OECD economies accompanied the great energy shock of the 1970s, and this downturn was transmitted to developing economies via falling OECD absorption. While an energy price contagion is very unlikely, the growth drag of steadily rising prices will likewise be shared by both energy-intensive countries and their trading partners.

The composition of adverse energy price effects will be determined by a combination of adaptability (already mentioned) and purchasing power. For example, if the PRC currency were to appreciate by 20%, this would substantially discount dollar-denominated energy from a PRC perspective, but not for other countries. Another concern would be a reversal of economic convergence, the fortuitous global trend where lower-income countries have grown faster than higher-income countries. Rising energy prices could ration energy access and its growth benefits in poorer countries.

These perspectives may be unduly pessimistic, but it is clear that the rapid emergence of populous Asian economies portends a new global landscape of energy use. We know the conventional resources to meet these needs are increasingly constrained, and the promises of greater efficiency, renewable alternatives, and nuclear power remain uncertain. For these reasons, global energy markets will continue to arbitrate access to conventional resources, and efforts by economists to elucidate the implications of this can make essential contributions to more effective policy. Much of this work remains to be done, but the authors have made a very important contribution to our understanding of the economics of global energy linkages.

Reference to Commentary

Kahrl, Fredrich and David Roland-Holst. 2006. "China's Carbon Challenge: Insights from the Electric Power Sector." Working Paper 110106, Department of Agricultural and Resource Economics, University of California, Berkeley. November.

Projected Economic Growth in the People's Republic of China and India:
The Role of Demographic Change

Rod Tyers, Jane Golley, and Iain Bain

8.1 INTRODUCTION

As the third decade of economic reforms in the People's Republic of China (PRC) draws to an end, its remarkable growth performance appears almost unstoppable. Between 1995 and 2005, gross domestic product (GDP) and per capita GDP grew at average annual rates of 8.8% and 8.0%, respectively. The central Government's ambition to raise the level of GDP in 2020 to four times the level in 2000, which requires an annual growth rate of 7.2%, seems well within reach. India's economic reforms began in earnest in the early 1990s and, like the PRC's, signal a systemic shift toward an increasingly market-driven economy. Despite the fact that India's average annual GDP growth performance of 6% in the last decade is enviable by virtually any standards Indian authorities have increased their growth target to 8%, indicating some degree of disappointment with the growth rates achieved in the first decade of reforms (Ahluwalia, 2002). In both countries, there is no question that achieving high and sustainable rates of GDP growth is a major policy objective.

In the PRC, a potential threat to GDP growth in the future is low fertility and the associated aging of the population. The United Nations (UN, 2005) projects a rise in the proportion of over 60s in the PRC's population from 10% in 2000 to 20% in 2025, and further to 31% by 2050. Meanwhile, the proportion of the population of working age (15–59 years) is predicted to fall from 65% in 2000 to 62% in 2025 and 53% in 2050. By 2020, the growth of the working-age population will be negative, suggesting that GDP growth will suffer as a consequence. India, by contrast, began the millennium with a much younger population than the PRC. Its aged population was only 7.5% of the total in 2000 and is predicted to rise to 12% in 2025 and 21% in 2050. The share of India's working-age population will rise from 58% in 2000 to a peak of 64% in 2035. India's relatively youthful population and high fertility rate suggest that its "demographic dividend" could continue for another two decades at least, in stark contrast with the PRC's.

The demographic transition to slower population growth and the associated aging of the PRC's population have been profoundly affected by the one-child policy. Yet fertility rates would have declined anyway, affected, as they have been in the PRC's Asian neighbors, by urbanization, female education, increased labor force participation rates, and improved life expectancy of new-born children. Indeed, while the associated fall in fertility has not been as spectacular as the PRC's, India's fertility rates have also declined steadily since the 1970s. Critically, however, the different age structures of the world's two most populous countries have elicited different population policy responses: in the PRC, with a transition to a declining and aging population in prospect, there is now public discussion of more relaxed family planning policies, while in India, with a rapidly growing population and high youth dependency rates, the focus continues to be on fertility reduction (*Xinhuanet*, 2005; Padmadas et al., 2005).

In this chapter, the linkages between demographic change and economic growth in the PRC and India are explored using a new global demographic sub-model that is integrated with an adaptation of the GTAP-Dynamic global economic model in which regional households are disaggregated by age and gender. The chapter is organized as follows. Section 8.2 discusses the theoretical and practical links between demographic change and economic growth in the PRC and India. In Section 8.3 the demographic sub-model and the GTAP-Dynamic economic model are described. The composite model provides a means to examine quantitatively the interactions between demographic change and economic performance.

Section 8.4 constructs a baseline scenario for the global economy through 2030, while Section 8.5 presents alternative fertility scenarios for the two nations. In the PRC, a transition to a two-child policy is considered, while in India, the alternative scenario explores the possibility that fertility could decline more quickly than in the baseline. Simply put, while more rapid population growth in the PRC might ultimately ease some of the burden of an aging population and contribute to higher rates of growth in GDP, it is shown to be contradictory to the goal of delivering improvements in real per capita income. For India, the benefits of reduced fertility, in terms of real per capita income, are shown to be substantial. Conclusions are offered in Section 8.6.

8.2 DEMOGRAPHIC CHANGE AND ECONOMIC GROWTH

At a basic level, faster population growth should yield stronger GDP growth, but lower per capita income growth. This expectation stems from the standard Solow-Swan model of growth that realistically incorporates diminishing factor returns, but less realistically assumes constant labor participation rates across an ageless population. This ensures that faster population growth generates faster-growing labor forces, which yield steady states with lower levels of capital per worker and hence lower per capita income.[1] In reality, changing populations have changing age distributions, and this alters average labor force participation rates and youth and aged dependency ratios. In a developing country with large numbers of dependent children, a fall in fertility not only slows population growth, it also reduces the total dependency ratio and raises the proportion of the working-age population. Income per capita is boosted by the fall in dependency so that the basic Solow-Swan result is strengthened, giving rise to a "demographic dividend."[2] As Bloom and Canning (2005a) point out, however, the per capita income boost is not an automatic consequence of changes in the age distribution, but instead depends on the wide range of economic policies that affect labor market flexibility, including education, child-care, pension, and immigration policies.

In addition to these supply-side effects of demographic change on growth, changes in age distributions also have demand-side implications. Lower fertility raises the average age of the population, changing the scale and product composition of final consumption to more strongly reflect the preferences of adults and the aged. More importantly, the associated rise in the proportion of the working-age population tends to raise the share of households' disposable incomes devoted to saving. In a developing country, following a fertility decline, this tends to increase the average savings rate. If investment is also raised, the demographic dividend is further bolstered. Higgins (1998) notes that the demographic "center of gravity" for investment demand occurs earlier in the age distribution than for savings supply, because the former is most closely related to the youth share in the population—via its connection to labor force growth—while the latter is most closely related to the share of mature adults—via their retirement needs.

The divergence between these two centers of gravity means that the effect of the demographic transition on savings and investment depends on the country's openness to capital flows. The more open is the capital account the more investment and capital growth depends on the economy's comparative performance and not, narrowly, on its savings behavior. Thus, as the PRC and India trend toward more open capital accounts, the effects of aging on their savings rates are likely to diminish.[3] Indeed, in affecting growth performance, the supply-side effects of demographic change, acting as they do through the size of the labor force, tend to dominate demand-side changes in average savings rates and in the product composition of consumption.[4]

Complexities arise, however, when the interdependence of fertility, longevity, labor force participation, and savings rates are fully accounted for. In one theoretical study, Bloom and Canning (2005b) predict that improvements in health and longevity will result in rising natural retirement ages (increased aged labor force participation) but declining average savings rates, the latter occurring because longer working lives reduce the need to save for retirement in each successive age cohort. However, this may not be observed in practice, particularly if policy regimes prevent or discourage later retirement, in which case increased longevity will require higher average savings rates in order to finance a longer retirement period. Consider the PRC, for example, where current retirement ages of 60 for men and 55 for women were set at a time when life expectancy was only 50 years, compared with over 70 years now. As longevity continues to rise, later retirement ages would be a simple way of expanding the proportion of workers and thereby reducing the burden placed on the fiscal system of a rapidly aging population.[5] Much more complicated is the impact of alternative pension systems on retirement decisions and savings, since different measures to deal with pension-related budgetary pressures will have profoundly different effects.[6]

Additional complexities include the link between labor force growth, capital returns, and foreign investment. While attracting investment from abroad boosts GDP growth, the new capital returns are repatriated and the contribution to per capita income growth then depends on real wage changes.[7] Faster labor force growth necessarily slows real wage growth even while it attracts foreign investment. Also dependent on the growth path of real wages is the pattern of migration. Both the PRC and India are substantial suppliers of (mainly skilled) migrants to the rest of the world. Growth due to boosted fertility, and its slower real wage growth path, would raise skilled emigration and reduce skill endowments in both. Finally, any labor supply-driven acceleration of GDP growth tends to shift the terms of trade adversely by raising output relative to consumption and exports relative to imports.[8] This also tends to weigh down the growth of per capita income. While the integrated model of demography and economic growth to be presented in the next section does not activate all of these interactions, it offers scope to experiment with alternative assumptions about each.

Fertility is obviously one of the key determinants of demographic change and, according to Padmadas et al. (2005), it is the main driving force of population change (in absolute terms) in both the PRC and India. They also argue that fertility rates are the most uncertain component of population change in both countries, largely because of rising gender imbalances, changing social attitudes toward reproduction and family structure, and the uncertain impacts of policy responses.[9]

In the PRC, while debates over the extent of fertility decline continue, it is widely accepted that by the turn of the century fertility rates had fallen to well below the replacement level of 2.1 births per woman. According to the National Bureau of Statistics, the total fertility rate in 2000 was 1.22 children per woman, although even the PRC Government recognizes that the true figure was more like 1.8 because of the incentive that the policy creates to underreport births in surveys and censuses (Sharping, 2003). Zhang and Zhao (2006) provide an extensive survey of the literature on fertility decline in the PRC during the last two decades and conclude that the total fertility rate probably fell to around 1.6 by the year 2000. There is no question that the one-child policy has been fundamental in facilitating this decline. Sharping (2003) controls for numerous other factors that affect population growth—including urbanization, female education, increases in labor force participation, and improved life expectancy, all of which would have contributed to declining fertility in the PRC, regardless of its population policy—and estimates that, in the absence of the state's birth control policies, the PRC's population would have been 1.6 billion instead of the 1.27 billion reported at the end of the 20th century.

The PRC's one-child policy has always been a highly controversial topic outside the PRC, and is now being openly challenged within the country on the grounds of related aging and gender imbalance issues.[10] The Government is certainly prepared to consider the implications of higher fertility rates, as indicated by research conducted by the Development Research Centre of the State Council of China (2000), which projects population under a variety of fertility scenarios including a "two-child policy." Of course, it is impossible to know the extent to which such a policy would impact on actual future fertility rates. According to Demeny (2003), in the past the family planning programs that have been most effective in reducing fertility rates in developing countries tended to work via "heavy-handed methods of persuasion, and, in the especially important case of China, by coercion backed by legal sanctions" (p. 14). The PRC Government is very unlikely to utilize such methods to raise fertility rates in the future, and would instead need to resort to fiscal measures (such as tax breaks and family allowances) and policies to make motherhood and the women's labor force more compatible (through day-care services and more flexible work-hours).[11]

Like the PRC, India has also sought to restrict population growth, although the policy mechanisms have clearly differed. India introduced a "target" oriented family planning program in the early 1970s, using a range of incentives to promote sterilization. The initial sterilization target was directed toward males but was ultimately deemed unsuccessful, because of political instability and administrative failures, with female sterilization later emerging as the predominant method of contraception among Indian couples. In 1996, the Government adopted a target-free approach, relying on family planning services to promote the spacing of births, smaller families, and improvements in female education and health (Padmadas et al., 2005). India has since entered a period of rapid fertility decline, particularly in the South where some states already have rates below replacement levels, which Sen (2000) cites as evidence that social policies can be more effective than administrative control measures. Leaving aside this debate, it is clear that Indian fertility rates have declined in the last three decades, from 5.4 in 1970–1975, dropping to 4.2 in 1985–1990 and further to 3.1 in 2000–2005 (UN, 2005).

The question of interest here is the speed with which fertility rates will fall in the future. The key factors impacting on India's fertility rates are the age of first marriage; the uptake of family planning, especially sterilization; and the vast discrepancies in levels across Indian states. Increases in the first two and convergence in the last one will all contribute to future fertility declines (Padmadas et al., 2005). Different assessments of the relative importance of these factors, along with different methods and data, have given rise to a wide range of forecasts regarding Indian fertility rates in the first three decades of the 21st century. The "high fertility" variant of the UN (2005) population projections, for example, implies a total fertility rate that falls to 2.45 in 2025–2030, while according to Dyson's (2002) "low fertility" variant it will reach 1.59 by that time.[12] Any assessment of the implications of demographic change on India's economy should therefore encompass this wide range of fertility outcomes. To do so, however, requires a model that integrates the demography with the economics. To this we now turn.

8.3 MODELING DEMOGRAPHIC AND ECONOMIC CHANGE

The approach adopted follows Tyers and Shi (2007), in that it encompasses demographic and economic change. A complete demographic sub-model is integrated within a dynamic numerical model of the global economy. The economic model is a development of GTAP-Dynamic, the standard version of which has single households in each region and therefore no demographic structure.[13] The version used has regional households with endogenous savings rates that are disaggregated by age group, gender, and skill level.

8.3.1 Demography
The demographic sub-model tracks populations in four age groups, two genders, and two skill categories, for a total of 16 population groups in each of the

14 regions listed in Table 8.1.[14] The four age groups are the dependent young, adults of fertile and working age, older working adults, and the mostly retired over 60s. The skill subdivision is between households that provide production labor (unskilled) and those that provide professional labor (skilled).[15] Each age-gender-skill group is a homogeneous subpopulation with group-specific birth and death rates and rates of both immigration and emigration, as illustrated in Figure 8.1.[16] If the group spans T years, the survival rate to the next age group is the fraction $1/T$ of its population, after group-specific deaths have been removed and its population has been adjusted for net migration.

Table 8.1 Regional Composition in the Global Model

Region	Composition of Aggregates
Australia	
North America	Canada, Mexico, United States
Western Europe	European Union, including Switzerland and Scandinavia but excluding Czech Republic, Hungary, and Poland
Central Europe and former Soviet Union	Central Europe includes Czech Republic, Hungary, and Poland
Japan	
China, People's Rep. of (PRC)	Includes Hong Kong, China and Taipei,China
Indonesia	
Other East Asia	Republic of Korea, Malaysia, Philippines, Singapore, Thailand, and Viet Nam
India	
Other South Asia	Bangladesh, Bhutan, Maldives, Nepal, Pakistan, and Sri Lanka
South America	Argentina, Bolivia, Brazil, Chile, Colombia, Ecuador, Peru, Venezuela, Uruguay
Middle East and North Africa	Includes Morocco through the Islamic Republic of Iran
Sub-Saharan Africa	The rest of Africa
Rest of World	Includes the rest of Central America, Cambodia, Lao PDR, small island states of the Pacific, Atlantic and Indian oceans, Mediterranean Sea, Myanmar, Mongolia, New Zealand, and former Yugoslavia

Source: The GTAP Global Database, Version 5.

The final age group (60+) has duration equal to measured life expectancy at 60, which varies across genders and regions. The key demographic parameters, then, are birth rates, sex ratios at birth, age-gender specific death, immigration and emigration rates, and life expectancies at 60. Immigration and emigration are also age and gender specific. The model represents a full matrix of global migration flows for each age and gender group. Each of these flows is currently

Figure 8.1 The Demographic Sub-Model

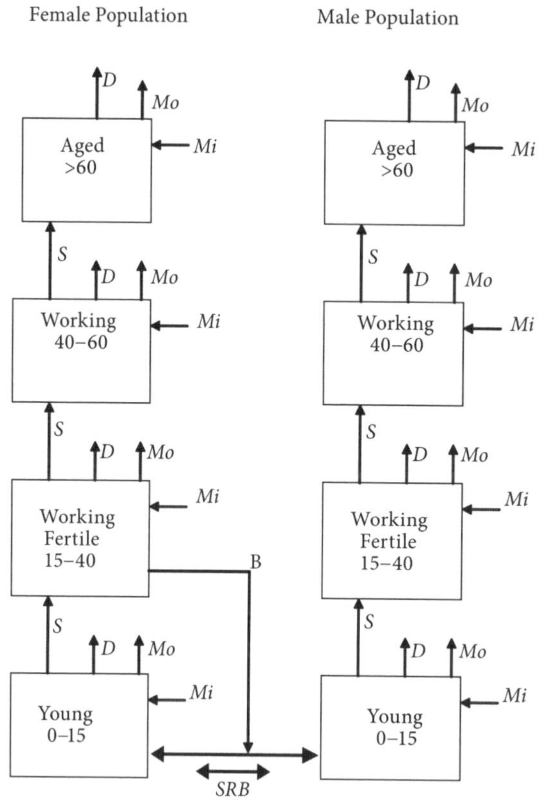

D = Deaths; S = Survival; B = Births; Mi = Immigration; Mo = Emigration; SRB = Sex Ratio at Birth.
Source: Authors.

set at a constant proportion of the population of its destination group, though for skilled workers the underlying migration rates are sensitive to interregional real wage divergences.[17] The birth rates, life expectancy at 60, and the age-specific mortality rates all trend through time asymptotically, as indicated in Tables 8.2–8.4. For each age-gender group and region, a target rate is identified.[18] The parameters then approach these target rates with initial growth rates determined by historical observation.

In particular, as indicated in Table 8.2, the declining trend in PRC fertility is noteworthy in that it extends the fall during the decade prior to the base year (1997) in an asymptotic approach toward, but not reaching, the birth rate observed in Japan in that year.[19] For India, the base year fertility rate is 3.5 and it trends asymptotically to a target of 2.56, slightly higher than the UN's (2005) "high" population projection for India.

A further key parameter is the rate at which each region's education and social development institutions transform production worker families into professional worker families. Each year a particular proportion of the population in each production worker age-gender group is transferred to professional (skilled) status. These proportions depend on the regions' levels of development, the associated capacities of their education systems, and the relative sizes of the production and professional labor groups. The resulting rates of transformation are based on changes during the decade prior to the base year, 1997, in the composition of aggregate regional labor forces as

Table 8.2 Baseline Birth Rates in the People's Republic of China, India, and Japan

Sex Ratio at Birth, Male/Female	PRC 1.10		India 1.08		Japan 1.06	
	Birth Rate[a]	Fertility Rate[b]	Birth Rate[a]	Fertility Rate[b]	Birth Rate[a]	Fertility Rate[b]
Base year, 1997	76	1.91	139	3.47	61	1.53
2010	62	1.56	114	2.86	59	1.48
2020	59	1.47	106	2.65	57	1.43
2030	58	1.44	102	2.56	56	1.40

Note: Birth rates are based on UN estimates and projections as represented by the US Bureau of the Census. The latter representation has annual changes in rates while the UN model has them stepped every 5 years. Initial birth rates are obtained from the UN model by dividing the number of births per year by the number of females aged 15–39. These rates change through time according to annualized projections by the US Bureau of the Census.

a Birth rates are here defined as the number of births per year per 1,000 women of fertile age. They are modified to allow for the modeling simplification that the fertile age group spans 15–39.

b Fertility rates are the average number of children borne by a woman throughout her life.

Source: Aggregated from UN (2003), US Department of Commerce–US Bureau of the Census "International Data Base," as compiled by Chan and Tyers (2006).

Table 8.3 Age-Gender Specific Death Rates in the People's Republic of China, India, and Japan

Deaths per 1,000	PRC		India		Japan	
	Males	Females	Males	Females	Males	Females
0–14						
Initial (1997)	1.10	0.90	8.2	9.4	1.20	1.00
2030	0.54	0.49	3.8	4.5	0.72	0.66
15–39						
Initial (1997)	0.80	0.30	2.4	2.4	0.70	0.40
2030	0.57	0.19	2.0	2.1	0.55	0.77
40–59						
Initial (1997)	3.90	2.00	12.3	8.5	3.50	2.00
2030	2.81	1.78	7.6	5.7	2.60	1.39

Note: Projections of these parameters to 2020 assume convergence on target rates observed in comparatively "advanced" countries, as explained in the text. Only the end point values are shown here but the model uses values that change with time along the path to convergence.

Source: Values to 1997 are from UN (2000) and WHO (2003).

between production and professional workers. They are constant within each region and through time.[20]

Labor Force

To evaluate the number of "full-time equivalent" workers we first construct labor force participation rates, by gender and age group for each region from International Labour Organization (ILO) statistics on the "economically active population." We then investigate the proportion of workers that are part-time

Table 8.4 Life Expectancy at 60 in the People's Republic of China, India, and Japan

Deaths per 1,000	PRC		India		Japan	
	Males	Females	Males	Females	Males	Females
Initial (1997)	16	18	15	18	22	26
2030	17	21	16	19	27	33

Note: Projections of these parameters to 2020 assume convergence on target rates observed in comparatively "advanced" countries, as explained in the text. Only the end point values are shown here but the model uses values that change with time along the path to convergence.

Source: Values to 1997 are from UN (2000).

and the hours they work relative to each regional standard for full-time work. The result is the number of full-time equivalents per worker.[21] For each age-gender group and region, a target country is identified whose participation rate is approached asymptotically. As with birth and death rates, the rate of this approach is determined by the initial rate of change. Target rates are chosen from countries considered "advanced" in terms of trends in participation rates. Where female participation rates are rising, therefore, Norway provides a commonly chosen target because its female labor force participation rates are higher than for other countries.[22]

For the PRC, India, and comparator nation Japan, the trends in labor force participation rates are summarized in Table 8.5. The PRC's aged labor force participation rises slightly to allow for the expected shortfall in pension income as more retirees leave private sector employment.[23] This, combined with the effects of aging, raises the trend of the labor force above that of the population, as indicated in Figure 8.2. Both India and Japan have substantially higher aged participation rates, lacking the PRC's central planning history. The other striking pattern is that India's female labor force participation rates are considerably lower in the 15–59 age groups than those in either the PRC or Japan. This reduces India's recorded labor force relative to that of the PRC.

The Baseline Population Projections for the PRC and India

The baseline population and labor force projections for both the PRC and India are illustrated in Figure 8.2 and the associated changes in the age and gender structure of each are summarized in Table 8.6. A dramatic contrast between the projections for the PRC and India is clear from Figure 8.2. While the PRC labor force falls short of a 10% increase over the three decades, and declines after 2015, the Indian labor force grows strongly, with expansion continuing beyond 2030.

This contrast is primarily due to the relative youth of India's population and its higher initial fertility rate. Even though the two populations are projected

Table 8.5 Age-Gender Specific Participation Rates in the People's Republic of China, India, and Japan, Base Year (1997) and Projected, 2030

Full-time Equivalent Workers per Person	PRC		India		Japan	
	Males	Females	Males	Females	Males	Females
15–39						
Initial (1997)	0.79	0.60	0.81	0.35	0.77	0.55
2030	0.77	0.61	0.83	0.36	0.76	0.57
40–59						
Initial (1997)	0.91	0.43	0.95	0.38	0.97	0.67
2030	0.93	0.45	0.96	0.40	0.97	0.68
60+						
Initial (1997)	0.24	0.04	0.55	0.14	0.46	0.22
2030	0.27	0.08	0.55	0.15	0.52	0.25

Note: Projections of these parameters to 2020 assume convergence on target rates observed in comparatively "advanced" countries, as explained in the text. Only the end point values are shown here but the model uses values that change with time along the path to convergence.

Source: Values to 1997 are from UN (2000).

Table 8.6 Baseline Population and Labor Force Structure in the People's Republic of China and India

Population	PRC			India		
	Millions	% Female	% 60+	Millions	% Female	% 60+
Initial (1997)	1,272	48.5	9.7	955	48.2	6.9
2010	1,364	48.7	14.8	1,146	48.4	10.6
2020	1,375	48.8	18.4	1,263	48.5	13.0
2030	1,353	49.0	21.2	1,349	48.5	14.8
Labor Force	Millions	% Female	% 40+	Millions	% Female	% 40+
Initial (1997)	570	37.2	33.9	356	27.4	36.3
2010	618	36.7	41.2	459	27.1	41.7
2020	624	36.4	45.4	522	27.2	45.1
2030	613	36.1	48.2	568	27.5	47.9

Source: Projections using the baseline simulation of the model described in the text. The labor forces are measured in full-time equivalent workers.

to reach rough parity in 2030, the Indian labor force remains smaller, due mainly to lower female participation rates. Accordingly, the projected Indian labor force has proportionally more male workers. Interestingly, the more rapid aging of the PRC population notwithstanding, the projected labor forces of the two nations maintain very similar proportions of older workers. This is explained by India's comparatively high participation rates of 60+ workers, which are close to double the PRC's for both men and women.

Figure 8.2 Projected Populations and Labor Forces, People's Republic of China and India

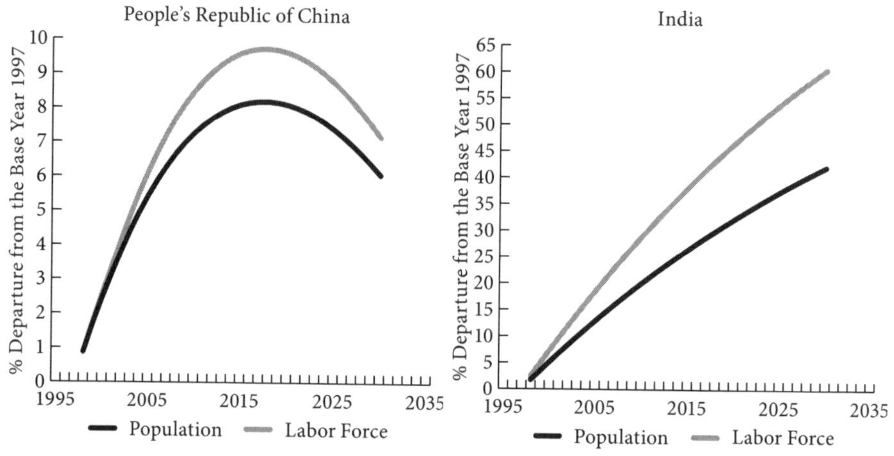

Note: Projected population and labor force data are cumulative percentage departures from the base year 1997, drawn from the baseline simulation in which the fertility of the People's Republic of China is projected to decline faster than India's and in which India starts with a much younger population.
Source: Projections using the baseline simulation of the model described in the text.

8.3.2 The Global Economic Model

GTAP-Dynamic is a multiregion, multiproduct dynamic simulation model of the world economy. Money is not included and the prices of goods and assets are set relative to a global numeraire. In the version used, the world is subdivided, consistent with the demographic sub-model, into the 14 regions indicated in Table 8.1. Industries are aggregated into just three sectors, food (including processed foods), industry (mining and manufacturing), and services. To reflect composition differences between regions, these products are differentiated by region of origin, meaning that the "food" produced in one region is not the same as that produced in others. Consumers substitute imperfectly between foods from different regions.

As in other dynamic models of the global economy, in GTAP-Dynamic the endogenous component of simulated economic growth is physical capital accumulation. Technical change is introduced in the form of exogenous productivity growth that is sector and factor specific. Skill (or human capital) acquisition is driven by the constant transformation rates of production into skilled worker households introduced in the previous section. A consequence of its capital accumulation dynamics is the property of all dynamic models of the Solow-Swan type that incorporate diminishing returns to factor use, namely that an increase in the growth rate of the population raises the growth rate of real GDP but reduces the level of real per capita income. What distinguishes the model from this simpler progenitor is the endogeneity of savings rates and its multiregional structure. All regional capital accounts are open and investors have adaptive expectations about real regional net rates of return on installed capital. These drive the distribution of investment across regions. In each, the level of investment is determined by a comparison of net rates of return on domestic installed capital with borrowing rates yielded by a global trust, to which each region's saving contributes, adjusted by calibrated region-specific interest premiums.

To capture the full effects of demographic change, including those of aging, the standard model has been modified to include multiple age, gender, and skill groups in line with the structure of the demographic sub-model. In the complete model, these 16 groups differ in their shares of regional disposable incomes, consumption preferences, savings rates, and their labor supply behavior. While the consumption-savings choice differs for each age-gender group, it is dependent for all on group-specific real per capita disposable income and the real lending rate. Governments balance their budgets while private groups save or borrow.[24] The high initial rates for the elderly are partly due to the complication that a comparatively large proportion of consumption spending by the PRC elderly is probably financed from the income of younger family members, but it also reflects high pension payments to retirees from state-owned enterprises.[25]

8.4 CONSTRUCTING THE BASELINE ECONOMIC SCENARIO

The baseline scenario represents a "business as usual" projection of the global economy through 2030. Although policy analysis can be sensitive to the content of this scenario, our focus is the extent of departures associated with alternative assumptions about demographic change in the PRC and India. Nonetheless, it is instructive to describe the baseline, not only because it has some limited forecasting value but primarily because all scenarios have in common a set of assumptions about future trends in key exogenous variables and because some exposition of the baseline makes the construction of departures from it clearer.

8.4.1 Shifts in Consumption-Savings Preferences

Consumption-savings preferences are represented by age-gender specific consumption equations that relate real per capita consumption to real per capita income and the real lending rate in each region. There is no endogeneity of savings rates to longevity even though death rates decline through time and 60+ life expectancy increases in both nations, as indicated in Tables 8.3 and 8.4.[26] Consumption-savings preferences are shifted through time, however, in

Table 8.7 Baseline Saving Rates from Personal Disposable Income (%)

| | 15–39 | | 40–59 | | 60+ | |
	Male	Female	Male	Female	Male	Female
North America						
1997	14	14	19	19	-30	-30
2030	14	14	19	19	-30	-30
Japan						
1997	24	24	28	28	22	22
2030	24	24	28	28	10	10
PRC						
1997	35	35	40	40	31	31
2030	53	35	40	40	10	10
India						
1997	19	19	28	28	19	19
2030	19	19	28	28	19	19

Source: These depend on initial values, compiled from studies of consumption behavior in particular countries, including Mexico: Attanasio and Szekely (1998); Japan: Kitamura et al. (2001); US: Attanasio et al. (1999), and on changes in real per capita disposable income and real lending rates that occur during the simulation.

the few regions where changes are expected to stem from developments not represented in the model. Baseline savings rates for four regions are listed in Table 8.7. Aged savings rates in East Asia are projected to decline. Unlike the aged dissaving of Europe and North America, the aged of Asia are positive savers, due to high, aged labor-force participation rates and the mixing of incomes in extended families. In Japan, aged participation rates are the highest in the industrialized world and unlikely to increase. As Japanese family sizes fall, the aged savings rates are likely to trend toward European levels. In the case of the PRC, the 60+ age group has low labor force participation but high state-financed retirement incomes. Because the proportion of the aged retiring on relatively generous state pensions is declining, the 60+ groups are assumed to have underlying savings rates that fall through time. There is no a priori reason to think that India's underlying savings rates will rise or fall, and so these are held constant.

8.4.2 Exogenous Factor Productivity Growth

The model simulates growth due to the accumulation of labor, skill, and physical capital. Other sources of growth, including all that passes for "technical change," are introduced via exogenous productivity growth shocks. These are applied separately for each of the model's five factors of production (land, physical capital, natural resources, production labor, and professional labor). The overall rate of economic growth proves quite sensitive to these exogenous shocks since the larger these are for a particular region, the larger is that region's marginal product of capital. The region therefore enjoys higher levels of investment and hence a double boost to its per capita real income growth rate.[27] Baseline agricultural productivity is assumed to grow more rapidly than that in the other sectors in the PRC, along with Australia, Indonesia, Other East Asia, India, and Other South Asia. This allows continued shedding of labor to the other sectors.[28] In the other industrialized regions, the process of labor relocation has slowed and labor productivity growth is slower in agriculture. In the other developing regions, the relocation of workers from agriculture has tended not to be so rapid. Labor productivity in services is

Table 8.8 Baseline Factor Productivity Growth in the People's Republic of China and India (%)

Country/Sector	Primary Factor					Regional and Sectoral Averages
	Land	Production Labor	Skilled Labor	Capital	Natural Resources	
PRC						3.1
Food	1.8	5.0	7.0	1.6	0.0	3.6
Industrial Products	0.0	4.0	8.5	1.6	0.7	3.2
Services	0.0	2.1	6.0	1.6	0.0	2.8
India						2.3
Food	2.1	3.0	6.0	1.6	0.0	2.4
Industrial Products	0.0	3.5	7.0	1.6	0.7	2.5
Services	0.0	2.0	4.0	1.6	0.0	2.0

Note: Productivity growth is specified by primary factor. For display, sectoral averages are weighted by factor cost shares in each sector and regional averages by sectoral value-added shares in each region.

Source: Tyers et al. (2005).

particularly difficult to measure. In general, baseline productivity growth rates in services are assumed to be slower than in the tradable goods sectors in all regions. The baseline values of each productivity growth rate for the PRC and India are given in Table 8.8.

8.4.3 Interest Premiums

The standard GTAP-Dynamic model takes no explicit account of financial market maturity or investment risk, and so tends to allocate investment to regions that have growing marginal products of physical capital. These tend to be labor-abundant developing countries with still rapidly expanding labor forces. Although the raw model finds these regions attractive prospects for this reason, we know that considerations of financial market segmentation, depth, and risk limit the flow of foreign investment at present and that these are likely to remain important in the future. To account for this we have constructed a "pre-base" simulation in which we set the relative growth rates of investment across regions as exogenous. This allows us to capture the implied investment premium changes between the base year, 1997, and 2005, for which we have data on actual investment patterns. Thereafter, of course, while the pre-base path of investment in each region remains exogenous, values are judgmental. Global investment rises and falls depending on the level of global saving, but its allocation between regions is thus controlled. To do this, the interest premium variable (GTAP-Dynamic variable *SDRORT*) is made endogenous. This creates wedges between international and regional borrowing rates. The results from the pre-baseline simulation show high interest premiums for the populous developing regions of Indonesia, India, South America, and Sub-Saharan Africa. In regions where labor forces are falling or growing more slowly premiums fall through time.

Most significant is a secular fall in the PRC premium. This is because the pre-base simulation incorporates the extraordinary rise in PRC investment of the 2000–2005 period and allows it to continue growing in real terms, albeit at declining rates thereafter, and notwithstanding the eventual decline in the PRC's labor force. On average, PRC investment is financed at an initial rate substantially above the PRC Government's long-term bond rate (which exceeds the corresponding US rate by 40%). The pre-base path of the PRC's domestic interest rate declines initially, wiping out most of the initial PRC premium.[29] This has the important consequence that the rental price of physical capital in the PRC declines in the early years of the pre-base simulation. In the case of India, the pre-base domestic interest rate is stable through time. Since the global interest rate rises gradually, this implies a decline in its interest premium, though one that is less spectacular than for the PRC. India's capital rental rate is nonetheless stable through time while those of the industrial economies, with more open capital markets, are rising with the global interest rate. Relatively competitive capital costs are therefore factors that lead both economies to have advantageously depreciating real exchange rates.[30]

Once the regional interest premiums are calibrated, they are rendered exogenous while actual investment in each region is made endogenous. The baseline simulation is then constructed, yielding results that are identical to the pre-baseline simulation and that then form the basis for comparison with subsequent simulations in which PRC and Indian fertility levels are altered.

8.4.4 The Baseline Projection

Overall baseline economic performance is suggested by Table 8.9, which details the average GDP and real per capita income growth performance of each region from 1997 to 2030. In part because of its comparatively young population and hence its continuing rapid labor force growth, India attracts

Table 8.9 Baseline Real GDP and Per Capita Income Projections to 2030

	Change in 2030 Over 1997, %		Implied Average Annual Growth, %	
	Real GDP	Real per Capita Income	Real GDP	Real per Capita Income
Australia	401	275	5.0	4.1
North America	350	255	4.7	3.9
Western Europe	227	276	3.7	4.1
Central Europe and former Soviet Union	337	331	4.6	4.5
Japan	214	313	3.5	4.4
PRC	743	578	6.7	6.0
Indonesia	253	243	3.9	3.8
Other East Asia	410	468	5.1	5.4
India	892	435	7.2	5.2
Other South Asia	424	157	5.1	2.9
South America	267	205	4.0	3.4
Middle East and North Africa	319	152	4.4	2.8
Sub-Saharan Africa	373	150	4.8	2.8
Rest of World	498	277	5.6	4.1

Source: The (low fertility) baseline projection described in the text.

Figure 8.3 Baseline GDP Growth Rates in the People's Republic of China and India

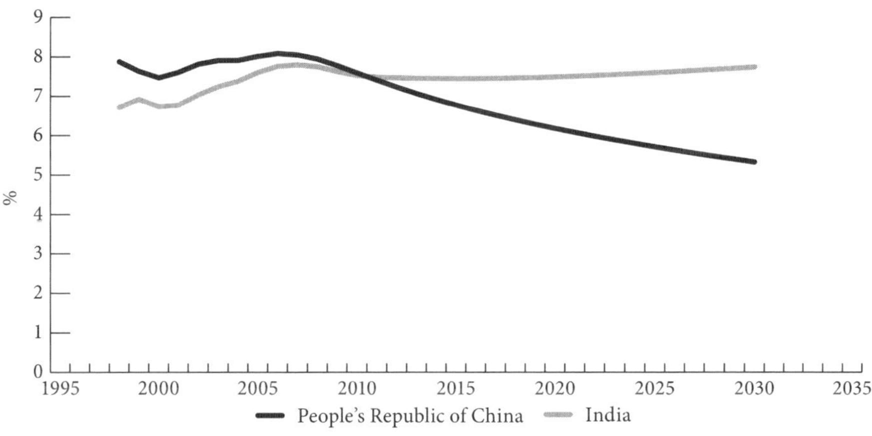

Note: GDP growth rates are annual growth rates of real GDP. They diverge in the later years due to slower labor force growth in the People's Republic of China.
Source: Model simulations.

substantial new investment and is projected to take over from the PRC as the world's most rapidly expanding region (Figure 8.3). Rapid population growth detracts from India's long-term real per capita income performance, however.

By this criterion, the PRC is the strongest performing region through the three decades. "Other East Asia" is also a strong performer, while the older industrial economies continue to grow more slowly. The emphasis hereafter is on quantifying the departures from this baseline projection due to changes in PRC and Indian fertility.

8.5 ALTERNATIVE FERTILITY POLICIES

The alternative scenario considered for the PRC is a path toward a two-child policy. That for India is a fertility decline that is faster than our baseline assumption. The effect of each is described in turn and, for the economic bottom line, a set of elasticities is constructed that enables the two scenarios to be compared.

8.5.1 A Two-Child Policy for the PRC

Following Sharping (2003) and the Development Research Centre of the State Council of China (2000), a higher-fertility scenario is constructed that, unlike the baseline, which has declining PRC fertility, offers an asymptotic trend toward a fertility rate of 2.3. It is similar to the State Council's "two-child policy" and to Sharping's "delayed two-child policy." The implications for the PRC's total population are indicated in Table 8.10. The correspondence between our model simulations and State Council projections is close. A transition to a two-child policy would raise the 2030 population by 19% relative to the baseline. The implications for population and labor force growth are displayed graphically in Figure 8.4. Critically, the path of the PRC's labor force shifts up by substantially less than that of its population. By 2030, the labor force is larger by 13% and the population by 21%. This is because higher fertility first enlarges the youth population, which does not contribute to the labor force. The PRC population continues to age, however, though more slowly with the higher fertility rate. This can be seen from the non-working-age dependency

Table 8.10 Population in the People's Republic of China: Baseline and Two-Child Policy

Millions	Baseline: (Declining) Fertility, 1.91 to 1.45	Transition to Two-Child Policy	
		State Council	Our Model
2000	1,252	1,270	1,257
2010	1,311	1,369	1,369
2020	1,321	1,466	1,462
2030	1,296	1,518	1,536

Notes: 1. The base year for our simulations is 1997, when the PRC's fertility rate was approximately 1.91. 2. Our two-child policy simulation matches the fertility assumptions by Sharping (2003).

Sources: Development Research Centre of the State Council of China (2000) and simulations using the model described in the text.

Figure 8.4 Population and Labor Force, Alternative Scenarios

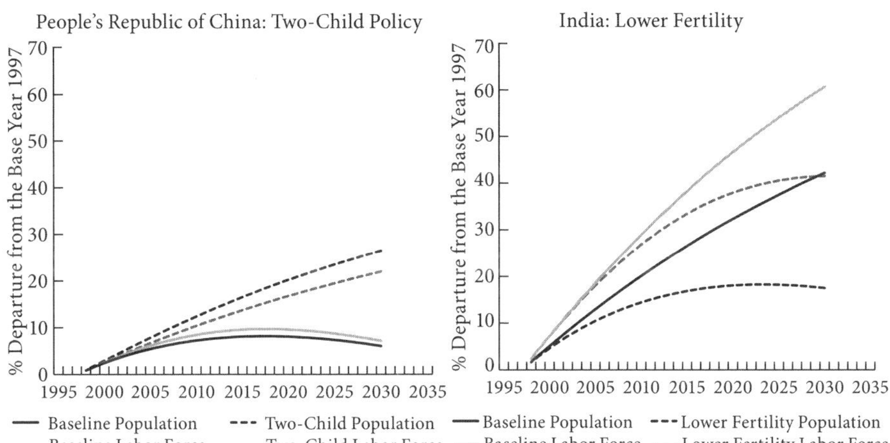

Note: Population and labor force data are cumulative percentage departures from the base year 1997.
Source: Model simulations.

Figure 8.5 Total, Youth, and Non-Working-Age (60+) Dependency Ratios

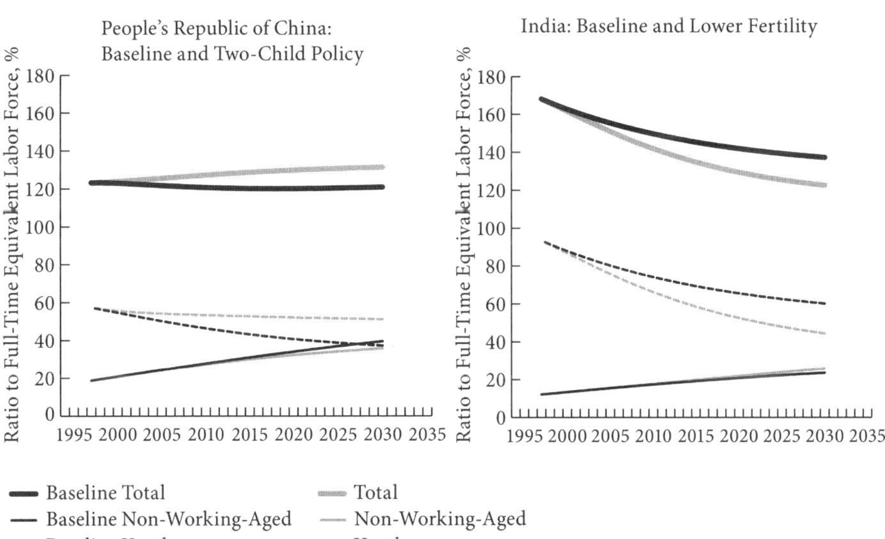

Note: The ratios are the simulated ratios of the total population, total youth population (0–15), and the non-working-age population, to the full-time equivalent labor force.
Source: Model simulations.

ratio in Figure 8.5 above. After 2015 there are discernible differences, with the two-child policy yielding a 2030 ratio that is lower by four percentage points than the low-fertility baseline. As the diagram shows clearly, however, rising youth dependency dominates declining aged dependency, ensuring that the total dependency rate is higher throughout the period.

The economic effects of this change bear out the generalizations of Section 8.2. In particular, supply-side labor force effects are dominant. The anticipated supply-side story is that the labor force expands, increasing capital productivity, and therefore the return on PRC investment. This attracts more of the world's savings into the PRC so that its capital stock grows more rapidly. The PRC's GDP might therefore be expected to be boosted substantially by increased fertility, through its direct and indirect influence over the supply of the two main factors of production, labor and capital.[31] In per capita terms, however, three forces would conspire to ensure that the average Chinese person bears an economic cost. First, the Solow-Swan predisposition (due to diminishing marginal returns) toward slower real wage growth would tend to slow the growth of income per capita. Second, the associated shift in the age distribution would cause a rise in dependency (a loss of the "demographic dividend") and hence a further slowing of per capita income growth. Finally,

Table 8.11 Economic Effects of Higher Fertility in the People's Republic of China, 2030 (% departures of the two-child policy from the baseline)

	Real Invest- ment	Real Capital Stock	Labor Force	Skill Inten- sity[a]	Real Skilled Wage	Real Prod- uction Wage	Skill Premium	Rate of Return[b]	Terms of Trade	Real GDP	Real per Capita GNP
2010	1.95	0.67	1.76	-0.26	-0.25	-0.65	0.41	0.05	0.04	1.15	-3.68
2020	7.77	3.65	6.51	-0.70	-1.01	-2.10	1.11	0.09	-0.29	4.73	-6.77
2030	15.87	8.87	13.85	-1.07	-2.53	-4.02	1.56	0.11	-1.13	10.52	-9.46

a Skill intensity is the ratio of the skilled to the total labor force. b On installed capital (percentage points).

Source: The baseline and the PRC two-child policy projections from the model described in the text.

because much of the new capital stems from foreign investment, there is a need to reward its foreign owners.

These expectations are indeed borne out in our simulations, as indicated in Table 8.11. The labor force increase is associated with a small decline in the skill intensity, due in part to the emigration of more internationally mobile skilled workers, which is boosted by lower skilled wages relative to destination regions.[32] The rate of return on installed capital in the PRC is raised and so, therefore, is the level of investment and the growth in the physical capital stock. Yet because the original stimulus is labor force expansion, this is insufficient to prevent a decline in labor productivity and hence in real wages. The terms of trade deteriorate slightly due to expansion in the PRC's core

Figure 8.6 GDP, Real Wages, and Real Per Capita Income, Alternative Scenarios

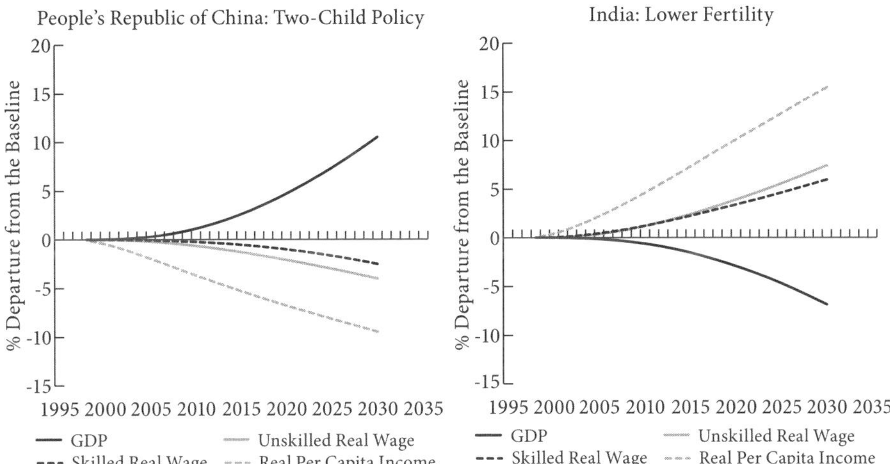

Note: The data are percentage departures from the baseline simulation for each year.
Source: Model simulations.

factors of production and the associated higher rise in the volume of exports than imports.

In the end, the PRC's 2030 GDP is higher by 11% compared with the baseline, as shown in Figure 8.6. Yet the faster growth this represents is still insufficient to keep pace with India's baseline growth rates.[33] And the rise in dependency, the slowdown in real wage growth, the repatriation abroad of an increased proportion of the income accruing to capital, the small addition to skilled emigration, and the terms-of-trade deterioration all conspire to slow the rate of growth in real per capita income. By 2030 it is smaller than the baseline by 10%. This represents a significant cost of "pushing the fertility button" to achieve higher GDP growth.[34]

8.5.2 Lower Fertility in India

The low fertility scenario for India embodies a fall in the total fertility rate to 1.55 by 2030, compared with 2.55 in the baseline simulation. It reduces fertility by one child per woman. The simulation is therefore similar to Dyson's (2002) "low fertility" variant cited in Section 8.2. As shown in Figure 8.4, it offers substantial slowdowns in both the population and the labor force, with both tending to stabilize by around 2030. As in the fertility shock to the PRC, the effect on the labor force is proportionally smaller than that on the population. Again, this is because fertility changes first affect the youth population, and not those of working age. In contrast with the PRC, however, in India

Table 8.12 Economic Effects of Reduced Indian Fertility, 2030
(% departures of the Indian low fertility scenario from the baseline)

	Real Invest- ment	Real Capital Stock	Labor Force	Skill Inten- sity[a]	Real Skilled Wage	Real Prod- uction Wage	Skill Premium	Rate of Return[b]	Terms of Trade	Real GDP	Real per Capita GNP
2010	-1.06	-0.32	-1.65	0.28	1.24	1.22	0.02	-0.04	0.05	-0.63	4.63
2020	-4.62	-2.23	-5.92	0.76	3.42	3.92	-0.48	-0.08	0.67	-2.92	10.07
2030	-9.65	-6.04	-11.93	1.18	5.97	7.42	-1.35	-0.09	1.87	-6.86	15.45

a Skill intensity is the ratio of the skilled to the total labor force. b On installed capital (percentage points).

Source: The baseline and low Indian fertility projections from the model described in the text.

the difference is made larger by its young population, its large population of women of fertile age, and its high, aged labor-force participation rates. The diminished slowing impact on the labor force results in a substantial decline in the total dependency ratio, which is the combination of a minimal rise in non-working-age dependency combined with a dramatic decline in youth dependency, as shown in Figure 8.5.

The economic implications of this are indicated in Figure 8.6 and Table 8.12. Slower labor force growth yields slower capital productivity growth and therefore slower investment and capital accumulation. With slower primary factor accumulation comes slower GDP growth—real GDP reaches a 2030 level that is 7% lower than the baseline. By contrast with the PRC's fertility increase, however, the forces influencing real per capita income are all positive. Dependency is substantially lower, the Solow-Swan effect sees real wages grow faster, the repatriation of capital income to foreign owners is less, skilled emigration is less, and the terms of trade improve. The last improvement is due to increased consumption relative to GDP and therefore increased imports relative to exports. In per capita terms, then, the Solow-Swan predisposition toward inverse proportionality between population and per capita income growth is amplified here. Even though aged dependency rises slightly, overall dependency falls substantially and slower population growth makes the average Indian better off. By 2030, the cost in GDP is 7% relative to the baseline but the gain in real per capita income is 15%.

8.5.3 Comparing the Implications of Fertility Change in the PRC and India

A glance at Figure 8.6 reveals that the cost of 10% more GDP in the PRC by 2030 is about the same in real per capita income. In India, by contrast, 15% more real per capita income can be gained through fertility decline at the expense of only 7% of GDP. To clarify this asymmetry, we extract the elasticities of GDP and per capita income to the target fertility rate—that rate toward which fertility is assumed to trend asymptotically.[35] This yields unitless measures that are independent of the directions of the fertility shocks. As shown in

Figure 8.7 Elasticities of GDP and Per Capita Income to Target Fertility Rate

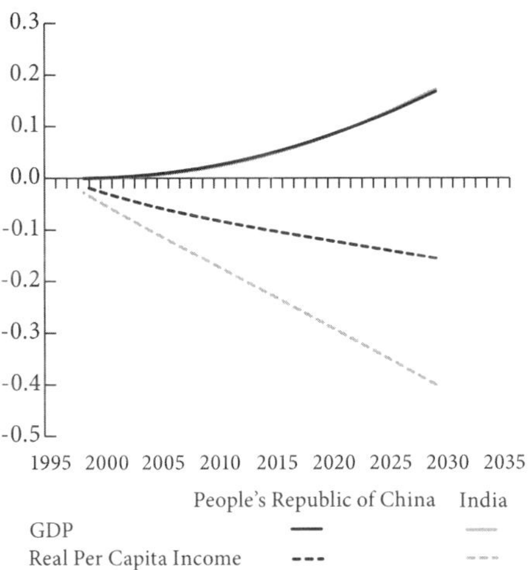

Note: The data are the percentage changes in real GDP and real per capita income for each corresponding percentage change in the target fertility rate, calculated from the results in Figure 8.6 and from target fertility rate changes of 59% for the People's Republic of China and -37% for India.
Source: Model simulations.

Figure 8.7, these elasticities change through time, because, following a shock to the target fertility rate, the economic implications enlarge with departures from the baseline population and labor force. While the effects of fertility change on GDP are found to be very similar for the two countries, those on income per capita are widely divergent. The benefit in per capita terms of reducing fertility in India is more than twice as large as in the PRC. This stems primarily from India's comparatively young population and the more considerable demographic dividend it can therefore derive from fertility decline.

In the analysis here, per capita income provides a simple measure for comparing the costs and benefits of alternative fertility policies in the PRC and India. This may provoke the criticism that changes in per capita income will not necessarily concord with changes in other social and economic indicators. There is no guarantee, for example, that the relatively high per capita income benefits of fertility decline for India will translate into corresponding improvements in health and consumption that are distributed evenly across the population and throughout the life cycle. Instead, this will hinge on the capacity of the respective governments to implement appropriate policies in the spheres of education, health care, and pensions, to name a few. While recognizing this caveat, the link between fertility and per capita income growth is of intrinsic interest in that rising levels of per capita income indicate the potential to deliver more broadly defined welfare improvements.

8.6 CONCLUSION

Within the next decade, the PRC's labor force will begin to contract, while that of India will expand faster than its population. A straightforward consideration of this in a neoclassical model with diminishing factor returns leads to the expectation that the impact of these changes will be lower GDP and higher per capita income growth in the PRC, and the reverse in India, and this general pattern does in fact emerge from the analysis provided above. However, the story is considerably more complex than this. In particular, population structure plays a critical role in determining the relative magnitudes of labor force growth to total population growth and the consequent change in dependency ratios, which in turn impact significantly on per capita GDP growth. Moreover, real wage trends influence skilled emigration from these regions and therefore the skill composition of their labor forces. With increasingly open capital accounts, other things equal, both countries stand to attract more foreign investment the faster their labor forces grow. This complements the positive association between fertility and GDP, but the necessity to compensate foreign capital owners detracts from the per capita income result. Finally, faster GDP growth tends to shift the terms of trade adversely, which also detracts from per capita performance. Our integrated model of global demography and economic growth offers some insight into all of these complexities.

A relaxation of the one-child policy has been proposed by some as a way of combating the negative impact that the slowdown and aging of the PRC's population will have on GDP growth in the future. Our simulations indicate that a two-child policy would indeed achieve the twin goals of increasing GDP and reducing the proportion of the aged population (from 21% to 18%) and, by a similar proportion, the aged dependency ratio. They also imply, however, that per capita income by 2030 would be reduced by almost as much as GDP would rise, a result that stems primarily from an associated large rise in the youth dependency ratio as well as from adverse changes in skilled emigration, capital income repatriation, and the terms of trade. If higher fertility rates are considered desirable for the PRC to achieve its GDP growth and other (libertarian) objectives, policy efforts will need to be directed toward mitigating the negative impact of higher population growth on per capita income by raising labor market participation rates and increasing retirement ages.

With India set to become the world's most populous country by around 2030, its population policy continues to be directed toward promoting fertility decline. While our simulations demonstrated that faster fertility decline would necessarily lead to lower GDP growth, they also indicate that the benefits in terms of per capita income could be substantial. While lower fertility reduces GDP and increases per capita income in both countries, India gains substantially more per capita income than the PRC per unit change in fertility, a result that depends critically on India's higher youth dependency. India therefore has considerably more to gain, at least in per capita terms, from further reducing its fertility.

ENDNOTES

1   See Solow (1956) and Swan (1956), and the detailed analytical review offered by Pitchford (1974, Chapter 4).

2   See Bloom and Williamson (1998) for a generic discussion of the demographic dividend in developing countries, Bloom and Canning (2003 and 2005a) for recent reviews, Bloom et al. (2000) for a detailed examination of the implications for Asia, and Cai and Wang (2005) for implications for the PRC.

3   The problems that arise in the closed capital markets that are common in developing countries are weak intermediation and hence maldistributed investment and a low level of embodied technical change. These are just two of the reasons for the switch to openness that is under way in the PRC and India.

4   See, for example, Tyers and Shi (2007).

5   Indeed, this recommendation was made in a World Bank report (1997).

6   Heller's (2006) recent review of Asian countries' preparedness for future population aging suggests that both the PRC and India lag behind the more advanced but smaller Asian economies in the development of policy regimes to cover pensions, health insurance, and labor market change. See Golley and Tyers (2006) for details on the PRC's pension system reforms.

7   See Tyers and Golley (2006).

8   Equivalently, lower wage costs relative to other regions tend to cause real depreciation.

9   The gender issue is particularly critical in the PRC, where the ratio of males to females in the 0–9 age group reached 1,147 per 1,000 in the year 2000. This is significantly higher than the ratio of 1,092 per 1,000 in the 10–19 age group, suggesting that the issue is getting worse, not better. India's ratio is also very high relative to international standards, with a ratio of 1,058 males to 1,000 females in the 0–9 age group in 2000, but at least this figure has fallen slightly from the ratio of 1,070 to 1,000 in the 10–19 age group. See Padmadas et al. (2005) for further details.

10   A *Xinhuanet* (2005) news article reported that a number of PRC scholars challenged the family planning policy at a forum on the PRC's population and economy at Beijing University, where the main issues were the "expanding gray generation" and the gender issue.

11   See Demeny's (2003) excellent discussion of population policy in low-fertility countries for further details.

12   See Padmadas et al. (2005) for further details.

13   The GTAP-Dynamic model is a development of its comparative static progenitor, GTAP (Hertel, 1997). Its dynamics are described by Ianchovichina and McDougall (2000).

14 The demographic sub-model has been used in stand-alone mode for the analysis of trends in dependency ratios. For more complete documentation, see Chan and Tyers (2006).

15 The subdivision between production and professional labor accords with ILO's occupation-based classification and is consistent with the labor division adopted in the GTAP Database. See Liu et al. (1998).

16 Mothers in families providing production labor are assumed to produce children who will grow up to also provide production labor, while the children of mothers in professional families are correspondingly assumed to become professional workers.

17 See Tyers et al. (2006a) for further details.

18 In this discussion the skill index, s, is omitted because birth and death rates, and life expectancies at 60 do not vary by skill category in the version of the model used.

19 Since 1997, the Japanese fertility rate has fallen further, to 1.25. These projections are slightly lower than those by the Development Research Centre of the State Council of China (2000) and Sharping (2003), yet the latter two make no attempt to allow PRC fertility to follow the declining trends observed in neighboring countries.

20 Note that, as regions become more advanced and populations in production-worker families become comparatively small, the skill transformation rate has a diminishing effect on the professional population. These transformation rates are held constant in this analysis but made endogenous to real per capita incomes and to the skilled wage premium in Tyers et al. (2006).

21 See Tyers et al. (2005, Tables 11 and 12) for further details.

22 The resulting participation rates are listed by Chan and Tyers (2006, Table 10).

23 This differs from the assumption of constant aged labor force participation rates made in Golley and Tyers (2006).

24 Unlike the standard GTAP models, in which regional incomes are split between private consumption, government consumption, and total saving via an upper-level Cobb-Douglas utility function that implies fixed regional saving rates, this adaptation first divides regional incomes between government consumption and total private disposable income and then allows endogeneity of group saving rates depending on real disposable income levels and real interest rates.

25 New research by Kinugasa and Mason (2005) and Feng and Mason (2005) offers useful results on the relationship between age and saving in the PRC.

26 This endogeneity is suggested by Bloom and Canning (2005b).

27 The importance of productivity notwithstanding, the empirical literature is inconsistent as to whether productivity growth has been faster in agriculture, manufacturing, or services and whether the gains in any sector have enhanced all primary factors or merely production labor. The factor productivity growth rates assumed in all scenarios are drawn from Tyers et al. (2005).

28 Wang and Ding (2006) have recently estimated that there are 40 million surplus workers in the PRC's agricultural sector. While underemployment is not explicit in our model, the assumption of high labor-productivity growth in agriculture implies that agriculture is capable of shedding labor more quickly than other sectors. This essentially mimics the surplus labor problem, which is thereby accounted for implicitly.

29 See Tyers and Golley (2006) for further details.

30 For an analysis using the same model of real exchange rates and their determinants, see Tyers et al. (2006b).

31 This result could have a number of economic implications that are not captured in our model, including that higher fertility might reduce pressure on fiscal policy and so the growth-retarding effects of tax distortions might be reduced. Our scenarios maintain constant tax rates and fiscal deficits.

32 This effect is too small to give it more space here. More details about the migration behavior embodied in the model are provided by Tyers et al. (2006a).

33 Even with the two-child policy and lower fertility in the PRC, India's 2030 growth rate is faster by 1.2% a year.

34 Empirical evidence for such terms-of-trade effects from growth is variable. In many cases, developing country expansions have not caused adverse shifts in their terms of trade because their trade has embraced new products and quality ladders in ways not captured by our model. See the literature on the developing country exports fallacy of composition argument, including Lewis (1952), Grilli and Yang (1988), Martin (1993), Singer (1998), and Mayer (2003).

35 Virtually the same result emerges when the contemporaneous fertility rate is used.

REFERENCES

Ahluwalia, M.S. 2002. "Economic Reforms in India since 1991: Has Gradualism Worked?" *The Journal of Economic Perspectives* 16(3):68-88.

Attanasio, O.P., J. Banks, C. Meghir, and G. Weber. 1999. "Humps and Bumps in Lifetime Consumption." *Journal of Business and Economic Statistics* 17(1):22-35, January.

Attanasio, O.P. and M. Szekely. 1998. "Household Savings and Income Distribution in Mexico." Inter-American Development Bank, Office of the Chief Economist. Documento de Trabajo 390, December.

Bloom, D.E., D.Canning, and P. Malaney. 2000. "Demographic Change and Economic Growth in Asia." *Population and Development Review* 26:257-90.

Bloom, D.E. and D. Canning. 2003. "How Demographic Change Can Bolster Economic Performance in Developing Countries." *World Economics* 4(4):1-14.

______. 2005a. "Global Demographic Change: Dimensions and Economic Significance." In *Global Demographic Change: Economic Impacts and Policy Challenges*. Federal Reserve Bank of Kansas City.

______. 2005b. "The Effect of Improvements in Health and Longevity on Optimal Retirement and Saving." NBER Working Paper 10919. Cambridge, MA: National Bureau of Economic Research, April.

Bloom, D.E. and J.G. Williamson. 1998. "Demographic transitions and economic miracles in emerging Asia." *World Bank Economic Review* 12(3): 419-455.

Cai, F. and D. Wang. 2005. "Demographic Transition: For Growth." In R. Garnaut and L. Song (eds.), *The China Boom and its Discontents*. Asia-Pacific Press, Canberra.

Chan, M.M. and R. Tyers. 2006. "Global Demographic Change and Labor Force Growth: Projections to 2020." Centre for Economic Policy Research Discussion Paper, Research School of Social Sciences (RSSS), Australian National University, December.

Demeny, P. 2003. "Population Policy: A Concise Summary." Population Council, Policy Research Division Working Paper 173.

Development Research Centre of the State Council of China. 2000. *China Development Studies: The Selected Research Report of the Development Research Centre of the State Council*. China Development Press.

Dyson, T. 2002. "On the Future of Human Fertility in India." Paper presented at the "Expert Group Meeting on Completing the Fertility Transition." United Nations Population Division, New York.

Feng, W. and A. Mason. 2005. "Demographic Dividend and Prospects for Economic Development in China." UN Expert Group Meeting on Social and Economic Implications of Changing Population Age Structures, Mexico City, August 21-September 2.

Golley, J. and R. Tyers. 2006. "China's Growth to 2030: Demographic Change and the Labor Supply Constraint." Chapter 8 in R. Garnaut and L. Song (eds.), *The Turning Point in China's Economic Development*. Asia-Pacific Press, Canberra.

Greenspan, A. 2004. "Alan Greenspan on the Economic Implications of Aging." *Population and Development Review* 30(4), December:779-82.

Grilli, E. and M.C. Yang. 1988. "Primary Commodity Prices, Manufactured Goods Prices and the Terms of Trade of Developing Countries: What the Long Run Shows." *World Bank Economic Review* 2(1), January:1-47.

Heller, P.S. 2006. "Is Asia Prepared for an Aging Population?" IMF Working Paper WP/06/272. International Monetary Fund, Washington DC, December.

Hertel, T.W. (ed.). 1997. *Global Trade Analysis Using the GTAP Model*, New York: Cambridge University Press. Available: http://www.agecon.purdue.edu/gtap.

Higgins, M. 1998. "Demography, National Savings and International Capital Flows." *International Economic Review* 39(2), May: 343-69.

Ianchovichina, E. and R. McDougall. 2000. "Theoretical Structure of Dynamic GTAP." GTAP Technical Paper 17, Purdue University, December. Available: http://www.agecon.purdue.edu/gtap/GTAP-Dyn.

Kinugasa, T. and A. Mason. 2005. "The Effects of Adult Longevity on Saving." Mimeo, University of Hawaii at Manoa.

Kitamura, U., N. Takayama, and F. Arita. 2001. "Household Savings and Wealth Distribution in Japan." Discussion Paper 38, Project on Intergenerational Equity, Institute of Economic Research, Hitotsubashi University, Tokyo, September.

Lewis, W.A. 1952. "World Production, Prices and Trade, 1870–1960." *Manchester School of Economic and Social Sciences* 20(2), May:105-38.

Liu, J., N. Van Leeuwen, T.T. Vo, R. Tyers, and T.W. Hertel. 1998. "Disaggregating Labor Payments by Skill Level in GTAP." Technical Paper 11, Center for Global Trade Analysis, Department of Agricultural Economics, Purdue University, West Lafayette, September.

Martin, W. 1993. "The Fallacy of Composition and Developing Country Exports of Manufactures." *The World Economy* 23: 979 1003.

Mayer, J. 2003. "The Fallacy of Composition: A Review of the Literature." UNCTAD Discussion Paper 166, February.

Padmadas, S., G. Wang, J. Brown, and B. Li. 2005. "Birth Planning and Population Prospects in China and India." Paper Presented at the IUSSP XXV International Population Conference, Tours, France, 18–23 July.

Pitchford, J.D. 1974. *Population in Economic Growth*. Amsterdam: North Holland Publishing Co.

Sen, A. 2000. *Development as Freedom*. New Delhi: Oxford University Press.

Sharping, T. 2003. *Birth Control in China 1949-2000: Population Policy and Demographic Development*. London: Routledge Curzon.

Singer, H.W. 1998. "Beyond Terms of Trade: Convergence/Divergence and Creative Destruction." *Zagreb International Review of Economics and Business* 1(1), May:13–25.

Solow, R.M. 1956. "A Contribution to the Theory of Economic Growth." *Quarterly Journal of Economics* 70(1):65-94.

Swan, T.W. 1956. "Economic Growth and Capital Accumulation." *Economic Record* 32(2):334-61.

Tyers, R., Q. Shi, and M.M. Chan. 2005. "Global Demographic Change and Economic Performance: Implications for the Food Sector." Report for the Rural Industries Research and Development Corporation, Canberra, September.

Tyers, R., I. Bain, and J. Vedi. 2006a. "The Global Implications of Freer Skilled Migration." Working Papers in Economics and Econometrics 468, Australian National University, Canberra, July.

Tyers, R., J. Golley, Y. Bu, and I. Bain. 2006b. "China's Economic Growth and its Real Exchange Rate." Working Papers in Economics and Econometrics 476. Australian National University, November.

Tyers, R. and J. Golley. 2006. "China's Growth to 2030: The Roles of Demographic Change and Investment Premia." Working Papers in Economics and Econometrics 461, May; version in Chinese 2007 in the *Chinese Journal of Population Science*.

Tyers, R. and Q. Shi. 2007. "Global Demographic Change, Policy Responses and their Economic Implications." *The World Economy* 30(4), April:537-66.

United Nations (UN). 2000. *1997 United Nations Demographic Yearbook*. UN Department of Economic and Social Affairs, New York.

______. 2003. *World Population Prospects: The 2002 Revision*. UN Population Division, February. Available: www.un.org/esa/population/publications/wpp2002.

______. 2005. *World Population Prospects: The 2004 Revision*. UN Population Division. Available: http://esa.un.org/unpp/.

Wang, J. and S. Ding. 2006. "A Re-estimation of China's Agricultural Surplus Labor— The Demonstration and Modification of Three Prevalent Methods." *Frontiers of Economics in China* 1(2):171-81.

World Bank. 1997. *China 2020: Old Age Security*. Washington, DC: World Bank.

World Health Organization (WHO). 2003. "Mortality Database: Table One: Number of Registered Deaths." Geneva: World Health Organization.

Xinhuanet. 2005. "Family Planning Becomes Controversial Topic." 30 December.

Commentary on Chapter 8

David Canning

1 Introduction

This chapter examines how changing fertility rates in the People's Republic of China (PRC) and India may affect those countries' economic growth over the next 20 years. In particular, it focuses on the likely economic impact of an increase in fertility in the PRC that might occur if it abandons its "one-child policy," and the effect of a faster than expected reduction of fertility in India. It investigates these questions using a general equilibrium model that allows for interactions between countries.

Before turning to the issues that need to be addressed when forecasting future economic growth, I want to spend some time looking at the economic takeoffs in the PRC and India over the last 25 years. Before 1980, economic growth in both the PRC and India, as measured by per capita income (in purchasing power parity terms) was relatively slow. However, after 1980 growth in both countries accelerated, dramatically in the case of the PRC, and more modestly in the case of India (Figure C.8.1). The PRC rapidly overtook India, and now has substantially higher per capita income.

How can we explain the modest economic takeoff in India and the rapid

Figure C.8.1 Income per Capita, People's Republic of China and India

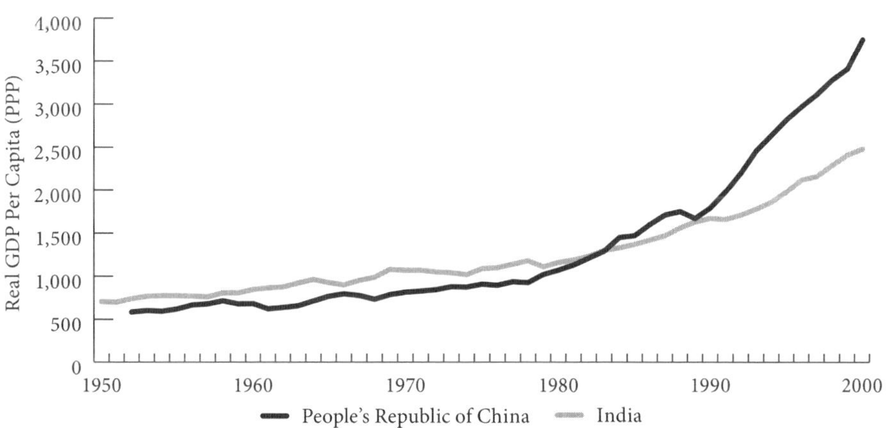

Source: UN (2004).

one in the PRC after 1980? Bloom et al. (2006) investigate the determinants of economic growth in the PRC and India by fitting a model of economic growth to a cross-country panel of data over the period 1960–2000. The model predicts the "takeoffs" in growth in per capita income in the PRC and India after 1980 reasonably well, based on changes in domestic factors in each country. The major sources of increased economic growth in the two countries are found to have been, in order of magnitude, rising health and longevity, increased openness to international trade, and a higher labor force ratio per capita due to falling fertility rates and dependency ratios.

Rather than using a general equilibrium model, Bloom et al. (2006) estimate the impact of different variables that may affect growth in a panel of countries and then apply the results to the PRC and India to see how well the fitted values compare with the actual growth experiences of these two countries. One advantage of doing this is that they can include in their analysis some variables, such as measures of institutional quality and openness to international trade, that may matter enormously for economic growth, but whose effects are difficult to calibrate using microeconomic data.

The two demographic factors they emphasize are the rapid increases in life expectancy and the declines in fertility that have occurred in both the PRC and India, though in each case the magnitude of the effects has been greater in the former. Figure C.8.2 shows the improvements in life expectancy over the last 50 years with projections out to 2050. These improvements have various economic effects. Life expectancy can be thought of as a proxy for population health. To the extent that health affects labor quality and productivity, we would expect the rising standard of labor inputs in the PRC to have an effect on

Figure C.8.2 Life Expectancy at Birth, People's Republic of China and India

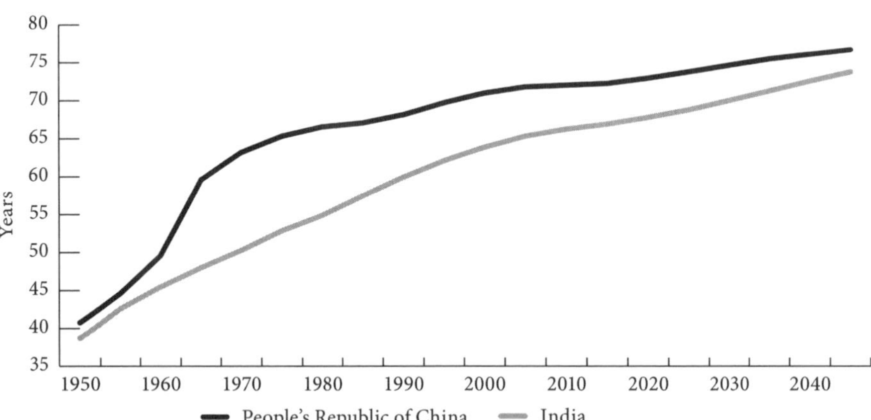

Source: UN (2004).

GDP per worker. Fogel (1994) emphasizes the role played by better health and nutrition in the Industrial Revolution, and Fogel (2004) argues that this effect, particularly the decline in chronic illness that accompanies improvements in population health, has led to a substantial improvement in productivity in the PRC. Bloom et al. (2004) estimate the effect of health as a form of human capital in a cross-country study of growth rates. In addition to this effect of health on worker productivity, an increase in health and prospective longevity can also be a driving force for increased saving for retirement (Bloom, Canning, and Graham, 2003), and for higher rates of foreign direct investment (Alsan et al. 2006) as well as domestic investment, savings, and educational enrollment (Lorentzen et al., 2005).

The second major demographic change has been the rapid declines in fertility that have taken place in both countries but again, especially in the PRC (Figure C.8.3). The decline in mortality in the two countries included large falls in infant and child mortality, which produced large cohorts of young people. The subsequent decline in fertility has produced a "bulge" generation. When this large generation reaches working age, a country will experience a demographically induced economic boost, provided that this demographic cohort is productively employed. Bloom and Williamson (1998), Bloom et al. (2000), and Mason (2001) have investigated the role of this "demographic dividend" in the successful East Asian "tiger" economies. Cai (2004) does so for the PRC, as do Bloom and Canning (2003) for the recent economic boom in Ireland. Figure C.8.4 shows the ratio of workers to dependents in the PRC and India. The more rapid improvements in health and reductions in fertility

Figure C.8.3 Total Fertility Rates, People's Republic of China and India

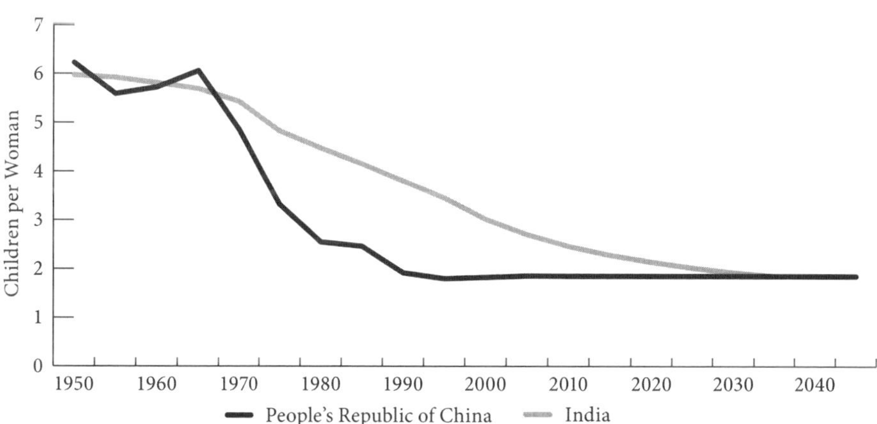

Source: UN (2004).

Figure C.8.4 Ratio of Workers to Dependents, People's Republic of China and India

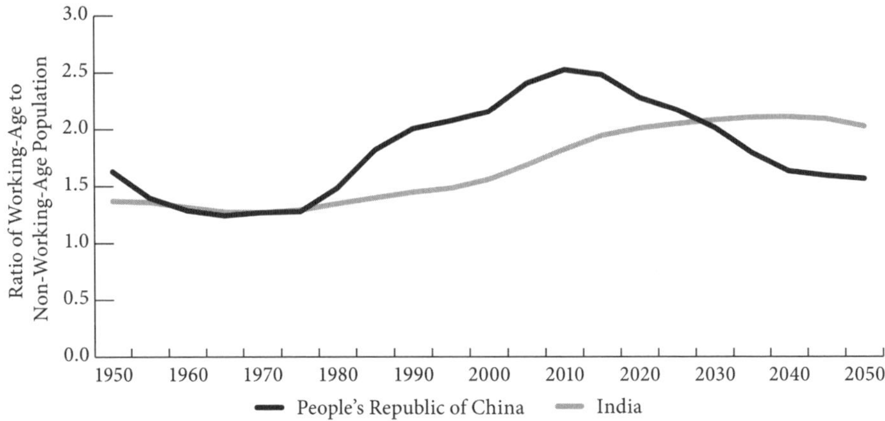

Source: UN (2004).

in the PRC have meant that its demographic dividend has been more rapid, but will also be reversed as population aging sets in.

East Asia's macroeconomic performance is tracked very closely by its demographic transition and resulting changes in age structure. Estimates indicate that as much as one third of its "economic miracle" can be accounted for by the demographic dividend (Bloom and Williamson, 1998). By contrast, the absence of demographic change also accounts for a large portion of Africa's economic debacle (Bloom, Canning, and Sevilla, 2003; Bloom and Sachs, 1998). In addition, the introduction of demographics has reduced the need for the argument that there was something exceptional about East Asia or idiosyncratic to Africa. Once age-structure dynamics are introduced into the economic growth model, these regions are much closer to obeying common principles of economic growth (Bloom et al., 2000).

In 1975, the ratio of working-age (15–64) to non-working-age (0–14 and 65+) people in both the PRC and India was around 1.3. Put simply, there were only modestly more working-age people than there were people who, by virtue of their age, were most likely dependents. In the 1970s, the PRC began to call for couples to have fewer children and to have them later. This culminated in the 1980 adoption of its one-child policy, encouraging and very often requiring couples to have only one child (though the policy was less rigorous in rural areas and among ethnic minorities). This policy propelled the sharp decline in fertility that began in the 1970s, which triggered a subsequent sharp rise in the ratio of working-age to non-working-age people, with this ratio heading toward an expected peak of 2.5 in 2010. India is changing demographically in the same direction, but much more slowly, with an expected peak of 2.1 in

2035, a level that the PRC reached in 1995. India still has the main portion of this potential demographic dividend ahead of it. The PRC, by contrast, can see a very rapidly rising elderly population in the not too distant future.

It is also clear, both theoretically and empirically, that there is nothing automatic about the link from demographic change to economic growth (Bloom, Canning, and Sevilla, 2003; Bloom and Canning, 2003). Age distribution changes create a supply-side effect and a potential for economic growth. Whether or not this potential is captured depends on the policy environment, as reflected, for example, by the quality of government institutions, labor legislation, macroeconomic management, openness to trade, and education policy. This realm is where Latin America seems to have stumbled. During 1965–1990, its demographics resembled those of East Asia, but its economic performance conformed more closely with that of Sub-Saharan Africa (especially during the latter part of this period). Poor macroeconomic management and weak governance seem to have prevented much of Latin America from exploiting its demographic window of opportunity, at least in its early phases. The PRC and India's institutional arrangements appear to be more average, and their ability to quickly absorb an increase in the labor force is better than that found in parts of Africa or Latin America, but perhaps not as good as that found in Ireland during its recent economic boom.

The PRC and India's remarkable economic growth has several additional possible explanations. Both countries embarked on economic reform, characterized by deregulation and liberalization, in the process opening up the economy to export orientation and attracting foreign investment. The PRC reformed earlier and much more aggressively than India, beginning in the 1980s; only in 1991, in response to a fiscal and balance-of-payments crisis, did India launch widespread economic policy reforms. The main consequences of economic reform and opening, such as the growth of private enterprises, the large inflow of foreign direct investment, and the increasing volume of foreign trade, appear to have made a significant contribution to economic growth. This relationship of economic reform, the opening-up of trade, and economic growth in the PRC has been discussed by Chen and Feng (2000); and for India by Chopra et al. (1995) and Sachs et al. (1999). The PRC and India have also made improvements in education. The contribution of human capital, proxied by the education level, to economic growth is examined by Cai and Wang (1999), Wang and Yao (2001), and Chopra et. al. (1995). Labor reallocation from agriculture to other sectors has been singled out for attention as a source of economic growth in the PRC and India. In these two countries, as in many others, there was surplus labor in agriculture, with a large differential in labor productivity between agriculture and industry. As a consequence, the intersectoral shift of labor (away from agriculture) increased overall productivity and, therefore, aggregate output. The effect of labor reallocation has been investigated by Sachs and Woo (1997) and Cai and Wang (1999) for the PRC.

2 Explaining the Takeoff in Economic Growth in the PRC and India

Bloom et al. (2006) take the change in the predicted growth rate between the period 1960–1965 and the period 1995–2000 and decompose the sources. The results are shown in Table C.8.1. Predicted growth in the PRC rose by 2.7 percentage points over the period, while predicted growth in India rose by 1.9 percentage points. In both cases, the major source of this rise is the large increase in the life expectancy proxy for health human capital.

The second principal source of the rise is the increased openness of both economies. Bloom et al. measure openness based on the residual of a regression of trade on population and per capita income. High-income countries tend to have more trade while large countries have less need for international trade, given the trade opportunities that exist internally. They construct a measure of "expected" trade given each country's size and income level; the gap between actual trade and this expected trade gives a measure of the country's degree of openness. This measure of openness is shown for the PRC and India in Figure C.8.5, which illustrates the rapid rise in international trade in these two economies.

The next important contributory factor found by Bloom et al. (2006) is the rise in the level and growth rate of the working-age share of the population. Schooling has had a positive impact on economic growth in both countries, though it should be noted that this is the effect imposed by calibration rather

Table C.8.1 Sources of the Increase in Predicted Growth Rates, People's Republic of China and India (percentage points)

	China, People's Rep. of	India
Increase in Predicted Annual Average Percentage Growth in GDP per Capita between 1960–1965 and 1995–2000	2.7	1.9
Effect of Higher Life Expectancy	2.5	1.3
Effect of Increased Trade	1.1	0.6
Effect of Increase in Working-age Share	0.9	0.7
Effect of Higher Levels of Schooling	0.5	0.5
Effect of Improved Bureaucratic Quality	0.2	0.2
Effect of Industrialization	0.0	0.1
Effect of Investment Rate	0.1	0.0
Effect of Higher Level of Per Capita Income	-2.4	-1.5

Figure C.8.5 Trade (residual from expected trade), People's Republic of China and India

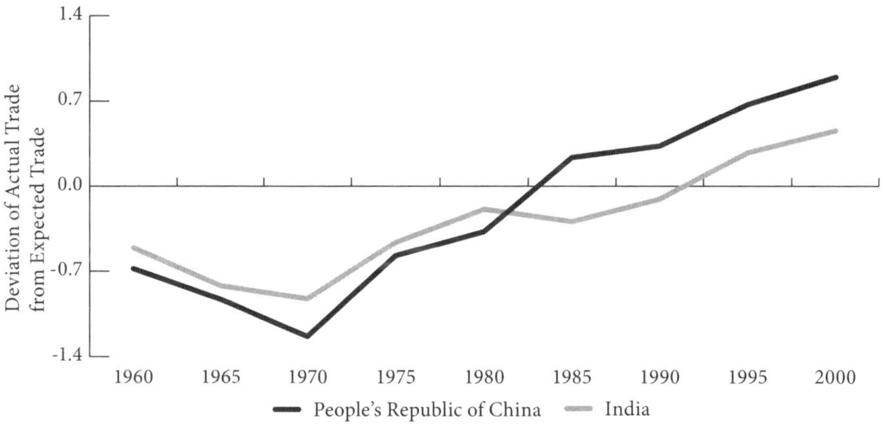

Source: Bloom et al. (2006).

than estimation. The rise in bureaucratic quality is estimated to have a small positive effect on growth rates.

Sectoral change in the form of industrialization appears to have had surprisingly little effect on economic growth in either country. While there has been a movement out of agriculture and into industry, the pace of this movement has been relatively modest in the PRC and India compared with Japan or the Republic of Korea during their growth spurts. Similarly, the investment rate seems to have had remarkably little effect in either country: this rate is almost exactly the same in 1960 and 1995 for both countries, making this an improbable source of change in growth rates.

Against these factors that have tended to raise the rate of economic growth in both the PRC and India, the one negative factor has been the effect of rising income levels in slowing the growth rate. The model has a self-correcting property that anything that causes economic growth tends to raise incomes in the long run, leading growth rates to stabilize again. The rapid increases in income levels between 1960 and 1995, particularly in the PRC, are estimated to have had a large dampening effect on the growth rate.

3 Forecasting the Future

While we appear to have a reasonable explanation for the takeoff in growth in the PRC and India, the chapter attempts the more ambitious task of projecting into the future. It investigates some demographic scenarios based on changes in future fertility rates. A first question is how likely these changes in fertility are. Even if the PRC abandons its one-child policy, it is unclear that fertility will rise substantially. Figure C.8.3 above shows that fertility in the PRC fell dramatically before the introduction of the policy in 1979, suggesting that other forces have also been at work. In addition, fertility is sensitive to cultural norms as well as to economic incentives, and having established a norm of low fertility it may be difficult to undo it. Fertility in India has been falling slowly but steadily, and an acceleration of the fertility reduction is possible there. However, rather than thinking of fertility as an exogenous driving force in economic development, I regard it more as an endogenous variable that responds to development as well as causes it.

In terms of using age structure to forecast future economic growth, two mechanisms are at work. The first is an accounting effect. Holding age- (and sex-) specific behaviors constant, changing the number of people in each age group will change aggregate outcomes. This effect is relatively easy to forecast, based on current age-specific behavior and projections of future age structure. While easy to forecast, this accounting effect can be very large and can capture most of the impact of demographic changes.

More difficult is the problem of assessing the impact of demographic changes on individual behaviors. If small, these changes probably do not affect aggregate outcomes substantially. However, there is the possibility of large induced behavioral effects that may undo the expected accounting effects. The possibility of changes in behavior in general could also impact the forecasts.

By far the most important complicating factor for labor market and savings behavior are social security arrangements. Public provision of pensions has a large impact on individual and aggregate savings (Bloom et al., 2007). The retirement incentives embedded in public pension programs can also have a large impact on the labor supply of older workers. While the chapter allows for such effects—for example, by assuming a high and rising level of labor supply for older workers in the PRC because of a lack of public pension provision in the private sector—it would be interesting to focus some projections on the likely effects of providing state pensions or mandatory private pensions in the private sector.

The most important likely consequence of changing fertility rates in the PRC and India will be on female labor supply. Any policy or force that changes fertility is likely to affect female labor supply, particularly in urban areas where work and production are separated from home and consumption. This is a key behavioral response seen in fertility changes. However, it is likely to augment rather than offset the accounting effect, since lower fertility is likely to lead to higher female labor market participation, boosting per capita income.

In the forecasts to 2030 set out in the chapter, the main effect of changing fertility is on the youth dependency rate and income per capita via the accounting mechanism. In the case of the PRC, raising the fertility rate increases youth dependency and lowers the growth rate of income per capita.

However, a longer time horizon, out past 2030, would see the effect of higher fertility today on working-age population in the future. Below replacement fertility is leading to population aging in the PRC and increasing fertility is one possible way to address this issue. In the "short run" (20 years) used in the forecasts, the effect of higher fertility is lower per capita income, but this should be compared with the longer-run (over 20 to 80 years in the future) beneficial effects of higher fertility today on future working-age populations.

4 Welfare

The chapter focuses on income and per capita income. While these are clearly interesting, they are not welfare measures. A broader notion of "full income" would measure health as well as consumption using a lifetime utility function. Becker et al. (2005) put monetary values on gains to life expectancy, based on value-of-life studies, and compare these gains with those from rising consumption levels. The continuing health improvements in India mean that full income has been rising faster than its consumption level, making its performance relative to the PRC, where population health has been stagnating since 1980, better than simple economic growth calculations would suggest. In the case of the PRC, a focus on per capita income suggests a takeoff in growth after 1980. However, using a full-income measure includes the welfare gains due to health improvements between 1960 and 1980. This gives a more balanced picture, with large welfare gains occurring over the whole period 1960–2000, mainly in the form of health gains before 1980 and income gains after 1980.

The issue of fertility raises a further complication. Should the number of children, and the desire for children, appear in an individual's utility function (as in Becker and Barro, 1988)? In this case the fertility policy has direct effects on welfare, as well as any induced effects on income. In addition, in thinking about fertility policy it would be useful to separate the welfare effects within the household where fertility decisions are made, from any externalities on people outside the household. The rationale for government fertility policy must be based on externalities; the costs and benefits at the level of the family should already be internalized in family fertility decisions.

References to Commentary

Alsan, M., D.E. Bloom, and D. Canning. 2006. "The Effect of Population Health on Foreign Direct Investment Inflows to Low- and Middle-Income Countries." *World Development* 34(4):613-30.

Becker, G.S., and R.J. Barro. 1988. "A Reformulation of the Economic Theory of Fertility." *The Quarterly Journal of Economics* 103(1):1-25.

Becker, G.S., T.J. Philipson, and R.R. Soares. 2005. "The Quantity and Quality of Life and the Evolution of World Inequality." *American Economic Review* 95:277-91.

Bloom, D.E., and J.D. Sachs. 1998. "Geography, Demography and Economic Growth in Africa." *Brookings Papers on Economic Activity* 2:207-95.

Bloom, D.E., and J.G. Williamson. 1998. "Demographic Transitions and Economic Miracles in Emerging Asia." *World Bank Economic Review* 12:419-56.

Bloom, D.E., D. Canning, and P. Malaney. 2000. "Demographic Change and Economic Growth in Asia." *Population and Development Review* 26:257-90.

Bloom, D.E., and D. Canning. 2003. "Contraception and the Celtic Tiger." *The Economic and Social Review* 34:229-47.

Bloom, D.E., D. Canning, and B. Graham. 2003. "Longevity and Life-cycle Savings." *Scandinavian Journal of Economics* 105(3):319-38.

Bloom, D.E., D. Canning, and J. Sevilla. 2003. *The Demographic Dividend: A New Perspective on the Economic Consequences of Population Change.* Santa Monica, California: RAND, MR–1274.

Bloom, D.E., D. Canning, and J. Sevilla. 2004. "The Effect of Health on Economic Growth: A Production Function Approach." *World Development* 32(1):1-13.

Bloom D.E., D. Canning, L. Hu, Y. Liu, A. Mahal, and W. Yip. 2006. "Demographic Change and Economic Growth: Comparing China and India." Processed. Program on the Global Demography of Aging, Harvard University.

Bloom, D.E., D. Canning, R. Mansfield, and M. Moore. 2007. "Demographic Change, Social Security Systems, and Savings." *Journal of Monetary Economics* 54(1):92-114.

Cai, F. 2004. "Demographic Transition, Demographic Dividend and the Sustainability of the Economic Growth." *Population Research* (in Chinese) 128(12):2-9.

Cai, F., and D. Wang. 1999. The Sustainability of China's Economic Growth and the Contribution of Labor." *Economic Research* (in Chinese), 10.

Chen, B., and Y. Feng. 2000. "Determinants of Economic Growth in China: Private Enterprise, Education, and Openness." *China Economic Review* 11:1-15.

Chopra, A., C. Collyns, R. Hemming, K.E. Parker, W. Chu, and O. Fratzscher. 1995. "India: Economic Reform and Growth." Occasional Paper, IMF, Washington, DC, December 1995.

Fogel, R.W. 1994. "Economic Growth, Population Theory, and Physiology: The Bearing of Long-Term Processes on the Making of Economic Policy." *American Economic Review* 84(3):369-95.

———. 2004. "High Performing Asian Economies." NBER Working Paper 10752, Cambridge, MA.

Lorentzen, P., J. McMillan, and R. Wacziarg. 2005. "Death and Development." NBER Working Paper 11620, Cambridge, MA.

Mason, A. (ed.). 2001. *Population Change and Economic Development in East Asia: Challenges Met, Opportunities Seized.* California: Stanford University Press.

Sachs, J., A. Varshney, and N. Bajpai. (eds). 1999. *India in the Era of Economic Reforms*. Oxford University Press.

Sachs, J., and W. T. Woo. 1994. "Structural Factors in the Economic Reforms of China, Eastern Europe and the Former Soviet Union." *Economic Policy* 18:1-102.

———. 1997. *Understanding China's Economic Growth*. Canberra, ACT, Australia.

United Nations (UN). 2004. *World Population Prospects: The 2004 Revision*. New York.

Wang, Y., and Y. Yao. 2001. "Sources of China's Economic Growth, 1952-99: Incorporating Human Capital Accumulation." World Bank Policy Research Working Paper 2650, Washington, DC.

9

Global Growth and Distribution: Asia and its Progression to Developed Status

Maurizio Bussolo, Rafael E. De Hoyos, Denis Medvedev, and Dominique van der Mensbrugghe

9.1 INTRODUCTION

During the 1980s, developing countries accounted for around one sixth of global production; in 2005 this share reached almost one quarter. This shift is to a great extent explained by the progressive economic expansion of the People's Republic of China (PRC) and India, the world's most populous countries. Over the last 25 years, average incomes in the two countries have grown at the impressive rate of 9% and 4%, respectively. Their increasing level of integration with the global economy—together with their importance in terms of world population (37.5% in 2005) and market size (6.4% of world output in 2005)—makes economic performance in these two giants an important element of global development: between 1995 and 2005, growth in these two countries accounted for 16% of global growth (Winters and Yusuf, 2006).

Though the PRC and India dominate their respective regions (respectively East Asia and South Asia) in terms of both economic output and population, the other countries in these two regions have also done remarkably well—both in historical terms as well as relative to other developing regions.[1] The unweighted average growth of output in East Asia and South Asia, respectively, was nearly 6% and 5% between 1980 and 2005. Even correcting for population growth, these are high outturns. By comparison, the (weighted) growth in Latin America over the same span was only 2.3% and in Sub-Saharan Africa 2.6% (and negative in per capita terms).

The initial low level of per capita incomes in the PRC, India, and other parts of Asia and their subsequent rapid growth has meant that, over the last quarter century, the global income distribution experienced drastic changes.

Between 1990 and 2005, it saw a significant decrease in its lower tail, pulling more than 450 million out of poverty.[2] This world exodus out of poverty could also be seen as an increase in the world's population in the middle-income range. The ascent of hundreds of millions of developing-country nationals into what can be named the *global middle class* is producing a large group of people in the developing world who can afford, and demand access to, the standards of living previously reserved mainly for the residents of high-income countries. This has two major implications for the global economy: (i) the demand for international goods and services will rise, and (ii) pressures for policies favoring global integration will increase.

Very likely, growth rates in Asia will decelerate in the future; nevertheless, their growth path will still outperform growth attainments in other countries. Meanwhile, the process of global market integration—at the core of Asia's astonishing performance—is very likely to continue in the next 25 years (World Bank, 2007a). It will therefore come as no surprise to observe further reductions in poverty and an increase in the global middle class in the coming years. The objective of this chapter is to analyze, in an ex ante fashion, the effects that economic expansion in Asia will have on global growth and the global middle class, and on poverty within Asia.

Our empirical results rely on the newly developed World Bank tool for Global Income Distribution Dynamics (GIDD).[3] GIDD is a tool for ex ante analyses of the distribution and poverty effects of changes in macroeconomic policy, of changes in trends in global markets, or both. It combines a global computable general equilibrium (CGE) model with a global microsimulation analysis based on standardized household surveys. The tool pools most of the currently available household surveys covering 1.3 million randomly sampled households in 64 developing countries. When data on income or consumption at the household level are not available (16 countries), GIDD uses grouped data (vintiles). The final dataset represents 91% of the world's population.

The methodology followed allows assessing the importance of Asia for global growth and its impact on the world income distribution. A scenario for the world economy in 2030 is simulated and the performance of Asia is analyzed. Thanks to the micro information available in GIDD, we can identify the position of Asian citizens in the world income distribution in 2000 and track their change through 2030.

The chapter is organized as follows. In the next section we briefly sketch the methodology, assumptions, and data behind GIDD. Section 9.3 presents the macroeconomic results of the baseline scenario, showing the importance of Asia for future global growth. Section 9.4 assesses the importance of growth in Asia for the changes in the global income distribution and the emergence of a global middle class. The last section offers some conclusions.

9.2 METHODOLOGY

The empirical analysis in this chapter relies on two tools developed at the Development Economic Prospects Group of the World Bank: the Linkage CGE model and GIDD, which combines a consistent set of price and volume changes from the CGE model with expected changes in demographic structure to create a counterfactual distribution of income in 2030. We begin with a brief description of the Linkage model and then proceed to introduce the GIDD framework and its ability to map macroeconomic outcomes to disaggregated household survey data.

9.2.1 Linkage: A Global Dynamic Multisectoral Model

The forward-looking scenarios in this chapter have been produced with the World Bank's Linkage model. At its core, Linkage is essentially a neoclassical growth model, with aggregate growth predicated on assumptions regarding the growth of the labor force, savings/investment decisions (and therefore capital accumulation), and productivity. Unlike more simple growth models, however, Linkage has considerably more structure (see van der Mensbrugghe, 2006 for a detailed description). First, it is multisectoral. This allows for more complex productivity dynamics, including differentiating productivity growth between agriculture, manufacturing, and services and picking up the changing structure of demand (and therefore output) as growth in incomes leads to a relative shift into manufactures and services. Second, it is linked multiregionally, allowing for the influence of openness—via trade and finance—on domestic variables such as output and wages. The model is also worldwide, with globally clearing markets for goods and services and balanced financial flows. Third, the Linkage model has a more diverse set of productive factors, including land and natural resources (in the fossil fuel sectors), and labor is split between unskilled and skilled categories.

The Linkage model has a 2001 base year and relies on the Global Trade Analysis Project (GTAP) 6.1 database[4] to calibrate initial parameters. A scenario is developed by solving for a new equilibrium in each subsequent year through 2030. The growth in the labor force is driven by demographics—essentially given by the growth of the working age population. Differentiated growth of skilled versus unskilled workers is partly driven by demographics and partly by changes in education rates. As education levels rise (in the younger populations), they eventually drive higher relative growth of skilled workers once they enter the labor force (and older unskilled workers retire). Savings decisions are partly driven by demographics—rising as youth dependency ratios fall and falling as elderly dependency ratios rise. Investment rates are driven by changes in growth rates (the accelerator mechanism) and differential rates of return to capital. Net foreign savings is the difference between domestic savings and investment.

Productivity is derived by a combination of factors, but is also partly judgmental. First, agricultural productivity is assumed to be factor neutral and exogenous, and is set to estimates from empirical studies. Productivity in manufacturing and services is labor augmenting, and a constant wedge is imposed between productivity growth in the two broad sectors with the assumption that productivity growth is higher in manufacturing than in services. Finally, the model assumes that energy efficiency improves autonomously by 1% a year in all regions and that international trade costs also decline by 1% a year.

9.2.2 GIDD: Linking Macroeconomic Outcomes to Micro Survey Data

The GIDD framework is based on microsimulation methodologies developed in the recent literature, including Bourguignon and Pereira da Silva (2003); Ferreira and Leite (2003, 2004); Chen and Ravallion (2003); and Bussolo, Lay, and van der Mensbrugghe (2006). The starting point is the global income distribution in 2000, assembled using data from household surveys for 84 developed and developing countries and data on income groups (usually vintiles) for the remaining countries; the final sample covers 91% of the world population (see the Appendix for a detailed list).[5] The hypothetical 2030 distribution is then obtained by applying three main exogenous changes to the initial distribution: (i) demographic changes, including aging and shifts in the skill composition of the population; (ii) shifts in the sectoral composition of employment; and (iii) economic growth, including changes in relative wages across skills and sectors.

The empirical framework is depicted in Figure 9.1. Our simulations include the expected changes in the shares of population by groups formed by age and education characteristics (top boxes of Figure 9.1). The future change in population shares by age group is taken as exogenous from the population projections provided by the World Bank's Development Data Group (upper left part of Figure 9.1). Therefore, we assume that fertility decisions and mortality rates are determined outside the model. The change in shares of the population by education group incorporates the expected demographic changes (linking arrow from top left box to top right box in Figure 9.1). Next, new sets of population shares by age and education subgroup are computed, and household sampling weights are rescaled according to the demographic and educational changes above (larger box in the middle of Figure 9.1). In a second step, the demographic changes will change the overall labor supply by age and skill group. These changes are incorporated into the CGE model to simulate overall economic growth, growth in relative incomes by education group, and

Figure 9.1 Global Income Distribution Dynamics Methodological Framework

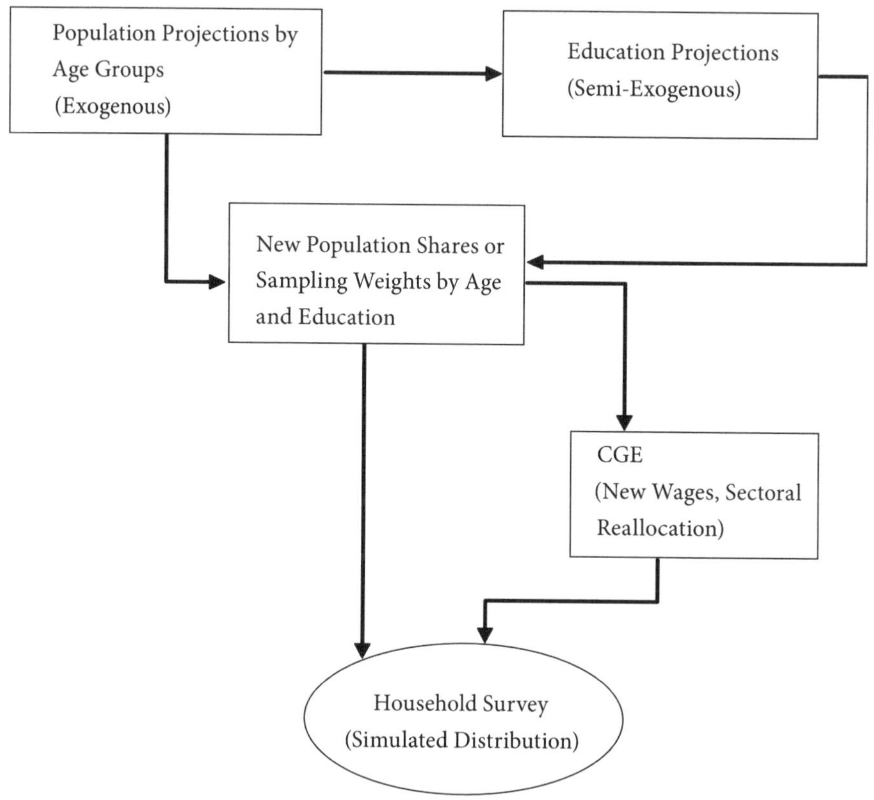

Source: Authors.

sector reallocation of labor (link between the middle and bottom rectangles). Finally, the results of the CGE model are passed on to the household survey for distributional analysis (bottom link in Figure 9.1).

In reality, these changes take place simultaneously, but in GIDD's simplified framework they are accommodated in a sequential fashion. In the first step, the total population in each country is expanded until it reaches the World Bank's projections for 2030. The structure of the population is also changed; for example, as fertility rates decrease and life expectancy increases, older age cohorts will become larger in many countries. To accommodate these changes in the survey data, larger weights have been assigned to older people than have been assigned to younger individuals.

In the next step, workers move from traditional agriculture sectors to more dynamic industry and services sectors, and new incomes are estimated for these movers. Finally, consistent with an overall growth rate of real income per capita, changes in labor remuneration by skill level and sector are applied to each worker in the sample, depending on their education and sector of employment. The number of workers changing sectoral occupation and the differential growth rates in wage rewards used to "shock" the study's microdata are consistent with the results of the global CGE model described in the previous section. (Note that the outcomes of the CGE model are also influenced by the same demographic changes described above.)

The sequential changes described above reshape national income distribution under a set of strong assumptions. In particular, income inequality within population subgroups formed by age, skills, and sector of employment is assumed to be constant over the period. Moreover, data limitations affect estimates of the initial inequality and its evolution. In particular, consumption data are not available for all country surveys, so, to get a global picture, the study had to include countries for which only income data were available. Consumption expenditure is a more reliable welfare measure than income, and its distribution is normally more equal than the distribution of income. Finally, measurement errors implicit in purchasing power parity exchange rates, which have been used to convert local currency units, also affect comparability across countries.

The resulting income distribution should thus not be seen as a *forecast* of what the future distribution might look like; instead it should be interpreted as the result of an exercise that captures the "other things being equal" distributional effect of demographic, sectoral, and economic changes. Although the results of this exercise provide a good starting point for debating potential policy trade-offs, they should not be used as the basis for detailed policy blueprints.

9.3 THE WORLD ECONOMY IN 2030

9.3.1 Doubling of Global Economy in the Next 25 Years

Under the baseline scenario of this chapter, global gross domestic product (GDP) grows at an average annual rate of 2.9% between 2005 and 2030. Measured at constant 2001 prices the global economy would reach $75 trillion in 2030, up from $35 trillion in 2005, some 2.1 times as large (Figure 9.2). The developing-country share would jump from $8 trillion to $24.3 trillion in the period—a tripling of output and an increase in global output share from 23% to 33%.

This represents a modest acceleration of what was observed between 1980 and 2005. For high-income countries, the projection represents a slight decrease with growth in per capita GDP at 1.9% on average a year compared with 2.0% in the earlier period, but a significant acceleration for developing countries (from 2.4% to 3.1%). Part of this acceleration is due to compositional

Figure 9.2 Developing Countries' Increasing Share of World Output, 2005–2030

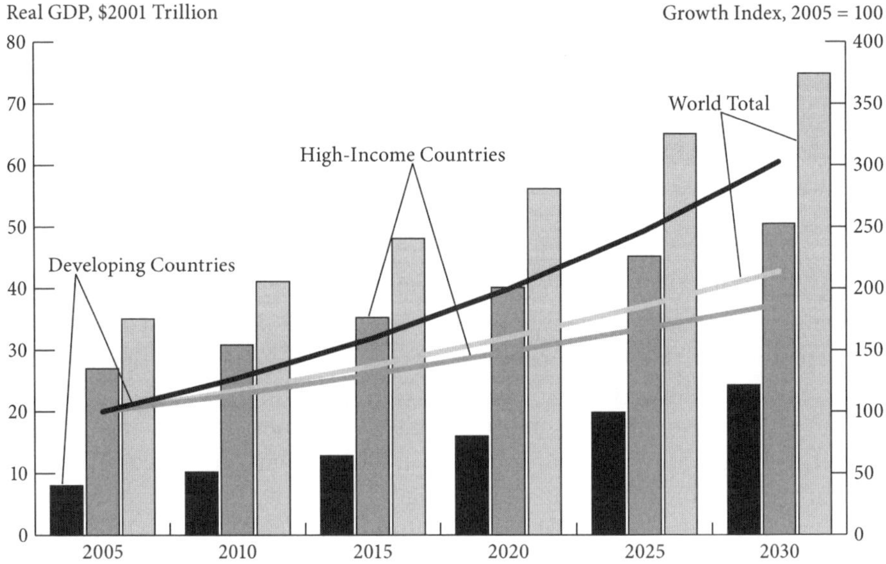

Note: Bars are measured on the left axis; lines are measured on the right axis.
Source: World Bank simulations using the Linkage model.

factors—higher-growth developing countries have higher weights today than back in 1980. However, it is mostly based on the authors' judgment that many developing countries are on an accelerated growth path as a consequence of the combination of improved initial conditions, better policies, and the still wide gap in productivity with high-income countries. Moreover, developing countries have greater capacity and incentives to adapt new technology as communications technology continues to improve, foreign direct investment remains a force in overall development, and education and skill levels improve.

If one decomposes the last 25 years into two periods—1980–2000 and 2000–2005—average growth in developing countries jumped from 3.2% a year in the first period to 5.0% a year in the second. This recent acceleration has not been shared by all countries—nor is it exclusively a PRC and India phenomenon (Figure 9.3). At the same time, the two giants played a major role in the quickening pace of growth: the contribution of the PRC and India to growth of low- and middle-income countries increased from 45% in the first period to 50% in the second. The baseline scenario envisages a slight slowing of this recent performance: over the next 25 years, the PRC and India are likely to account for 18% of growth in global output and 46% of growth in real output of today's low- and middle-income countries.

9.3.2 Productivity and Demography: Driving Forces in World Growth

The central scenario of GDP growth rates described above is built up from a number of key driving forces—notably demographic trends, savings, investment behavior, and the role of technological change, as well as how these trends interact with globalization (see Section 9.2 for more details). Some of these forces are, in turn, influenced by the quality of domestic and international policies.

While demographic trends are fairly predictable, assumptions about technological changes and ensuing productivity growth are subject to a wider band of possibilities. There is no agreement on how to interpret recent productivity growth, let alone how to anticipate future patterns. For example, in the view of Gordon (2000), recent inventions—such as cell phones, the Internet, or new drugs—are relatively normal incremental changes to productivity and are unlikely to have the same impact as the new technologies at the beginning of the 20th century—electricity, the internal combustion engine, telephones, radio, television, and indoor plumbing. Other observers, for example David (1990), suggest that it takes time for new discoveries to have their full impact— either because initial costs are too high, or because there are network externalities, or because it takes time for organizations to change their management practices to fully benefit from the new technologies.

Figure 9.3 Developing Countries' Increasing Share of World Output, 1980–2005

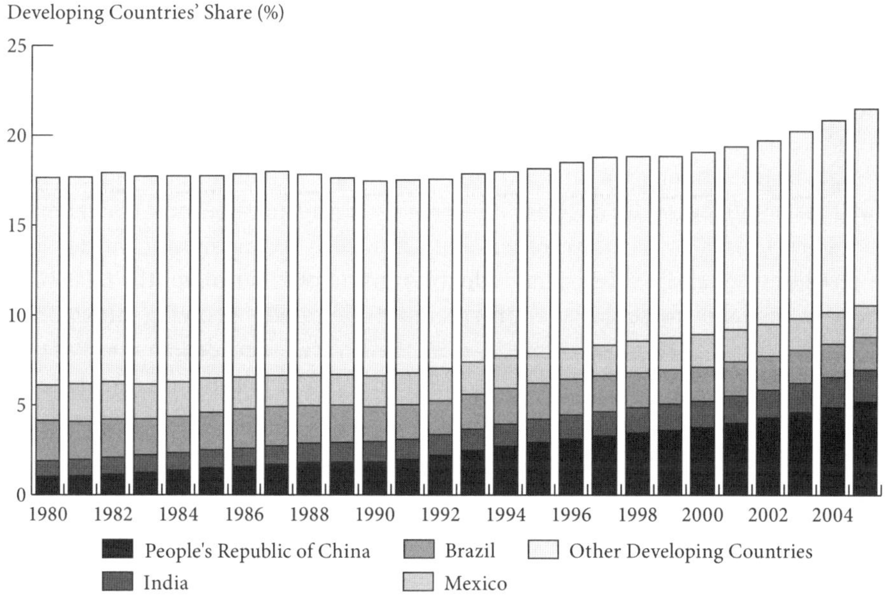

Developing Countries' Share (%)

Source: World Bank, *World Development Indicators*.

Whether one takes a sanguine view of new technologies or not, large parts of the developing world have yet to benefit from "old" technologies.

The macro assumptions on productivity built into the forecast are largely consistent with the estimates of total factor productivity (TFP) growth from the literature (see, for example, Bosworth and Collins 2003). The world saw a period of very rapid TFP growth in the 1960s, followed by a decade of stagnation coinciding with the energy crisis of the 1970s, recovery to an estimated rate of 0.8% a year in the 1980s and 1990s, and an acceleration in the 2000s. There have been large variations across regions and over time. The central scenario assumes a long-term rate of TFP growth in the range of 1.0–1.4% for high-income countries, somewhat on the high end of the Bosworth and Collins estimates. The range for developing countries is somewhat wider—between 0.7% and 2.9% toward 2015 and declining slowly thereafter as the positive impacts of rural-to-urban migration fade.

TFP improvements are modeled as labor-augmenting productivity (Harrod-neutral technical change), which is skill neutral but sector biased. Consistent with the existing literature, productivity in agriculture expands at an average annual rate of 2.5% in all countries. Improvements in labor productivity take place at a much faster pace in manufacturing, where countries in Asia register annual increases of 15% for manufacturing (for comparison, US manufacturing productivity grows at 2.5% a year over the same period).

Two significant demographic changes are occurring at the moment: (i) virtually all of the increase in global population will be in developing countries, and (ii) today's high-income countries and the PRC will become significantly older. Changing demographics weigh heavily on the results influencing the growth of employment, demand trends, and changes in savings and investment behavior (and even productivity). Developed economies have seen a huge decline in fertility rates (to well below replacement rate), a stable labor force that will begin to decline, and rapidly aging populations. Developing countries—some earlier than others—are now also seeing significant declines in fertility rates and a substantial reduction in the number of youths relative to those in the labor force. Most countries still have rapidly growing labor forces owing to the large number of births over the last two decades, and are seeing only modest increases in the share of the elderly in the population. The latter is because rising life expectancy largely impacts current (and larger) generations rather than past ones.

The world will add 1.5 billion people to its population between 2005 and 2030, going from (about) 6.5 billion to about 8 billion (Figure 9.4). Roughly 12% will be living in high-income countries, down sharply from the 18% in 1980 and 14.5% in 2005. Due to the differential in fertility rates, all but 40 million of this growth in population will occur in developing countries.

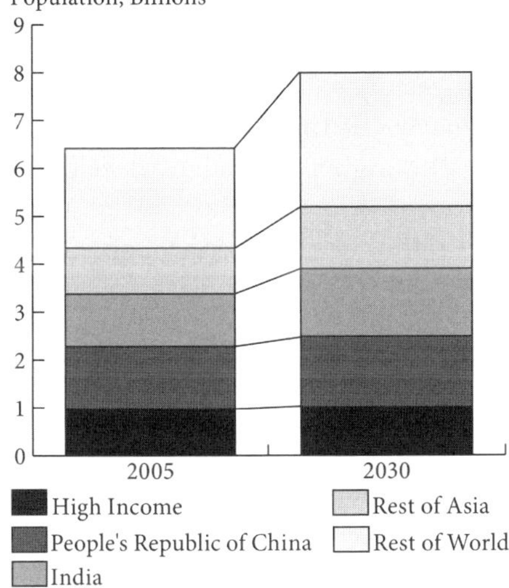

Figure 9.4 Concentration of World Population Growth in Developing Countries

Sources: UN Population Division; World Bank Data group; authors' calculations.

While this represents a substantial increase in the number of people—with concomitant effects on already scarce resources—it also represents a slowing of world population growth, which added 2 billion between 1980 and 2005.

The largest contribution to the nearly 1.5 billion increase in developing regions can be attributed to India, representing 320 million additional people, and to Sub-Saharan Africa (excluding Nigeria and South Africa), with a similar increment of 320 million; each contributes 20% to the global increase. Despite the PRC's one-child policy and overall aging population, the momentum of the current population will generate 170 million additional citizens by 2030, for another 11% of the global increase.

For developed economies, the standard economic impacts of slowing population growth and of aging suggest that aggregate savings will decline, all else being equal, as aging populations tend to dissave or consume out of existing assets. This would tend to decrease the amount of savings available for developed countries. The evidence for this dissaving is mixed and other factors—such as current levels of public or international indebtedness—may influence the long-term patterns of savings and investment.

Lower rates of employment growth could have mixed impacts on investment. Lower labor supply could lessen the need for investment in sectors where labor and capital are close complements. But more intense investment may counteract this effect in sectors where labor and capital are substitutes and labor-saving technology is an option.

Population aging can have other consequences. Productivity growth could be higher in economies with rapid increases in the number of youths joining the labor force. Population aging can also be associated with changes in consumer behavior, with less demand for food and educational services and more demand for leisure and health services (McKibbin, 2005; Bryant, 2004; Helliwell, 2004; Tyers and Shi, 2005). There could also be fiscal implications as promises to earlier generations in terms of social welfare benefits prove hard to finance from a lower tax base. This eventually may involve a combination of lower benefits and delayed retirement age or other forms of higher labor force participation among the elderly.

For developing countries, some of these impacts are reversed. With a lower proportion of youths to care for—including provision for housing, education, and nourishment—more can be saved and invested, particularly because many countries still have a low proportion of elderly. To the extent that available savings from developed countries decline, the higher savings in developing countries would tend to offset the decline.

Developed countries' employment growth, though positive through 2010 at about 1.2 million new jobs a year, becomes negative thereafter, with an average loss of about 700,000 jobs between 2010 and 2015, jumping to an annual average loss of over 3.2 million between 2025 and 2030. This latter number represents a decline of about 1% a year.

Labor force growth is still rapid in developing countries, though on a declining trend throughout the period. Currently, developing countries need to increase employment by nearly 50 million jobs a year to keep up with working age population growth, under the proviso of no change to the labor force participation rate (including females). This latter assumption may be dubious given that fertility is declining rapidly in developing countries.

The largest needs are in the largest countries, with the PRC and India having to create 8 million–10 million jobs each year. This may be easier in these rapidly growing economies. Countries in Sub-Saharan Africa also need to create close to 10 million jobs a year, but in a context of lower economic growth and relatively small urban populations, the task appears to be much harder. The trends for the PRC also show the impact of its decades-long population policies limiting births. In the relatively near future, employment growth will decline precipitously from over 5 million between 2010 and 2015 to under 500,000 between 2015 and 2025, and will turn negative thereafter.

The rest of Asia (excluding the PRC and India) faces rapid labor force growth, particularly early in the period—on par with both the PRC and India—and will need to create about 10 million jobs annually. Even later in the period, the rest of Asia will still need to add some 6.5 million jobs annually, compared with 5.4 million for India and a potential loss of over 2 million a year for the PRC.

For developing countries, aging populations (as defined by the number of elderly per 100 workers) will rise only slowly from current levels (starting from 12 in 2005) through about 2020, but will start accelerating modestly afterward to reach a level of nearly 19. This is still well below the developed-country average of 30 today and differs widely across regions. The PRC will see a sharp rise in its elderly dependency rate, moving from 12 currently to 25 by 2030. This can be contrasted with India, which has a level similar to the PRC's at

11, but which rises to only 16 by 2030. The rest of Asia remains younger on average with a dependency ratio of 15 in 2030. An interesting highlight of the demographic projections is that nearly 50% of the elderly on a worldwide basis will be living in developing Asia in 2030.

9.3.3 Importance of Per Capita Income Growth

Economic size has its importance, not least in terms of determining power relations, be it at the global, regional, or bilateral level. But from a welfare point of view, what really matters is per capita income. Using the market dollar exchange rate of an economy provides a biased estimate of individual well-being because prices differ substantially across economies—particularly for nontraded goods such as personal and housing services. For this reason, it is more appropriate to use the purchasing power parity (PPP) exchange rates, since they take into account these differences in prices. Even using PPP exchange rates, the speed of convergence between developing- and developed-country incomes would be modest under this scenario. At today's income in PPP terms, the average developing-country resident receives about 16% of the average income of high-income countries—$4,800 versus $29,700 (Figure 9.5). This ratio would rise to 21% in 25 years' time, representing an average developing-country income of $11,200, versus $53,200 for high-income countries.

There is, perhaps needless to say, great variance across countries. PRC incomes would rise from 19% of the average high-income level to 39% (in PPP terms), a significant narrowing of the gap that would give an average income close to the lower range of today's poorest high-income countries. Per capita incomes in India are likely to rise much more slowly—from 10.5% in 2005 to 15% in 2030—due to faster population growth and more measured expansion in real GDP. The rest of Asia would also only witness a modest decline in the income gap, from 12.4% to 15.3%. There would be a further falling behind in Sub-Saharan Africa with its modest per capita income growth below the high-income average, and Latin America would see little if any convergence on average. As the previous 25 years have shown, there is plenty of scope for surprises and countries doing significantly better, even compared with countries having similar initial conditions.

The rather modest level of convergence overall nevertheless obscures the fact that market opportunities for both developed and developing countries will increase dramatically as the sheer size of the population of the latter ensures the growth of a very significant middle and upper class likely to rival the purchasing power of today's high-income consumer.[6] Thus, notwithstanding the challenge that poverty will continue to hold for the global community, the wider spread of wealth globally will also provide

Figure 9.5 Convergence in Per Capita Incomes

Index: High Income = 100 in Each Year

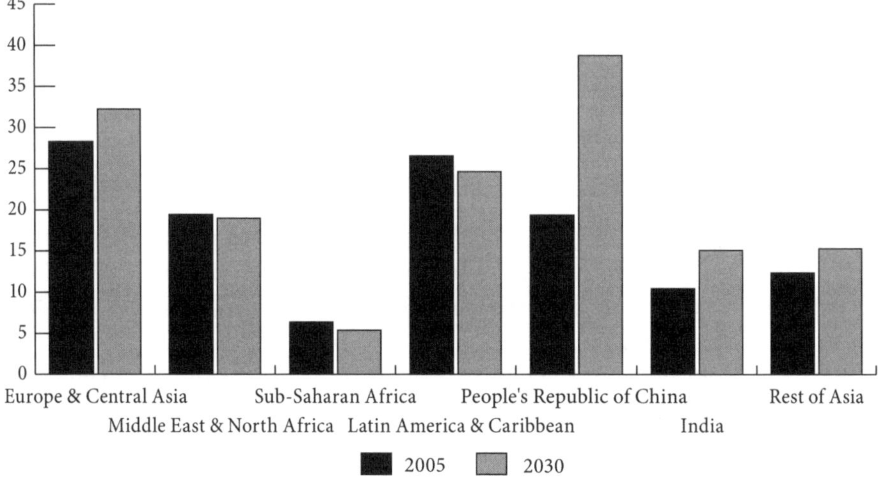

Note: Ratio of PPP-adjusted per capita incomes relative to high-income average. PPP is fixed at base year (2001) level.
Source: World Bank simulations with Linkage model.

greater means to deal more substantively with poverty and other global concerns, such as the environment and health.

9.3.4 Changes in Production Structure and Deepening Trade Integration

The previous sections have shown that under baseline conditions, growth in Asia will account for an increasing share of global output. Similarly, as the Asian countries are already major participants in the global trade arena, the continued expansion of these economies is likely to have far-reaching consequences for world trade. This section highlights four main developments: increasing orientation of the Asian economies toward services, growing demand for skilled workers, further improvements in competitiveness of manufactured goods, and rising imports of agricultural products from high-income countries.

As average incomes of developing countries converge to OECD levels, demand for services in the developing world is likely to increase faster than in high-income countries because services tend to have higher income elasticities than agricultural and manufactured products. Some of this catch-up will be moderated by growing demand for health and public services by the aging OECD populations, but overall, faster growth in low- and middle-income countries—and particularly the PRC and India—is likely to translate into a more pronounced shift of production toward service activities (Figure 9.6).

In order to accommodate this growing share of services in total output, the contribution of other sectors to aggregate production will decrease. For developing countries, the expansion is likely to come at the cost of agricultural output: the PRC's output share is likely to decrease by more than one half, and India's could decline by one third. The fast pace of productivity growth in manufacturing signifies a declining manufacturing share in value terms as factor prices rise rapidly, but relative costs rise more rapidly in services that do not benefit from the same growth in productivity.

The changing sectoral structure of Asian economies is likely to have profound effects on factor returns. Because services tend to be more skill intensive than other sectors, increasing demand for services is likely to exert upward pressure on skilled wages. In 2005, 79% and 91% of the total skilled wages bill in the PRC and India was paid to services workers, and these shares could rise much further by 2030. Demand for skilled workers over the coming decades is likely to be particularly acute in the PRC, where slower population growth will add to the relative scarcity of white-collar employees. However, improvements in education service provision, and the fact that younger cohorts tend to be better educated than their older colleagues, are likely to ameliorate some of the pressures in the labor market. Nonetheless, our baseline scenario envisages an increasing relative scarcity of skilled workers in Asia (as well as most of the developing world) and as a result the skill premium is expected to rise (Figure 9.7). This widening of wage gaps could lead to increasing inequality

Figure 9.6 Pronounced Asian Shift into Services

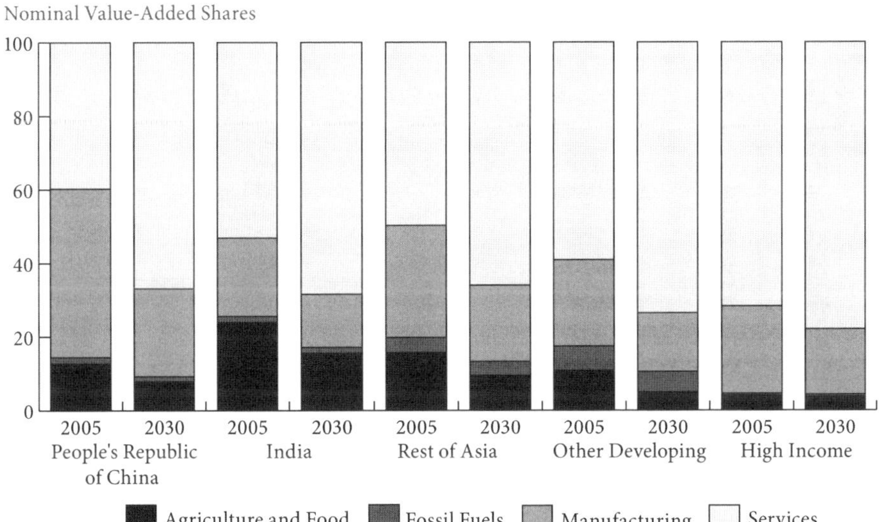

Source: World Bank simulations with Linkage model.

within fast-growing economies, although such pressures could be counteracted by a host of effects including falling rural-urban wage differentials, decrease in the gender wage gap, or changing returns to other worker characteristics.

Productivity growth, changing sectoral structure, and widening skill premiums lead to important changes in international competitiveness of developing countries. Low- and middle-income nations solidify their comparative advantage in exports of manufactured goods, which rise from 79% to 88% of total merchandise exports between 2005 and 2030 (Figure 9.8). The trend is even more pronounced in the PRC and India, which benefit from a TFP growth significantly above the developing country average. In our scenario, 97% of PRC and 95% of Indian merchandise exports are likely to originate from manufacturing. Still, as high-income countries lose competitiveness in manufacturing due to their lower productivity, the share of manufacturing products in their total exports is likely to decline significantly.

The result that agricultural products become a more important component of high-income countries' exports may seem counterintuitive at first glance. There are two main reasons for this development. First, our baseline does not include any significant removal of domestic support in agriculture, which allows high-income farm producers to sell a significant portion of their output in world markets. Second, as developing countries, led by the PRC and India,

Figure 9.7 Likely Rise in Skill Premiums Across the Developing World

Skilled Wages Relative to Unskilled Wages

Source: World Bank simulations with Linkage model.

Figure 9.8 Increasing Concentration of Manufactured Goods in Developing-Country Exports

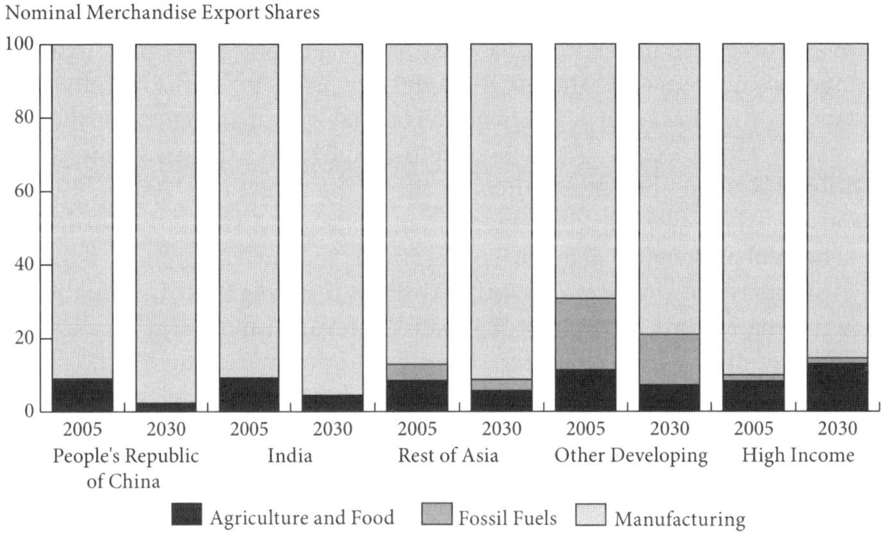

Nominal Merchandise Export Shares

Source: World Bank simulations with Linkage model.

gain competitiveness in manufacturing, the relative price of agricultural products imported from high-income countries declines.

This growing importance of developing countries is also reflected in changes in the direction of trade, which is also likely to undergo significant shifts over the next 25 years. Under the baseline scenario, the faster pace of growth in developing countries translates into their rise as destinations for Asian exports. At the same time, Asian countries buy many more of their manufacturing imports from developing countries, while agricultural imports are increasingly sourced from high-income countries (consistent with the analysis above). Much of the growing trade dependence between developing countries is due to trade in intermediate goods—today, 63% of the PRC's imports are classified as intermediate goods, with roughly half of them coming in the form of parts and components. With the increasing orientation of developing countries toward manufacturing, these linkages are likely to become even stronger by 2030.

The scenario outlined above is intended to illustrate deep changes that the global economy is likely to exhibit over the next 25 years. Actual outturns, particularly for individual countries, may be quite different, but the scenario highlights some of the underlying trends and stresses that will dominate international policy making in the future—including global equity issues, to which we now turn.

9.4 GLOBAL INCOME DISTRIBUTION: IMPACTS IN ASIA AND THE EMERGING MIDDLE CLASS

As briefly described in Section 9.2 above, the demographic shifts and economic changes simulated with the CGE model are used to "shock" individual household incomes, and a new counterfactual global income distribution for 2030 is estimated. This is then used to quantify the changes in the global middle class and the importance of the rapid growth in Asia for these changes.

The global income distribution captures income differences between all citizens in the world; we may think of the resulting global inequality as showing the income differences that would prevail if the world was seen as a single country.[7] Given that there is no global polity, i.e., there is no single global government or civil society, one might think that the relevance played by global inequality is, at least, debatable. Nevertheless, with the rapid increase in globalization, people's perception regarding their relative position in society is no longer based solely on a national yardstick, but is influenced by the increasing awareness of living standards of people around the world (Milanovic, 2006).

9.4.1 Global and Asian Income Inequality

In Table 9.1, global income inequality is measured using two well-known inequality indexes, the Gini coefficient and the Theil index (generalized entropy with aversion parameter equal to 1). The results indicate that if the world were a single country, it would have an inequality index higher than almost all existing countries,[8] with a Gini coefficient of 0.68, well above the world's simple average of 0.39 and the population-weighted average of 0.35. A level of global inequality higher than the inequality level within most countries is the outcome of disparities in average incomes *between* countries. A simple way of evaluating the importance of a particular factor in total income inequality is to separate or partition the population (in this case the world population) into mutually exclusive groups and see how much inequality is accounted for by difference in incomes *between* groups versus that *within* these groups (Mookherjee and Shorrocks, 1982). The importance of a particular characteristic determining the partition rule will be captured by the proportion of inequality that can be accounted for by differences in average incomes *between* groups (Cowell and Jenkins, 1995).

Table 9.1 shows the decomposition results for two different population subgroups (coming from two different partition rules): (i) all the countries in the world and (ii) the PRC and India versus the rest of the world. The results show that a measure of international inequality based on the countries' average

Table 9.1 Subgroup Decomposition of Global Income Inequality

| Year | Global Inequality | | Subgroups | | | |
	Gini	Theil	Countries		PRC–India versus Rest of the World	
2000	0.68	0.93	Between	0.69	Between	0.17
				(0.75)		(0.18)
			Within	0.23	Within	0.76
				(0.25)		(0.82)
2030	0.63	0.77	Between	0.54	Between	0.03
				(0.70)		(0.04)
			Within	0.23	Within	0.74
				(0.30)		(0.96)

Notes: 1. Decomposition results are based on the Theil index decomposition. 2. Proportion of total income inequality within parentheses.

Source: Authors' calculations.

incomes, completely ignoring within-country differences in incomes, would be able to capture three quarters of total global inequality in 2000 (Table 9.1). In other words, eliminating all within country income differences would only bring global income inequality down by 25%. In a second exercise, the world's population is partitioned in two subgroups, one containing the populations of the PRC and India and the other those of the rest of the world. This decomposition shows that in 2000, comparing average income in the PRC and India with average income in the rest of the world (RoW) would be enough to capture 18% of total income inequality (Table 9.1).

Consider now the global income distribution for 2030: global income inequality will be 5 Gini points lower by 2030.[9] *According to the decomposition results, the reduction from 0.93 to 0.77 in the Theil index is entirely accounted for by a reduction in disparities in average incomes across countries.* Since reductions in average income differentials are weighted by population, a rapid growth of poor countries like the PRC and India can have a great impact on global inequality. As a matter of fact, the decomposition results for the PRC and India versus the rest of the world shows that 14 out of a total of 16 points reduction in the Theil index between 2000 and 2030 are explained by a reduction in inequality in average incomes between the PRC and India versus the rest of the world (compare the share of 18% between the component in the decomposition regarding the PRC and India in 2000 with the result of 4% for 2030).

Doing the same calculation for Asian economies alone (including Hong Kong, China; Republic of Korea; and Singapore) the Theil index for the region is measured at 0.53 in 2000, thus there is much more equality shown than at the global level. This is hardly surprising since most countries in Asia are in a much narrower band of income. Within-country inequality accounts for around 50% of the total regional inequality, again very different from the global picture where within-country inequality only explains 25% of global inequality. Inequality rises perceptibly in 2030, with the regional Theil index jumping to 0.56 and the regional Gini coefficient climbing 4 percentage points to 0.54. However, there is little change in the decomposition between within- and across-country inequality.

Regional inequality in 2000 varies significantly, and more so in East Asia than in South Asia (Figure 9.9). The full range (for the surveyed countries) is a low of 0.26 for Pakistan and a high of 0.54 for Papua New Guinea. The regional average is between 0.36 (population weighted) and 0.37 (simple average), that is, somewhat below the global average. The average is much higher for East Asia, measuring about 0.4, some 10 percentage points higher than South Asia at 0.29.[10] The two largest countries dominate their respective regions and the differences between East Asia and South Asia are mirrored in the Gini coefficients of the PRC and India, respectively. It is now a well-established fact that inequality has risen rapidly in the PRC—particularly as income growth has lagged in rural and interior regions. As India accelerates its development, a similar pattern may arise with urban areas gaining significantly more than rural areas.

Figure 9.9 Inequality in Asia, 2000

Gini Coefficient in 2000

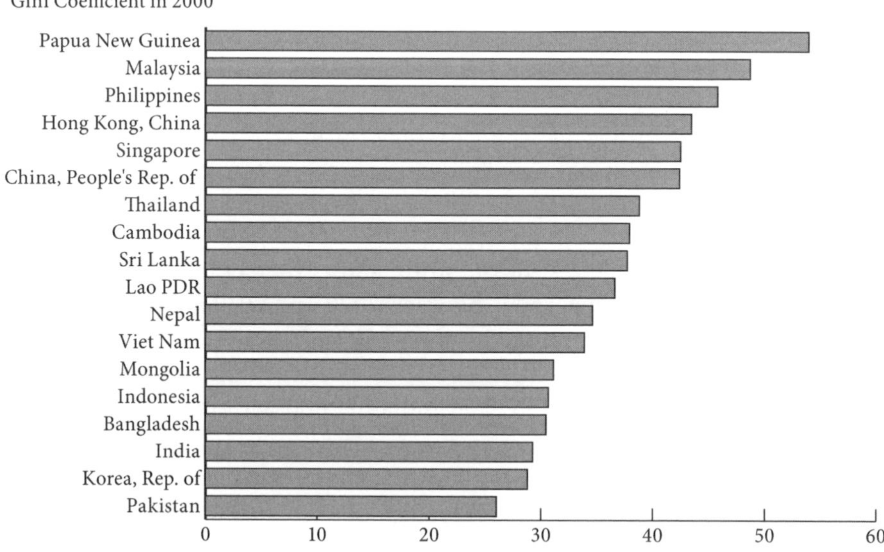

Source: World Bank, Global Income Distribution Dynamics.

9.4.2 More Within-Country Inequality

More than two thirds of low- and middle-income countries in the study sample, accounting for 86% of the population in the developing world, are projected to experience a rise in inequality by 2030. For some countries, the increase is quite significant (Figure 9.10). So, even if average incomes rise, a reduction in poverty could be attenuated by rising inequality.

Within-country inequality is driven by two main factors—shifts in the demographic structure of the population, in terms of aging and education attainment; and changes in rewards for individuals' characteristics, such as their education level, experience, employment sector, and so on. Although in the real world these demographic and economic shocks occur simultaneously and jointly determine inequality changes, this analysis applies to each of them sequentially and decomposes the total change into various components.

Controlling for other factors, both the level and dispersion (inequality) of household income tend to increase with the age and education of the household head. Therefore, as the population shares of groups with more income inequality rise, one may expect to see higher inequality. However, as shown by black tick marks in Figure 9.10, there is no clear pattern in changes in inequality driven by demographic forces. One explanation is that countries with relatively large public sectors and relatively high education levels (such as countries in Europe and Central Asia) tend to have a more egalitarian distribution of

Figure 9.10 Changes in Inequality and Economic Shifts

Variation of Gini Coefficient between Base Year and 2030

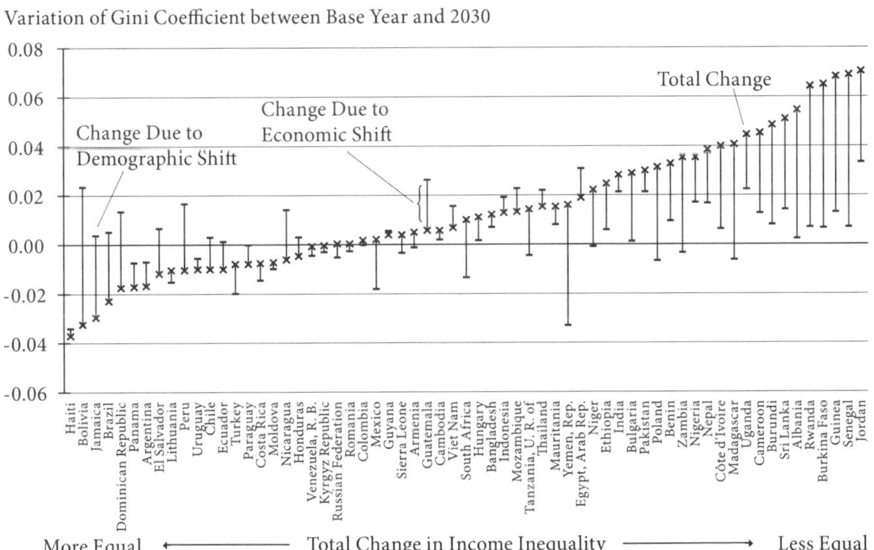

Source: Authors' calculations.

income among skilled workers, possibly because their governments and other bureaucracies have more compressed wage structures. Hence, changes in the demographic structure work to reduce income inequality. By contrast, many countries in Latin America and Sub-Saharan Africa experience an increase in inequality as the shares of older and more skilled workers rise, since wage dispersion within these groups tends to be high. Although aging and the accumulation of human capital imply important changes in the demographic structure of many countries, the overall effect of demographic changes on inequality varies within a narrow band (Figure 9.10).

On the other hand, widening gaps in factor rewards, and particularly in the premium paid for higher skills, tend to produce larger changes in inequality and generally determine the overall direction of the effect. This is shown in Figure 9.10, where for large changes in inequality, the distance between the black crosses and tick marks—that is, the change in inequality attributable to changes in economic factors—increases, a sign that economic factors are the most important determinant for the final level of inequality. The initial skill premiums and the pattern of growth experienced by each country determine the consequences for inequality of the economic factors. Those consequences are obtained by applying the changes in the factor rewards to the income sources of individual households as determined by the Linkage model.

Countries in East and South Asia will experience widening inequality, driven by low initial skill premiums and high per capita growth rates. Faster income growth generates more demand for skill-intensive products and requires higher rates of investment, both of which increase the returns to skilled labor. For example, one of the largest increases in inequality in the sample is observed in India, a country with low initial inequality (the incomes of unskilled-headed households are 52% of the skilled-headed incomes) and an average per capita growth of more than 4%, which together lead to a substantial rise in the skill premium. The rise in inequality is somewhat mitigated by convergence between farm and nonfarm incomes, but this effect is quite small because growth is concentrated in the nonagriculture sectors.

In sum, changes in income inequality over the next 30 years are likely to be driven mainly by changes in the rewards for individual characteristics and investment in education, rather than by globalization in isolation. Countries with low initial inequality and fast growth are likely to experience a worsening distribution of income, while countries with slower growth rates and greater initial inequality in income are likely to see inequality narrow. The results therefore illustrate a "convergence" of income distributions across countries, which can be interpreted as a manifestation of the Kuznets hypothesis, or as a consequence of the globalization-induced equalization of factor prices. Of course, these trends are driven by the assumptions of the baseline scenario and are far from inevitable.

9.4.3 Emergence of a Global Middle Class

Given some absolute thresholds determining a middle income range (or certain ambit of purchasing power) a concept of a *global middle class* can be concretized. The thresholds defining the middle class can be applied to either countries or citizens. If the thresholds are applied to countries, the global middle class will encapsulate all citizens of countries with average incomes within the thresholds, regardless of their personal income level; if applied to citizens, this class will be formed by citizens with personal incomes within the middle class range, regardless of their country's average income. In this study, the thresholds are defined as in Milanovic and Yitzhaki (2002). The authors proposed disaggregating the world population into three categories—poor, middle class, and rich—where the middle class is defined as citizens living in *countries* with an average income falling between the per capita incomes of Brazil and Italy.[11] The authors showed that, in 1993, the population in countries classified as middle class accounted for 8% of global population and 12% of global income. Moreover, they showed that income differences between countries classified as rich, poor, and middle class captured 90% of income asymmetries between countries and almost 70% of global inequality.

Following the class definition of Milanovic and Yitzhaki (2002), i.e., merging populations of *countries* within the same class, in 2000, differences in average incomes between the three classes accounted for 87% of total between-country differences and 65% of global inequality. Comparing this result with the figures for 1993 (reported above), we can conclude that the asymmetries in incomes between the three classes are decreasing over time. Figure 9.11 shows a graphical representation, using nonparametric kernel densities, of the global income distribution and the distributions by class of country (poor, middle class, and rich). The densities in Figure 9.11 consistently show the proportion of the global population to the population in countries within the same class; the area below the density for poor countries is equal to 81% of the area below the global density, showing that 81% of the world's population lives in a country classified as poor. One can also interpret the densities in Figure 9.11 as the probability of being within a particular income range *and* being a citizen of a country categorized into one of the three classes. For instance, the probability of being within a log income range of 2 and 4 while being a citizen of a rich country is equal to zero (the area below the density for rich countries within this range is zero).

Figure 9.11 also illustrates what Quah (1996) called the "twin peaks," i.e., convergence or agglomeration among poor and rich countries, and hence a

Figure 9.11 Global Distribution and Distribution by Class in 2000

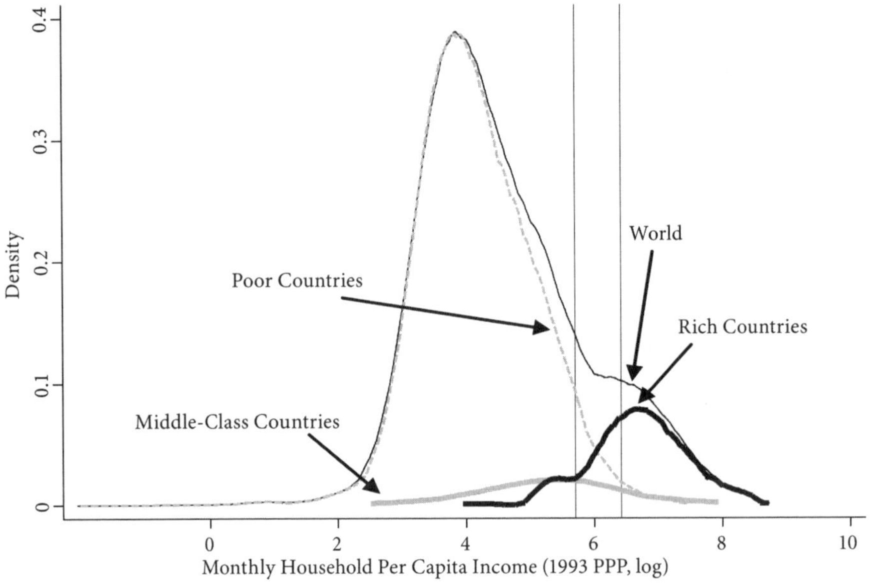

Source: Authors' calculations.

shrinking middle class. Notice that defining the international middle class as countries with per capita income between those of Brazil and Italy[12] captures the bipolar convergence process pointed out by Quah (1996), i.e., agglomeration in poor and rich countries' densities. Interestingly enough, most of the *citizens* forming the international middle class are actually *not* nationals of a country classified as such.[13] The explanation for this is the highly unequal distribution of incomes within middle class countries. The Gini coefficient for the agglomeration of poor countries was equal to 0.48, 0.38 for rich and 0.51 for middle class.[14]

The example above illustrated the differences between definitions of middle class which classifies countries as opposed to individuals as middle class members. The concept of *global middle class* used in the present study assigned class membership based on the individual's income. An individual (as opposed to countries) is classified as part of the global middle class if his or her income falls between the per capita incomes of Brazil and Italy. Using this definition of class, in 2000, 82% of the world population was defined as poor (regardless of their country of citizenship), 7.6% was part of the middle class and 10.5% was rich (Table 9.2).[15] Out of the 7.6% of the world population in the middle class, slightly less than half of them (i.e., 3.4 percentage points) were citizens of developed countries and the rest where citizens of a developing country.[16] The income shares controlled by the different classes can also provide us with an idea of how skewed is the global income distribution, with the poorest 82% of the global population receiving only 28.7% of total income whereas the richest 10% controls 57.5% of total income (Table 9.2).

According to our projected scenario, the situation will change significantly by 2030. Between 2000 and 2030, the middle class will experience a huge expansion, with 740 million new entrants (making it the fastest growing class) ending up with a total of 1.2 billion members or 16.1% of the world's population (Table 9.2). The great majority of the new entrants are citizens of developing countries—hence tomorrow's global middle class will be formed by today's citizens from developing countries. The total increase in the global middle class is explained by (i) population growth rates of cohorts within this class above the world average and (ii) higher economic growth rates in developing countries, which pull their citizens out of poverty and into the global middle class. The population growth rates of the global middle class (as classified in 2000) was relatively low, with an average rate of 18% compared with the world average of 32%. Therefore, the great majority of the increase in the global middle class is explained by high economic growth rates in developing countries—but how much of this increase is attributable to the PRC, India, and Asia more broadly?

Figure 9.12 divides the global middle class into citizens of the PRC, India, the rest of Asia, and the rest of the world. In 2000 only 17% of the global middle class were citizens of developing Asia—the majority were in the PRC, and virtually none in India.[17] By 2030, citizens from developing Asia will constitute 55% of the global middle class with the great majority (37%) from the PRC; in fact, half of the total 740 million new entrants into the global

Table 9.2 Growth and Changing Composition of Global Middle Class

| | Shares | | | | Growth Rates, % | |
| | 2000 | | 2030 | | (2000–2030) | |
	Pop.	Income	Pop.	Income	Pop.	Income
Poor	82.0	28.7	63.0	17.0	2	29
Middle Class, of which:	7.6	13.8	16.1	14.0	178	0
Developed-Country Nationals	3.4	6.8	1.2	1.0	-52	-2
Developing-Country Nationals	4.2	7.0	14.9	12.9	363	3
Rich	10.5	57.5	20.9	69.0	163	28
Total	100	100	100	100	32	109

Notes: 1. Totals may not sum to 100 because of rounding. 2. Poor are defined as individuals with an income below the average of Brazil; the middle class was defined as individuals with an income between the per capita incomes of Brazil and Italy; rich are those individuals with incomes at or above the average income in Italy. 3. Thresholds of Brazil and Italy are annual per capita incomes (2000 PPP) of $3,914 and $16,746.

Source: Authors' calculations.

middle class will be PRC nationals. The importance of developing Asia in the global middle class will depend not only on its economic and population growth rates but also on initial and final within-country income inequality.

Figure 9.12 Developing Asia Dominates the Global Middle Class in 2030

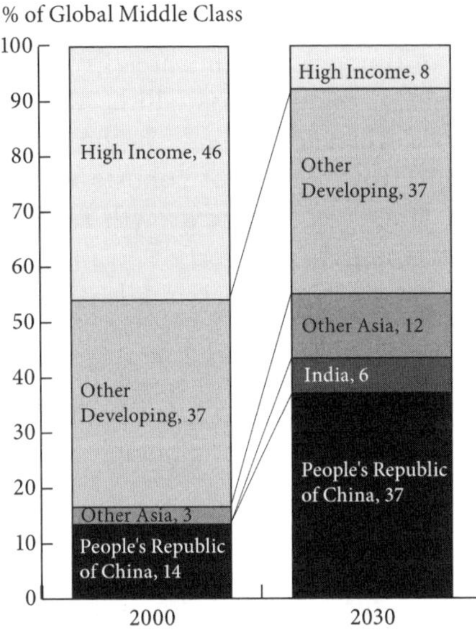

Source: Authors' calculations.

For instance, in the PRC, 56 million people belonged to the global middle class in 2000, earning more than 90% of all PRC citizens, i.e., they belonged to the richest decile. By 2030, assuming that inequality in the PRC remains constant, there will be 361 million in the PRC in the global middle class, and their earnings will range from the sixth to the ninth decile of the PRC national income distribution. PRC members of the global middle class will no longer be among the richest citizens of that country, but will probably be considered upper middle class there. A lower inequality in the PRC, increasing the population among the middle deciles of their population, would imply a considerable increase in the global middle class.

9.4.4 Consequences of a Growing Global Middle Class

The ascent of hundreds of millions of Asians and nationals from other developing countries into the global middle class will produce a large group of people in the developing world who can afford, and will demand access to, the standards of living that were previously reserved mainly for the residents of high-income countries. This has two major implications: the demand for international goods and services will rise, and pressures for policies that favor global integration will increase.

Much of the effect of the middle-class expansion on the world economy will be realized through a changing demand for goods. The fact that the middle class will be growing at a much faster rate than the overall population (Table 9.2 above) implies that multinational enterprises will be able to sell their products to a much larger market in 2030 than they do today. Furthermore, the rules of this new global marketplace will be increasingly determined by the tastes and preferences of the developing world, particularly the desires of consumers in the PRC and, to a lesser extent, India and other parts of Asia.

Therefore, while most of the world's purchasing power will continue to be concentrated in the OECD countries, the global economic influence of those countries will vastly diminish. By 2030, marketing to the developing world will be a much more important strategy for multinationals than it is today.

The rise of the global middle class will also affect demand for services. For example, given the strong correlation between income and determinants of human capital accumulation, like health and education levels, the growing middle class is likely to demand more and better health and education. Therefore, the increased emphasis on health and education among the middle class will deepen the human capital stock, so establishing the foundations for continued growth in the developing countries. However, the increasing demand for education and health is likely to put pressure on the budgets of developing-country governments and will require heightened policy attention.

Today, the median voter in most developing countries is unlikely to be a member of the global middle class; by 2030, the likelihood of finding the median voter in that class will have increased. In the PRC, for example, the median and mode earner will be members of the global middle class in 2030. These changes are likely to have an impact on the domestic policy arena. Some evidence points to a correlation between rising incomes and a shift in demand toward policies that are more supportive of globalization. Other policy goals—among them improved transparency, intensified anticorruption efforts, and demand for a more open society and cleaner environment—are also likely to move to the forefront of the policy agenda with the expansion in the size of the middle class.

9.4.5 Persistence of Poverty

Since 1990, the developing world in aggregate has made only slight progress in reducing the *number* of poor, though has made a more marked reduction in the *share* of developing countries' populations living in poverty (Table 9.3).[18] For the purposes of international comparison, the World Bank measures poverty with two distinct poverty lines—$1 a day and $2 a day per capita.[19] Most national poverty lines fall between them.

The regional variation is great. East Asia has seen the most dramatic drop—both in terms of the number of poor as well as the share of poor. Using the more-encompassing $2-a-day poverty line, the number of poor in East Asia has dropped from 1,113 million in 1990 to 684 million in 2004, and taking into account population growth, this translates into a reduction in the share of the poor from 70% to 37%. Progress in South Asia has been less favorable, with a higher initial level and less growth. The percentage living on $2 a day fell from 86% to only 81%, and this modest progress could not compensate for population growth, and so we observe a rise in the absolute number of poor.

Table 9.3 Regional Breakdown of Poverty in Developing Countries

| | Millions of People Living on: | | | | | | | |
| | Less than $1 a day | | | | Less than $2 a day | | | |
Region	1990	2004	2015	2030	1990	2004	2015	2030
East Asia and Pacific	476	169	48	12	1,113	684	312	148
PRC	374	128	37	9	819	452	196	76
Rest of East Asia and Pacific	102	41	11	3	294	232	115	72
South Asia	479	462	304	191	954	1,124	1,015	962
India	376	386	282	180	734	876	853	754
Rest of South Asia	103	76	22	11	220	248	162	207
Europe and Central Asia	2	4	2	2	20	46	23	9
Middle East and North Africa	5	4	3	3	49	59	40	26
Sub-Saharan Africa	240	298	326	326	396	522	597	656
Latin America and the Caribbean	45	47	38	38	115	121	109	87
Total	1,247	985	721	571	2,647	2,556	2,095	1,889
Excluding PRC	873	857	684	562	1,828	2,104	1,899	1,813

| | % of Population Living on: | | | | | | | |
| | Less than $1 a day | | | | Less than $2 a day | | | |
Region	1990	2004	2015	2030	1990	2004	2015	2030
East Asia and Pacific	29.8	9.1	2.4	0.6	69.7	36.6	15.3	6.7
PRC	33.0	9.9	2.6	0.6	72.2	34.9	14.1	5.2
Rest of East Asia and Pacific	22.1	8.8	2.5	0.4	63.7	50.2	25.1	9.7
South Asia	43.0	32.0	18.0	9.7	85.7	77.7	60.1	49.0
India	44.3	35.8	22.1	12.8	86.4	81.1	66.9	53.5
Rest of South Asia	38.9	28.8	8.3	1.9	83.4	94.2	61.6	37.4
Europe and Central Asia	0.5	0.9	0.5	0.2	4.3	9.8	4.8	2.0
Middle East and North Africa	2.3	1.5	0.8	0.3	21.7	19.7	10.9	5.4
Sub-Saharan Africa	46.7	41.1	35.4	30.5	77.1	72.0	64.7	58.3
Latin America and the Caribbean	10.2	8.6	6.0	3.5	26.3	22.2	17.3	12.1
Total	28.7	18.4	11.8	6.4	60.8	47.7	34.2	21.1
Excluding PRC	27.1	21.1	14.5	7.5	56.8	51.8	40.1	24.3

Source: The historical poverty estimates and the 2015 forecast come from the World Bank's Global Monitoring Report 2007; the 2030 poverty forecast is based on the economic forecast from the Linkage model.

South Asia made better progress on reducing the incidence of extreme poverty, with the number of poor living in extreme poverty declining after 1990.

Looking ahead, the percentage of the poor in East Asia would drop to 15% in 2015 (compared with 37% in 2004) and drop further to 6.7% by 2030—translating into a level of 150 million poor in 2030, of which one half would be in the PRC.[20] Thus the number of poor living on $2 a day would decline to less than 10%—a remarkable achievement over a span of two generations—and extreme poverty would be limited to some isolated pockets and account for less than 1% of the population. Again, South Asia lags, though the percentage of poor would drop to less than 50% averaged over the region and somewhat higher in India. Nonetheless, extreme poverty would drop considerably, to less than 10% on a regional basis.

Globally, poverty would be concentrated in two regions in 2030. South Asia would still have nearly 1 billion living in $2-a-day poverty and Sub-Saharan Africa would have about 660 million. These two regions together would account for 85% of the world's poor. East Asia would have about 8%. So, despite the rapid rise of a large middle class in Asia, the region, particularly South Asia, would still face the considerable challenge of pulling a significant portion of its population above the poverty line.

9.5 CONCLUSIONS

This chapter has analyzed, in an ex ante fashion, the effects that economic expansion in Asia will have on global growth and the global income distribution. Our empirical results rely on GIDD, a tool combining a global CGE model (Linkage) with microsimulation analysis. GIDD is used to "roll" the world economy to 2030 and assess the importance played by Asia during the projected development. Our results should not be interpreted as forecasts or predictions of future economic development; they should rather be seen as scenarios representing a set of plausible and mutually consistent assumptions.

The results under the baseline scenario show that, between 2005 and 2030, global GDP more than doubles, with the PRC and India accounting for a significant share (18%) of global expansion. In terms of per capita income, in 2005 the average person in the PRC had an income one fifth of the average citizen of a high-income country; this gap narrows significantly to two fifths by 2030. Due to faster population growth and more measured expansion in real GDP, per capita incomes in India are likely to rise much more slowly than in the PRC, catching up from one tenth of average incomes in rich countries in 2005 to less than one sixth in 2030.

The continued expansion of Asian economies is likely to translate into a more pronounced shift of production toward service activities. Because services tend to be more skill intensive than other sectors, the PRC's and India's increase in demand for services is likely to exert upward pressure on skilled wages, leading to a rise in wage inequality within fast-growing economies.

In the second part of the chapter, Asia's effect on the global middle class was analyzed. Constructing a global income distribution for 2000, we show that if the world were a single country, it would be one of the worst distributed (relative to the countries on the planet today), with a Gini coefficient of 0.68. A subgroup decomposition by countries shows that a measure of international inequality based on countries' average incomes—completely ignoring within-country differences in incomes—would be able to capture three quarters of total global inequality in 2000; a similar decomposition partitioning the world into the PRC and India versus the rest of the world would be able to account for 18% of total inequality. The central projections for the global economy in 2030 will have as a consequence a decrease in global inequality—with a decline in the Gini index of 5 points. This reduction in global inequality is *entirely accounted for by a reduction in disparities in average incomes across countries*; moreover, 86% of the total reduction is accounted for by the difference in average income between the PRC and India versus that in the rest of the world.

Forthcoming growth in Asia and the changes in global distribution described above will increase the proportion of the world population that are members of the *global middle class. Over the next 25 years, the global middle class will grow from 440 million to 1.2 billion. The PRC, by itself, accounts for almost half of the total increase in the middle class (310 million out of the total 740 million new entrants).* The expansion in the global middle class will increase demand for human capital-related services like health and education; perhaps more important, the global middle class members (the majority of them being PRC nationals), will have a say in global and domestic policies, demanding more transparency, globalization, anticorruption efforts and, in general, a more open society. A rising middle class will also provide the countries in Asia with more resources to confront the still considerable poverty challenge the region will have in 2030, particularly in South Asia.

ENDNOTES

1   The term Asia encompasses the World Bank's definition of developing Asia—both East Asia and Pacific and South Asia. Unless indicated otherwise, it does not include high-income economies in East Asia, such as Hong Kong, China; Japan; Republic of Korea; and Singapore. Our definition also excludes the countries of Central Asia that are part of the World Bank's Europe and Central Asia region.

2   Where poverty is measured using the World Bank's standard measure of $1 a day in international prices.

3   See Bussolo, De Hoyos, Medvedev, and Sulla (2006) for details.

4   See www.gtap.org for details.

5   Throughout the chapter, when we talk about the global distribution, we are indeed referring to GIDD's sample covering 91% of the world population.

6   See Section 9.4 for a more detailed discussion of the expanding middle class.

7   This measure of global inequality follows a growing literature, including the recent studies of Bourguignon and Morrison (2002), Milanovic (2002), and Atkinson and Brandolini (2004).

8   Haiti had a Gini coefficient of 0.71 in 2000.

9   It is worth noticing that the results of our model are not a forecast of future income distribution; the GIDD creates, within a global CGE model, a hypothetical income distribution accommodating assumptions regarding the future rate of growth of the population, human capital accumulation, and GDP.

10   Simple and population-weighted averages are very close.

11   Italy's per capita income was used as the upper threshold because it was the country with the lowest income among the G7; Brazil's per capita income corresponded with the official poverty line used in rich countries like the US and Germany (about $10 PPP per capita per day).

12   The middle class threshold is represented by the two vertical lines in Figure 9.11. The lower threshold is the log of monthly per capita income of Brazil ($322 international dollars) and Italy ($1,395 international dollars).

13   A total of 83% of the world *citizens* within the middle class thresholds live in either a poor or a rich country.

14   Middle-income countries are largely in Latin America, and include Argentina, Brazil, Chile, Czech Republic, Croatia, Dominican Republic, Guyana, Malaysia, Panama, Portugal, Slovak Republic, and Slovenia.

15   Notice that the definition of poor used here is not equivalent to the standard $1-a-day definition since it is based on the threshold defined above relating to the average per capita income of Brazil.

16   For clarity purposes, countries are classified as developed or underdeveloped on the basis of the World Bank definition. Individuals can therefore be citizens of a "poor" country as defined by Milanovic and Yitzhaki (2002) that could be classified as "developed" by the World Bank, yet they could be part of the global "middle class" when this is defined at the individual level.

17   Given the collection and statistical treatment of the Indian Household Survey, the initial situation underestimates the number of Indians within the middle and high income ranges.

18   The historical poverty estimates and the 2015 forecast come from the World Bank's *Global Monitoring Report 2007*, with the 2015 poverty forecast based on the economic forecast from the Linkage model.

19   Measured in PPP prices.

20   The methodology used for the poverty forecast differs from that used to forecast the middle class, even if the same underlying surveys are used. The poverty forecast is based on the World Bank's standard poverty forecast as provided in the annual *Global Economic Prospects* reports. It essentially assumes distribution neutrality except for the PRC and India. An assumption of some income convergence between rural and urban households is provided for the PRC.

India's poverty forecast is based on region-specific growth rates. The forecast from 2004 to 2015 is based on parametric Lorenz curves, thus the poverty elasticity with respect to growth is not constant. From 2015 to 2030 the poverty forecast is based on a constant poverty elasticity approach, with the poverty elasticity implicitly derived from the 2004/2015 outcome. These forecasts should be seen only as indicative of orders of magnitudes. As shown in the text, wage gaps between skilled and unskilled workers in many countries could increase in the future, leading to potentially worse poverty outcomes, though this could be offset somewhat by internal migration. Domestic policy could also help reduce long-term poverty to the extent that it provides greater opportunities for the poor, for example through financing of health and education.

REFERENCES

Atkinson, Anthony B. and Andrea Brandolini. 2004. "Global World Inequality: Absolute, Relative or Intermediate." Paper prepared for the 28th Conference of the International Association for Research in Income and Wealth, Cork, Ireland, 22-28 August.

Bosworth, Barry P. and Susan M. Collins. 2003. "The Empirics of Growth: An Update." *Brookings Papers on Economic Activity* 2:113-206.

Bourguignon, François and Luiz Pereira da Silva (eds.). 2003. *The Impact of Economic Policies on Poverty and Income Distribution: Evaluation Techniques and Tools.* Washington, DC: World Bank and Oxford University Press.

Bourguignon, François and Christian Morrison. 2002. "Inequality among World Citizens: 1890–1992." *American Economic Review* 92(4):727-44.

Bussolo, Maurizio, Rafael E. De Hoyos, Denis Medvedev, and Victor Sulla. 2006. "Demographic Change, Economic Growth, and Income Distribution: An Empirical Analysis Using Ex-Ante Microsimulations." *Background paper for Global Economic Prospects 2007: Confronting Challenges of the Coming Globalization.*

Bussolo, Maurizio, Jann Lay, and Dominique van der Mensbrugghe. 2006. "Structural Change and Poverty Reduction in Brazil: The Impact of the Doha Round." *World Bank Policy Research Working Paper* 3833, Washington, DC.

Bryant, Ralph C. 2004. "Cross-Border Macroeconomic Implications of Demographic Change." Brookings Discussion Papers in International Economics No. 166, September.

Chen, Shaohua and Martin Ravallion. 2003. "Household Welfare Impacts of China's Accession to the World Trade Organization." World Bank Policy Research Working Paper 3040, Washington, DC.

Cowell, F.A. and S.P. Jenkins. 1995. "How Much Inequality Can We Explain? A Methodology and an Application to the United States." *The Economic Journal* 105:421-30.

David, Paul A. 1990. "The Dynamo and the Computer: An Historical Perspective on the Modern Productivity Paradox." *The American Economic Review* 80(2):355-62. May.

Ferreira, Francisco H. G. and Phillippe G. Leite. 2003. "Meeting the Millennium Development Goals in Brazil: Can Microsimulations Help?" *Economía* 3(2):235-79.

———. 2004. "Educational Expansion and Income Distribution: A Microsimulation for Ceará." In Anthony Shorrocks and Rolph van der Hoeven (eds.), *Growth, Inequality and Poverty*. London: Oxford University Press.

Gordon, Robert J. 2000. "Does the 'New Economy' Measure Up to the Great Inventions of the Past?" *Journal of Economic Perspectives* 14(4):49-74.

Helliwell, John F. 2004. "Demographic Changes and International Factor Mobility." National Bureau of Economic Research Working Paper 10945. Cambridge, Mass.

McKibbin, Warwick J. 2005. "The Global Macroeconomic Consequences of a Demographic Transition." Centre for Applied Macroeconomic Analysis, Australian National University. Processed. August.

Milanovic, Branko. 2002. "True World Income Distribution, 1988 and 1993: First Calculation Based on Household Surveys Alone." *Economic Journal* (Royal Economic Society) 112(476), January: 51-92.

———. 2006. "Global Income Inequality: What it is and Why it Matters." World Bank Policy Research Working Paper 3865. Washington, DC.

Milanovic, Branko and Shlomo Yitzhaki. 2002. "Decomposing World Income Distribution: Does the World Have a Middle Class?" *Review of Income and Wealth* 48(2), June:155-78.

Mookherjee, Dilip and Anthony Shorrocks. 1982. "A Decomposition Analysis of the Trend in UK Income Inequality." *Economic Journal* 92:886–902.

Quah, Danny T. 1996. "Twin Peaks: Growth and Convergence in Models of Distribution Dynamics." *Economic Journal*, Royal Economic Society 106(437), July:1045-55.

Tyers, Rod and Qun Shi. 2005. "Global Demographic Change, Labour Force Growth and Economic Performance." Faculty of Economics and Commerce, Australian National University. Processed. June.

van der Mensbrugghe, Dominique. 2005. "The Linkage Model Technical Documentation." World Bank, Washington, DC.

Winters, L. A. and S. Yusuf. 2006. *Dancing with Giants: China, India and the Global Economy*. The World Bank and the Institute of Policy Studies.

World Bank. 2007a. *Global Economic Prospects 2007: Confronting Challenges of the Coming Globalization*. Oxford University Press for the World Bank, Oxford and New York.

———. 2007b. *Global Monitoring Report 2007*. Washington, DC.

APPENDIX

Appendix Table A9.1 Household Surveys

Region	Covered Population	World Population	Coverage Share
World	5,513,066	6,034,889	91.35
East Asia and Pacific	1,806,041	1,879,471	96.09
South Asia	1,336,923	1,339,150	99.83
High-Income countries	706,783	860,336	82.15
Latin America and the Caribbean	503,418	517,446	97.29
Sub-Saharan Africa	491,234	661,679	74.24
Eastern Europe and Central Asia	473,313	474,244	99.80
Middle East and North Africa	195,355	302,564	64.57

Economy	Covered Population	World Population	% of Total	Group
Sub-Saharan Africa	491,234	661,679	74.24	
Nigeria	117,608	117,608	17.77	3
Ethiopia	68,527	68,527	10.36	3
South Africa	45,610	45,610	6.89	3
Tanzania, United Rep. of	34,761	34,761	5.25	3
Kenya	30,688	30,688	4.64	1
Uganda	24,309	24,309	3.67	3
Ghana	19,867	19,867	3.00	1
Côte d'Ivoire	16,734	16,734	2.53	3
Madagascar	16,196	16,196	2.45	3
Cameroon	14,855	14,855	2.25	3
Zimbabwe	12,680	12,680	1.92	1
Zambia	12,594	12,594	1.90	3
Niger	11,781	11,781	1.78	3
Malawi	11,512	11,512	1.74	1
Burkina Faso	11,291	11,291	1.71	3
Senegal	10,342	10,342	1.56	3
Guinea	8,433	8,433	1.27	3
Rwanda	8,024	8,024	1.21	3
Burundi	6,488	6,488	0.98	3
Sierra Leone	4,509	4,509	0.68	3
Lesotho	1,787	1,787	0.27	1
Mauritania	2,643	2,643	0.40	3
Congo, Dem. Rep. of		50,053	7.56	2
Sudan		32,901	4.97	2
Afghanistan		23,734	3.59	2
Angola		13,841	2.09	2
Mali		11,647	1.76	2
Chad		8,214	1.24	2
Togo		5,366	0.81	2
Central African Republic		3,779	0.57	2
Eritrea		3,557	0.54	2
Congo, Rep. of		3,440	0.52	2
Liberia		3,066	0.46	2
Namibia		1,895	0.29	2
Botswana		1,755	0.27	2
Guinea-Bissau		1,367	0.21	2
Gambia, The		1,315	0.20	2
Gabon		1,272	0.19	2

Economy	Covered Population	World Population	% of Total	Group
Mauritius		1,186	0.18	2
Swaziland		1,023	0.15	2
Cape Verde		452	0.07	2
Equatorial Guinea		447	0.07	2
São Tomé and Principe		140	0.02	2
East Asia and Pacific	1,806,041	1,879,471	96.09	
China, People's Rep. of (rural)	866,670	866,670	46.11	1
China, People's Rep. of (urban)	407,755	407,755	21.70	1
Indonesia	209,173	209,173	11.13	3
Viet Nam	78,670	78,670	4.19	3
Philippines	75,140	75,140	4.00	1
Thailand	62,387	62,387	3.32	3
Korea, Rep. of	46,778	46,778	2.49	1
Malaysia	22,996	22,996	1.22	1
Cambodia	12,744	12,744	0.68	3
Hong Kong, China	6,639	6,639	0.35	1
Lao People's Dem. Rep.	5,278	5,278	0.28	1
Papua New Guinea	5,298	5,298	0.28	1
Singapore	4,018	4,018	0.21	1
Mongolia (urban)	1,576	1,576	0.08	1
Mongolia (rural)	921	921	0.05	1
Myanmar		47,723	2.54	2
Korea, Dem. People's Rep. of		21,861	1.16	2
Fiji Islands		811	0.04	2
Timor-Leste, Dem. Rep. of		721	0.04	2
Solomon Islands		420	0.02	2
Marshall Islands, Rep. of		385	0.02	2
Brunei Darussalam		333	0.02	2
French Polynesia		237	0.01	2
New Caledonia		215	0.01	2
Vanuatu		191	0.01	2
Samoa		175	0.01	2
Guam		155	0.01	2
Micronesia, Fed. States of		107	0.01	2
Tonga		100	0.01	2
Eastern Europe and Central Asia	473,313	474,244	99.80	
Russian Federation	146,560	146,560	30.90	3
Turkey	68,234	68,234	14.39	3
Ukraine	49,117	49,117	10.36	1
Poland	38,649	38,649	8.15	3
Uzbekistan	24,725	24,725	5.21	1
Romania	22,117	22,117	4.66	3
Kazakhstan	15,034	15,034	3.17	3
Yugoslavia, former (Serbia and Montenegro)	12,555	12,555	2.65	1
Czech Republic	10,267	10,267	2.16	1
Hungary	10,226	10,226	2.16	3
Belarus	10,028	10,028	2.11	1
Azerbaijan	8,143	8,143	1.72	1
Bulgaria	7,999	7,999	1.69	3
Tajikistan	6,158	6,158	1.30	3
Slovak Republic	5,402	5,402	1.14	1
Kyrgyz Republic	4,952	4,952	1.04	3

Economy	Covered Population	World Population	% of Total	Group
Georgia	4,521	4,521	0.95	1
Croatia	4,506	4,506	0.95	1
Turkmenistan	4,501	4,501	0.95	1
Moldova	4,275	4,275	0.90	3
Lithuania	3,499	3,499	0.74	3
Armenia	3,082	3,082	0.65	3
Albania	3,062	3,062	0.65	3
Latvia	2,374	2,374	0.50	1
Slovenia	1,968	1,968	0.41	1
Estonia	1,366	1,366	0.29	3
Cyprus		786	0.17	2
Channel Islands		145	0.03	2
High-Income Countries	706,783	860,336	82.15	
United States	284,155	284,155	33.03	3
Germany	82,343	82,343	9.57	3
United Kingdom	58,669	58,669	6.82	3
France	59,279	59,279	6.89	3
Italy	57,573	57,573	6.69	3
Spain	40,719	40,719	4.73	3
Canada	30,692	30,692	3.57	3
Netherlands	15,898	15,898	1.85	3
Greece	10,976	10,976	1.28	3
Belgium	10,305	10,305	1.20	3
Portugal	9,960	9,960	1.16	3
Sweden	8,877	8,877	1.03	3
Austria	8,096	8,096	0.94	3
Israel	6,085	6,085	0.71	3
Denmark	5,339	5,339	0.62	3
Finland	5,178	5,178	0.60	3
Norway	4,582	4,582	0.53	3
New Zealand	3,821	3,821	0.44	3
Ireland	3,803	3,803	0.44	3
Luxembourg	437	437	0.05	3
Japan		127,034	14.77	2
Australia		19,071	2.22	2
Switzerland		7,167	0.83	2
Iceland		282	0.03	2
Latin America and Caribbean	503,418	517,446	97.29	
Brazil	173,860	173,860	33.60	3
Mexico	100,088	100,088	19.34	3
Colombia	42,120	42,120	8.14	3
Argentina	36,897	36,897	7.13	3
Peru	25,953	25,953	5.02	3
Venezuela, R. B. de	24,418	24,418	4.72	3
Chile	15,412	15,412	2.98	3
Ecuador	12,306	12,306	2.38	3
Guatemala	11,166	11,166	2.16	3
Bolivia	8,318	8,318	1.61	3
Dominican Republic	8,265	8,265	1.60	3
Haiti	7,941	7,941	1.53	3
Honduras	6,423	6,423	1.24	3
El Salvador	6,281	6,281	1.21	3
Paraguay	5,468	5,468	1.06	3
Nicaragua	4,958	4,958	0.96	3

Economy	Covered Population	World Population	% of Total	Group
Costa Rica	3,928	3,928	0.76	3
Uruguay	3,343	3,343	0.65	3
Panama	2,949	2,949	0.57	3
Jamaica	2,585	2,585	0.50	3
Guyana	744	744	0.14	3
Cuba		11,124	2.15	2
Trinidad and Tobago		1,286	0.25	2
Suriname		433	0.08	2
Bahamas, The		302	0.06	2
Barbados		266	0.05	2
Belize		240	0.05	2
St. Lucia		153	0.03	2
St. Vincent and the Grenadines		116	0.02	2
Virgin Islands (US)		110	0.02	2
Middle East and North Africa	195,355	302,564	64.57	
Egypt, Arab Rep. of	67,288	67,288	10.17	3
Iran, Islamic Rep. of	66,366	66,366	21.93	1
Morocco	29,230	29,230	4.42	1
Yemen, Rep. of	17,936	17,936	5.93	3
Tunisia	9,564	9,564	1.45	1
Jordan	4,973	4,973	1.64	3
Algeria		30,464	10.07	2
Iraq		25,075	8.29	2
Saudi Arabia		21,485	7.10	2
Syrian Arab Rep.		16,814	5.56	2
Libya		5,305	1.75	2
Lebanon		3,397	1.12	2
Oman		2,442	0.81	2
Kuwait		2,228	0.74	2
South Asia	1,336,923	1,339,150	99.83	
India	1,021,083	1,021,083	76.25	3
Pakistan	142,650	142,650	10.65	3
Bangladesh	128,914	128,914	9.63	3
Nepal	24,430	24,430	1.82	3
Sri Lanka	19,847	19,847	1.48	3
Bhutan		1,938	0.14	2
Maldives		289	0.02	2

Groups: 1 = only grouped data (vintiles) are available; 2 = data are not available; 3 = data at the individual household level are available.

Source: Authors.

Commentary on Chapter 9

Rod Tyers

The chapter offers a projection of global economic performance to 2030 to a very high level of detail, encompassing 87 regions and countries (69 are individual countries) and, for each, 57 economic sectors. This projection is the outcome of an immense effort in careful scenario building and economic modeling. The results are clearly presented and sensibly explained. In its second half, the chapter then offers the results from a yet more heroic exercise in projection: the linking of model simulations to income distributional data from expenditure surveys from countries covering almost all of the global population. This linkage yields associated projections of global income distribution through 2030.

1 Key Findings

The key findings are striking, yet not surprising. Trade and global economic integration are projected to increase. Populations will grow more slowly and age, and international migration will rise. These will ensure that there continues to be comparatively rapid per capita economic expansion in the developing world and, therefore, that poverty levels decline overall. Two caveats to this positive story, however, are that a concentration of poverty is projected to remain in Sub-Saharan Africa and that Kuznets curves will see domestic inequality in many developing countries increase. Most striking, however, is the conclusion that, by 2030, the global "middle class" will more than double.

2 Careful "Futurology"

Projection into the future for its own sake is always a treacherous task. In this case it is done, at least in part, to enhance the World Bank's identification of future development priorities and to provide a context for recommended future policy changes. One step toward careful practice is the use of multiple scenarios. Even this, however, cannot anticipate unforeseen shocks, which are anything but smooth. Nonetheless, the weight of the simulations shows that there is undeniable potential for higher developing-country incomes. The optimistic scenario is therefore important as a benchmark.[1]

3 The Baseline Modeling

Although the judgment of experts has been central to the scenario building, the use of a numerical model of the global economy is very sensible. This is because the model ensures that accounting consistency is preserved and that the complexities of cause and multiple effect are captured to the best of the modeler's knowledge. What follows are some brief comments on technical aspects of the modeling.

Capital–Skill Complementarity

This is innovative and useful for capturing the expected continuation of the growth in the skilled wage premium. Another important determinant of this growth is the relative expansion of the service sector and the relative skill-intensity of services. What is not included, but which would make the modeling still more realistic, is skill-augmenting technical change and changes in the composition of capital stocks to reflect the relative rise in the share of ever-cheaper skill-augmenting equipment in total capital use.

Services Productivity Growth

This is the key to long-run real exchange rate changes, which affect the relative performance of economies. Yet it is poorly understood for lack of good measures of the output and quality of many services. The assumption that services productivity growth is slower than that of tradables, which is made throughout this analysis, is not always borne out.[2]

Rural–Urban Labor Transformation

It is important in a dynamic model to incorporate transformation lags in conforming the skills of rural–urban migrants. The blanket, single-parameter approach adopted here is fraught with difficulty, however, because the labor non-substitutability is heterogeneous. It is due to skill mismatches, pipeline lags when urban capital is growing quickly, and urban registration restrictions.[3] It is further complicated in the early stages of development by peak rural labor demands. The pace of urbanization therefore depends on the rate of physical capital accumulation and the stage of development, as indicated by training capacity and the depth of urban and rural labor markets, as well as on technical change in agriculture.

Stories Not Captured in the Modeling

Many of the development stories told in the chapter are not readily modeled globally. Some of these would make a difference to projected economic performance. They include, first, the links between aging and savings rates on the one hand (portfolio risk effects and retirement income policies) and labor force participation (incentives for the aged to continue working) on the other. Research on the PRC economy has shown that modest changes in aged saving and aged labor force participation rates make a large difference to economic performance.[4] Second, the variously documented links between the age of labor forces and productivity growth on the one hand and investment on the other are mentioned but not modeled. Third, since ageing affects both savings and investment, it is unclear whether it has effects on investment financing costs, the capital account, or interest premiums.[5]

Fourth, much appears to depend on the sustainability of the US current account deficit and, by association, the US private savings rate, yet this is really endogenous. Should foreign purchasers of US assets diversify, US yields will rise faster and US asset prices more slowly. This will induce greater savings from private disposable income. Finally, quite a bit is made of rises in the shares of output traded. The projected rises could not stem from the underlying modeling since its structure does not capture the increased horizontal and vertical specialization that is required. The one thing in the model that does contribute to this is the assumption that trade costs will fall through time.

4 The Distributional Analysis

The Herculean task of concording so many expenditure surveys with national accounts and with the global database on which the modeling rests deserves considerable credit. The task is made more difficult because, even when they are accurate, expenditure surveys ignore wealth and therefore understate income disparities. Moreover, the resulting modeling depends heavily on the skill-acquisition process and this is notoriously difficult to quantify even in the most advanced countries. Skilled wage premiums are sensitive to both skill transformation rates and rates of immigration and emigration.[6] They also depend on technology assumptions, key among which is the lack of factor-specific productivity growth shocks. Once the skill composition of the labor force is projected, it is not clear from the chapter how income from physical capital is then distributed across households that are principally endowed with skilled and unskilled labor. One expects skill-abundant households to own more physical capital than low-skill households.

A difficulty with distributional dynamics is that the families inhabiting each income percentile are not the same through time. Generational changes and the graduations that occur with overall income growth and development mean that it is not possible to claim that a percentile group in one year is better or worse off a decade later, as if the per capita income of a particular group of people has risen or fallen. For this reason, the growth incidence discussion in Section 4 of the chapter seems misleading. When the urban or middle class does better, so do many previously rural or poor, along with their remaining family members, who have graduated in that decade.

The fact of Kuznets inequality is undisputed, but the experience of the industrial countries shows that it is temporary. Care is required to avoid obscuring the benefits of *average* gains when considering distribution. Would we wish to *unwind* the growth in Mexico because that would hurt the rich or the urban middle class more than the (mainly rural) poor? Is it better to have slower growth that makes fewer people rich? The middle-income rise in inequality is necessary, since it is urbanization and industrial development that raise capital returns in the first place and it is the subsequent rise in the (mainly urban) capital stock that lifts urban labor productivity, attracting rural workers. The inequality, and the associated urban-rural productivity gap, drive the expansion of the urban middle class and provide the incentive for the young to commit time to education. The departure of workers from agriculture is then what fosters rural productivity growth. In essence, the chicken and egg go together—high-productivity urban growth (and therefore inequality) is needed to raise rural productivity.

Endnotes to Commentary

1   In an earlier draft, a discussion was included about projections of economic performance made a century earlier. History is an excellent teacher and, in this case especially, it warns the reader that much can go wrong.

2   See, for example, Miyajima (2005), Tyers et al. (2006b).

3   Registration restrictions influence rural-urban migration in the People's Republic of China and Viet Nam.

4   See, for example, Golley and Tyers (2006).

5   See, for example, Tyers and Shi (2007).

6   The links between immigration and emigration rates and skill acquisition is explored by Tyers et al. (2006a).

References to Commentary

Golley, J. and R. Tyers. 2006. "China's Growth to 2030: Demographic Change and the Labour Supply Constraint." Chapter 8 in R. Garnaut and L. Song (eds.), *The Turning Point in China's Economic Development*. Asia-Pacific Press. September.

Miyajima, K. 2005. "Real Exchange Rates in Growing Economies: How Strong is the Role of the Non-tradables Sector." IMF Working Paper 05/233, Washington, DC.

Tyers, R., I. Bain, and J. Vedi. 2006a. "The Global Economic Implications of Freer Skilled Migration." Working Papers in Economics and Econometrics No 468, Australian National University, Canberra. June.

Tyers, R., J. Golley, Y. Bu, and I. Bain. 2006b. "China's Economic Growth and its Real Exchange Rate." Working Papers in Economics and Econometrics No. 476, Australian National University, Canberra. November. Presented at the All China Economics International Conference, City University of Hong Kong, 18-20 December.

Tyers, R. and Q. Shi. 2007. "Global Demographic Change, Policy Responses and their Economic Implications." *The World Economy* 30(4), April:537-66.

Index

V

vertical specialization
  rationale for 15

W

World Bank model 118 *see also* Linkage
    model

WTO-minus 69

WTO-plus 56, 68-69

WTO rules 103-106